The History of Civilization

Edited by C. K. OGDEN, M.A.

Mesopotamia

Mesopotamia

The Babylonian and Assyrian Civilization

By

L. DELAPORTE

Late Attaché to the National Museum
Professor in the Catholic Institute of Paris

Translated by

V. GORDON CHILDE

NEW YORK

BARNES & NOBLE, INC.

First published in 1925
Reprinted 1970

Published in the United States of America 1970
by Barnes & Noble, Inc., New York, N.Y.

SBN 389 04018 5

Printed in Great Britain

FOREWORD

THE SEMITES AND CIVILIZATION

M. MORET'S From Tribe to Empire *has revealed the Mesopotamian peoples and empires in the general history of the Ancient East ; it has assigned them their place in that complex evolution when social organization was beginning and civilization developing through the accords and conflicts of human groups which the contradictory tendencies to mutual aid and to imperialist greed evoke.*

As M. Moret's volume on the Nile and Egyptian Civilization is destined to do for Egypt, this volume sets out to define the rôle of Babylonia and Assyria, to determine their contributions to human progress.

Here will be seen how, by patient excavation and by laborious decipherment, this remote past has been conjured up gradually— conjured up with all the gaps of a shadow. L. Delaporte gives in abridged form the results of the latest works on the kings, the dynasties, the perpetual wars, the sacks of towns, the deportations of the conquered, the monotonous destructions of the products of collective labour. Maspero's Histoire ancienne des peuples de l'Orient classique *has inevitably become out of date. The period prior to Hammurabi has never yet been treated as it deserves in any French work. Abroad, although great tomes have been consecrated to partial syntheses, the present state of our knowledge has not been fixed taking the two great Mesopotamian empires as a whole. Moreover, if in doing so, this book leaves the same impression as certain ancient tapestries frayed by time where fragmentary scenes and mutilated figures alone are visible, that is just what the author intended. Continuous knowledge in the case of these past ages is neither possible, nor, happily, essential.*

An argument against history is often based on these gaps which exist and will always exist. But what is vital for history—one must not weary of repeating it—is not to know all the facts, but to solve the problems. Individual facts in infinite number have, for the most part, left no trace ; but for the solution of the problem, an integral knowledge of them, far from being necessary, would be a crushing burden. A restricted number of data can suffice for the establishment of general facts.

Undoubtedly in the case of Mesopotamia the main chronological framework is not yet established with all the rigour that could be wished. Still, already the history of Babylonia and that of Assyria are assuming a reasonably precise and articulate form from the beginning of the third millennium before Christ in the one case and during the first millennium in the other.

Undoubtedly the racial problems are far from being solved and perhaps they never will be completely solved.[1] Asia Minor, as A. Moret has remarked, has been a sort of Germany, " a reservoir of peoples, disparate in origin, reflecting the shock and recoil of the ceaseless migrations which were going on further north on the plains which stretch from the present Russia to Tibet."[2] In these movements of groups whose ethnic origins are diverse, it is the Semites who appear in the first place, although behind them are seen other elements of different races and less sharply defined : the Sumerians who have been absorbed by the Semites, the Elamites, Kassites, Hittites, and Mitannians, who have "blocked" the latter and limited an expansion which will start anew later in the Mohammedan epoch.[3]

Undoubtedly we are not fully informed about this Mesopotamian civilization on which the Semitic element has stamped its mark. Still, many precious documents have been collected. The main object of this book is to define exactly what is and what is not known about the institutions and mental acquisitions of the Babylonians and Assyrians. And its deepest interest—corresponding to the deepest interest of history—is to show as far as possible how amid varied chances, thanks to favourable contingencies (certain ethnic endowments, a certain natural environment, certain individuals), the logical treasury of humanity was enriched in this portion of space and time.

---

[1] Methodical excavation might remove many of the uncertainties. See Moret, From Tribe to Empire, and the conclusion of the present volume.

[2] Ibid. Contrary to A. Moret, J. de Morgan is inclined to place the cradle of the Semites in Arabia. Cf. an article by J. de Morgan on "The Origins of the Semites and those of the Indo-Europeans " in Révue de Synth. hist., Tome XXXIV.

[3] See Moret, op. cit. Are the Sumerians and Elamites Turanian, the rest Aryan ? They were in any case mixed with Aryans.

The imperialist spirit as defined in the Foreword to From
Tribe to Empire *found its fullest incarnation among the Semitic
population of Mesopotamia. Among these peoples—above all
among the Assyrians—war played a preponderant rôle ; their
military institutions were specially developed ; the " exploitation of the weak by the strong "[1] has been the current practice—
and it was pitiless. They were not content with victory ; conquests and raids were accompanied by systematic massacres and
wholesale deportations.[2] At Babylon the king reserves to himself
the satisfaction " of tearing out the eyes of the conquered king."[3]
In Assur war was not only a means, it seems often to have been
an end—battle for the exercise of violence, victory for the pleasure
of torturing. It is useless to know all the wars which the Babylonians and Assyrians unleashed, but, to know the people themselves, one must catch a glimpse of their garden of torments by
the help of some examples.*

*The inscriptions—and there are many of them—in which the
Assyrian kings immortalize their triumphs represent the most
frightful expression of human " wickedness."[4] "These warriors
who had sinned against Ashur and had plotted evil against me,
the Great One who worship him, from their hostile mouths have
I torn their tongues and I have compassed their destruction. As
for the others (Babylonians) who remained alive, I offered them
as a funerary sacrifice at the feet of the great* shêdê *and* lamassê
*(winged bulls and lions) between whom Sennacharib my father's
father had been assassinated ; their lacerated members have I
given unto the dogs, the swine, the wolves, the birds of prey, the
fowls of the air, and the fishes of the waters to devour. By accom-
plishing these deeds I have rejoiced the hearts of the great gods,*

---

[1] Ibid.

[2] *J. de Morgan describes the condition of Chaldœa when it received its first
non-Semitic colonists, thus :—*"The soil, of extreme richness and perpetually
moist, was covered with tamarisks, willows, acacias, and date-palms, presented
impenetrable thickets and wide glades where grew cereals—among them wheat,
barley, and oats, of which these lands are the original home. *The lagoons,
quite shallow, muddy, sometimes several kilometres wide, fringed with a girdle of
gigantic reeds, and choked with aquatic plants, were breeding-places for an
immense abundance of fishes and clouds of waterfowl. It is here in this privi-
leged region surrounded by deserts on every hand, that the imagination of the
Orientals placed the terrestrial paradise* " (Les premières civilisations, *p.* 179).
*This "garden of Mesopotamia," this Eden (cf. Moret, op. cit.), must have
attracted the Semites in large numbers when they began their movements—the cause
of which J. de Morgan finds in the desiccation of Arabia. Cf. the article cited
above in* Rév. de Synth. hist.

[3] *See below, p.* 70.   [4] Ibid.

my lords." [1] *It must not be forgotten moreover that the triumphal stelæ constitute at once monuments of pride and of terror ; there may be an element of cynical bluff in these inventories of massacres.*

These masters of war, this strange people of Assyria who, in that respect like the Huns, have written a blood-stained page in history, have been, as so often happens, vanquished by the vanquished. From the point of view of human evolution, the Assyrians are of interest just in so far as they have been agents in the transmission of Babylonian influence. Through them and not only directly, Babylon has acted upon Israel, upon the Phœnicians and Lydians ; through the latter and through the Hittites it has acted upon Greece.

Babylon owes to the mixture of the Semitic element with the Sumerian element—undoubtedly pacific and inventive—an original civilization which with Egypt[2] is the oldest and most notable.[3] In the Sumero-Akkadian empire, " it seems," says J. de Morgan, " that governmental conceptions, such as administration, finance and war, must be attributed to the Semites, while the arts, writing, industry, cultivation and all branches of knowledge based upon care bestowed upon the earth, were due to the aborigines."[4] What the Assyrians have transmitted are then certain advances in social organization, some techniques and an art, finally myths and sciences—a false knowledge and a true knowledge.

In Chaldæa and Assyria the social structure of human life was consolidated. Egoistic and practical, these people, although they moved in the religious atmosphere of which we have spoken,[5] although they always ascribed a religious origin to power and a sacred character to the kings,[6] gladly used religion as an instrument, and it was open to them to free themselves from its bonds more easily than others. They have endowed the family with rigid cohesion. They have perfected administration. Among

---

[1] J. de Morgan, op. cit., *p.* 363, *note* 1 (*the text quoted above has been revised by L. Delaporte*) ; *cf. pp.* 340, 349, 350, 357 *and, in this volume, p.* 342.

[2] *See Moret,* op. cit. *Cf. J. de Morgan,* op. cit., *pp.* 209 *ff. and the conclusion to this book.*

[3] *"The Semites have only risen to the first rank in countries where they have been mixed with other peoples such as the Sumerians in Mesopotamia " R. Kreglinger,* La réligion d'Israël, *p.* 12).

[4] Op. cit., *p.* 227 ; *cf. p.* 239.

[5] *Foreword to* From Tribe to Empire.

[6] *See Moret,* op. cit. ; Année Sociologique, *Vol. XII, pp.* 457 *ff.*

*them economic organization was exceptionally advanced and the
contract particularly played a rôle undoubtedly quite as important
as " in Attic law of the fourth century B.C., in Roman law at
the beginning of our era, or in French law at the beginning of
the Renaissance."* [1] *Legislation very consciously retained a
purely social character. The Code of Hammurabi—discovered
by J. de Morgan in 1902 and translated by V. Scheil—the oldest
legislative text of the same importance in our possession, " is
entirely free from any religious formula, almost from any religious idea at all, a surprising fact in those days when, among
all other peoples, legislation was only a department of the precepts of cult."* [2] *The penalties it inflicts are very severe, often
cruel.* [3] *Its spirit is in the strictest sense juridical, not moral.
Mesopotamia was thus as positivist as Egypt was idealist.* [4]

*Art for art's sake, science for the sake of knowledge itself, only
arise—we have pointed this out already, and we shall insist upon
it subsequently—in a late phase of human evolution. Here art
and science have progressed just by reason of deep-seated utili-
tarianism and the appetite for enjoyment.*

*" The cities of Marduk, of Ishtar, and of Assur, the gardens
of Babylon, the palaces of the Sargonids and of Nebuchedrezzar
have endowed the sanguinary and voluptuous despotism with a
grandiose and inhuman setting. . . . With greater knowledge
than Egypt . . . with a more studious attention to detail,
Chaldœa was less nobly artistic, her thought less lofty, her taste
more sober and less pure, her touch less delicate and less light ;
but her defects as much as her merits have served her for the
creation of that Asiatic art—sensuous, sumptuous, and colossal.
Superb cities, temples and palaces of unheard-of luxury,
dazzling ziggurats. . . . Blue battlements crown walls of green,
white, yellow, and red ; from black to gold, white, purple, blue,
vermilion, silver, the seven storeys mottled with changing lustre
add variety to the ascent of the tower ; the towns gleam like
polychrome enamels in the flames of the sun." A wealth of detail
corresponds to the magnificence of the whole—" glazed bricks,
friezes of figures in relief, the glittering treasure of the miner's
toil, cunning workmanship in iron, silver and bronze, an extra-*

---

[1] Ibid., *Vol. XII*, p. 500; cf. *p.* 517.
[2] J. de Morgan, op. cit., *p.* 273 ; cf. *Moret*, op. cit.
[3] *See below, pp.* 98 *ff.*
[4] J. de Morgan, op. cit., *p.* 251.

B

vagance of jewels, embroideries, stuffs, fringed robes, haughty tiaras, furniture resting on pedestals like palaces on basements, a glory of tapestries, those ' Babylonian fabrics' renowned throughout Antiquity, the famous ancestors of the Oriental carpets."[1]

A part of the legends which have formed the imaginative explanation of things and which have helped to regulate the conduct of men—the Creation, the victory of light over dark chaos, Paradise Lost, the Deluge—have come down from the Babylonians, although their division between the Sumerian and the Semitic element[2] *cannot be accurately apportioned. At the same time they have been pioneers in the positive advances whereby human society has been perfected and man's empire over his environment has been enlarged. For industrial techniques, the means of communication and the transmission of ideas, for the knowledge of nature and especially of the heavens, mankind as a whole is indebted to them. Our scientists have remote precursors among their scribes and magicians. The latter have been attracted by the brilliance of the eastern nights. Astrology rests on these two principles*[3]—*" the starry heaven is the visible countenance of the sacred world*[4] *; a necessary relation subsists between astronomical phenomena and the events of terrestrial life." But astrology has been the nurse of astronomy since the false idea has led to true observations. Primitive science, when it does not spring directly from practice, is born of speculations which turn the spirit towards nature.*

Calculation, writing, cosmology—in that gradual formation of the psychism of which we have already spoken—these are the new and pregnant elements, these are the fertile inventions of Mesopotamia.

Across the successive volumes of this work what is to ensure their unity is the general plan, the continual preoccupation with the problems of history and the anxiety to verify some great explicative hypotheses. It is also solid knowledge, the indis-

---

[1] *Paul Lorquet,* L'Art et l'Histoire, *pp. 205–213, esp. 208 and 211*

[2] *On Israel's debt to Babylonian mythology, see Kreglinger, op. cit., pp. 22 ff. In his conclusion, L. Delaport makes some reservations as to the originality of the Babylonians.*

[3] *Année Sociologique, IV, p. 183. Cf. Kreglinger, op. cit., p. 25.*

[4] *See* Prehistoric Man, Language, A Geographical Introduction to History, The Earth before History, *and* Race and History, *in this series.*

pensable basis for any historical construction. But the method of exposition in history cannot be completely independent of the author's personality. Does not that play some part even in the explanation of the natural sciences and of the truths of mathematics themselves without infecting the foundation of Science? On the same basis of profound erudition one historian proceeds by generalizations and extensive scenes, another by fine shades, by an accumulation of details and typical quotations. Properly handled the two procedures end by calling forth a similar image. We believe that the reader of this book, replete as it is with facts, while he views the general outline of the past in Mesopotamia, will at the same time arrive unconsciously, but inevitably, at the heart of that reanimated civilization.

HENRI BERR

CONTENTS

xiii

CONTENTS

LIST OF ILLUSTRATIONS

INTRODUCTION

THE sources from which we derive our knowledge of the Babylonian and Assyrian civilizations which flourished in the Tigris-Euphrates plains before the Christian era, are almost exclusively the inscriptions and monuments of the two civilizations themselves. To M. Botta, French Consul at Mosul, is due the distinction of having first undertaken systematic excavations to recover traces of the ancient Assyrian Empire. He was responsible for the discovery in 1842, on the site of Khorsabad, of Dûr-Sharrukîn, the town built by Sargon at the end of the eighth century before our era. A little later, the Englishman, Layard, took up works which Botta had abandoned and revealed the important library of King Ashurbanipal (seventh century B.C.) together with the ruins of ancient Niniveh.[1] It lies outside the scope of our subject to recall all the researches conducted by French, English, German and American archæologists after these happy beginnings. But as far as Babylonia is concerned, we cannot forget the work of Ernest de Sarzec. Appointed French vice-consul at Basra, and two months after having taken up his duties in January, 1877, he attacked the mounds of sand named Tello and carried on till his death fruitful campaigns at the site, which were continued by Col. Cros. They have yielded tens of thousands of texts and the history of Lagash, an important city throughout the third millennium. We must also mention the *Délégation Scientifique en Perse du Ministère de l'Instruction Publique*. Between 1897 and 1912, under the able direction of M. Jacques de Morgan, it exhumed from the ruins of Susa, the capital of a country bordering on, and often hostile to, Babylonia, numerous artistic and epigraphical documents which throw brilliant light on Babylonian civilization; it will suffice to cite the triumphal stele of Narâm-Sin (twenty-eighth century) and the Code of

[1] LXXII.

1

Hammurabi (twenty-first century), the most important text
of ancient law yet discovered.

Hardly any information upon our subject that deserves
attention is to be found in classical traditions. Most of the
time the sources used by the Greek authors are the narratives of travellers, and, when they can be tested by Assyrian
or Babylonian documents, many mistakes, many errors, are
found in them. For instance, on the testimony of Herodotus,
"the soil of Babylonia is so favourable for cereals that they
yield a two-hundredfold harvest, and in soils of exceptional
quality a three-hundredfold return." The Greek historian
had visited the country himself and his testimony is quite
honest, but he had undoubtedly been shown some experi-
mental plot from which a yield far above the average had
been obtained by suckering. It has recently been possible
to cite the case of some stalks of wheat, cultivated in
excellent land at Mérignac (Gironde), which have produced
2250 grains from one,[1] but one could not infer from this
that such a result is obtained under normal conditions of
cultivation to-day. In the plains of the Lower Euphrates
the yield of wheat, at present from thirty to forty times
the sowing, has scarcely varied since antiquity ; at most,
judging from the account-tablets, it may have been slightly
higher during the third millennium in the region round
Lagash near the Persian Gulf.[2]

The beginnings of the decipherment of the Babylonian
and Assyrian script, called cuneiform (from the Latin
cuneus, wedge, and *forma*, form), because each element in
the signs resembles a wedge, go back beyond the discoveries
of Botta. The first attempts were, in fact, made on the total
of forty-one characters derived from the Babylonian script
which compose the syllabary of the Achæmenid Persian
inscriptions.[3] After Pietro della Valle, who in 1621 had
copied five signs in the ruins of Persepolis, and had recognized the direction of the writing, Chardin (1673), Kaempfer
(1712), and Corneille de Bruyn (1718) had brought back
more important summaries of the texts. About 1765 Niebuhr

---

[1] G. Heuzé, *Les plantes céréales, Le Blé*, p. 182.
[2] **LXXVIII,** p. xlvi.   [3] **LXXXIX.**

transcribed several complete inscriptions, proved that they were grouped by threes, that in each group there were three different types of script, and that, if they were inscribed on the same line, the simplest was always on the right, the most complicated on the left. In 1798 Tyschen recognized that words in texts of the first type were separated by a sign, the oblique wedge. Münter, in 1802, opined that the language of this first script must be related to Zend, which separates the words in the same way. In the same year Grotefend took his stand on archæological considerations in attempting the analysis of this first script. He found the word in which Tyschen and Münter thought they discerned the royal title, often repeated twice near the beginning of the inscription, the second time with a termination in which he saw the mark of the plural; the whole group would mean " king of kings." The preceding word was certainly the king's name itself. Hence the formula " X king of kings." The group " king " sometimes appeared again as the third word after this whole. We must then in this case have the name of the father preceded by a term which meant son. Hence the formula " X king of kings, son of Y king." Elsewhere, for comparison, " Y king of kings, son of Z," occurred without the latter being himself a king. Since it was a question of the inscriptions of Persepolis, the second formula must give the name of the founder of the dynasty of the Achæmenids. If it were a question of Cyrus, whose father and son bore the same names, X and Z would be identical; Y then represented Darius and the translations must read :

> Xerxes, king of kings, son of Darius king . . .
> Darius, king of kings, son of Hystaspes, . . .

To decipher the three proper names Grotefend turned to the ancient transcriptions. He definitely identified two vowels and determined the phonetic value of ten syllabic signs. Eleven savants, among them Lassen and Burnouf, Hincks and Rawlinson, perfected his work. The syllable *la* was only recognized in 1851 by Oppert, and the ideogram under which the name of Ormuzd, the national god of the Achæmenids lay hid, resisted decipherment till 1878.

The second of the scripts of Persepolis presented greater difficulties, but it was rightly believed that the three texts must each recite the same theme in different languages. The presence of a distinctive sign in front of proper names was at once demonstrated, and much ingenuity was devoted to classifying the signs in accordance with the number and direction of their elements. The first serious attempt at translation was made in 1844 by the Dane, Westergaard. Hincks discovered the syllabism and some elements (1846), and Saulcy (1850) studied the grammatical forms. In 1853 Norris published the *Inscription of Behistun* recovered by Rawlinson, and the decipherment proposed by Westergaard was tested. The excavations of the Délégation en Perse were needed to increase the number of texts drawn up in this language, called Elamite, or Anzanite, spoken by the non-Semitic inhabitants of Elam.

The third script remained. To Grotefend again is due the credit of having determined the first words. He succeeded in isolating the groups of signs which must correspond to the names of Cyrus, Hystaspes, Darius and Xerxes. Having demonstrated the analogies of this script to that on some bricks picked up among the ruins of Babylon, a happy intuition enabled him to determine the group representing the name of Nebuchadrezzar. Such roughly was the state of decipherment when Botta announced his discoveries. In the third type of script it had only been possible to identify twenty proper names known from the two others. Löwenstern tried to analyse them ; he demonstrated the existence of variants of signs and suggested the principle of *homophony*, i.e. the existence of different signs for the same sound. Longpérier deciphered the protocol of Sargon on the monuments discovered by Botta, and the latter classified 642 different signs. Like Löwenstern he discovered homophones. He identified the script of Khorsabad with those of Persepolis and Babylon, and finally proved that the tongue was Semitic. Saulcy picked out from the texts of Persepolis short phrases corresponding to phrases in the Persian text. He determined 120 characters and found their phonetic value. Hincks of Dublin discovered the principle of *syllabism*, i.e. the equivalence of some signs to a syllable and not just to a single letter. Saulcy at length devoted himself to the texts from Khorsabad, convinced himself that the same inscription was repeated several times, made some comparisons and, utilizing his former readings of the signs, succeeded in translating ninety-six lines. Rawlinson, who had just published without commentary the introduction to the *Obelisk of Nimrûd*, proposed a translation differing only very slightly. In 1851 Rawlinson transcribed and translated the *Inscription of Behistun* from the version in the third script; he assigned their value to 246 characters and discovered the principle of polyphony or the existence of signs which each have several values, several sounds. The following year Hincks recognized that certain signs formed composite syllables. The more one struggled with the decipherment, the more complications arose. It was then that the Royal Asiatic Society conceived the idea of inviting several savants to decipher a text of over eight hundred lines, each according to his own particular method and principles. Rawlinson, Hincks, Fox Talbot, and Oppert sent in their manuscripts, which were unsealed on May 25th, 1857. The result was very satisfactory. The four translations of this inscription of Tiglath-Pileser I, king of Assyria, were engraved on four columns to let the world see that the key had been found to the third script of the Achæmenid inscriptions, the script of the Assyrians and Babylonians.

Babylonian and Assyrian literature is extremely varied. The thousands of texts, either originals or ancient copies, now preserved in European and American museums, range over a period beginning before 3000 B.C. and extending down to the first century. Among them are to be found historical texts : annals, fasti, dedications of monuments, votive inscriptions, chronological tables ; religious texts : hymns, prayers, psalms of penitence ; magic formulæ : incantations, talismans, presages based upon observations of the stars, of the movements of men and animals, of entrails, of oil dropped on to water ; poetry : epics, legends, fables ; juridical texts : laws, judicial decisions ; all sorts of contracts : sale and purchase, loan, commerical partnership, marriage, divorce, adoption ; accounts : archives of temples, palaces, families ; correspondence, official or private ; epigraphical, grammatical, lexicographical collections; geographical lists; mathematical, astronomical, astrological tables; medicine.

Art and archæology are no less well represented; statues and statuettes in stone or metal in bas-relief or in the round; stelæ of victory, figurines of metal or terra-cotta; engraved vases, seals ornamented with religious scenes, painted pottery, are the witnesses at different epochs to progress achieved, or a reversion to the most primitive conceptions. The excavations have further revealed the methods of construction, the plan and the arrangement of cities, and such data in an ancient text can sometimes, even to-day, be checked by comparison with the ruins of the monument, a description of which it provides.

However, the thousands of documents of all sorts are far from constituting a continuous series throughout the ages. The chance of the diggings has brought to light collections each of which forms a whole for a specific epoch and place in a particular category, but the equivalent of which for another epoch or another place cannot at present be reconstituted. So temple accounts have come down to us chiefly from the third millennium; family archives from the time of the first dynasty of Babylon and others from that of the Achæmenid kings. Assyrian art is scarcely revealed to us save between the ninth and seventh centuries, while the history of Assyria begins before 2400 B.C.

The first care in the study of a civilization, whatever it be, must be to classify the documents by epochs. Great social and political upheavals do not happen without modifying manners and customs more or less profoundly, without leaving traces on art and literature. So we must now determine the chronological framework within which Babylonian and Assyrian institutions developed.

The framework is double according as we consider the temporal relation connecting the events among themselves, or that which unites those events to the present.

A natural division, that of the day, is imposed upon all peoples; the succession of night and day, whatever starting-point—the rising or setting of the sun, its passage across the

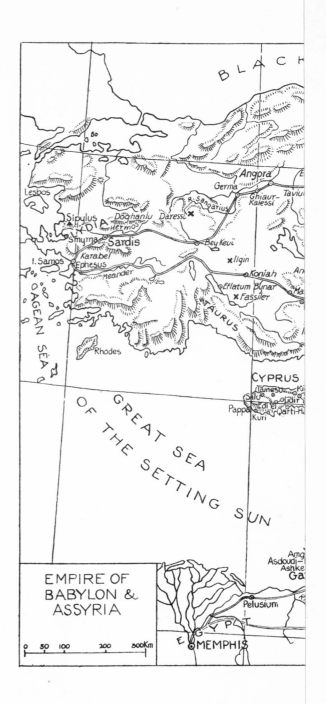

BLACK

Lesbos

Angora
Germa
Taviu
Ghiaur-
Kalessi

Sipylus
LYDIA   Doghanlu Daressi ×
Hermo
R. Sangarius
Smyrna   Sardis
Bey Kevï
Karabel
I. Samos   Ilgin ×
Ephesus   Koniah
Meander   An
Eflatun Bunar
× Fassiler   Ha

AEGEAN SEA

TAURUS

Rhodes

CYPRUS
Tamesu   Ki
Silu   Idir
Pappa   Qarti-Ha
Kuri

GREAT SEA
OF THE SETTING SUN

Amg
Asdoudi-
Ashke
Ga

Pelusium

EMPIRE OF
BABYLON &
ASSYRIA

EGYPT
E   MEMPHIS

0   50 100   200   300Km

meridian, or the middle of the night—be adopted, is the primordial element of every chronology.

A second division springs from the recurrence of the seasons. After a certain number of days the same phenomena are repeated in nature in regular procession. That is the result of the obliquity of ecliptic in respect of the terrestrial equator ; its consequence is the solar year whose duration has been only lately determined, and does not correspond to an exact number of days.

The peoples of antiquity had therefore to have recourse to a third division of time, and adopted the phases of the moon whose four quarters are distributed over a small number of days, but do not correspond, any more than the solar, to a whole number. The Babylonians and Assyrians employed an empirical method, and the month, now of 29, now of 30 or 31 days, had its beginning fixed after the first appearance of the crescent in the heavens. As it was impossible to find a common measure between the lunar month and the revolution of the sun, the year was normally reckoned as twelve months, and equilibrium was restored by intercalating a thirteenth month from time to time.

In the oldest documents, called pre-Sargonic, because they are earlier than the accession of Sargon, king of Agade (twenty-ninth century), the years of each reign were indicated by a simple number. The practice of giving each year a name after some event worthy of commemoration in the previous year began with the epoch of Agade ; it lasted till the Kassite kings, who adopted the system of computation by regnal years, maintained in Babylonia thereafter till the collapse of the empire. In Assyria, the king and the high functionaries were successively eponymous ; this custom goes back to a very remote antiquity, at least to the twenty-fourth century, an epoch when the existence in Cappadocia of a colony of worshippers of Ashur is proved by tablets.

FIRST PART

BABYLONIAN CIVILIZATION

BOOK ONE

HISTORICAL OUTLINE

CHAPTER I

THE LAND AND ITS RESOURCES

EXCEPTING the district of Eridu (Abu Shahreïn), the southernmost city built on an island in the Persian Gulf and separated from the Euphrates valley by sandstone cliffs, the Babylonia of classical writers corresponds precisely to the plain created by the Tigris and Euphrates on their arrival at the sea through the alluvial deposits whose constituents are derived from the Armenian mountains where the rivers rise. Formed in the quarternary epoch after the glacial period, its natural boundaries are : on the west the Arabian desert, inhabited by nomads who make raids upon the sedentary populations : on the north the high plain of Mesopotamia, where the Assyrians were to establish themselves and from which Babylonia is separated by a line commencing at Hit, on the Euphrates, and reaching the Tigris above its junction with the Adhem ; on the east the last outposts of the hills which form the present frontier of Persia, with diverse tribes established in all their valleys ; thence come stone, metals, timber for building ; finally, towards the south the Persian Gulf with its lagoons beyond which navigation scarcely proceeds. At the beginning of historical times this plain did not extend far below the present canal of the Shatt-el-Hai : the country of Lagash, a city whose ruins lie an hour-and-a-quarter to the east of this canal and two hundred kilometres from the gulf, was included in the maritime region.

The regime of the two rivers is not identical. The Tigris, with higher and more resisting banks, has a rapid current.

11

Its flood commences at the beginning of March, reaches its maximum in the first days of May and ends towards the middle of June. The Euphrates carries half as much water ; its flood begins about a fortnight later and does not subside before September ; its banks being lower, it overflows more readily on to the plain, and spreads there a beneficent inundation. So the first inhabitants preferred its banks for the foundation of their cities. The present course of the Euphrates does not wash the ruins of the greater number of these ancient cities ; if Babylon (Hille) and Ur (Muqayyar) are still near its bed, the others are found on the plain much further to the east. But the evidence of the ancient texts proves the change of the river's course due to the looseness of the soil and the crumbling of the banks during the inundation. The ideogram for Euphrates means Stream of Sippar ; then Sippar (Abu Habba) stood upon its banks. One of the years of Samsu-Iluna, a king of the First Dynasty of Babylon, commemorates the building of the walls of Kish (El Oheïmir) on the banks of the Euphrates. The ruins of Kish lie on a canal, the Shatt-el-Nil, which also passes Niffer, the ruins of Nippur ; it was still at the time of Darius II a branch of the Euphrates, the " river of Sippar and Nippur." Shuruppak (Fara) was likewise on the banks of the Euphrates, according to the legend of Gilgamesh. For Larsa (Senkereh) the same information is given by the correspondence of Hammurabi with Sin-idinnam, governor of that town. The river's branches were numerous ; Umma (Yokha) stood on the arm which flowed not far from Lagash. In the earliest historical period, when the two cities were in continual conflict, Entemena, prince of the latter city, cut a canal which connected the two rivers. The Tigris, which was thereby diverted eastward, followed at that epoch almost the course of the Shatt-el-Amâra to-day.

The men who established themselves in these localities, as soon as they were habitable, already possessed a high culture. To put themselves beyond the reach of the flood, they built cities upon artificial escarpments. They constructed houses and temples of brick, they possessed numerous flocks and herds of stock ; they could irrigate their culti-

vated land, cut canals and constructed watering machines.
They worked copper and silver, fashioned arms in metal.
If their sculpture was still rude and naïve, their script bears
witness to great development : it was no longer simply
pictographic, and beside ideographic signs purely phonetic
characters are to be met. In the lowest strata, however,
traces of neolithic industry, chipped flints imported from
the mountainous regions, are found.

The naturalist, Olivier, visiting Mesopotamia at the
beginning of the nineteenth century, found barley, starch
and wheat growing wild on soil unsuitable for cultivation
to the north-west of Anah, on the right bank of the Euphrates.
This region is the original habitat of these three plants, and
from the most remote times they were spread thence in
Babylonia. Barley, the basis of the nourishment of men
and animals, has been the commonest grain at all periods
in history. It formed a highly-prized medium of exchange,
and a loan of barley remained till the end of the Neo-
Babylonian Empire more expensive than a loan of silver.
Millet was also sown, but rye and oats seem to have been
unknown. Sesame was valued for its edible oil, and for a
drink which could be extracted from it ; the tamerisk for
its sugary gum, the vine for raisins and wine. The fig tree
is mentioned with the pomegranate tree in pre-Sargonic
texts, and its fruit was considered worthy to be offered to
the gods by Gudea.[1] The date palm is one of the principal
riches of the land. In the words of Strabo, " it suffices for
all the needs of the population. From it they make a sort
of bread, wine, vinegar, honey, cakes, and a hundred kinds
of tissues ; smiths use its stones in the form of charcoal,
and the same stones crushed and soaked are used in feeding
cattle and sheep which are being fattened." In the gardens
the onion, the cucumber, and many another plant still
unidentified were cultivated. A tablet of the epoch of Agade [2]
(about the twenty-eighth century B.C.) mentions plantations
of onions having an area of a quarter, a half, or even a
whole *gan* [3] (35 ares or $\frac{7}{8}$ acre). In the reed beds gigantic

---

[1] **CXI**, p. 123. [2] **XXIV**, Vol. II, No. 3070.
[3] The relation between the ancient measures and the metric system are
indicated on pp. 224 ff.

rushes served for the construction of shelters and hedges, the fabrication of pens and that of the cinders necessary for the lye.[1]

The animals whose existence is attested by the ancient texts or graphic representations are : among the domestic species, the ass, cattle, sheep, the goat, the pig, the dog and some sorts of poultry ; among the wild species, the lion, the bison, the buffalo, the deer, the leopard, the wild goat, the antelope, the eagle, the snake, the scorpion, several species of fishes and crustaceans.

Two varieties of animals, grouped with the ass species and carefully distinguished from the earliest epoch, represent perhaps the horse and the mule, in any case some species of equidæ.

The ancient inhabitants seem to have had some notion of apiculture ; the existence of bees in the Lower Euphrates valley is certain ; for honey was gathered and used for food.

The fauna and flora of Babylonia originated and developed on an alluvial soil formed by the deposits laid down by the Tigris and Euphrates, and fertilized every year by the beneficent overflow of the two rivers. Man had to found his dwelling above the level of the flood, and to that end to form artificial mounds on which he built a hut of reeds or a house of earth. The clayey soil furnished him with material for making bricks, which he baked or simply left to dry in the sun. From it, too, he fashioned all his pottery for domestic purposes—dishes, drinking vessels, jugs, and jars. From it he shaped tablets on which, with a pen cut from a reed, he commemorated public events or jotted down private memoranda. Of shells and bones he put together ornaments ; but he found no stone, no metal on his territory. The door sockets of the palaces, the diorite or marble blocks from which statues of deities and kings were to be carved, the precious stones from which engraved seals were made, the cedar-wood so highly prized for the decoration of sanctuaries, gold and silver, iron and copper for all sorts of implements, all these had to be imported by the Babylonian.

This necessity led to relations with other ethnic groups. To the south swamps extended to the seashore, and navigation was never destined to reach a high development. In

the south-west all was inhospitable wilderness which imagination peopled with terrifying demons. A natural route
opened towards the north; ascending the Euphrates you
reached, beyond the junction with the Habur, mountains
where diorite was abundant; further on in the Taurus,
west of the bend of the river, were silver mines exploited
from a high antiquity; in the Amanus and the Lebanon
grew forests of cedars and other trees to serve as rafts for
the transportation of stone blocks, and then to be used
themselves in building. The caravans from Babylon will
descend along the Mediterranean coast to the Nile delta,
preparing the path for the Assyrians and Nebuchadrezzar.
In Asia Minor, during the course of the third millennium,
the cuneiform script inscribed upon a clay tablet was adopted
by some Semitic worshippers of Ashur, whose art already
manifested certain characteristics which were to distinguish
the works of the Assyrians and Hittites. By the same way,
in the opposite direction, foreign influences were going to
penetrate to Babylonia; towards the end of the third
millennium, after a gradual infiltration, Amorites grasped
the sovereignty and achieved the unity of the empire; still
later the Hittites will come and ruin their power, but will
not succeed in annihilating their work.

To the north, at the end of the third millennium, Babylon
maintained garrisons in the cities where the Assyrian power
was growing up and kept it in subjection for a time. Eastward, beyond the Tigris, stretched a mountainous region
rich in stone and metal. Diverse ethnic groups dwelt there,
against whom a continuous struggle with varying success
would have to be waged. A Sargon, a Narâm-Sin, a Dungi,
could subdue them to the yoke, but reactions would follow.
Awan and Gutium were to exercise dominion over the
lowlands; the Elamites from Emutbal founded a kingdom
at Larsa; a Kassite dynasty was to be established for five
centuries at Babylon, and finally Cyrus, the Anzanite, was
destined to descend from these regions to destroy the Neo-
Babylonian Empire.

CHAPTER II

PEOPLES AND DYNASTIES

THE plain was inhabited by two distinct races, in the south by non-Semites, in the north by Semites. Which were the first comers ? Had they to surrender part of their territory ? Tradition preserves no memory of the answers ; it only notes that now a city of the north, now a city of the south, now even a foreign city, won the hegemony and exercised a more or less ephemeral supremacy. One of the oldest documents testifies to the intervention of a king of Kish, a city of the northern division, between the people of Umma and those of Lagash, who belong to the southern group.

It looks, indeed, as if the non-Semites had originally occupied not only the whole alluvial plain, but also the middle course of the Tigris, where the Assyrian power was destined to arise later on. The Semites appear to have subsequently come from Syria, descending the course of the Euphrates, as their kinsmen, the Amorites, did at a later date, and then settled in the northern region as far as the neighbourhood of Nippur.

The non-Semites are called Sumerians from the name, Sumer, by which their Semitic neighbours designated their territory. Often, too, in the oldest documents this region, called Kengi in Sumerian, is simply named *kalam*, "the Land," in opposition to *kurkur*, "the Countries," an expression applied in general to the whole inhabited world, but more especially to what was not Sumer. Enshakushana I calls himself "Lord of Sumer and king of the Countries." Two centuries at least after him, Lugalzaggisi of Uruk (twenty-ninth century) assigns to himself the title, "king of the Land," after having united under his sceptre all the cities of the region, and he is, so he says, established by the gods as their vicegerent in the sanctuaries of Sumer. His

16

domination extended over Nippur, the religious capital and most northerly city, Ur, Uruk, Larsa. . . . Lagash formed part of the same territory; Gudea, one of its princes, prays that "Sumer should be at the head of the countries," and he received from the god of his city the assurance that oil should flow in abundance in Sumer when the foundations of his temple had been laid. In more ancient times, in the peace treaty dictated by Eanatum of Lagash to the inhabitants of Umma, the goddess of Kesh was included among the deities of Sumer who were to receive the oaths of the vanquished. Shuruppak and Eridu are likewise included in this region.

To the Semites belonged, from a period which cannot yet be determined, Babylon, Sippar, Kish, Opis, Akshak, Kuta, and Akkad or Agade. The latter city, founded or restored by Sargon in the twenty-ninth century, gives its name to the whole north country, and the inhabitants are called Akkadians. Sargon of Agade became also "king of the Land" when, after defeating Lugalzaggisi, he succeeded in conquering it; but apparently it was the kings of Ur who, in the twenty-fourth century, first took the title, "kings of Sumer and Akkad"; and this title was preserved even in the inscriptions of Cyrus after the fall of the Neo-Babylonian Empire. The Amorite kings, who founded the First Dynasty of Babylon, finally united the two regions under one sceptre, and the Sumerian race came to be annihilated to a large extent during the struggle with Elam: Lagash, Umma, Kissura, and Adab were destroyed by fire and scarcely rose again upon their ruins; the Sumerian language disappeared, and was only preserved for liturgical and legal purposes. The name of Akkad was extended to both countries. Geographical unity answered to the political unity, and when a little later an independent power was being formed in the southern region it no longer took the name of Sumer, but declared itself established in the "Land of the Sea."

For the period preceding the First Dynasty of Babylon no absolute chronology exists. The oldest exact date, fixed by astronomical observations, is that of the reign of Ammizaduga, the last but one of the Amorite kings. Yet even this date is not at the time of writing determined beyond all possibility of doubt. The Jesuit, Father Kugler, has carried out researches to discover in what years the occultations of the planet Venus, mentioned in a tablet of Ammizaduga, long preserved in the British Museum, and especially that of his sixth year coinciding with a new moon, could have occurred. Among the dates recognized by him as theoretically possible he had at first adopted 1972–1971 B.C. as that of this sixth year, thus pushing the beginning of the Amorite dynasty back to 2225 B.C. His results were thus in agreement with the data given by Berosus, and with the figures thus proposed by various Assyriologists. Recently, however, he has revised this demonstration and, relying on a new fact, has chosen 1796–1795 instead of 1972–1971. The consequence of this is to reduce by 176 years the whole First Dynasty and all previous events, and to eliminate almost entirely the effective domination of the Second Dynasty in Babylon itself. Its first and last kings can hardly have exercised their sway beyond the region of the Persian Gulf. The First Dynasty will on this view have begun in 2049 B.C., a date very close to the 2057 adopted by the German, Weidner, on the strength of other considerations. The English astronomer Froteringham, for his part, calculates that the only date that could satisfy the data for the sixth year of Ammizaduga, furnished by the cuneiform document, is 1916–1915 B.C. Hence his date for the beginning of the First Dynasty is 2169. Provisionally, we shall retain the chronology formerly accepted, placing the initial year of the First Dynasty in 2225 B.C., until the astronomers come to an agreement or some new discoveries come to light to confirm one thesis or another. Still, it is important to note that there is a very marked tendency among historians and Assyriologists to adopt the lower dates.

The most important sources for the determination of the relative chronology are first of all the monuments of the early kings themselves, discovered in the ancient towns. They give genealogies and the names of princes who governed other cities ; from them the order of the reigns can be deduced and a synchronism established between the activities of diverse centres. To supplement them we turn to the dates derived from account-tablets and from chronological lists drawn up by the ancient scribes. The method of designating each year by an event has the advantage of furnishing us with precious information, but was not without drawbacks for contemporaries ; they had to make use of the systems of nomenclature for the years and as, on the other hand, each city had its own calendar, these lists had to be established and studiously preserved. Some tablets drawn up in the twenty-first century give the succession of the oldest dynasties and, when combined with other texts, furnish an almost unbroken series from an epoch anterior to the most archaic inscriptions. The dates of the first dynasty of Babylon being fixed in the universal calendar, on the theory here adopted, the year 2225 is that when it was founded by Sumu-abum. A tablet in the Louvre gives the chronology of a dynasty which reigned at Larsa for 262 years, and disappeared in the 29th year of Hammurabi, 2095 B.C. The beginning of this series of kings then goes back exactly to 2357. That would allow us to determine the dates of events relating to a contemporary dynasty established at Isin for about 225 years, were there not some obscurity about its last year ; it had begun between 2357 and 2352 B.C., and provisionally, the first of these dates has been taken as the starting-point. Immediately before the dynasty of Isin the tablets indicate the Third Dynasty of Ur, and assign it 117 years. There is a mistake about the fourth king.; his reign is reckoned as seven years, but the contemporary documents prove that he governed two years longer. On the other hand, fifty-eight years are attributed to the reign of another king, Dungi ; a chronological list of events in his reign, unfortunately mutilated, does not look as if it could cover such a large number of years. However that may be, and making, moreover, reservations about the twenty-five years of Ibi-Sin, the last king, we obtain as approximate limits for this dynasty 2474 and 2358 B.C. Before the kings of Ur went the period of alien rule from Gutium intervening between two dynasties of Uruk, both of short duration. Going back still further we come at once to the dynasty of Agade, whose twelve kings ruled 197 years (*circa* 2845–2649) ; the founder of this line, Sargon, had established his kingdom on the ruins of the power of Lugalzaggisi of Uruk, who had been king of Sumer for a quarter of a century. The latter had conquered Urukagina of Lagash, from whose time contemporary documents enable us to trace events back to the reign of Ur-Ninâ. An ancient epigraphic monument containing a reliable datum is the mace-head ornamented with animals, dedicated to the god Ningirsu, patron of the town ; its legend reads : " Mesilim, king of Kish, builder of the temple of Ningirsu, has set (this) for Ningirsu, Lugal-shag-engur being ishakku [1] of Lagash." At this archaic epoch, therefore, a king of the northern region performed an act of suzerainty over a city of the south and built a temple there. At Nippur an ex-voto, dedicated to the god Enlil by Utug, ishakku of Kish, bears still more archaic writing.

At Tell el'Obeid, near Ur, recent excavations have brought to light the foundation tablet of a temple of Ninhursag, bearing the name of A-an-ni-padda, son of Mes-an-ni-padda, of the First Dynasty of Ur, and it may belong to a rather earlier age.

If we wish to penetrate still further into the past, contemporary written documents fail us almost entirely, and it is necessary to refer to later traditions. Sumerians and Akkadians, probably come, the latter from Syria, the former from the mountainous regions east of the Tigris, seem to have forgotten their original homes ; they believed themselves to be autochthonous in the Euphrates Valley. The mythical epoch includes first seventy-two sars (259,200) of years, during which, according to Berosus, no chief existed. Then " royalty descended from the heavens," and for a period extending down to the Flood, we have two traditions based on the sexagesimal system.[2] The one with a long chronology estimates the duration of the ante-diluvian era at 126 sars 4 nêr (i.c. $(2 \times 60 + 6) + 4$, or 456,000 years), corresponding to the information gathered by Berosus (120 sars) ; the other assigns to it only 67 sars, or 241,200 years. The three lists which have come down to us differ similarly in the number of the royal cities and the number of kings, giving 3, 5 or 6 towns, and 8 or 10

---

[1] Formerly the transcription *patesi* was used ; cf. p. 64 note (1).
[2] **XXXVIII**, Vol. II. See VII, 33m année (1924), p. 534 ff.

princes. The oldest city—other traditions also assert this—
was Eridu, the southernmost town. Its name means " the
good city," and was afterwards applied to Babylon—one
source of the confusion in the text of Berosus which caused
this latter town to be regarded as the oldest seat of royalty.
Supremacy passed next to Bad-Tibira (Semitic, Dûr-ququrri,
to-day, Tell-Sifr), later on a mere dependency of Larsa
and the Pantibiblia of Berosus. One of its kings was the
god Dumuzi, " the shepherd " (Berosus' Daos), first of the
six children of Enki, god of Eridu, and also god of vegetation,
the lover of the goddess Ishtar. The third royal town was
Larak, on the former course of the Tigris (to-day the Shatt-
el-Haï). The fourth was Sippar, in the northern region,
where Enmeduranki (the Evedorachos of Berosus) reigned,
to whom tradition ascribed the institution of the priesthood.
Finally, the sceptre passed to Shuruppak (Fara) in the
south. Here Ubar-Tutu (Berosus' Opartes) was directly or
ultimately succeeded by Ziusudu, the Xisuthros of Berosus,
whose name was translated in Semitic by Uta-napishtim-
rûqu, Uta-napishtim the remote. In the days of Ziusudu
the gods decreed the annihilation of mankind and caused
them to perish in the Flood. The royal lists, to which
allusion has already been made, carry on the series of
dynasties which succeeded one another in Sumer and Akkad,
from the Deluge to the kings of Isin. Ten cities were in
turn the centre of a more or less extensive empire, and a
hundred and twenty-three kings are mentioned before those
of Isin. Four times the foreigner had imposed his sway—
Awan and Hamazi, cities of Elam, Mari (Uerdi), a town
situated on the Middle Euphrates, and finally Gutium. At
Kish, a city of the north, twenty-three princes followed
one another during a fabulous period of 24,510 years, 3
months, $3\frac{1}{2}$ days [1]: one of them, Etana, a divine hero in
a legend, was carried up to heaven by an eagle. The next
dynasty had its seat at Uruk in Sumer : the third king,
Lugal-marda, was honoured as a god by later generations,
as was his successor, Dumuzi, the fisher. After them ruled
Gilgamesh, the type of Sumerian greatness and hero of a
magnificent epic, commemorated by several princes for the
works he had carried out in his city. After some other

[1] **XXXVIII**, W–B, 144.

dynasties [1] we reach the historic age, that for which we possess contemporary written documents.

In 1923 the joint expedition of the British Museum and the Museum of the University of Pennsylvania discovered at Tell-el'Obeid a foundation-tablet in the name of A-an-ni-padda, son of that Mes-an-ni-padda who appears in the dynastic lists as the founder of the First Dynasty of Ur. The writing is very little older than that on the mace of Mesilim (Fig. 2); this is fresh evidence that the chronology

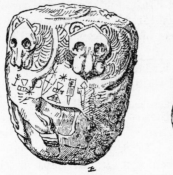

FIG. 2. Votive mace-head of Mesilim (Tello, Louvre).

of these lists rests on no sure foundation. Perhaps their compilers just placed one after the other the houses of local princes partly or even wholly contemporaneous. At present we can scarcely go back further than Mesilim, king of Kish, in the northern region, who extended his dominion over Sumer. If a dispute arose between rival cities, he intervened as sovereign and restored peace. Entemena of Lagash reports that he ought to exercise his royal prerogative as the result of a conflict between that city and Umma, to lay down a frontier between them, and erect there a stele commemorating the peace treaty. In accordance with the religious ideas of the period, he only intervened at the behest of the goddess of Kish, and to transcribe upon a stele the text of the treaty the details of which had been determined by the gods when Enlil, the chief god of Sumer, had bidden the deities of Lagash and Umma to make peace and fix the limits between their territories.

Ur-Ninâ was the founder of a local dynasty of Lagash.

[1] **XIII**, 1921, pp. 241 ff.; **XXXI**, vol. I; **XXXVIII**, W–B, 144; cf. p. 61 below.

This prince does not seem to have been of a warlike temperament. All his inscriptions refer to works of peace : he restores the ramparts, constructs or rebuilds temples and other public buildings, consecrates statues for the gods and cuts canals, one of which is dedicated to Enlil, the chief god of Sumer. In the quarter of Girsu he built a granary, the substructure of which has been recovered. On some sculptured slabs he had himself represented carrying on his head a basketful of building material. He had timber

FIG. 3.   Ur-Ninâ and his family (Tello, Louvre).

felled in the distant mountains, transported it by water, and employed it for the gates and roofs of buildings. His reign was an epoch of prosperity and growth for the city of Lagash. Akurgal, his son, succeeded him, but he appears soon to have been replaced by Eanatum. The latter found it necessary to restore the quarter of Girsu, rebuild that of Ninâ, and raise anew the ramparts of the sacred city. Lagash must have suffered some disaster during the reign of Akurgal, and that prince had abandoned the title of king and adopted instead that of ishakku.

Without any provocation on the part of the people of
Lagash, Ush, ishakku of Umma, at the behest of his god,
Shara, removed the stele of Mesilim, broke the treaty once
sworn before all the gods of Sumer, and invaded the Guedin,
the sacred territory of Ningirsu. The god of Lagash ordered
his vicegerent to defend him, and Enlil, the supreme god of
Sumer, took the part of Eanatum. However, the citizens
of Lagash did not take the field at once; the attack
apparently had been unexpected and had taken the form
of a lightning raid: villages were pillaged and burned,
serfs, flocks and other spoils were carried off to Umma.
Eanatum made careful preparations for avenging the outrage.
He presented himself in the temple of Ningirsu and lay there
prostrate, face to the ground. The god appeared to him in
a vision, promised him victory and the aid of the sun-god.
At word of his approach the people of Umma hastened to
advance to meet him so as to protect their own land and
give battle upon the territory of Lagash. The conflict was
frightful, the carnage immense; to indicate its importance
the official narrative puts at 3600 the number of warriors
left upon the field. The citizens of Umma retire; the men
of Lagash arrive before the walls of their city, attempt an
assault and succeed in scaling the rampart. Then the
carnage is renewed; on every hand is ruin and destruction.
Umma surrenders at last to the mercy of the victors; the
carcases of her soldiers are to be the prey of vultures, those
of the men of Lagash will be gathered together at twenty
points on the plain and receive funerary honours. Eanatum
had a canal cut on the frontiers of the two districts as a
line of demarcation. It was at the same time a barrier in
case of a fresh attack. On its banks the stele of Mesilim was
set up again, and close by a monument was erected to
commemorate the new treaty of peace. Umma had to pay
a tribute in the form of grain, and Lagash exacted immediate
payment. The treaty was confirmed by an oath and placed
under the protection of the gods. The citizens of Lagash
raised chapels in honour of the gods who had aided them,
and erected the monument known as the *Stele of the Vultures*.[1]

This conflict with Umma was not the first campaign of
Eanatum. He had defeated Elam and Urua, whose ishakku

[1] Cf. Fig. 8, p. 70 below.

had been taken prisoner and exposed at the gate of Lagash to the jeers of the populace. In a fourth campaign he made himself master of Uruk. Ur and Ki-Babbar subsequently fell under his sway, which soon extended over all Sumer. Beyond the frontiers of the land he attacked Uruaz, Mishime and Arua, pillaged them and set fire to them. Zuzu, king of Akshak, became alarmed at the success of the king of Lagash; he came and attacked him on the territory of the god Ningirsu, but he was driven back and his army, pursued to the very walls of the capital, was annihilated. A great part of the region of the north fell into the hands of the men of Lagash, and the goddess Innana, by the mouth of the priests of her sanctuaries, had Eanatum proclaimed king of Kish. The period of peace which ensued was to be employed in the digging of a canal and a basin fed by the canal. The prosperity was such that it could be said, " In those days Ningirsu loves Eanatum." The last years of that prince seem to have been darkened by a fresh conflict with Elam. Eanatum lost successively the title of king of Kish, then that of king of Lagash, and became simple ishakku once more. He was reduced when dedicating a mortar to the goddess Ninâ to express the wish that " the king of Kish might not get possession of it."

He died without leaving heirs. Enanatum I, his brother, succeeded him.

Umma renewed the conflict and delivered a violent attack. An indecisive battle was fought on the territory Lagash. Let us pass on to the reign of Entemena; we then find Umma trying once more to shake off the yoke, but her ishakku, pursued into the town, was put to the sword; a foreigner was enthroned in his stead.

Since Enanatum I the priests had been extending their influence considerably : Ur-Halub inscribed his name beside that of the king ; Dudu himself dedicated to the god whose high priest he was, a support for a mace, the bas-relief of which, decorated with his own portrait and the city arms, recalls those which Ur-Ninâ had had carved. And when six hundred Elamites came to ravage the territory of Lagash, in the reign of Enanatum II, Luenna, the priest of Ninmar, who had repulsed them, did not inform the prince directly of his success. It was to Enetarzi, the priest of Ningirsu,

C

that he addressed his message. This Enetarzi seized the
throne. He had as successor the priest, Enlitarzi, and the
son of the latter, Lugalanda, was himself ishakku for some
years. These usurpers abused their position and took upon
themselves to modify to their private advantage the laws
and customs. A reaction ensued. Lugalanda was over-
thrown and replaced by Urukagina, who after a few years
reassumed the title of king. This prince reformed the
abuses; his inscriptions bear testimony to this, the account-
tablets confirm the accuracy of the official texts, and the
sum of these documents reveals the real life of a Sumerian
town at the beginning of the third millennium.[1]

The account of this prince's reforms, drawn up in true
literary style, describes first the hapless condition of the
inhabitants "since the earliest times, since the beginning,"
the exactions of which they were the victims, the injustices
which they suffered. Then the prince describes his reforms
and boasts in conclusion of having " established liberty "
in the realm.[2] The chief officials, following the example
of the ishakku, had been very corrupt. In order to secure
themselves impunity in imposing exactions upon the people,
the higher clergy had adopted the custom of sharing with
the prince and chief dignitaries the temple revenues—
barley, garments, fruit. " In the garden of the mother of
the poor the priests were wont to remove the trees, to despoil
the fruits." " Into the garden of the mother of the poor he
entered no more; he no longer removed her trees, he no
longer despoiled her fruits." " The oxen of the gods were
employed raising water for the lands given unto the ishakku.
As for the barley, among the men of the ishakku would
the priests distribute it . . . the garments . . . cloth . . .
birds . . . kids—the priests were wont to bring as tribute."
" Of the tribute which the priests used to bring unto the
ishakku, he withdrew the overseer thereof. In the house
of the ishakku, and in the field of the ishakku, he reinstated
the god, Ningirsu, their master; in the house of the wife
(of the ishakku), and in the field of the wife he reinstated the
goddess Baü, their mistress; in the house of the children
and in the field of the children he reinstated the god Dunsha-
gana, their master." The useless officials were suppressed;

[1] Cf. **LXXVIII.**   [2] **CV**, pp. 74 f.

others who had not been unfaithful were continued in office. So the intendent, Eniggal, " scribe of the house of the wife " (of the ishakku) since the second year of Lugalanda, became "scribe of the goddess Baü," and continued to enjoy the prince's favour. Moreover, numerous account-tablets witness to his activity in respect of the great undertakings of the state. Urukagina fixed the fees of the clergy. One priest used to receive for a burial 7 urns of fermented liquor, 420 loaves, 120 qa of grain, 1 garment, 1 kid, 1 bed ; in future he would only be entitled to 3 urns of liquor, 80 loaves, 1 kid and 1 bed. Another, to whom he had allowed 60 qa of grain, found his share reduced by half. The sooth-sayers were salaried officials of the temples, but they had been accustomed to charge for their services ; they had now to return to the ancient practice and give their consultations gratis. The abuses of the rich were checked. Whether he wanted to specify in the law the obligation of paying for any property, real or personal, which they desired to appropriate, or wished to forbid seizure by force, Urukagina selected the concrete cases of the ass or the house : " If a good ass be born unto a subject of the king, and if his lord say unto him ' I would buy it,' in the case that he shall buy it, let him say : ' Pay in good silver,' and in the case that he shall not buy it, the lord must not (take it)." And each enjoyed liberty in accordance with his station.

Urukagina moreover represents himself in his inscriptions as a royal builder. He commemorates the reconstruction of several temples, particularly of the Eninnu, the sanctuary of Ningirsu. Some labels in the form of perforated olives show the care with which precious objects belonging to the temples, the gods, or the high officials were hidden in a bastion of the ramparts under the reign of this prince, perhaps at the time when the city was invested by the men of Umma ; for the latter shook off the yoke, tore up the treaty dictated by Entemena, and under the leadership of their ishakku, Lugalzaggisi, carried fire and sword among their hereditary foes. The kingship of Lagash was destroyed, and a little later a scribe wrote a lament upon the devastation of the town which forms one of the most beautiful pages of Sumerian literature.[1]

[1] Cf. p. 205.

In the royal lists compiled in the twenty-first century, Lugalzaggisi by himself constitutes the Fifteenth Dynasty, and a reign of twenty-five years (*circa* 2870–2846) is attributed to him. Before him the Fourth Dynasty of Kish is mentioned, not Urukagina, whose power seems scarcely to have extended beyond his own town.

After his success against Lagash, the ishakku of Umma seized various cities in Sumer, and had himself proclaimed king of the Land and priest of Anu in Uruk. He abandoned his old title of ishakku of Umma, but kept that of prophet of Nisaba. Nippur fell into his hands ; he became high ishakku of Enlil, to whom he dedicated some stone vases and a statue. " Enlil hath subjected the countries to his power ; from the east unto the west he hath conquered all." He fought his way to the Persian Gulf and northward raided even the coasts of Syria. He concerned himself besides with works of public utility—for instance, the irrigation of the territory of Larsa. He besought the gods " to bestow upon him generously soldiers like the grass of the field in multitude," not to change his happy destiny, and to maintain him for ever as shepherd of his people. His hegemony scarcely extended over Akkad as far as we can judge. There a rival Semitic power was growing up which was destined to unite both regions under a single sceptre. Later, legend was to represent Sargon as brought into the world in secret, exposed on the Euphrates in a basket of reeds caulked with bitumen, and picked up by the irrigator Akki, who brought him up as his own son. Sargon, according to another tradition, was first the gardener, then the libation-bearer of Ur-Zababa, a king of the Fourth Dynasty of Kish. This Sargon founded the dynasty of Agade. The inscription on the base of a monument, erected in the temple of Enlil at Nippur, celebrates the downfall of Lugalzaggisi. Sargon had taken Uruk, probably by surprise, and had removed its walls. He strove next with the forces of the men of Uruk and defeated them. In a second battle he took Lugalziggisi himself prisoner and brought him in chains before Enlil, the chief god of Sumer, to obtain the dethronement of the old king and the transfer to himself of the title of high ishakku. He was thus master of northern Sumer. In another campaign he crushed the forces of Ur and dismantled that city. The whole territory of Lagash next fell into his hands and, reaching the shores of the Persian Gulf, he washed his arms in the sea, following a religious rite which was to be repeated till the last days of the Babylonian Empire. On his return he completed the conquest of Sumer by taking Umma, which he dismantled.

The same inscription relates how, by the grace of Enlil, Sargon became master without rival from the upper sea (the Mediterranean) to the lower sea (the Persian Gulf). The legend on a statue gives some details of the political situation to the north-west of Sumer and Akkad. It names three realms—Mari, on the Middle Euphrates, which once had ruled as far as the Persian Gulf, and in Eanatum's time had been allied with Kish against the king of Lagash ; Iarmuti, west of the bend of the Euphrates, and finally Ibla, on the slopes of the Taurus. Across these territories Sargon's power extended to " the cedar forests " (Lebanon or Anti-Lebanon) and " the mountains of silver " (Taurus). These had been the objective of the expedition. His own country, an alluvial land, yielded the inhabitants neither timber for building nor stone nor metal ; it had been necessary from the beginning to try to assure a supply from outside, either among the mountains east of the Tigris, inhabited by hostile peoples, or in the direction of the Taurus and Lebanon, following the natural route offered by the Euphrates.

In the third year of his reign, at the request of a colony of Semitic merchants established at Ganes (Gul-tepe (?) in Cappadocia), who were oppressed by Nûr-Dagan, king of Bursahanda, he marched against that town, whence he sent to Akkad two species of fig trees, vines, rose trees and other plants.[1]

Sargon constructed or rebuilt Agade, or Akkad, the site of which has not been identified ; he made it the capital of his empire. His court was most gorgeous : sometimes he describes in detail the princes who are in his presence, and sometimes he mentions that 5400 men took meat before him every day.

The inscription on another monument from Ekur, mentions two victorious conflicts with Elam and Barahse ;

[1] **XLI**, *fasc.* 6.

sculptures depict the vanquished, the despoiled, the tribes
of the subjugated cities. Kazallu, at the foot of the mountains of Elam, was also conquered. Another campaign
reached Shirihum, on the shore of the Persian Gulf and,
according to the Neo-Babylonian tradition, Sargon may
have embarked his troops to go and conquer Dilmun.
Towards the end of his life a general revolt occurred.
Besieged in Agade he defeated his enemies and offered an
enormous booty to the goddess Ishtar. Subartu, the region
north of Akkad, had given help to the rebels ; it was conquered. The city of Babylon is now mentioned for the first
time in history. It, too, had participated in the revolt ;
it was sacked. However, peace was not re-established.
Sargon disappears and his son only receives the title of
shar kish(shatim), king of the totality, which was connected
with the cult of Anu and corresponded in Akkad to the
lugal kalama of Sumer.

Urumush had to face foes on every hand. Against the
armies of Ur and Umma he gave battle, slew 8040 men,
and took prisoner the king of Ur, his ishakkê, and 5460
warriors. He pursued his victorious march as far as the
sea, ravaged the fields, destroyed the cities, took back
hostages. On his return he captured Kazallu and spread
terror in Elam. Umma reconstituted a coalition with Dêr ;
he overthrew it, put 8900 warriors to death and took 3500
captives. Hallab and Lagash had taken part in the struggle ;
their ishakkê and ministers were among the prisoners. He
subdued Elam and conquered Abalgamash, king of Barahse ;
a great battle was fought on the river Kabnitum, between
Awan and Susa. Anshan and Sirihum were conquered.
Like his father, Urumush could declare that he had subdued
to Enlil the upper sea and the lower sea and all the mountainous regions. However, he only assumed the title of
shar kish, and did not call himself king of Agade. He set
up monuments of victory in the temple of Nippur, placed
his own leaden statue in front of the statue of the god,
dedicated part of the booty to him and fixed foundations
for the offerings.

Manishtusu smote Anshan and Sirihum, traversed the
Persian Gulf to attack thirty-two petty kings on the Elamite
coast, but above all to assure the exploitation of the silver

mines and stone quarries. In the neighbourhood of Agade
he acquired large tracts of land and had his proprietary
title engraved on a diorite obelisk. Susa recognised his
authority; its ishakku dedicated a statuette in his honour.

FIG. 4.   Stele of Narâm-Sin (Délégation en Perse, Louvre).

Narâm-Sin (*circa* 2768–2712) extended his sway from the
Persian Gulf to Asia Minor. Several monuments bear
witness to his glory and the development of the fine arts in
his reign. At Pir-Hussein, on the Ambar-Su, four and a half
hours north of Diarbekir, a stele has been found in place
where he set it up. On another stele, carried to Susa by a
conquering Elamite, a clever sculptor has made the struggle

against the kings of Suduri and Lulubu live again.[1] During
his lifetime he was deified : the inscriptions on several
cylinders belonging to high officials expressly call him
" god of Agade." Numerous account-tablets date from his
reign and that of his grandson, Shargalisharri (*circa* 2711–
2688).

Uruk revolted and had to be reconquered. The Elamites
reached Umma, but were driven back. Northward war
with Gutium, north-east with Basar. One year-name
commemorated the capture of the king of Kuta and the

FIG. 5.   Statue of Gudea (Tello, Louvre).

laying of foundations of temples at Babylon ; another, the
continuation of the building of the Ekur at Nippur, begun
in the previous reign ; some inscribed door-sockets and
stamps for bricks have been found among the ruins. On
the death of Shargalisharri anarchy prevailed. " Who was
king, who was not king ? " Four reigns in three years !
Dudu, who has left an alabaster vase, and his son, Gimil-
DUR-KIB (*circa* 2656–2649), close the list of princes of
Agade.

A dynasty of Uruk with five kings recovered the su-

[1] Fig. 4.

premacy for twenty-six years (*circa* 2648–2623). But the hordes of Gutium, who less than a century earlier had been repulsed by Shargalisharri, descended upon the plain from the eastern mountains and subdued Sumer and Akkad (*circa* 2622–2498). One of the kings of this race, Lasirab, had a legend in Akkadian engraved on a votive mace. In it he invokes Innina and Sin with the gods of his own land. After one hundred and twenty-five years, Utu-hegal, proclaimed king of Umma and the four regions, placed himself under the auspices of Enlil, of Innana, the goddess of Uruk, and of Gilgamesh the old legendary king ; he gathered together the forces of Uruk and Kullab against the foreigner. Tiriqan, king of Gutium, lost the battle and fled towards his fortress of Dubrum. Abandoned by his men, he was taken prisoner with his wife and children. Independence was re-established. From this still obscure period a few names have survived, those of ishakkê of Lagash. Among them was Gudea, whose influence extended well beyond his own city. Of him the Louvre possesses eleven statues, two statuettes, some fragments of a stele, two cylinders of terra-cotta commemorating the rebuilding of the great temple of Lagash, some bricks, some clay nails, tablets, vases, maces, a votive lion and seal impressions. He rebuilt the Eninnu on a magnificent scale : the inscription on the cylinders describes at length the preparations for this work, its execution, and the dedicatory festivals. In each restored temple he placed his own statue in a humble and respectful attitude before the deity. In the court of the Eninnu he set up seven stelæ, two of which have been partially recovered. In addition, we have a mace of Taurus marble, decorated with lions' heads and covered with a layer of gold ; a vase decorated with dragons, the prototype of those which are to be the emblem of Marduk, god of Babylon, and which continue to figure on the bas-reliefs and paintings even under the new empire ; and a lion dedicated to the goddess Gatumdug.[1] The temples restored, he took care to re-establish the old pious foundations and to increase the majority of the ritual offerings. His inscriptions only make curt reference to military events—a war with Anshan. Possibly Gudea was deified during his life. Certainly, soon

[1] Cf. Figs. 5, 18 and 19.

after his death, he was the object of a cult, and regular
foundations were established for offerings to his statue. He
had as successor his son, Ur-Ningirsu, soon displaced as
ishakku by Ur-Engur, king of Ur, but retained as priest of
Anu and Enki till the reign of Dungi.

It was about 2474 B.C. that there arose at Ur the Third
Dynasty founded by Ur-Engur.[1] Ur had been laid waste, its
palace burnt, its walls pulled down. The new king reconstructed his city, rebuilt the temple of Nannar. He became lord
of Uruk and installed his son there as high priest of Innana,
captured Lagash, deposed its ishakku and replaced him by
Ur-Abba and cut a canal there. Becoming king of Sumer
and Akkad he rebuilt many a temple—at Larsa that of the
sun-god, at Nippur those of Enlil and Ninlil. He cut canals,
reformed the law, and " made justice reign." The seal
cylinder of Hashhamer, ishakku of Ishkun-Sin and vassal
of the king of Ur, one of the best known specimens of the
glyptic of the period, is the only proof of his power in Akkad.
A date during his reign commemorates a campaign "from
the low land to the high land."

Dungi,[2] son of Ur-Engur, succeeded him about 2456 B.C.
His long reign of fifty-eight years falls into two periods.
During the first the king seems to have devoted himself
exclusively to the works of peace. Each year commemorates
a religious event or public works : the foundations of
temples, the construction of sacred furniture, the induction
of deities into their restored sanctuaries, the appointment
of high priests by means of omens, the restoration of monuments. However, he neglected no opportunity for extending
his hegemony. When the thirty-third year came, it witnessed
the beginning of a series of campaigns against the lands
lying in the mountainous region east of Sumer and Akkad.
Monuments of his reign have been discovered on many sites,
such as Nippur, Muqayyar, and Tello. Building bricks
found at Susa indicate that his sway extended effectively
over that city. Tablets from Tello, belonging to the series
of " provisions for the journey," show that the central

[1] Some Assyriologists read this name Ur-Nammu.
[2] There is a tendency among Assyriologists to prefer the reading Shulgi.

power was directly concerned with the details of administration in the most distant cities, and that it had organized a service of couriers with relays to transmit orders and insure their execution. The king was further at pains to tighten the bond of union among his vassals by imposts which were at the same time religious links. About his forty-eighth year he reorganized the park near the temple of Enlil, chief god of Sumer. There, for thirty years, till the last days of the dynasty, were to be gathered, together with voluntary offerings, the feudal dues imposed upon the cities and their governors. The latter, even when they kept the title of ishakku, are quite often only officials appointed by the king. Umma, Babylon, Marad (Wannet-es-Sadun, near Afej), Adab (Bismaya), Ur, Shuruppak and Kazallu (between Marad and Agade) had to make provision for certain offerings each for one month in the year; the ishakku of Girsu pays by himself four monthly contributions each year; the twelfth part belongs to the ishakku of the feast of Dungi. The other cities, such as Nippur in Sumer, Kish in Akkad, Harshi east of the Tigris, Mari and Ibla on the Euphrates in the west, furnished occasional contributions, dues, taxes. The bureaucracy, already highly developed in the towns in the time of Lugalanda and Urukagina, had expanded enormously. No business could be transacted in the public magazines without a tablet being written out which was carefully preserved by the archivists and listed in the indices covering the finances of one or more years. No opportunity was lost which might serve to the aggrandizement of the royal power: in year 25, Princess Nialimmidashu, the king's daughter, became the queen of Marhashi, in the mountainous region; in year 39, the ishakku of Anshan espoused one of the royal princesses, but friendly relations did not last long, and four years later his terrority was ravaged.

Dungi, like Narâm-Sin before him, caused divine honours to be paid to him. Temples were built for him, offerings were offered to his statue at the new moon and at the full moon. In some calendars one of the months was even called that " of the feast of Dungi." Hymns were composed in his honour, and it was this god-king whose name was used in forming the names of his subjects—Dungi-ilî (Dungi is my god), Dungi-bâni (Dungi is creator), Dungi-abî (Dungi is my father).

Bur-Sin, son of Dungi, succeeded him and reigned nine years. He had to carry on the war with the peoples beyond the Tigris. The devastation of Urbillum in his year 1, of Sharu and Huhunuri in years 5 and 6, served as marks in the calendar. The other dates belong to the sphere of religion. At Eridu he restored the apsu of Enlil; at Ur he set up a statue and executed many works in the temple of the moon-god; at Nippur he constructed a building for the sacrifices of honey, butter, and wine to Enlil. "The god who gives life to his land," " the sun-god of his country," he, like his father, received offerings in temples consecrated to him. He kept his place in the pantheon, and in the seventh century he reappears in the retinue of the god of Ur. Assyria now appears for the first time in the history of Sumer and Akkad : Zariku, shakkanak of Assur, makes a dedication for the life of his lord, " Bur-Sin, mighty king of Ur, king of the four regions."

A door-socket in one of the temples, raised in honour of the reigning king in Ur itself, bears a dedication by Lugal-maguri, ishakku of Ur, in honour of Gimil-Sin, " his god," the son and successor of Bur-Sin. According to contemporary documents this king, like his father, reigned for nine years (*circa* 2389–2381). He devastated Simanum on the east, and had to construct a wall running from the Tigris to the Euphrates, near Sippar, which would protect his territory against the incursions of the Amorites. In year 6 the overthrow of the land of Zabshali. He, too, restored temples and embellished them. In his reign the centralization progressed ; the chief minister, Arad-Nannar, confirmed in the office which his father and grandfather had held, can call himself ishakku of six cities and governor of five others, and of two lands in the inscription on the door-sockets of the temple which he raised at Girsu in honour of the king.

Ibi-Sin, son of Gimil-Sin, is the last king of the dynasty (*circa* 2380–2358). The known documents all refer to the first two or three years of his reign. He wasted Anshan and married one of his daughters to the ishakku of that land. Hard pressed by Ishbi-Ira, the chief of the Amorites of Mari, on the Middle Euphrates, and by the Elamites under

Kutur-Nahhunte, who were eager to free themselves from his yoke and occupy the plain, he was unable to maintain his power. Taken prisoner, he was carried away to Mari. Two new realms rose on the ruins of the empire of Ur, one at Isin, the other at Larsa.

Ishbi-Ira established an Amorite dynasty at Isin, whose princes styled themselves kings of Sumer and Akkad, and had divine honours paid them. The third king of this line counted Sippar among the cities subject to his dominion. His son, Ishme-Dagan (*circa* 2294–2275) extended his sway over Nippur, Ur, Eridu, and Uruk. His brother, Lipit-Ishtar, succeeded him (*circa* 2274–2264) and was replaced by Ur-Inurta (*circa* 2263–2236). On building bricks the latter bears the same titles as his predecessors. However, during his reign, Gungunum, fifth king of Larsa (2264–2238), consolidated his power, captured Ur, and ended by adopting the title of king of Sumer and Akkad. Enanatum, son of Ishme-Dagan, was confirmed in his office as high priest of Nannar at Ur by him, and in gratitude therefor erected a temple to Babbar, the god of Larsa, for the life of Gungunum, "king of Ur." The capture of Ur was anterior to the year 9 of the reign; for in that year the king caused emblems to be placed in the temple of Nannar, and in the following year enthroned a copper statue there. The chief events recorded belong to the civil or religious sphere. Two military operations are, however, mentioned in the dates: the devastation of Bashime in year 2 and that of Anshan in year 4. Abî-sarê (2237–2227) succeeded Gungunum. He, too, cut canals, adorned the temples of the gods; Nannar of Ur received two statues, one of silver, the other of cornelian and lapis lazuli. In year 9 a battle against the army of Isin, whose king was Bur-Sin (*circa* 2235–2215). Bur-Sin adopted the titles of his predecessors and claimed the suzerainty over Nippur, Ur, Eridu, Uruk, and Isin. A cylinder, whose legend bears his name, shows already the characteristics of the glyptic of the First Dynasty of Babylon. However, Sumu-ilum (2226–2198), the successor of Abî-sarê, had kept the title of king of Ur and possessed Lagash, where a votive dog in steatite was vowed to the goddess, Nin-Isin, in his honour.[1] He waged war against Kazallu

[1] Fig. 20, p. 182.

(year 3, year 21), Ka-ida (year 2), and Kish (year 10) ; cut canals, offered a silver statue to Shamash.[1]

The year following that in which the accession of Sumu-ilum took place, is one of the most important dates in the history of the Orient. In 2225 B.C. the Amorite Sumu-abum had himself proclaimed king at Babylon. The dynasty which he founded will destroy the dynasties of Isin and Larsa, extend its power over all Sumer and Akkad, and realize the final unity of the two lands under a single sceptre, so often attempted for more than two thousand years by the principal cities. The Sumerian race will be partly annihilated, partly assimilated. The very name Sumer will be only preserved in protocols ; that of Akkad will embrace the whole region. Babylon will become not only the political capital, but also the religious capital of the Empire.

Sumu-abum (2225–2212) was attacked by Ilushuma of Assur. Although known to Babylonian tradition, the conflict seems to have been indecisive, since the king did not commemorate its conclusion. He made haste to fortify his city and encircled it with a rampart of unbaked brick, then he aimed at expansion. In year 3 he constructed the wall of Kibalbarru in the immediate vicinity of the capital. In year 9 he incorporated Dilbat, twenty-seven kilometres away, the centre of an agricultural region which would assure the supply of provisions for the capital. Sippar recognized his suzerainty, since the name of the king of Babylon was inscribed in the oath-formula there, but it enjoyed some degree of independence ; it had its own kings, its own calendar, its own judicial practice. Kish resisted for eight years ; to reduce it Sumu-abum allied himself with the king of Larsa and in his tenth year performed an act of suzerainty in the stubborn town by offering a crown to the god Anum. Then he turned to the east, attacked Kazallu, upon which Sumu-ilum had made war, about 2224 B.C. and laid it waste (2214). He died two years later and Sumu-la-ilum succeeded him (2211–2176). Kish had then recovered a certain independence. An inscription of Ashduni-erim, the opponent

[1] Cf. **CV.**

of Sumu-abum, refers to a war lasting eight years against
" the four regions." In the eighth year the king of Kish had
only three hundred warriors left, but by the help of his gods,
Zababa and Ishtar, he had won back, so he says, the supremacy in forty days after fighting a day's march from home—
that would correspond to the distance from Kish to Babylon.
Under Manama in 2212 B.C. it was in the name of that prince
and not that of Sumu-abum that oaths were taken. Some
tablets bear the dates current at Babylon, others local dates.
After Manama came Sumu-ditana and Iawium, in whose
reign the city was taken and laid waste by Sumu-la-ilum
(2200).

In his first year Sumu-la-ilum had had the canal, Shamash-
hegallu, cut. He had built the great wall of Babylon (2208),
raised the temple of Adad (2205) and, the year before the
destruction of Kish, cut a new canal to which he gave his own
name. In 2195 B.C. Iazir-el of Kazallu revolted, marched
against Babylon, and embroiled Kish in the conflict. The
latter city was taken the next year, its ramparts were razed
to the ground. The walls of Kazallu were levelled (2193), and
its army beaten. Iazir-el had made good his escape. He was
not to be recaptured and put to death till 2188 B.C. The
years 22, 24, and 26 of the reign commemorate religious
events—the adornment with gold and silver of the throne
of Marduk ; statues to Zarpanitum, Ishtar, and Nana. In
2185 B.C. the king of Babylon made himself master of Kutha
and restored its walls. In the same year he set foot in Sumer
and annexed Dur-Zakar, one of the defences of Nippur. He
died after a reign of thirty-six years, bequeathing to his son,
Zabium (2175–2162), a realm which embraced the whole of
the territory of Akkad, whose frontier on the south was
defended by four fortresses, and the region of Dur-Zakar in
Sumer.

Zabium apparently did not seek to enlarge his realm ; only
one military expedition undertaken by him is known, and it
was directed against a restored Kazallu whose ramparts
he destroyed (2165). He applied himself to the rebuilding
of temples, erected a bronze statue of himself in the E-Babbar
at Sippar (2164), cut a canal, fortified Kar-Shamash. Abil-
Sin (2161–2144) restored the walls of Babylon, constructed
temples, cut canals, offered a precious throne to Shamash.

Sin-idinnam, king of Larsa (2181–2176), son and successor
of Nur-Adad (2197–2182), had won back from Zambia,
twelfth king of Isin, the title of king of Sumer and Akkad.
He had employed the six years of his reign in constructing
fortifications and in insuring the irrigation of his territory.
His successors, Sin-eribâm (2176–2174), Sin-iqîsham (2173–
2169), Tsilli-Adad (2168) pass across the pages of history,
leaving scarcely any mark. Tsilli-Adad was probably over-
thrown by Muti-abal, the king of Kazallu, who next attacked
the *adda* (father) of Emutbal, Kudur-Mabug, son of Simti-
Shilhak. The army of Kazallu was cut to pieces. Kudur-
Mabug contented himself with adding to his title of *adda* of
Emutbal, that of *adda* of the West and secured the recognition
of his son, Warad-Sin, as king of Larsa (2167) in the days of
Zabium, king of Babylon. Then begins a war of the races
which will continue for over seventy years. The stake
is the rich plain of Sumer to the possession of which Elam
finally lays claim. Thirty years later Rîm-Sin, the second
Elamite king of Larsa, will have crushed Isin and put an end
to its independence (2132) ; but in his path will arise the king
of Babylon. In 2095 B.C. he will be defeated by Hammurabi
and next year will fall into his hands.

In 2131 B.C. Sin-muballit (2143–2124) gave battle against
the army of Ur and Larsa. Isin had lost her king, but kept
a certain, albeit precarious, independence between two rivals,
neither of whom probably was strong enough to hold her.
Three years later (2128) the king of Babylon boasted of
having taken the town. Next year Rîm-Sin " in a single
day " captured Dunnum " the principal city of Isin," probably by surprise, made captive its men of war, but spared the
townsfolk. Soon (2126) Isin herself was annexed to the realm
of Larsa. Sin-muballit died in 2124 B.C. His son Hammurabi,
the most illustrious of the kings of Babylon, true founder of
the empire's unity, was destined not only to pursue the policy
of his ancestors, but also to codify the laws and customs, to
reorganize the administration of justice, to centralize the
power. Going further than Dungi, king of Ur, he could
afford to carry through a religious revolution, reduce the
number of gods by compelling rival deities to amalgamate,
and even depose Enlil of Nippur who had enjoyed the
supremacy from time immemorial, in favour of Marduk, the

god of Babylon. Five years after his accession, in 2118 B.C., he captured Uruk and Isin, but it was only in 2095 that he put an end to the dynasty of Larsa by giving battle against the troops of Elam. Rîm-Sin fled to the land of Emutbal whence his father, Kudur-Mabug, had originally come. Next year he was taken prisoner, but the war was not yet finished; the forces of Ashnunnak united with those of Emutbal and it needed a fresh compaign (2093) to reduce them. Twenty years later (2072) in the reign of Samsu-iluna,

Fig. 6. Hammurabi before Shamash
(Délégation en Perse, Louvre).

a pretender was to impersonate Rîm-Sin; he was destined to raise a revolt in Idamaraz, Emutbal, Uruk, and Isin, but not to establish a lasting power.

No sooner had Hammurabi come to power than he set about " establishing justice," and throughout his reign he laboured to collect " the decisions of equity " which he had engraved on stone. The " Code " discovered at Susa is one of those collections, published after the fortieth year of his reign, in which the king proclaimed the remodelled rules of tradition and ancient Sumerian law which were to be applied to the new society in which the Amorites had just fused with the old

inhabitants of Sumer and Akkad. The prologue to this
" Code " enumerates a certain number of cities subjected to
Babylon. Its power extended from Lagash and Eridu near
the Persian Gulf to Assur and Nineveh, two cities in Assyria.

The Sumerian race was tending to disappear, to be confused with the Semitic race, the Akkadian element of which
had received fresh blood from the Amorite immigration.
Sumerian inscriptions were still being composed, but Sumerian
was becoming a dead language and its translation began to
present difficulties. Religion retained it as a sacred language ;
justice kept its formulæ consecrated by use. The scribes then
spent much ingenuity in composing interlinear translations,
lists of signs, words, ideograms, phrases, which were to be
copied again and again and developed down to the end of
the Neo-Babylonian Empire and even in the days of Seleucids.
Hammurabi knew how to take advantage of the decadence
of Sumer for the consolidation of his own power. He conceived the idea of having the ancient legends modified and in
the new versions, adapted to the new political situation,
Marduk, god of Babylon, who formerly had been a second-
class god, the son of the god Enki of Eridu, acquired the first
place in his own right and had the sovereign might of the
supreme god Anu assigned to him by the assembly of the high
gods. So Babylon, the political capital, instead of Nippur,
became the undisputed religious capital to which the Assyrians would come to ask after the theological tradition.

Hammurabi was at pains to develop trade with the west,
with those Mediterranean regions whither people had gone
from the beginning to seek stone, metals and woods containing various essences, which were completely lacking in the
low plains of the Tigris and Euphrates, and where those western
Semites were quartered, from whom his own race was sprung.
In the interior of his realm he had canals cut as much to
facilitate traffic as for the development of cultivation. His
correspondence with governors of cities shows that he took
a personal interest in the administration of justice, in works
of public utility, as much as in the exploitation of his personal
estates and the care of his enormous flocks.

The excavations have revealed that from this epoch rules
existed for the planning of the city of Babylon which, despite
revolutions, despite periods of foreign domination, continued

to be applied till the fall of the Neo-Babylonian Empire. The city of Hammurabi's epoch has been covered up by the Kasr, Tell Amrân-ibu-Ali and the Merkes. In the district north of the Merkes, partly below and partly above the present water-level, rose a private quarter. Its houses were built of unburnt bricks, resting on a foundation of burnt bricks, as was always the practice in future. A thick layer of ashes proves that this quarter was destroyed by a fire, perhaps at the time of the Hittite invasion. The temple of Ishtar of Agade there was tightly wedged in among the houses and already the main streets, parallel to the Sacred Way, were intersected at right angles by other roads, whereas in the old Sumerian towns the dwellings were grouped anyhow and the streets had no fixed direction.

After the destruction of Isin and the capture of Rîm-Sin, the battle against Ashnunnak and Emutbal (2093), Hammurabi had to turn westward and attacked Mari (2090), the walls of which he dismantled. Two years later he gave battle against the forces of Turukku, Kakmu, and Subartu in the north. Finally, in 2086 B.C. he defeated the whole of the hostile lands in Subartu.

Samsu-iluna (2080–2043) maintained the wise traditions of his father. Like him he exercised a keen supervision over his officials and took an interest in great public works. In the eighth year of his reign the Kassites, a people who probably belonged to the Aryan race and seem related to the Mitannians, established in northern Mesopotamia, showed themselves hostile on the eastern frontier. They were defeated and driven back, but soon they began to filter into the land as labourers and workmen. Three centuries later, about 1761 B.C., they were to establish a dynasty in Babylon, which would not be assimilated to the autochthonous element. In the south the recent deposits of the two rivers had formed a marshy region partly covered with reeds and partly cultivated, whose inhabitants, some Sumerian, others Akkadian, to judge by the names of their kings, had perhaps taken refuge there at the time of the infiltrations of the Amorites. This was the " Land of the Sea." Iluma-ilum reigned there and defied the king of Babylon. Two campaigns were undertaken against him but without success. On the contrary, from year 30 of Samsu-iluna the king of the Land of the Sea seemed to be master of Nippur, where a tablet bearing his name has been found, and the king of Babylon was constrained to restore the line of forts which Sumu-la-ilum had planted on the frontier of Akkad. In year 36 Sumu-iluna had to repel an attack by Amorite bands, who tried to come and settle in Babylonia. However, relations with the western regions were generally friendly ; ten years before he had imported a monolith from the great mountain of Amurru.

A later chronicle relates that Abêshu (2042–2015), the son and successor of Sumu-iluna, had recommenced the struggle with Iluma-ilum. To reach him he managed to divert the waters of the Tigris, but he could not catch his enemy. He founded the fortress Dur-Abêshu near the Tigris and built the city of Lukaia on the canal Arahtu in the vicinity of Babylon. He adorned his capital with fresh temples. One was dedicated to Enlil of Nippur, probably to support the king's claim to the old religious capital, now fallen into the hands of the people of the Land of the Sea ; another in honour of Nannar, representing the great temple of Ur. At least five statues of the king were placed in the sanctuaries of the gods and that of the old ishakku of Lagash, Entemena, who also had a chapel at Babylon, was renewed. Abêshu moreover deified himself as his predecessors had done since the conquest of Nippur ; had not the supreme authority passed from Enlil to Marduk and had not the king of Babylon inherited all the prerogatives which the chief ishakku of Enlil had once enjoyed ? The political and social organization founded by Hammurabi was upheld. Despite the loss of a great part of Sumer and the continual menace of difficulties with the Land of the Sea, good relations were successfully maintained, both with Elam and with Syria, and a flourishing trade with both these regions was kept up.

Ammiditana (2014–1978) undertook great public works —a canal Ammiditana, forts, walls, palaces in the suburbs of Babylon on the banks of the Arahtu. He fought with the Land of the Sea ; recaptured Nippur and Isin whose walls he destroyed (year 36). Two years later Ammizaduga (1977–1957) ascended the throne. In year 9 he was in conflict with his neighbours ; in year 10 he built the fortress Dur-Ammizaduga on the banks of the Euphrates ; in year 15 he cut a canal. At the end of his reign and under Samsu-ditana (1956–1926) allusion was made to military struggles. The dynasty disappeared beneath the pressure of the Westerners. According to a Neo-Babylonian chronicle the Hittites, who dwelt in Asia Minor and had had relations with Sumer and Akkad for several centuries, descended from their mountains, followed the course of the Euphrates and came to pillage Babylon, and one of their inscriptions has been discovered there. Marduk and his consort Zarpanitum were carried away captive to Hana[1] where an Amorite realm flourished, the customs of which had been deeply influenced by Babylonian civilization.

For a century and a half (from 1925 to about 1762 B.C.) the kings of the Land of the Sea exercised a more or less precarious authority over the region of Akkad. When the Kassites felt themselves sufficiently strong they seized the power. Gandash (*circa* 1761–1746), founder of the Third Dynasty, calls himself king of Babylon, king of the four regions, king of Sumer and Akkad. He restored the temple of Marduk bereft of the presence of the god. Agum, his son, reigned twenty-two years (*circa* 1745–1724). He had as successor his son, Kashtiliash I (*circa* 1723–1702). Another son, Ulamburiash, conquered the Land of the Sea, whose last king, Ea-gâmil, had made an expedition against Elam. Later it was necessary to reconquer the region. This was done by Agum, a younger son of Kashtiliash I, while his elder brother, Ushshi, occupied the throne of Babylon. The latter's successors were Abirattash, Tashshigurumash, son of Abirattash, and Agumkakrime, son of Tashshigurumash. Agum had the good fortune to recover the statues of Marduk and Zarpanitum, and escorted them back in state to a restored and embellished Esargil. Gold, precious stones, and the rarest timbers vied with one another in the adornment of chapels, in the fabrication of statues and emblems. The clergy was reorganized, the cult re-established, the properties of the gods exempted from all taxes. Agum extended his power eastward over Padan, Alman, Gutium, and Ashnunnak.

For a century and a half we knew nothing of the history of

---

[1] Capital Tirqâ (Tell Ishâra) between Dêr-ez-Zôr and Tsalihiya.

Babylon, save that eight kings followed one another upon the throne ; among them were Kurigalzu I and Melishipak I.

When we can pick up the thread of events again, it is far from the ruins of Babylon that contemporary documents have been found. The chance of excavation has lighted on them in Egypt at Tell-el-Amarna, the site of the city of Akhutaten, built by Amenophis IV, who took thither the diplomatic archives belonging to his father and himself. There we have dug up the correspondence of these two kings with the princes of Syria, with the kings of the Hittites, Mitanni, Assyria, and Babylon. It was written on clay tablets in cuneiform characters, either in Babylonian or in a closely-allied dialect. The influence of Sumer and Akkad on the Mediterranean coast and Asia Minor had been maintained and developed since the expeditions of Sargon of Agade, fourteen centuries before.

Eleven letters from Tell-el-Amarna bear directly on Babylonian affairs. We learn from them that relations had existed between the two countries since the reign of Thothmes III of Egypt. Karaindash I (*circa* 1425), sixteenth king of the Kassite dynasty, had corresponded with Amenophis III. His second successor, Kadashman Enlil I, was on most friendly terms with the Egyptian court, and one of his sisters entered Pharaoh's harem. This was the period when Canaan (Southern Syria) and Amurru (Northern Syria), subjects of Egypt, tried to rebel under the influence of Shubbiluliuma, king of the Hittites. He had passed the Euphrates and ravaged northern Mitanni ; later he had descended into Amurru and carried off thence a rich booty. On the succession of Amenophis IV he sent greetings to the Pharaoh, but when Aziru, a Syrian prince, performed an act of homage to Egypt, he occupied Amurru and by a treaty secured recognition for his suzerainty over it. Babylon was indifferent to these political changes ; what she demanded was security for her merchants on the highways. When his subjects were the victims of robberies or murders in Canaan, the king of Babylon laid the responsibility at the door of the king of Egypt. "Canaan is thy land, and its kings are thy vassals." Moreover, when Canaan had tried to rebel,

Kurigalzu II had refused to assist its revolt. Egypt, on the other hand, was encouraging Assyria against Babylon, and Burnaburiash II (*circa* 1375) complained that Amenophis IV had received an embassy from the Assyrians whom he claimed as his own subjects. The same king reminded Pharaoh that their fathers had exchanged numerous presents. He himself had already received two minæ of gold. He wrote, " Send me much gold, as much as thy father," and promised in return to despatch all that the Egyptian monarch might desire from the products of his own country. In fact, the very day he protested against the robbers on the highways through Canaan, he re-enforced his claims by a substantial present—three minæ of lapis lazuli, five equippages for horses, and five chariots.

Kara-indash (*circa* 1425) had come to an agreement with Ashur-rîm-nishêshu of Assur about their mutual frontiers. Burnaburiash and Ashur-uballit made a similar convention. Later on Burnaburiash married Muballitat-Sherûa, Ashur-uballit's daughter. The son of Burnaburiash, Ashur-uballit's grandson, was slain by the Kassite faction, perhaps because of his relations with Assyria, and replaced by a certain Nazibugah.

The king of Assyria invaded Babylonia and set another of his grandsons, Kurigalzu III, upon the throne (*circa* 1357–1335).

Kurigalzu III conducted a lucky campaign against Elam. He carried his victorious armies to Susa. There he captured as a trophy an agate tablet, dedicated long before by an ishakku to the goddess Ninni for the life of Dungi, king of Ur, carried it off, and offered it to Ninlil of Nippur. Hurpatila, king of Elam, had sent him a challenge : " Come," said he, " let us do battle, thou and I." The issue had been favourable to the Babylonian ; with his own hand he took his adversary prisoner. After the death of his grandfather, Ashur-uballit, Kurigalzu attacked Assyria, but he was defeated at Sugagi on the Zalzallat by Enlil-nirari, who forced him to submit to a rectification of the frontier. Nazimaruttash, his son (*circa* 1334–1309), was defeated at Kâr-Ishtar, and obliged to cede some territory east of the Tigris. Like his father, Kadashman-Turgu (*circa* 1308–1292) left several inscriptions at Nippur. On his death the Hittite

king, Hattusil, wrote that he would break off the alliance with
Babylon unless the young Kadashman-Enlil (1291–1286)
were proclaimed king. Itti-Marduk-balâtu, the prime minister,
objected—" the tone of thy letter is not that of an ally, but
rather that of a master "—and relations between the two
lands were suspended till the prince attained his majority.
At this time the Hittites had lost Canaan which Seti I had
recovered from Mursil, son of Shubbiluliuma, but they still
held Amurru which Rameses II was to reconquer by the
battle of Qadesh. A treaty of offensive and defensive alliance
between the Hittites and Egypt would be the outcome ; the
Babylonian original was engraved on a silver tablet, but a
copy has been discovered among the ruins of Hatti, accompanied by the minute of the letter which tells us of Hattusil's relations with Kadashman-Enlil. Some Babylonian
merchants proceeding in caravan to Amurru and Ugarit,
a city of Phœnicia, while Amurru was still under the
suzerainty of the Hittites, had been massacred, Kadashman-
Enlil appealed to Hattusil to secure the punishment of the
offenders. An Amorite prince also was accused of stirring
up trouble in Babylonia. Hattusil invited his correspondent
to pursue the charge in person. The accused would have to
prove his innocence by oath before the gods in the presence
of the Babylonian ambassador. Hattusil did his best to keep
up friendly relations and urged the king of Babylon to attack
a mutual enemy whom unfortunately he did not mention by
name. The fame of Babylonian science had induced foreign
princes to summon thence doctors, exorcists and scribes to
their courts. Mutallu, Hattusil's brother and predecessor,
had secured the services of a doctor and an exorcist, but they
had never come home. Kadashman-Enlil demanded their
return. The reply states that the exorcist was dead ; as to
the doctor he would be ordered to go back.

His son, Kudur-Ellil (*circa* 1285–1277), his grandson,
Shagarakti-Shuriash (*circa* 1276–1264) and his great-grandson,
Kashtiliash III (*circa* 1263–1256), succeeded Kadashman-
Ellil II. The last-named was defeated by Tukulti-Inurta I
of Assyria, who took him prisoner and brought him in chains
into the presence of the god Ashur. The walls of Babylon
were razed to the ground, her defenders were put to the sword.
The treasures of the Esargil, the spoils of the city, were taken

away to Assyria; even Marduk himself was carried away captive. The king of Assyria died in the course of an insurrection and Babylon took advantage of the occasion to recover some measure of independence. Two kings followed one another there in three years—Ellil-nadin-shum and Kadash-man-Harbe II. The first attacked Kidin-Hutrutash, king of Elam, who had seized the opportunity offered by the Assyrian success for pillaging Dêr and Nippur; he compelled him to retreat behind his own frontiers. Adad-shum-utsur (*circa* 1246–1217), who succeeded Adad-shum iddin(*circa* 1252–1247), secured the restitution of the statue of Marduk by the king of Assyria and perhaps also the return of the seal of Shagar-akti-Shuriash which Sennacherib later recovered from the treasuries of Babylon. When the Assyrians, rebelling against their king who had gone to Babylon, expelled Ashur-shum-lishir, the regent, and requested the delivery of their sovereign, Adad-shum-utsur refused, attacked the new king, defeated him, and slew him in single combat; he pursued the enemy to the walls of Assur, besieged the town, but failed to reduce it.

The throne of Babylon was handed on from father to son by Melis-shipak II (*circa* 1216–1202), Marduk-apal-iddin I (*circa* 1201–1189), and Zababa-shum-iddin. The latter was attacked by Ashur-dân I of Assyria who captured Zaban, Irria, Akarsallu, and carried off an enormous booty. The same year Shutruk-Nahhunte, king of Elam, invaded Babylonia, defeated and slew Zababa-shum-iddin. With his son, Kutir-Nahhunte, he pillaged Sippar and a hundred other towns or villages. He took home a large number of monuments which have been discovered among the ruins of Susa—stelæ of Sargon and Narâm-Sin, the Obelisk of Manish-tusu, the Code of Hammurabi, Kassite " kudurrus," etc. Ellil-nadin-ahê, thirty-sixth and last king of the Kassite dynasty, reigned only three years (1187–1185). For 576 years the Kassites had occupied the throne of Babylon. They had introduced the use of the horse, little known in the plain before their days. They had changed the system of counting the years; from their time each year was designated not by a complicated formula recalling some recent event, but by the number of the place it occupies in the reign of each king, a practice maintained till the fall of the Babylonian Empire. The royal power was no longer strong enough to

ensure the protection of private property ; the aid of religion
must be invoked. So people were not content with establishing titles to property; in addition, upon the great domains
bestowed as rewards by the king on princes or subjects whom
he wished to requite for their services, stones were set up
with divine symbols, the history of the property, and imprecations against anyone who should alter or move the monument, engraved upon them.

It is possible that Shutruk-Nahhunte was proclaimed king
of Babylon after the fall of Zababa-shum-iddin, but the royal
lists give the name of the Kassite Ellil-nadin-ahê and after
him mention the Fourth Dynasty called the house of Pashe.
Its eleven kings occupied the throne for 132½ years. The
second prince of this dynasty, Inurta-nadin-shumi, shook
off the yoke of Elam. The third, Nebuchadrezzar I (*circa*
1140) had to recommence the conflict ; he was defeated at
first by the king of Elam at Dur-Apil-Sin, but he succeeded
in reconquering all his own territory and went so far as to
carry the war beyond his own frontiers. He conquered
Lullumu in the mountainous region east of Babylonia, and
westward made a raid, in consequence of which he adopted
the title " conqueror of Amurru." Ashur-rêsh-ishi, the king
of Assyria, attempted an invasion. Nebuchadrezzar drove
him back and laid siege to the frontier fortress of Zanki, but
was forced to retreat and his munitions were burned by the
enemy. He returned to the charge and was defeated ; his
camp was taken ; the commander-in-chief was made prisoner,
and forty chariots fell into the hands of the Assyrians.
Ellil-nadin-apli (*circa* 1120), the son of Nebuchadrezzar,
occupied all Babylonia ; for he gave some land in the neighbourhood of Edina to the Land of the Sea.

Tiglath-pileser I of Assyria was twice at war with the
king of Babylon. In the first conflict he perhaps already
met Marduk-nadin-ahê (*circa* 1110) ; the Babylonian carried
off in captivity the statues of Adad and Shala, deities of
Ekallatê, which Sennacherib was to discover in a shrine at
Babylon in 689 B.C. In the second war the Assyrian took
Babylon, Dur-Kurigalzu, Sippar, and Ophis, but did not
establish his dominion there. Ashur-bêl-kala, son of Tiglath-

pileser, put an end to the conflict which had raged between the two countries for three centuries with hardly any intermission. He was on excellent terms with Marduk-shapik-zêrim, the successor of Marduk-nadin-ahê. An age of prosperity for Babylon ensued ; her walls were rebuilt, the temple of Marduk enlarged.

A rebellion put an end to the reign of Marduk-shapik-zêrim. Adad-apal-iddin, who took his place upon the throne, married his daughter to the king of Assyria. The peace, or rather the truce, lasted for half a century longer. During that period Sumer and Akkad became the prey of the Sútæans, half nomad Aramæans encamped on the right bank of the Euphrates whence they made raids to plunder the towns and their temples. At Sippar, for instance, the sanctuary of Shamash was devastated by them, and it was only under Shimmash-Shipak, who came from the Land of the Sea and founded the Fifth Dynasty, that the worship could be re-established. This last-named prince died at the sword's point after a reign of eighteen years. An usurper, Ea-mukin-shumi, lived a few months, and during the three years of Kashshu-nadin-ahê there was nothing but civil war, foreign war, and famine. At Sippar the cult of Shamash could not be practised, the foundations had disappeared, the observances were falling into desuetude.

The next dynasty, the Sixth, lasted twenty years and three months (1031–1012) and includes three reigns. It was an epoch of disaster and misery, of storm and floods. An Elamite, Mâr-bîte-apal-utsur, constitutes by himself the Seventh Dynasty and remained six years on the throne (1011–1006).

Nabu-mukîn-apli (*circa* 1005–970), whose portrait is preserved to us on a *kudurru*, founded the Eighth Dynasty. A number of omens collected during his reign have been preserved. The Aramæan tribes beyond the Euphrates were restless and harassed Babylonia : in the seventh year Nabu could not proceed from Borsippa to Babylon for the New Year festivals. Many times during the reign, and even for several consecutive years, the Babylonians had to abandon those religious celebrations to which they attached the utmost importance.

Shamash-mudammiq (*circa* 910), third successor of Nabu-shum-ukîn, defeated by Adad-nirâri of Assyria, lost his cavalry and his chariots. He was killed by Nabu-shum-ukîn, who seized the power. Adad-nirâri invaded Babylonia, took several cities, and carried home a substantial booty. Later on peace was concluded between the two princes ; they delimited their respective territories and interchanged daughters in marriage.

Nabu-apla-iddin, son of Nabu-shum-ukîn, was afraid of being cut off from the markets of Syria by Ashur-nâtsir-apla II,

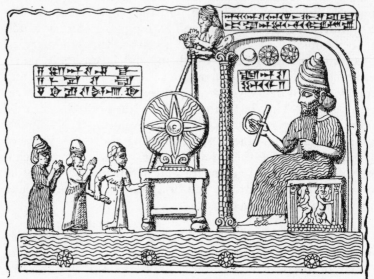

FIG. 7.   Tablet of Nabu-apla-iddin (British Museum).

king of Assyria. He made an alliance with the Aramæans of Suhi (879), above the junctions of the Habur, and sent them troops. But his brother, Tsabdanu, the general Bêl-apla-iddin, and 3000 men fell into the hands of the enemy The king was constrained to make peace with Assyria. Thereafter he could only devote himself to restoring the ruins of his own land. A stone tablet records his works upon the temple of Shamash and the re-establishment of the cult in the thirty-first year of his reign. He had himself portrayed upon it, led into the presence of the god, seated in his sanctuary, by the priest and accompanied by the goddess Aïa (Fig. 7).

Marduk-zakir-shum, son and successor of Nabu-apla-iddin, offered a lapis cylinder engraved in low relief to Marduk. On this *kunukku* the god is depicted standing accompanied by his sacred dragon.[1] In 852 B.C. the same king requested the intervention of Shalmaneser III, king of Assyria, against his brother, Marduk-bêl-ushatê, who had rebelled and proclaimed himself an independent king in the eastern provinces. Shalmaneser ravaged the territory occupied by Marduk-bêl-ushatê and next year he caught the rebel himself and put him to death. The king of Babylon did homage; the Assyrian as sovereign came and paid his respects to the high gods in their temples at Kutha, Borsippa and Babylon and offered rich gifts to them. Then he descended upon Chaldæa, captured the frontier fortress of Bagâni, received the submission of Adini, its chief, and Yakîn, king of the Land of the Sea. He had this campaign illustrated on the bronze reliefs of Balawat; the Chaldæans bring as tribute vases, cattle, and tent poles.

However, Babylon could not long endure this state of submission. Shamshi-adad V, son of Shalmaneser, had to undertake a campaign against Marduk-balâtsu-iqbi, who had formed a league with Chaldæans, Aramæans, Elamites, and warriors of the Namri. A great battle was fought at Dur-Papsukal, and the Assyrians carried off immense spoils. After the death of Marduk-balâtsu-iqbi there may have been an interregnum. Some Aramæans came and settled on the cultivated lands of Babylon and Borsippa. Erba-Marduk, a descendant of Marduk-zakir-shum, put them to the sword, and restored the fields and orchards to their rightful owners. He became king, but he could not "take the hand of Bêl" till the second year of his reign. Another king, Bau-ahê-iddin, was carried away to Assyria by Adad-nirâri III, who seized his treasures. The whole land was conquered; some gods were deported; those of Kutha, Borsippa, and Babylon received offerings from the Assyrian monarch, who came down right into Chaldæa, whose princes paid him tribute.

The *Synchronous History* stops at that point. We know neither the end of the Eighth Dynasty nor the beginning of the Ninth for sixty odd years. The central authority was

[1] Fig. 13, p. 140.

weak in Babylonia, Shamash-rêsh-utsur, in the name of the king of Assyria governor of Mari and Suhi on the Middle Euphrates, acted virtually as an independent sovereign.

In 748 B.C. began the reign of Nabonassar (Nabu-natsir) (748–734), the starting-point of the canon of Ptolemy. In his third year (745) the Assyrian general, Pulu, the fomenter of a military rebellion, had himself proclaimed king of Assyria under the name of Tiglath-pileser III ; he inaugurated the last period of expansion, that which was to ensure for more than a century dominion over Babylon, but was destined to end in 606 B.C. with the fall of Nineveh, the final collapse of Assyria. Without any loss of time he invaded Babylon and compelled Nabonassar, against whom Borsippa and Sippar had revolted, to recognise his authority. The principal cities submitted ; he marched down as far as Nippur and had himself proclaimed king of Sumer and Akkad.

Nabu-nadin-zêr, son of Nabonassar, was killed after reigning two years by Nabu-shum-ukîn, who governed for one month and twelve days and ended the Ninth Dynasty.

The Tenth Dynasty is represented by the names of nineteen kings of diverse origins who occupied the throne between 732 and 606 B.C., during the period when Babylon was almost entirely dependent on Assyria. Nabu-ukîn-zêr (732–730) was deported by Tiglath-pileser, who became king under the name of Pulu (729–727). Shalmaneser V succeeded him, and had himself called Ululaï in Babylonia (727–722). On his death Merodach-Baladan II (721–710), the Chaldæan king of the Bît-Yakîn, in the Land of the Sea, who called himself a descendant of Erba-Marduk, a king of the Eighth Dynasty, appointed a governor at Babylon and claimed to act as sovereign. Sargon II of Assyria, advanced against Akkad. Merodach-Baladan, with the aid of Humbanigash, king of Elam, gave battle to him under the walls of Dêr and inflicted a defeat upon him. He was to reign uncontested for twelve years while the Assyrian was engaged fighting in Syria and Urartu. Still, it was no era of prosperity for the inhabitants of Akkad, since their lands were divided up among the Chaldæan and Aramæan soldiers. So when Sargon, conqueror of the Egyptians and Urartians, returned in 710 B.C. to attack Merodach-Baladan, the latter fled to the south, taking notables from Babylon, Sippar, and Nippur as hostages. The capital was over-joyed at the departure of the tyrant, and organised fêtes in honour of the Assyrian, who was acclaimed as a liberator. On New Year's Day (709) Sargon "took the hand of Bêl" and became the legitimate sovereign of Babylon (709-705). Pressed by his foe, Merodach-Baladan retreated by stages towards the Bît-Yakîn, where he let loose the floods in front of his pursuers ; but the Assyrian foiled his manœuvre and found a passage. Merodach-Baladan fled to Elam, while the Puqudians and the Sutæans coming to reinforce him were annihilated. The Bît-Yakîn was ravaged ; the Baby-lonian hostages were rescued and restored to freedom ; the inhabitants of the land were deported and replaced by prisoners captured in Commagene. Sargon restored the cities and their temples, Ur, Uruk, Eridu, Larsa, and Kish.[1] He enlarged Babylon, and had a quay covered with asphalt constructed between the Ishtar Gate and the Euphrates. An angle of this quay, with a circular bastion, has been uncovered to the north-west of the citadel, the two encircling walls of which, likewise constructed by Sargon, were sub-sequently restored several times.

According to a Greek tradition, Sargon had destined the throne of Babylon for one of his sons. When he died a violent death in 705 B.C., Sennacherib, who succeeded him in Assyria, was in conflict with Armenia and could not intervene in Akkadian affairs. According to one royal list a slave seized the power and kept it for one month. Merodach-Baladan, supported by Hallushu, king of Elam, returned and reigned for a few months. Sennacherib defeated him before the walls of Kish and entered the capital with-out difficulty. He ravaged the whole of Chaldæa and deported 208,000 inhabitants. Bêl-ibni, a Babylonian prince educated at the Assyrian court, was installed as viceroy. Three years later he allied himself with Merodach-Baladan. The latter, among the marshes whither he had retreated, had persuaded the Chaldæan, Mushezib-Marduk, to stir up a revolt. Sennacherib deposed Bêl-ibni and

[1] I, vol. X, pp. 83 ff.

replaced him by his own son, Ashur-nadin-shumi (700–694).
Mushezib-Marduk retreated to his marshes; Merodach-
Baladan, after an attempt at resistance, embarked his gods
and his people and sought refuge at Nagiti, on the coast of
Elam. The king of Assyria resolved to pursue him across
the sea. He had a fleet built, traversed the Persian Gulf
and attacked the Chaldæans in their refuge. The king of
Elam, whose territory had been violated, threw himself
upon Babylonia, ravaged Sippar, took Ashur-nadin-shumi
prisoner, and installed in his place the Chaldæan, Nergal-
shêzib (694–693). The latter marched southwards to bar
the passage of the Assyrian army on its way back from
Nagiti. A great battle was fought; Nergal-shêzib was
defeated and carried off to Assyria. Sennacherib meant to
take advantage of troubles in Elam to invade that land,
but he was prevented by the winter (693). Mushezib-
Marduk (693–689) seized the power at Babylon, despoiled
the treasuries of Esargil in order to send rich presents to
the king of Elam, Humban-menanu, with whom he contracted an alliance. Chaldæans, Aramæans, Babylonians,
Persians, Puqudians, and Gambulicians awaited the Assyrians at Halule, east of the Tigris. Sennacherib declared
himself the victor, but could not profit by his success at
once. Two years later (689), after the death of Humban-
menanu of Elam, he took Babylon, reduced its defences
to ruins, destroyed temples, palaces, and houses, deported
the citizens, carried the god Marduk away into captivity,
and converted the region into a vast lagoon—" That in
future no man might find again even the soil of this city
and of the gods' temples : to that end I destroyed it by
water and left it like a swamp."

Esarhaddon, his son (681–669), deeply occupied by his
wars in the west, left to generals the task of repelling the
Elamites who had advanced as far as Sippar, and of resisting
Nabu-zêr-kênish-lishir, the son of Merodach-Baladan, who
had seized Ur. This prince fled to Elam, where he was
killed; his brother, Nâ'id-Marduk, submitted, and was
recognized as a vassal in the Land of the Sea. Babylonia
was reconstructed, the cities restored, the temples rebuilt,
cult re-established.

In 668 B.C. Esarhaddon chose his son, Ashurbanipal, to

succeed him in Assyria, and gave the governorship of Babylon to another son, Shamash-shum-ukîn. Marduk re-entered the Esargil in the month of Ayar (668), and at the New Year's feast of 667 Shamash-shum-ukîn took his hand. Ashurbanipal kept control over the southern regions and set up Assyrian governors there ; nor did he fail to pay his vows to the great gods of Kutha, Borsippa, and Babylon. The viceroy busied himself at first with works of peace ; when he thought himself strong enough to throw off allegiance, he formed a league against Assyria with Humbanigash II, king of Elam, with the Arabs, Aramæans, and Chaldæans, and forbade his brother to offer sacrifices in Babylonian cities. Ashurbanipal, after a brilliant victory in Arahsamnah (650), laid siege to Babylon, Borsippa, Kutha, and Sippar, while he rapidly reconquered Chaldæa. Babylon resisted till Ayar, 648 B.C. ; reduced by famine and disease rather than arms, it was put to fire and sword. Shamash-shum-ukîn died in the conflagration of his palace and was replaced by Kandalu. His successors enjoyed a more or less precarious authority over certain cities, notably Nippur, Ur, and Uruk.

In 625 B.C. the Scythians were threatening the empire, and Nabopolassar proclaimed himself king. He founded the Eleventh Dynasty called Neo-Babylonian. At first his power only extended over Babylon and Borsippa, but he knew how to take advantage of the rapid enfeeblement of Assyria for the enlargement of his own territory. He allied himself with Cyaxares, king of the Medes, and had a daughter of that prince betrothed to his son, Nebuchadrezzar. When the Medes entered Mesopotamia and besieged Nineveh, the Babylonians took part in the campaign. After a resistance of three years, the city was taken (606) and the Assyrian empire vanished.

Egypt, too, had broken the yoke of Nineveh, and since 608 B.C. had occupied Palestine and Syria ; Necho had reached as far as the Euphrates. Now Babylon had been fighting with Assyria for centuries just to protect her trade. Could she then tolerate Pharaoh's enterprise on the Syrian coast ? Nebuchadrezzar was sent to oppose the Egyptians' advance. In 604 B.C. he defeated them at Carchemish and

D

pursued them victoriously. Arriving at Pelusium he learned of his father's death, and found himself obliged to return to Babylon to take up the succession.

Nabopolassar had been a great builder. Nebuchadrezzar II (604–561) continued the restoration and embellishment of the cities. It is from his reign that the principal remains discovered at Babylon date—an outer city wall of stamped bricks, a palace where the influence of Hittite and of Assyrian art can be discerned, and above all the Ishtar Gate, the most important of the ruins. He rebuilt the Esargil, paved the Sacred Way, and created the hanging gardens, one of the seven wonders of the Ancient World.

The greater part of Syria had acknowledged the authority of Nebuchadrezzar in 604. Soon Judea ceased to pay tribute, and despite the objurgations of the prophet Jeremiah rebelled against her lord. Jerusalem was taken in 596 B.C. and some of the inhabitants were deported. Egypt wanted to try and recover her preponderance in Syria; Judea joined her, as did Tyre and Sidon. In 587 Nebuchadrezzar took up his position at Ribla, on the Orontes, and thence sent a force to besiege Jerusalem for the second time. In vain did Pharaoh Apries try to come to the aid of his ally; the city succumbed in the next year, and the majority of its population was carried off to captivity. King Zedekiah, captured while flying, was brought to Ribla; his sons were slaughtered before his eyes, he was robbed of his sight, loaded with chains, and led away to Babylon. Tyre held out longer—for thirteen years, on the evidence of Josephus (585–573).

As ally of the Medes, Nebuchadrezzar took part in a conflict with Lydia. On May 28th, 585 B.C., during a great battle with Cyaxares at Alyatte, on the Halys, an eclipse of the sun occurred. This event was regarded as a presage by both sides: peace was agreed upon, and the Babylonian king took part in the conclusion of the treaty, which fixed the Halys as the frontier between Medes and Lydians.

In the thirty-seventh year of his reign, according to a fragment of the Annals, Nebuchadrezzar made a campaign against Amasis of Egypt. He seems to have been victorious over the Egyptians and their Greek mercenaries; perhaps he

reached even Delta. He had left rock inscriptions in Syria—
at Wadi Brissa and at Nahr-el-Kelb.

His son, Evil-Merodach (Awil-Marduk), was restrained
neither by law nor by decency. Less than three years after
his accession the sacerdotal faction had him assassinated
and replaced by Neriglissar (Nergal-shar-utsur) (559–556),
the *rab-mag* who had been present at the siege of Jerusalem,
and had married a daughter of Nebuchadrezzar. Neriglissar
died without having re-established the military organization
of his country. He had restored the temples of Babylon
and Borsippa ; in the latter town he had had a palace built.
His son, Labashi-Marduk, a child, was deposed after reigning
nine months and replaced by Nabonidus (Nabu-nâ'id)
(555–539), the son of a priestess of Sin at Harran,[1] imbued
with traditions, wholly preoccupied with archæology and
the restoration of cult. He has been called the " sacristan
king." Babylonia, Mesopotamia, Syria as far as Gaza,
formed his empire. But in Elam a new power was rising.
In 550 B.C. Cyrus, king of Anshan, a vassal of Astyages the
Mede, revolted and deposed his liege lord. He attacked
Lydia, where the famous Crœsus had gathered in his capital
of Sardis the most cultured of the Greeks. After the battle
of Pterium, in Cappadocia (547), he captured that town and
put an end to the realm of Lydia (546). Then he turned
upon Babylon, which, in agreement with Egypt, had
supported Crœsus. The priestly faction and the people were
alienated from the king ; the latter did not deign to come
to the city, while without his presence the festival of the
New Year could not be celebrated. In his archæological
zeal, and under the pretext of bringing the gods into safety,
he had collected almost all their statues in the temples of
the capital. The business of the state and the command of
the army were in the charge of his son, Balthazar (Bêl-shar-
utsur). The Babylonian Kubaru (Gobryas), governor of
Guti, between the Zâb and the Diyala, took the part of the
king of Anshan and supplied him with recruits. Balthazar
was defeated at Opis ; he reformed his army—a new defeat ;
on the 14th of Tammuz, 539, Sippar opened her gates.
Nabonidus fled, and on the 16th Gobryas entered Babylon.
On the 3rd of Marheshvan next Cyrus was received there

[1] **I**, vol. XI, p. 170.

as liberator, and secured his popularity by the complete restoration of cult. Nabonidus died in exile in Carmania.

The king of Anshan aimed at preserving the customs of the peoples whom he had subdued. In Babylonia private documents were still drawn up in the same terms as before. When Cambyses (529–522), Cyrus' successor, died, two pretenders tried to shake off the yoke, but Darius the Mede, son of Hystaspes, a prince of the house of Cyrus, took command of the army, besieged Babylon and established his dominion firmly. At the end of his reign, and at the beginning of that of Xerxes (486–465), usurpers arose. Xerxes dismantled the city, pillaged it, and destroyed the Esargil. In 331 B.C., after the defeat of Darius III, Alexander chose Babylon as the capital of Asia, and proposed to rebuild the temple of Marduk. A tablet, dated in his sixteenth year, gives a receipt for the payment of ten minæ of silver for the removal of the debris. The Greeks built themselves a theatre of sun-dried bricks with beton pillars : their customs influenced the manners of the Babylonians, who, by royal privilege, might obtain permission to adopt Greek names. In 270 Antiochus Soter restored temples at Babylon, at Borsippa, and at Uruk. In the second century, Anu and Marduk were invoked together as a single deity under the name of Ana-Bêl, and dynasts constructed their dwellings with the materials of the ancient cities. Thus, on the site of Lagash, Adad-nahin-ahê had a palace built and utilized the bricks of Gudea. In the year 27, before the Christian era, the cult was still being celebrated in Babylon.

CHRONOLOGICAL SUMMARY OF THE HISTORY
OF BABYLONIA

MYTHICAL CHRONOLOGY.

Creation
Anarchy — 259,200 years
Ten antediluvian kings — 432,000 456,200
or 241,200 years
The Flood
1st Dynasty of Kish — 24,510 years 3 months 3½ days — Etana
1st Dynasty of Uruk (in Sumer) — 2310 years — Gilgamesh
1st Dynasty of Ur (in Sumer) — 171 „
Dynasty of Awan (in Elam) — 396 „
2nd Dynasty of Kish — 3792 (or 3195 ?) years
Dynasty of Hamazi (in Elam) — 17 years
2nd Dynasty of Uruk — 420 „
2nd Dynasty of Ur — 108 „
Dynasty of Adab (in Sumer) — 90 „
Dynasty of Mari (on the Middle Euphrates) — 136 „
3rd Dynasty of Kish — 100 „
Dynasty of Akshak (in Akkad) — 99 „

HISTORICAL EPOCH.

4th Dynasty of Kish — 106 years — Urukagina at Lagash
3rd Dynasty of Uruk — 25 „ — Lugalzaggisi
Dynasty of Agade (in Akkad) — c. 2845–2649 B.C. — Sargon, Narâm-Sin
4th Dynasty of Uruk — c. 2648–2623
Dynasty of Gutium (east of the Tigris) — c. 2622–2498
5th Dynasty of Uruk — c. 2497–2475 — Gudea at Lagash
3rd Dynasty of Ur — c. 2474–2358 — Dungi
Dynasty of Isin — c. 2357–2132
Dynasty of Larsa — c. 2357–2095
1st Dynasty of Babylon (Amorite) — 2225–1926 — Hammurabi
2nd Dynasty at Babylon (of the Land of the Sea) — c. 1925–1761
3rd Dynasty (Kassite) — c. 1760–1185
4th Dynasty — c. 1184–1053
5th Dynasty — c. 1052–1032
6th Dynasty — c. 1031–1012
7th Dynasty (Elamite) — c. 1011–1006
8th Dynasty — c. 1005–762
9th Dynasty — c. 761–732
10th Dynasty (Assyrian domination) — 732–625
11th Dynasty (Neo-Babylonian) — 625–539 — Nebuchadrezzar II
12th Dynasty (Achæmenid) — 539–331

BOOK TWO

INSTITUTIONS

CHAPTER I

THE STATE AND THE FAMILY

1. THE STATE

BEFORE the accession of Hammurabi, true founder of Babylonian unity, Sumer and Akkad were sometimes united under a single sceptre, more often divided by the rivalries of princes in autonomous cities.

The city with the more or less extensive territory depending on it formed in society a cell with its own peculiar life. Its foundation was a religious work which could not be undertaken without the order of the great gods ; for the city was above all a centre of cult. Its name and the god who deigned to make it his residence often had the same ideogram—at Nippur, for instance, the seat of Enlil, the lord of all Sumer. In other cases the deity marked his sovereignty differently ; that was the case with Lagash, the god whereof, Inurta, was always called Ningirsu, lord of Girsu, after the quarter where his temple rose. Babylon means the Gate of God, and when the kings of the First Dynasty of Babylon founded new towns, they still gave them theophorous names— Kar-Shamash, "fortress of the god Shamash," Nar-Adad, "light of the god Adad." However, the central power was consolidated, and recourse to religion was less necessary ; a certain tendency manifested itself to substitute for the divine name that of the king, who was, of course, himself deified. Hammurabi ordered the cutting of a "canal of Hammurabi" : Ammiditana and Ammizaduga built "the wall of Ammiditana," "the wall of Ammizaduga" ; under the Third Dynasty Kurigalzu would not hesitate to call a new town Dur-Kurigalzu.

The god was the real lord of the city. In the inscription
on the Stele of the Vultures, Eanatum relates how "the
king" appeared to him in a dream. One of his successors,
Entemena, calls Ningirsu "his king who loves him," and
Urukagina speaks expressly of "the subjects of the king,"
alluding to the time when Lagash was governed by ishakkê.
Ur-Ninsun vows to Ningirsu a plate the name of which is
"May the king prolong my life." The inscriptions of Gudea,
above all, abound in allusions to the royalty of Ningirsu.
When he has finished the construction of a temple he brings
the offerings to the god and addresses this prayer to him :
"O my king, O Ningirsu, I have built thy temple with joy
and wish to induct thee there." And, at the beginning of
the prologue to his Laws, Hammurabi recalls that Anu and
Ellil have decreed to Marduk an eternal kingship in Babylon.

The god inhabited the city with his wife, his children,
and his servitors. The temple was his house, the richest of
all. At great expense Ur-Ninâ had imported wood from the
mountains to adorn sanctuaries, and Gudea enumerates
with complaisance the diverse essences, the stones, the
precious metals gathered together for the reconstruction of
the E-ninnu, and how he had them worked by artists summoned from Elam. Special domains, granaries, stables and
slaves belonged to the gods. Eanatum made war upon
Umma to recover from her the Guedin—"cherished territory" of Ningirsu. Under Urukagina the gods re-entered
into possession of their properties which Lugalanda had
taken for himself and his families : we have the proof of
this not only in the inscriptions, but also in account-tablets
of this period. At the epoch of Ur, we can follow for thirty
years the deliveries of cattle made in the park of the national
temple of Enlil by the cities and principal tax-payers.
Much later, the Kassite king, Nazimaruttash, devoted a
great landed estate to the god Marduk, who became the
"lord of the field."

The god did not administer the city or the kingdom by
himself. He chose a vicegerent, a king or ishakku,[1] to

---

[1] *Ishakku* is the equivalent in Semitic of the ideogram PA-TE-SI. In
Sumerian the value of the sign, ending in *g*, seems to have been *issag*. No
term in modern languages corresponds exactly to this title, which was at once
civil and religious.

whom he entrusted pastorate of his people. Entemena of Lagash was the high ishakku of Ningirsu. Lugalzaggisi, whose power extended over all Sumer, was the ishakku of Enlil, the national god. The prince at the same time fulfilled sacerdotal functions; he was high priest of the god of the land or of the town. Gudea and Lugalzaggisi are evidence for this—the latter declares that "the gods in the sanctuaries of Sumer as ishakku of the countries, and at Uruk, as high priest, have established him." Civil and religious administrator, the prince was not slow to deify himself. A proper name on the Obelisk of Manishtusu is the earliest evidence for the practice: Sharru-kîn-ili means "Sargon is my god." Narâm-Sin, during his lifetime, was called "god of Agade." Dungi and his successors placed the divine determinative before their names; they had their temples and their statues. Hammurabi, one of whose contemporaries took the name Hammurabi-ilu (" Hammurabi is god "), styled himself " god of the kings," and the Kassites, who made so many other alterations in customs, nevertheless did not disdain these divine honours.

In the pre-Sargonic epoch, beside the prince, his wife possessed and administered considerable property herself. She had her own palace and took part in the affairs of the State; the royal children had their house and their servants—cup-bearers, seamstresses, cook, carpenter, ass-herd, musician, cultivators, hairdressers, and others. The chief official seems to have been the intendant of the palace— " at once the organizer of enterprises of public interest and agricultural works, the king's treasurer, the steward of the palace, and everybody's notary." [1] The tablets mention other *nubanda*, intendants—that of the god and that of the children—various classes of priests, business agents, judges, custodians of granaries, scribes, overseers, and other officials whose functions still remain obscure; women are priestesses, seamstresses, or holders of various offices. Among the workmen and artisans, the perfumer, the currier, the founder, the sculptor of statues, the gem-cutter, the mason, the excavator, and the gardener are mentioned.

All reappear in the epoch of Ur, but the house of a king, whose power extends far beyond the bounds of Sumer,

[1] **LXXVIII**, p. xxv.

requires a more imposing retinue than that of the ishakku of a single town. The *nubanda* devoted himself exclusively to all that related to the levy : be it a question of war or simply of cultivating fields, cutting canals, constructing walls, palaces or temples, he is to be found everywhere.[1] Beside the king there was a supreme minister, ishakku and governor of several cities [2] ; other ministers, supported by soldiers and couriers, travelled the country to carry the king's commands to the most distant cities of the empire. All the officials of this epoch seem to have been free men or slaves ; we have to come down to Hammurabi's time before we discern another division of classes in society without, however, being able to determine how far back it goes.[3]

The Babylonian code distinguished in the realm the free man, the *mushkinu,* and the slave. *Mushkinu,* from the same root as the French *mesquin,* indicates a citizen of lowly estate who ranks between the two other classes. He can own slaves. He can divorce his wife, giving her a third of a mina of silver, while in the same position a free man must pay a whole mina. The laws dealing with accidents and surgical aid specify very exactly his social situation in fixing fees and penalties respectively. If a *mushkinu* has an eye torn out or a limb broken by an aggressor, he is indemnified by the payment of a mina of silver ; if it had been a free man, the *lex talionis* would have applied ; for a slave the indemnity would only cost half his market value. If someone breaks his teeth, he will get a third of a mina ; if someone hits him over the head, it is only ten shekels as against a mina for a free man. If he is killed unintentionally in a quarrel, his family will get a third of a mina, and not half a mina as in the case of a free man's son. If his daughter is pregnant and a miscarriage befalls her as the result of blows, the aggressor must pay five shekels ; if she dies as a result of the accident, a half-mina of silver. Were her father a free man, the penalty would be ten shekels in the first case and the *lex talionis* would be applied in the second ;

---

[1] **LXXXIII,** p. 38.   [2] **CVI,** p. 213.
[3] A complaint older than the epoch of Ur distinguishes the simple citizen, the official, and the free man, but that does not prove that they form three classes in society. **I,** vol. XVII, p. 45.

for a slave's daughter the rates are two shekels and a third of a mina respectively. For surgical aid, where the free man pays ten shekels, the master is only bound to pay two shekels on behalf of his slave, and the *mushkinu* is taxed five shekels. The *mushkinu* is therefore certainly of inferior status to the *amêlu* or free man, but it is surprising to note that, in discussing theft, the flight of slaves, and the marriage of a free girl with a slave, the law makes no mention of a free man, but distinguishes only what belongs to the temple or palace on the one hand, to the *mushkinu* on the other.[1]

The slave was the property of his master, whether born in the house, bought, or made prisoner in war. Manishtusu acquired five men and three women at twenty shekels a head, and a girl for thirteen and a half shekels. In the era of Ur a whole family was valued at half a mina, a child at three and a half shekels. A slave could protest against his own sale, and the transaction was submitted to the consideration of judges. He could take oath at least in matters which concerned him. The serving-maid of a doctor, accused of having stolen a garment from a certain Bazi, asserted that the garment in question had been given her by one of this man's slaves named Lugaldurdug. In the temple of Ninmar Lugaldurdug affirmed and swore that he had had no part in the theft, and the maid was reduced to slavery in the service of Bazi. The sale of a slave was final if the buyer swore that he had really made the purchase, if there were witnesses, if the agreed price had been paid. A child could be sold as a slave by its father or mother ; on the other hand, a slave could be enfranchised by his master.[2] In the reign of Ellil-bâni, king of Isin (2201–2178)., Pidur-libur and his wife, Nim-Utumu, enfranchised a woman who was to remain in their service, but over whom their two sons and daughter would have no rights.[3] That gave rise to a ceremony of laving the brow. As a matter of fact marks of servitude existed, and Hammurabi's law punished

---

[1] M. Cavaignac considers that *mushkinu* denotes a Babylonian of free status who is neither an official nor attached to the service of a temple. He is mentioned in the Laws of Hammurabi only in cases where he does not enjoy the privileges granted to the *amêlu* ; the latter term would then have a restricted meaning and denote a citizen who holds a post in the temple or the palace. Cf. **I**, vol. XX, pp. 45–47.

[2] **XXIX**, Nos. 748, 838, 733, 746, 830, 832, 751, 752.

[3] **I**, vol. XIV.

with amputation of the hands a surgeon who, without the master's knowledge, deliberately placed upon a slave the "inalienable" mark. In the third millennium before the Christian era, at Uruk,[1] the name of the owner would be found on the right hand, and, if the slave changed masters, the name of the new possessor would be added beside that of the old.

The concubine by whom a man had had children might not be sold; her master had only the right of giving her, like his wife or son, as a pledge. In the case of the latter, in the age of the First Dynasty, servitude could not last longer than three years, a provision which was to disappear from legislation; in the Neo-Babylonian epoch a son remained for ten consecutive years in the service of two priestesses in order to work off a debt of his father's. Hammurabi fixed the market value of a slave at twenty shekels; that was the rate of indemnity to be paid in respect of death caused by an angry bull, or by misusage at the hands of the man to whom the slave had been given as a security; the life of a freeman in the same circumstances was, however, only valued at thirty shekels. According to their age, sex, and manual skill, some slaves were sold for not more than four or six shekels, while others fetched the high prices of from fifty-one to fifty-seven shekels, nearly a mina of silver. A free woman might marry a slave; the children would be born free according to the status of the mother, and only half the property of the household would be returned to the father's master. If a free man had taken a slave as concubine, the mother and children would be automatically enfranchised on the man's death, but the children could not be his heirs without an act of adoption.

The slave had opportunity to gather a peculium and to buy back his liberty for silver; if he was not in a position to provide the necessary sum, he could borrow: at Babylon, the temple of Marduk would grant him advances. Enfranchisement, like repurchase, was final; it could not be disputed. The fugitive slave must not be received or succoured by anyone under penalty of death; whoever captured him and returned him to his master could claim a reward of two shekels under Hammurabi's law. "If anyone have kept

[1] **XXVII**, vol. II, Nos. 6 and 25.

in his house a (runaway) slave," declared this law, " and if thereafter the slave be discovered under his roof, that man is punishable with death." An older Sumerian law[1] lays down milder penalties. " If the maid-servant or the slave of any man outside the city escape, his house in which he shall be found in asylum within one month (the proprietor thereof), shall be cónvicted and head for head shall he provide ; if he has no slave, twenty-five shekels of silver shall he pay."

2. THE ARMY

From the most remote ages the towns of the Lower Euphrates had been at strife to acquire hegemony the one over the other. The army was one of the most important institutions of society.

The *Stele of the Vultures* [2] erected on the territory of Lagash by king Eanatum, as a result of his victory over the men of Umma, shows in the scenes engraved upon its historical face what was the composition of a Sumerian army in that remote age and what its equipment was like.

The king marches to battle at the head of his soldiers. He is clad in a loin-cloth of kaunakes ; a finer stuff or a kid's skin covers his left shoulder. His head is protected by a helmet, slightly conical with a havelock ; that of the men-at-arms is plain, on the king's, the artist has copied a sort of chignon kept in place by a band, and has indicated the ears. Whether he fights on foot or in a chariot, the prince has as arms the lance and a sort of curved weapon formed of strips or blades held together by straps or rings.

The warriors form two bodies of troops. The shock troops, who fight a pitched battle with the king on foot, advance in files of seven. The first carries the defensive arm, an enormous rectangular shield ; the rest are equipped with lances and hold them with both hands almost at the end of the shaft. Those who press on in pursuit of the enemy behind the king mounted on his car are armed with a lance and a hoe. After the victory the prince celebrates his triumph by the immolation of an ox ; the soldiers proceed to the execution of the prisoners and pile up the corpses, while the king himself

[1] I, vol. XVII, p. 37
[2] **XCVIII**, pls. 3 ff. ; cf. Fig. 8.

retains the privilege of tearing out the eyes of the vanquished monarch.

Another weapon is depicted on the face of the stele which is engraved with mythological scenes : it is the mace the use of which is attested for a still older epoch by a bas-relief from Tello[1] and by the votive mace decorated with lions vowed by Mesilim to the god Ningirsu.

FIG. 8.   Fragment from the Stele of the Vultures (Tello, Louvre)

The armament of the king and the warriors at the epoch of Agade is illustrated by the triumphal stele of Narâm-Sin.[2] The scene represents the pursuit of the enemy in a mountainous region. The prince, clad in a short shawl, the edge of which hangs down to his knees, has sandals on his feet and on his head a helmet with a large havelock, decorated with horns symbolizing the deity. He holds in his left hand a doubly

[1] **XCVIII**, pl. 1.   [2] **XXIII**, vol. I, p. 144; cf. Fig. 4, p. 31.

curved bow and his arm clasps to his breast an axe with a
very narrow blade ; in his right hand is a long arrow plumed
and tipped with a sharpened head. The host is represented
by two columns of warriors protected by scouts. One of the
scouts carries a lance, the other a bow simpler than the
king's. At the head of each column marches a bearded chief
whose shawl, girt up like a petticoat, is shorter than that of
his men ; like them he wears a helmet. One captain is armèd
with the lance and an axe with convex blade, like that so
often illustrated on cylinders of the First Dynasty of Babylon
with a lion's head as ornament ; the other carries an axe.

FIG. 9.   Sumerian weapons
(Tello, Louvre).

The common soldiers, beside the axe, carry a lance or a standard. The enemy's armament is identical with that of the
men of Agade.

A tablet of this period bears witness to the manufacture
of helmets of leather, for which ox-hide, kid-skins, and wool
were employed, and others of bronze sometimes decorated
with silver. The axes were of copper-bronze and so were the
lance-heads. In the fabrication of the quivers leather and
wool were used.[1]

In the temple of Lagash, where the god's court is a faithful
reflexion of the prince's court, Gudea introduced a first and

[1] II, 1913

second lieutenant who ranked immediately after the two divine persons charged with justice and offerings.[1]

In the epoch of Ur the *nubanda* commanded soldiers and were further charged with the direction of the levies for public works. A class of people liable to military service was constituted by the *ukush* who had special chiefs.

Hammurabi's code regulates the privileges and fixes certain duties of two citizens summoned to participate in the royal expeditions—the *rêdum* or " conductor of slaves " (the Semite equivalent of the Sumerian *ukush*) and the *baïrum* or " fisher." It is impossible to give exact translations of these expressions, because we have no officials occupying analogous positions ; the former were charged with recruiting the ranks of the army and the latter seem to have been more specially connected with the police. Both when summoned to the king's service had to perform their duty in person ; it was in no wise permissible to escape this obligation ; by getting a mercenary to take his place, he would expose himself to capital punishment—so ran the law. In practice it underwent mitigation : a man might buy exemption by the payment of an annual tax called " the *ilku*-money."

The *ilku* was " service of the king," and by an extension a property of the State granted by way of a life pension to the *rêdum* and the *baïrum*. Two letters—one an order from king Samsu-iluna, the other the advice of the transmission of the first—show how the grant of these possessions was carried out.[2] A certain Ibni-Adad, possessor of eighteen gan (more than six hectares) of land, field and orchard, in the district of Sippar had abandoned this to obtain a more profitable concession. The king ordered the assignment of the first property to a new titular, the Elamite Walî ; a tablet was to be drawn up and the one which concerned Ibni-Adad sent to the palace. Marduk-natsir, chief officer of Sippar, received the royal letter, opened it, took cognizance thereof, replaced it in its envelope, and forwarded it to the two administrators of the domain with an advice of its dispatch in which he recalled in detail the royal prescriptions.

An *ilku*-property could neither be seized nor sold ; whoever bought it lost his money and his tablet had to be destroyed.

[1] **CV**, p. 183.　　　　[2] **XXX**, p. 156.

It could not be given by the titular to his wife or daughter, and that allows us to infer its transmission to the son on condition of the fulfilment of the obligations imposed ; it was likewise forbidden to use it as the security for a debt.

When the *rêdum* or the *baïrum* was absent on service, the administration of the property was entrusted to his son, or if his children were all minors, to his wife with the assignment of a third of the income in return for taking care of everything. Such a benefice had, moreover, to be maintained in good condition and cultivated. If the titular voluntarily neglected it and if another man had occupied it for three years, any attempt to reclaim it would be void ; the *de facto* beneficiary would become the beneficiary *de iure*. No provision regulated cases where the property was deserted for a brief period.

The *rêdum* enjoyed privileges both in respect of his person and of his properties. He was quite independent of the authority of the governor, and the latter incurred the death penalty if " he seized the property of a *rêdum*, caused it damage, let it out, delivered it in court into the possession of a stronger man, or took from him what the king had given him."

Rêdum and *baïrum* if captured in war and ransomed by a business-agent, had to redeem themselves if their movable property permitted it ; their real property was reserved. If they were incapable of paying the requisite sum, the temple of their city had to pay it, and if the temple did not possess sufficient resources, the debt became a charge upon the State. An order of king Hammurabi shows how this legal provision was applied ; it was the case of a man of Larsa : " On behalf of Imaninum whom the enemy has taken prisoner, give ten minæ of silver from the temple of Sin to his business-agent and ransom him." [1]

In the Neo-Babylonian epoch certain tax-payers were obliged to pay a war tax and to share financially in the up-keep of a soldier. One would pay seventy shekels in fifth year of Darius, another would pay the wages of a man for two years, or assure the upkeep of a horseman. At that epoch the Babylonian army must have been organized very

[1] **XXXVI**, vol. II, No. 32.

like the Assyrian army in the last days of the Sargonids' empire.

3. THE FAMILY

The family, rigidly constituted in society in Sumer and Akkad, was founded from the earliest times on a limited monogamy. A man could not in principle possess more than one legitimate wife, but law and custom allowed him one or more concubines.

Marriage rested essentially on a written document—a one-sided binding deed in which the husband laid down before witnesses the rights and duties of his spouse, fixed the sum he would pay in case of divorce, the penalty incurred by his wife for infidelity, and in general all the conditions of the agreement. Before the execution of the deed a preliminary agreement with the parents of the future wife was necessary.

The " law of Nisaba and Hani,"[1] in use at least in part of Sumer before the establishment of the Babylonian empire, declared that the seducer of an unmarried girl was obliged to ask her in marriage from her parents ; if he had seduced her after his suit had been rejected, he was liable to the death penalty.

At the epoch of Hammurabi the fiancée was usually chosen by the young man's father ; when the marriage had been arranged between the two families, the betrothal went on. The external sign of that ceremony was the despatch to the house of the future father-in-law of certain articles of furniture and the presentation to him by the young man or his father of a *tirhatu* offered on a dish. This *tirhatu* was a sum of money ; under the First Dynasty it sometimes fell to a shekel. sometimes rose to twenty shekels or even a half-mina. Survivals of an age when marriage was by purchase, the betrothal-gifts are mentioned in a text of Gudea. The ishakku, after reconstructing the temple of the goddess Bau, increased for the future the marriage gifts which had to be renewed at each New Year's festival—cattle, sheep, lambs, baskets of dates, butter, palm-kernels, pigs, cakes, barn-door fowls, fish, and tamarisk wood. In the epoch of Ur, five fat oxen,

[1] **XXXVI,** vol. I, No. 28.

thirty sheep, and five rams were driven out of the park of the temple of Enlil on the occasion the royal prince's betrothal ; five sheep, three ewes, and two goats formed the present of an intendant.[1]

The *tirhatu* was not absolutely obligatory—there were unions without a *tirhatu*—and it did not establish a definite engagement. If the young man withdrew from his promise, he sacrificed the money to the girl's father; if, on the other hand, it was the latter who broke his word, he returned the gifts intact. The tradition of the *tirhatu* was not without judicial consequences. If the fiancée remained in her father's house, a man who violated her became liable to the death penalty. On the other hand, if she took up her abode in the family of her future husband and had guilty relations with her future father-in-law without her betrothed's knowledge, she must recover her liberty and return to her father's house taking with her her dowry and an indemnity of a half-mina of silver ; but if her betrothed was privy to her behaviour, she could not plead good faith, both the guilty parties were punished and she was cast into the water.

The bride was usually provided with a *sheriqtu* or dowry by her father or, in case of his decease, by her brothers. Such property, delivered to the husband at the commencement of cohabitation, remained the wife's property until her death : she would bequeath it to her children or, if she had no heirs, it would revert to the paternal house.

The couple might have contracted debts before their marriage ; their respective legal positions would not be identical : the husband was in no case obliged to honour the previous commitments of his wife, while the latter, to shelter herself from her husband's creditors, must have had included in her tablet a specific provision that she could not be seized by them. For any debt contracted during married life both were jointly responsible, and often—we have an example from the days of the kings of Ur[2]—they were named together in a loan contract. The husband could not, however, dispose of the joint property without his wife's consent.

A certain juridical capacity was assigned to a married woman ; she might be a witness, and that was the case in the pre-Sargonic period when a wife witnessed the sale of a

[1] **LXXXIII,** Nos. 331, 370.   [2] **I,** vol. XIII.

house.[1] She might have private possessions, buy them and sell them without the consent of her husband ; she could sell her slaves and the law placed no obstacle in her way save in the case of a slave-woman, given by her to her husband as concubine who had born him children. In case of the husband's absence, for instance, during a term of military service as man-at-arms, if he had no adult son, the administration of the estate was left to the wife and a third of the revenue was granted to her personally. In one such case the wife claimed the return of a slave given as a pledge by her husband, and secured an order for his restitution from the judges when it had been proved that the services rendered exactly balanced the debt.[2] Hammurabi granted even a married woman the right if, " being a good housewife and without reproach," she complained of the absences of a husband who neglected her, to appeal to the judge for permission to recover her dowry, leave the conjugal domicile, and retire beneath her parents' roof. However, she made herself liable to be cast into the water by judicial decree, if she were not personally free from blame.

The husband had certain rights over his wife. He could reduce her to servitude with a creditor ; this very ancient custom was destined to persist and still existed under the new empire in the days of Nabonidus. Hammurabi's law limited such servitude to a maximum term of three years, after which the woman had to be set at liberty. The husband might further, as a punishment and under certain conditions on which we are very imperfectly informed, sell his unfaithful wife.

If there were no issue of the marriage, the husband had a choice of two alternatives : to take another wife of secondary rank or to divorce his spouse, surrender the *tirhatu*, and pay a certain sum of money, a mina or a third of a mina of silver according to his rank. In the individual cases of divorce which have survived, this law is scarcely applied; conventions always exist and, after Hammurabi, custom seems to have fixed the price of divorce at a half-mina. If he decided to take a wife of secondary status, the husband introduced her into the conjugal household, but he was not allowed to make her the equal of his consort. As a precaution, and in applica-

<hr>

[1] **XLVII,** No. 31.   [2] **I,** vol. XII.

tion of the law declaring void any marriage for which the husband had not laid down in writing the duties of the wife, he specified the exact situation on a tablet. In the reign of Sin-muballit, Hammurabi's father, a man decided that his second wife should " wash the feet of the first and carry her chair to the temple of the god Marduk."[1] In any case she would have the same rights as the legitimate wife in the event of a divorce.

Whether she were a mother herself or no, a wife might give her husband a concubine chosen from among her own personal slaves or bought in agreement with him. Such a woman would be enfranchised as soon as she had born a child, but her mistress would at all times retain the right to reduce her to servitude again if she aimed at being her rival and even to sell her if she had not become a mother. The husband who had thus received a concubine from his wife and had children by her, was no longer permitted to introduce another person into the conjugal domicile.

A chronic malady or infirmity in the wife which prevented the fulfilment of her duties, did not authorize a divorce. In such a case the husband might legally take a second wife, but the first had the right of staying with him with the assurance of honourable means of subsistence in conformity with her position ; if she preferred to withdraw, she was permitted to return to her father's house and take back her dowry intact. A wife who refused her conjugal duty, was to be thrown into the water according to ancient Sumerian law. Hammurabi made a distinction—if she was not a good house-wife, he applied the rule strictly to her case ; if, on the other hand, she proved that her husband deserted her, she was permitted to return to her paternal abode taking her dowry with her. If a wife conducted herself in a disorderly manner and turned out a bad housewife, if she neglected her husband, the latter had two ways out to choose from—to divorce her before the court, when she would be driven out with no indemnity ; or to declare before the judge that he would not divorce her, in which case she would remain as a slave. In either case it was permissible for the husband to contract a new marriage.

A woman, however, whether lawful wife or concubine,

[1] LVI, No. XIX.

might be divorced without any fault on her side, and that constituted a grave threat to the principle of monogamy. In such a case she would retire with her dowry ; the judge assigned to her the usufruct of certain property of her husband's and entrusted her with the custody of the children ; on their majority she received for herself the share of one child and became free to remarry. An old Sumerian law granted her a half-mina of silver.

Adultery on the part of the wife was punishable by death if she were caught *in flagrante delicto*. The guilty pair would be tied together and cast into the water, "unless the husband allowed his wife and the king his servant to live." If not taken in the act, the wife might prove her innocence on oath ; if only vexatious rumours concerning her were spread abroad, she had recourse to the ordeal, leaving to the river-god the task of vindicating her innocence.

It is apparently with adultery rather than with polyandry that we should connect the penalties previously laid down by Urukagina when he declared, " The women of yore by two men were possessed (with impunity) ; the women of to-day (in such a case) to the . . . are thrown."

It might happen that the husband was carried off to captivity. If the household resources were sufficient, it was not lawful for the wife to form a connection with another man ; she would be liable to be brought to justice and thrown into the water. But, " if there were nothing ·to eat in the house," she might remarry and if, later on, her first husband came back, she returned to him, leaving the offspring of her second union to their father. A deserted wife was never obliged to return to conjugal life and, if she remarried, had to stay with her new husband. The law also made provision for the case of a woman who had her husband assassinated in order to marry another man ; she would be sentenced to hanging.

During married life a husband might make a settlement on his wife so as to secure to her after his death more ample means than those which would come to her from her dowry and her child's portion in the estate assigned to her by law.

She had only the usufruct of the properties thus settled on her called *nudunnu*. She could not alienate them : " after her they belonged to the children."

If a free man chose a slave woman as wife or as concubine, she was enfranchised after her first child-bed. If a free man's daughter married a slave, she did not become a slave herself, and the husband's owner could make no claim upon the children born of the union. Furthermore, the wife's dowry, if it came from her father, would be restored intact on the death of her spouse, and she was entitled to half the earnings of the husband during his married life for his progeny; only the other half belonged to the slave's master.

Thus was the legal position of a married couple fixed by Hammurabi's law. Documents of varied origin—tablets of marriage, of divorce and of the constitution of a *nudunnu*—drawn up before or after the promulgation of that legislation allow us to reach more or less ancient traditions, to recognize innovations which in practice were not always applied with the rigour of law.

The position of the child in the family was likewise regulated by a certain number of articles in the Code of Hammurabi. It was born free if the mother was free ; enfranchised if the slave-mother was the concubine of a free man ; a slave, if both parents were in that position. If the father or mother lived by prostitution, the child was brought up by foster-parents and could not be reclaimed ; he must not know his origin and if, discovering it, he dared to desert the people who had cared for him in childhood and to go and live with his father and mother, the law condemned him to have his eyes torn out.

Adoption, the object of which was to perpetuate the family by securing a child to persons who had none and had abandoned hope of getting any, was largely practised in Babylonia despite the legal facilities for dissolving unfruitful marriages. Its application was even extended ; there is the case, exceptional indeed, of a father who already had five children, adopting a sixth.

In practice a distinction was made between the adoption of unrelated children and that of the offspring of a concubine. The latter, in fact, did not by birth enjoy all the rights of children born in wedlock. They were not legitimate children, and even if they were legitimated by a free deed emanating from the father, from husband and wife, or perhaps in certain circumstances from the wife alone, they would always remain in an inferior position. Adoption was made in writing by a contract or unilateral deed—a contract between the adopter and those who had reared the adoptive child, a unilateral deed, in the case of a concubine's children, or where the adopter had already acquired rights by taking charge of a child with the consent of the parents, either to relieve their necessities or to teach the child a trade. If the foster-parent had no children as yet, he would make provision against such eventuality in the tablet by stipulating that the adopted child should be considered as the elder brother of the children to come. If he was already a father, in the case of the legitimation of a concubine's offspring, he forbad his other sons disputing the claims of the adopted one. The law made provision for the case of a man who, having brought up a child, wanted to expel it because he had founded a family of his own; it granted the adopted child thus repudiated a third of a child's portion in the movable property, but denied it any title to the real estate. An adopted son denying his foster-father was marked on the brow with the sign of servitude, cast into chains, and sold; his tablet of adoption was broken, and were either of his parents prostitutes, his tongue was cut out.

The husband to whom the right of reducing his wife or concubine to servitude with a creditor had been granted, could equally dispose of his children, boys and girls, on the same terms and apparently irrespective of their age and status. That is to say, he was allowed under the law of Hammurabi to hand them over as pledges for a maximum term of three years. This provision was only aggravated with the passage of time, if we may judge from the single instance known from the Neo-Babylonian epoch.[1] A certain Ina-tsil-Bâbi-rabi remained in servitude for ten years to work off a loan of forty-two shekels of silver raised by his father, and he would have had to wait still longer to regain his liberty if the death of his father, procuring him his patrimony, had not allowed him to liquidate the debt. A baker by trade, he had had to enter the abode of the sagittum Ahata as a pledge. And the value of his service was reckoned at the

---

[1] I, vol. XII.

legal rate of six *qa* of barley a day, one *gur* a month. Four years later the lady Ahata died, Banât-ina-Esagil succeeded her in office and took over the debt and the security. Ina-tsil-Bâbi-rabi continued to serve at the same rate for six years. The young man's father, Ahushunu, died in the tenth year of his son's servitude ; the latter made up his accounts, offered his mistress twenty *gur* of barley in liquidation of the debt and, in 558 B.C., appealed to the tribunal at Uruk to secure his liberation. The judges calculated that the advance —originally forty-two shekels of silver—had grown by the accumulation of simple interest at 20 per cent—the legal rate —for ten years, was thus twice as much, and reached a total of two minæ six shekels; on the other hand they proved that the service rendered, valued at six *qa* of barley a day, and twenty *gur* of barley paid in kind would amount to a total of 140 *gur*, a sum admittedly equivalent to two minæ six shekels. As a result they had a tablet written out, and sealed with their seals, to cancel the debt and set free the pledge.

Hammurabi regulated the division of the inheritance on the decease of the parents, and the restoration to his family of the possessions of the defunct when he had no children or had been unable formally to designate an heir. According to private deeds the father of a family at this epoch was entitled during his life to assign part of his fortune to a stranger gratuitously and finally. It was sufficient to have an authentic deed of gift drawn up in the presence of witnesses, and the donation thus made was unimpeachable in law ; every time that the children tried to contest it, they were non-suited. A clause inserted in the text put any subsequent objections on their part out of court, and often their father took care to secure their actual presence as witnesses to the execution of the deed. The wife, likewise, according to the contents of one tablet, might receive a *nudunnu* from her husband, and such liberality put an end to her claim to share in the inheritance : it was the same in respect of any child to whom the father during his lifetime had made over part of his possessions : such was the position of his married daughters, priestesses, or prostitutes to whom he had assigned a dowry. Thus, according to the Sumerian laws of Nisaba and Hani, a child who wished to set up house for himself outside the paternal roof, received his portion and had no further claim on the inheritance.

On the decease of the head of the family a *tirhatu* was first put aside for the boys not yet of age, and then the estate—house, land, plant, slaves, furniture, and animals—was divided up according to the following rules : one part for the mother unless a *nudunnu* had been assigned her, one part for each of the boys, the usufruct of one part for each daughter who had not received a *sheriqtu*, the ultimate proprietary rights remaining vested in her brothers, one part, likewise in usufruct, for a daughter who had become a lay sister, a third of a part only, but in respect of the whole property, for the daughter who had entered the service of the god Marduk at Babylon. A dowry proportionate to the fortune of the house was set aside for the concubine's daughter who was still unmarried. As to the concubine's sons, although enfranchised and not liable to be claimed as slaves, they had nothing to hope for from the patrimony unless their father during his lifetime had given them a tablet of adoption. If he had admitted them as heirs, portions were allotted to them, but the children of the lawful wife exercised the right of choosing their portions.

If the head of the family had married twice, the offspring of both unions had personally equal claims on their father's estate, and the descendants of a son predeceasing his sire had to share between them what would have fallen to their parent. In default of descendants the succession of the defunct belonged to his brothers ; in default of brothers it went to the paternal uncles.

Before Hammurabi's time it was lawful not only to make benefactions at the expense of the children's portions, but also to disinherit them altogether. " If to a man," declared one of the laws of Nisaba and Hani, " his father and his mother say : ' Thou art no more our son,' out from the city shall he go." It was still so in the reign of Sin-muballit, but after the promulgation of the new law the courts had to be invoked, and a grave crime, sufficient to deprive him of his legal rights, had to be proved against the child.

The succession of the married woman was regulated according to the same principle as that of her husband—the retention of the fortune within the family. Without children she could not dispose of her possessions ; they would revert to the paternal house on her death, less the value of the *tirhatu* paid by the husband at the time of the betrothal, which must be repaid him by his father-in-law or which he might himself deduct from the dowry. If a mother of a family, widowed, and provided with a *nudunnu* or a child's share, she remained in her late husband's house and enjoyed her possessions, but might not part with them for money ; after her they belonged to the children. If in disagreement with her children she secured the permission of the judge to retire, she abandoned what came to her from her husband and took away only her dowry; when she died, each of her children would have a claim to an equal share in the succession if he had not been the object of any special liberality. When a woman had been twice married, the children of both marriages, and they alone to the exclusion of the second husband, were called on to divide the inheritance.

The division of the patrimony might be carried out by friendly agreement or by the courts. It was advisable to draw up a tablet for each of the co-participators so as to provide him with a proprietary title to the portion which fell to him. Thus, we have the three deeds executed for three brothers in the thirteenth year of Sin-muballit. In cases where the defunct had held some post, one did not omit to declare that the possessions he left were free of any charge— a necessary clause when he had held from the king properties not transmissible to the family such as the *ilku* estates assigned to men-at-arms.

The tablets of the Neo-Babylonian epoch contain an unique case of marriage by purchase. In the thirteenth year of Nebuchadrezzar II, Dâgil-ilî asks Hammâ, daughter of Nergal-iddin, " Give me thy sister, Latubashini ; let her be my wife ! " The business is arranged and Dâgil-ilî sends Hammâ in exchange for her sister a mina and a half of silver with a slave bought for half a mina. If the husband, it is prescribed, take a second wife, he will pay half a mina as the price of a divorce.[1] We have here, it seems, a survival of the Assyrian usage and no sort of proof of the existence of

[1] **XL,** p. 187.

marriage by purchase among Babylonian customs; for even under the Achæmenids a wife received a dowry from her father. Here is a case in the reign of Darius in which both husband and wife are of foreign blood. In the eleventh year of that prince, Patmu-ustu asks Saman-napir for the hand of his sister, Tahema-ushahtum; the girl received for the house an Akkadian bed, some chairs, a copper cauldron, and many other objects. Under Nebuchadrezzar II[1] the lady Silim-Ishtar made a present of all her goods to her son, Shanashîshu; she recalls in the deed how she had already arranged a dowry for her child's marriage, and gives details of it—five minæ of silver, two slaves, and some furniture. This dowry is called *nudunnu*, a name given in Hammurabi's days to the gift made by husband to wife, while the *sheriqtu* has now become the husband's gift. This interchange of meaning between two words deserves attention. The *nudunnu* consisted of goods and chattels; we see land, silver, slaves, and various utensils figure in it.[2] The father-in-law often postponed delivering it to his son-in-law; thence arose lawsuits. A law[3] of the seventh century compelled him to furnish what he had promised in accordance with his means : " between father-in-law and son-in-law there must be no trickery." An excellent means of regularizing the position was to determine in a contract the balance of the dowry and take a security for its payment. So acted Aplâ, son of Bêl-ahê-iddin, in the eleventh year of Nebuchadrezzar.[4] " Four minæ of silver, that is the balance of the *nudunnu* of Hammâ, daughter of Aplâ, wife of Balatsu due from Aplâ, her father. All his goods in town and in the country as much as he hath form the security for Hammâ. No creditor shall be able to obtain disposal, thereof, until Hammâ hath received four minæ of silver, the balance of her *nudunnu*."

The law as to the restoration to her family of the property of a wife dying childless, remained unaltered from Hammurabi's time. A childless widow recovered her dowry and took with her whatever her husband had settled on her in writing. If she had married without a dowry and had received nothing from her husband, she appealed to the tribunal; the judge

[1] CLXI, Dar. 301, Nbk. 283.
[2] CLIV. Nos. 19, 24, 92, 99, 100, 121.
[3] CXXXII, p. 72.   [4] CLXI, Nbk. 91.

valued the fortune of the deceased and assigned his wife a share in the estate.

A married woman disposed of her goods with or without the consent of her husband. Ina-Esagil-banâta had married Uballitsu-Gula in the sixth year of Nabonidus, and had received as dowry a mina of silver, some furniture, and three slaves. Five years later she agreed to a loan of twenty shekels to Itti-Bêl-abnu, a slave of her father-in-law. The scribe of the instrument was her own husband.

Divorce seems to have been very frequent and to have depended exclusively on the humour of the husband. At least the marriage-tablets often make provision for it and fix its price. Shamash-nâdin-shum, in the fourth year of Cyrus, wanted to marry Nadâ, daughter of Nabu-zaqip. The affair arranged, he made the following promise on oath : " The day that Shamash-nâdin-shum shall divorce Nadâ and take another wife, he shall pay six minæ to Nabu-zaqip." Other documents provided for the constitution of a pension for wife and children and seem to require the presence of a *shangu* (temple administrator) to validate the deed.

When a wife had no male child, but only a daughter, she might dispose of all her possessions in her favour. Thus did the lady Silim-Ishtar in the thirty-fifth year of Nebuchadrezzar II ; she retained the usufruct of her property and defined the situation very clearly ; thereafter she could no longer dispose of the ownership nor assign it to anyone ; on her death all her possessions will belong to Gula-qâ'ishat, her daughter, but with one reservation—the latter could dispose of nothing herself without the authorization of her husband.

The emancipation and adoption of a slave likewise required the presence of the *shangu*. In the ninth year of Cyrus, the lady Hibtâ, mistress of Bazuzu, announced to the shangu of Sippar her intention of acknowledging this slave as her son on condition that he provided her within the terms of a tablet with accommodation, food, unguents, and clothing. The temple-administrator himself determined the quantities of daily food, spices, fabrics, and other dues, the sum of which constituted the obligations imposed on the adopted child.

Simultaneous polygamy was not tolerated by law in the sense that a man could treat two wives as equals ; if he married two, though they were sisters, one of them would

rank below the other in the household. The law also foresaw
the second marriage of a woman whose first husband had been
captured by the enemy.

A wife who was also a mother, and who in widowhood wished
to remain in her husband's house, kept that right even under
the Achæmenid kings as in the days of the First Dynasty.
In the reign of Cambyses, Ummu-tâbat, widow of Shamash-
uballit, declared on oath before Bêl-uballit, a priest of Sippar,
that she did not wish to marry again, but would live with
her three children and bring them up till their majority[1]
The widow who preferred to retire from her children's house
and contract a second marriage, took away her dowry and
whatever her husband had given her in writing. On her
death all the boys took each an equal portion of her dowry ;
that was just the provision laid down in Article 173 of the
Code of Hammurabi. The law also prescribed the position
of the daughters, in what terms we do not know, as well as
for the patrimony of a father who had married twice and had
issue from both unions. Hammurabi, in Article 167, had
provided that the children should not share according to
their mothers, but should each take an equal part of the
property of the paternal house. In the seventh century that
was no longer the rule : the children of the first wife were
entitled to two-thirds of their father's total wealth, and those
of the second to one-third only.

The law which regulated in such detail the position of
married daughters, could not overlook those who remained
in celibacy—virgins dedicated to the gods or prostitutes.
At the epoch of Hammurabi such women had legal claims on
the patrimony. The father might allot a dowry to his
daughter either in full possession or in usufruct only. In the
first case, she did not have to give any account to her brothers
and might dispose of her possessions " after the wish of her
heart." In the second case, on her father's death, her brothers
took over the administration of her real estate and delivered
to her the revenue—barley, oil, and wool—according to the
value of her portion ; had she any complaint to make, she
chose a tenant, but might not execute any deed of alienation,
the absolute ownership rested with her brothers. A cloistered

---

[1] **CLXI**, Nbn. 1243, 498 ; Cyr. 183 ; Nbk. 283 ; Cyr. 339 ; Camb., 113, 273.

virgin or a harlot for whom the father had provided no dowry, inherited a child's portion in usufruct ; a hierodulos (*kadishtu*) or virgin (*zêr-mashitu*) in the same position obtained only a third of a portion in usufruct ; a priestess of Marduk in Babylon had likewise a third part, but of the whole estate—it was forbidden her personally to administer the estate, but she might alienate it or bequeath it as she liked.

Priestesses and virgins consecrated to the gods might lawfully contract marriages, but they were by no means always absolved from their vows. Deeds are numerous in which they appear as contracting parties in the city of Sippar, where a considerable congregation had grown up in the shadow of the temple of Shamash. Often they even entered into covenants—thus, in the reign of Hammurabi,[1] the priestess Ribatum acquired a sar of building land belonging to the priestess Aïa-inil-rishêtim for a third of a mina of silver.

Prostitutes appear in Sumer from the most remote antiquity. It was a courtesan who rescued the mythical personage Enkidu from savage life ; and in the city of Uruk, once consecrated to the supreme god Anu, the cult of the immodest Ishtar had taken the foremost place.

There are found three classes of *sacred prostitutes*—the *kizrête*, the *sanhâte*, and the *harimâte*, " for whom Ishtar hath preserved man and hath delivered him into their hands."

It was said of them :

" Marry not a harimâtu whose husbands are innumerable :
  In thy misfortune, she will not succour thee ;
  When men bring thee into court, she will slander thee ;
  Respect and submission are not in her,
  In sooth she will overwhelm a house : conduct her then
    outside,
  She who turneth her regard after the ways of strangers.
  Every house into which she entereth, crumbleth away ;
    he prospereth not who marrieth her."

In the days of the First Dynasty prostitutes, like the effeminate familiars of the palace, could not legally bring up

---

[1] **XCIX**, No. 67.

their children ; they were entrusted to foster-parents. If
they sought out their natural parents and wanted to live
with them, the judge would condemn them to death. In the
first millennium, according to the Book of Baruch, in Babylon
might be seen " women with cords about them, sitting in
the ways (who) burn bran for perfume : but if any of them,
drawn by some that passeth by, lie with him, she reproacheth
her fellow, that she was not thought as worthy as herself,
nor her cord broken."[1] Herodotus and Strabo alleged
that each woman had to yield herself once to a stranger.
He passed before them and cast a coin on the knees of whomsoever he had chosen ; she could not refuse and had to follow
him.

" However monstrous such practices introduced into cult
may seem to us, they had at least in their origin an import
and significance more lofty than the coarse gratification of
sensual appetites ; they were veritable sacrifices in which
the woman dedicated to the goddess the firstfruits of her
body by yielding herself to a stranger before giving herself
to a husband. Like any sacrifice that might be painful ;
nevertheless resignation was a duty, 'but,' adds Herodotus,
' when the woman has fulfilled what she owes to the goddess,
it is no longer possible to seduce her whatever sum one offer
her.' "[2]

Contracts dating from the reign of Nebuchadrezzar II[3]
reveal the descendants of Egibi, a rich Babylonian, making
profits from the prostitution of their slaves : thus Nabu-ahê-
iddin goes into partnership with a certain Kalbâ, gives him
some of his serving women, and will take three-quarters of
the earnings as his share.

In laying down the rules for succession and for the division
of goods, the Babylonian legislator at all periods tended to
give great cohesion to the family ; the rights of individuals
were determined in such a way that the family group should
be kept together as long as possible. Nevertheless no family
names were current, but about the seventh century we see
in private documents the name of an ancestor begin to appear

[1] Baruch vi, 42–43.   [2] **XCV**, p. 250.
[3] **CLXI**, Nbk. 409, 679.

after whom all his descendants are called—Egibi, Murashu. Before that epoch persons of free status were designated by their own name and that of their father—" So and so, son of So and so," slaves by one name only—" So and so." These names among the ancient Sumerians as among the Akkadians were a pious formula praising the deity or invoking his protection. In the pre-Sargonic epoch we meet Ur-Ninâ—" servant of the goddess Ninâ," Ninshubur-amamu—" the goddess Ninshubur is my mother," Sib-lagash-kiag—" the Shepherd of Lagash is faithful." Among the Semitic section at the epoch of Agade, we may cite Narâm-Sin—" beloved of Sin," and under the new empire, Nebuchadrezzar—" O Nabu protect the kudurru."

From the reign of Nabonidus[1] there exists evidence of the way in which a child sometimes got its name. On the testimony of a certain Ramua, guaranteed by Nadin-shum, the slave woman, Luballat, had " given the name Taddanu to the child she brought into the world." Other children had not yet received a name, even when three or four months old. At the same period certain persons would change their names in the course of their lives. The king, having raised his daughter to be high priestess of the temple of Nanna at Ur, gave her a new name—Bêl-shalti-Nanna. The Babylonian and Achæmenid kings forced the change on foreigners engaged in their service : the Seleucids introduced the use of Greek names which spread in good society without, however, ousting Babylonian names entirely.[2] These changes do not seem to have been innovations. In the time of the First Dynasty, under the kings of Ur, and even in the pre-Sargonic epoch,[3] some adult men bore names compounded of that of the reigning king, and one must admit, when the reign was very short, the substitution of one name for another ; moreover, under Lugalanda a high official bore the name Ninâ-ama-Lugalanda (the goddess Ninâ is the mother of Lugalanda), the name given the previous year to a statue of the prince.

---

[1] **CLXI,** Nbn. 343.   [2] **I,** vol. IX, p. 152.
[3] **XXVII,** pp. 15 ff

CHAPTER II

LEGISLATION

THE most important discovery relating to Babylonian legislation is that of the " Code of Hammurabi." This name is given to a block of diorite 2·25 metres high with a circumference of 1·90 metres at the base; it was found broken into three fragments among the ruins of Susa in December, 1901, and January, 1902. It is adorned with a bas-relief[1] representing the sun-god, Shamash, lord of justice, dictating to the Babylonian prince the " decrees of equity," the text of which is inscribed on the face of the stone. In the present condition of this monument, erected between the fortieth and forty-third year of Hammurabi's reign (about 2083 B.C.), we can read two hundred and fifty articles of law in forty-six columns, comprising approximately 3600 lines of text. Five other columns on the face have been erased in antiquity— probably at the command of the Elamite king, Shutruk-Nahhunte, whose intention may have been to have a legend in his own name engraved there as on other war trophies. This gap is partly bridged by fragments of ancient copies engraved on clay tablets, Assyrian works of the Sargonid epoch, and by some articles dealing with loans at interest, and trust-contracts found among the ruins at Nippur.

It is not a code in the sense we attribute to the word, a body of laws embracing a complete system of legislation ; it is a collection of royal decisions, of constitutions upon diverse subjects which it is well to compare with the deeds executed at the same epoch in order to obtain a more adequate idea of the jurisprudence then current. A certain order is recognizable in the arrangement of the articles of the law— charms and lots (1–2), injury to witnesses, subornation of witnesses (3–4), amendment of a judgment by the man who pronounced it (5), various categories of theft (6–25), position

---

[1] Cf. Fig. 6, p. 41.

and duties of officials (26–41), cultivation (42–65), then, after a blank, loans at interest (a–c), trust contracts (100–107), taverns (108–111), debts and their recovery (112–121), deposit contracts (122–127), family (128–191), blows and wounds (192–214), doctors, architects, and builders (215–240), animals, slaves, and rural property (241–252).

The Code of Hammurabi was not the oldest legislation promulgated in the Euphrates plains ; if he published new laws, he was most often proclaiming what had long been obligatory. When the early reforming king, Urukagina, boasted of having suppressed abuses in the city of Lagash and having delivered his subjects from robbery, murder, the wrong which the strong do to the weak, did he not allude to new regulations sanctioned by his royal authority ? Ur-Engur " made justice to reign." In the reign of Sumu-la-ilu, second prince of the First Dynasty of Babylon, the "king's law " was applied. There existed then legal decisions on a certain number of subjects : when there were none, judgment was given in accordance with local custom. It was so in a case of widowhood in Hammurabi's own reign ; the judges decided that " the law of the citizens of Sippar shall be the law applied to the parties."

Although it is certain there were legislators in the pre-Sargonic age, we know neither their names nor their cities, but we know part of the Sumerian work through later compilations. In the collection *ana ittishu* are to be read articles of law, applications of which can be traced in contracts and judicial decisions before Hammurabi. If a son said to his father, "thou art not my father," the latter would brand him, bind him and sell him. If a wife said to her lord, " thou art not my husband," she would be thrown into the water. Moreover, the recent publication of fragments of undated Sumerian codes encourages us to hope for the subsequent discovery of completer documents. Some of these fragments come from Nippur [1] ; the others, of unknown origin, formed part of a collection entitled " the laws of (the goddess) Nisaba, and (the god) Hani." [2]

Of the legislation subsequent to Hammurabi we likewise know little. A fragmentary text in the British Museum contains either judicial decisions or extracts from a code.

---

[1] I, vol. XVII, p. 35.   [2] **XXXII**, vol. I, No. 28.

The various articles may be compared with numerous cases of their application discovered in Neo-Babylonian tablets.

In the pre-Sargonic period at Lagash, we find mention of a judge named Ur-eninni. A judge, too, was that Gimil-ilishu, who had engraved on his cylinder-seal two episodes in the contest between the hero Gilgamesh and the lion and the bull. Judges were numerous in the epoch of Ur; a label on a tablet-basket mentions four in the first year of Gimil-Sin, and, in fact, they held sittings in a special place, sometimes four at a time, sometimes three, sometimes two, and sometimes one alone. In a suit about a cow, sentence was pronounced by a judge and the mayor of the city. We have another given by the chief minister, to whom the case had been taken by the plaintif, but this chief minister, Arad-nannar, was at the same time ishakku of Lagash, and it was probably in that capacity that he presided in the court; for many decisions, in which no mention is found of a judge, give the name of the ishakku, who, in any case, used certainly to intervene in person as judge of appeal. There existed at the same period a " place of oath by the name of the king." ¹ There, plaintiff, defendant, and witness respectively were obliged to take the oath in affirmation of the accuracy of their declarations.

Under the First Dynasty justice was administered by courts of first instance, and an appeal lay to the king against their decisions; but a judge was forbidden for any cause whatsoever to reverse the judgment he had given, and that under penalty of dismissal. " If a judge pronounce a sentence," decided Hammurabi, " formulate a decision, and draw up a tablet, if then he annul that sentence, he shall be summoned to answer for the annulment of the sentence which he pronounced; the amount at issue shall he pay twelve times, he shall be expelled from his seat of justice, he shall not return thither again, nor shall he sit any more with a judge in a case." The royal justice extended all over the empire. Sometimes the petitioners were invited to come in person to Babylon to plead their causes; sometimes a delegate was empowered to settle the dispute on the spot.

¹ **XXIV**, Nos. 810, 733, 748, 832, 920, 746, 932, 744, 963, 928, 1010, 960.

There were two sorts of courts of first instance, ecclesiastical and civil. Every temple was apparently in the full sense a place of justice, and its clergy might pronounce judgments. Priests and priestesses, according to the cases, sat at the gate of the holy place or in a special apartment ; as many as six judges heard a single suit. In the civil courts the sitting magistrates were no less numerous. Very often, if not always, they were professional men, for they kept the title of judge even apart from their functions—for instance, when they were simply witnesses to the execution of a deed.

In principle, judicial decisions had to be written ; the deed was drawn up by a scribe in accordance with a precise and concise formula, which was handed down by tradition in each city, but which varied from city to city. The special points of each case were entered therein, the scribe added a list of witnesses and usually his own name. Mention was made of the date, and the document was authenticated by the affixation of seals. Often the minute was then enclosed in an envelope, on which a transcript of every detail of the document was made, and which sometimes served alone to receive the impressions of the cylinder-seals. A copy was made out for anyone who in future might be interested to produce it, and another deposited in the archives ; to the last category the tablets from Ur probably belong ; for several decisions of different kinds are grouped together on them.

Under the new empire, as in earlier times, the sitting judges often numbered three or four ; sometimes, likewise, there was one judge alone. The process began with a plaint which the plaintiff presented in person, or by medium of a third party. His evidence was examined. The defendant was summoned to argue his case and judgment was pronounced. When a tablet could not be produced again, proof by the sworn testimony of the scribe who had drawn it up, or of one of the witnesses, was admissible. Under Cambyses, two brothers had sold two female slaves to a Babylonian ; a third person, a witness to the sale, came to swear that the price had actually been paid. However, certain difficulties were sometimes settled outside the courts. A remarried wife had a dispute with her son about

some slaves : the latter ended by returning to her those
whom he possessed and paying her four minæ as compensation for another who had died in his house. At other times
arbitrators—for instance, the eldest member of a family—
were appointed.

From the earliest times until the last days of the empire,
the elders of a town constituted a tribunal, the competence
of which we cannot determine exactly. At certain periods
they were chosen, or at least confirmed, by the royal authority,
and they recruited their ranks even among women, above all
priestesses of temples. Under the First Dynasty, Apil-ilishu
disputed the claims of Pala-Shamash to certain goods—a
house, a boat, slaves, and silver. The city elders before
whom the case was brought confirmed the title of Pala-
Shamash.

Witnesses in the courts were divided into two classes.
Some formed a sort of jury ; they were very often the
same persons, men or women, whose names appear in the
deeds. They composed the public before whom the execution of penal sentences—for instance, flogging, or the
expulsion of a judge who had reversed one of his own
decisions—were carried out. Others came to testify what
they knew of the case and affirmed their depositions on
oath. There are plenty of instances at the epoch of Ur.
Hammurabi's law provided for the case of a witness who
could not justify his statements. In serious cases involving
the death penalty the witness himself was liable to death ;
in money matters he would be made to pay costs. The
law also dealt with the case in which an object, disappearing
from the house of its lawful owner, was found on the
premises of someone who had acquired it from a third
party. Each had to call his witnesses to the tribunal.
" The judge will examine their statements ; the witnesses
before whom the purchase was made, and the witnesses
who knew the vanished object, will tell what they know
in the presence of the gods. The seller will be treated as a
thief. The owner will recover his article and the buyer

will recover the money paid from the house of the vendor."
In such a case two other hypotheses had to be faced, according as the one or the other of the parties fled at the moment
of administering the oath. That was the purpose of the
following articles : a purchaser, or vendor, who did not
bring forward witnesses, would be held guilty and become
punishable with death. The judge might, however, grant a
postponement when the witnesses were on a journey, or
did not live in the neighbourhood, but this postponement
was not to extend for more than six months.

Witnesses were requisite for a number of extrajudicial
deeds, which might eventually give rise to litigation or
disputes. They were often persons interested in cognizance
of the transaction. The purchaser of a slave or a house
would demand the presence of the vendor's children so as
to avoid inconvenience when the former owner's estate
came to be proved. Any purchase made from certain
persons required the execution of a deed and the presence
of a third person, otherwise the buyer ran the risk of being
considered a thief and incurring the death penalty. Such
was the case of the purchase of a sheep, an ox, or a slave,
from someone else's son or slave. Hammurabi's Law is
explicit on this point. A deposit of valuables had also to
be made before witnesses ; otherwise, in case of dispute,
the judge could not interfere.

If a civil case could not be amicably settled, one of the
parties would file a plaint. If the other party did not appear
voluntarily before the tribunal, he was summoned. Most
usually, however, they submitted their difference to the
arbitrament of the judges by common accord. That is why
in drawing up the tablets the unsuccessful party was
generally considered the plaintiff, the successful litigant
the defendant. The judge listened to the statements of the
parties, examined the documents produced, and received
the evidence of witnesses. In default of written documents,
or if their contents did not allow of a solution of the difficulty, he tendered the oath to one or other of the parties,
and in some cases to the witnesses. This oath was sworn
in the name of the gods, following a custom which went

back to the pre-Sargonic epoch, and very likely to an even earlier age. It was taken in the name of the king from the epoch of Ur till the days of the Achæmenids ; that did not in any way effect its religious character since the king was himself deified. Under the First Dynasty, the names of the gods and of the reigning monarch were most commonly united in the traditional formula. The oath was normally taken in the temple, even when the case was proceeding before the civil court, and in the presence of certain religious emblems. There were, however, circumstances under which these symbols were taken outside the sacred precincts. For instance, in a dispute about land with buildings on it, the defendant was obliged to affirm his title upon the site itself, and, in the consecrated phrase, to " lave the brow " of his house.

A plaintiff injured in his personal estate, plundered by a brigand, for instance, affirmed on oath the loss he had sustained in order to obtain compensation from the social group on whose territory he had suffered the outrage. In case of the deposit of crops, it was by oath that the depositor would sue for restitution of his property if the depositary disputed the total quantity received. A ferryman whose punt had been wrecked by a barge, likewise took an oath to obtain fair restitution. A man sued or prosecuted might secure acquittal by a declaration supported by an oath. That was the position of a man who had captured a runaway slave when the latter had died before being restored to his master, or of a wife accused of adultery by her husband if she had not been taken in the act, or of a man who unintentionally wounded or killed his adversary in a quarrel.

The oath played a part again after the delivery of the judgment. The parties pledged themselves before the gods to respect that pronouncement as final and irrevocable. A special clause was introduced in this connection to the effect that the subject in dispute would not be reviewed, that no new proceedings would be instituted. Sometimes even provision was made for a sanction, or fine, upon the transgressor.

The Neo-Babylonians often replaced mention of this oath by curses against the man who altered the decision given— " Let Marduk and Zarpanitum decree his ruin ! " in a deed of the reign of Nebuchadrezzar ; and, in the time of Cyrus the Anshanite, " Whosoever shall attempt to change this decision, may Anu, Ellil, and Ea curse him, may Nabu, scribe of the Esagil, cut short his fate ! ".

The judges' decisions concern all sorts of objects, and quite often no mention even is made of the causes of the litigation in the tablet of judgment. We see them intervening, for example, in a purchase of property disputed by the vendor's sons ; the latter were non-suited. After the sale of a house by a man and his two sons, in the reign of Sin-muballit, one of the sons tried to repudiate the transaction, and was condemned to be branded on the brow. Various revenues, especially those derived from titles to sacred offices, gave rise to lawsuits from time to time. The judges would determine the portions to which the petitioners were entitled, or would dismiss their plaint as groundless. Division of inheritances was also a cause for appeal to the courts. In the thirty-third year of Hammurabi, two brothers could not come to an agreement for the apportionment of their deceased father's possessions ; a certain Nidnat-Sin " made an equitable partition." Partnerships could not be dissolved without the intervention of the courts ; sometimes, in the course of their existence, they gave rise to difficulties which were solved in the same way. In the thirty-fourth year of Hammurabi, two brothers, Tsilli-Ishtar and Awil-ili, were arraigned in respect of a house and other possessions lately acquired by them. It had been bought with the money of a partnership made between them and him, maintained the plaintiff. The defendants proved that it was not so ; they had paid for it with money remitted to Tsilli-Ishtar by his mother and won their case.

The law made provision for the case of a man who abandoned his wife, went away to another town, and returning later on wished to resume conjugal life. He was denied that right, and, if his wife had married again, she would remain with her new lord. A judgment pronounced at Sippar, in the ninth year of Hammurabi, is a practical application of the old rule on which this provision in the law was based. A certain Sin-natsir had left his wife for twenty years ; when she died he came to claim the inheritance bequeathed to her daughter Hulatum, obviously a slave woman. The rabianu of Sippar and the Kar-Sippar met and determined that Sin-natsir had left his wife " to pursue his own destiny and had not loved her " ; they laid the blame upon him and refused to grant his request. The woman, Amat-Shamash, alleged that she was the adopted daughter of Shamash-Gâmil and his wife, Ummi-Arahtum. She had no tablet ; her witnesses brought no convincing proofs ; the judges tendered the oath to Ummi-Arahtum, the defendant, and rejected the claims of the plaintiff.

Babilitum sued Erish-sagil, Ubar-Nabium, and Marduk-nâtsir to secure a share in an inheritance : the judge granted it to him.

Not every tribunal was competent to hear all cases. In the twenty-eighth year of Hammurabi, the judges at Babylon refused to take a case because the plaintiff was domiciled at Sippar, and, consequently, was not entitled to bring his suit before them.

In a certain number of cases Hammurabi's Law fixed the penalties which the judges might inflict.

A capital sentence might be pronounced upon a man who cast a spell upon another and did not convict him of fault, upon the false witness for the prosecution in a criminal case, upon the robber of the treasures at a temple or the palace, and the receiver of the stolen objects, upon the thief who could not restore the movable object of value which he had appropriated and pay damages, on the vendor of the stolen object, the receiver, or anyone who bought or received a deposit without a deed or witnesses from the hands of a minor, or a slave, or who without proof claimed a stolen object. Opportunity of flight offered to a slave, shelter given to a runaway slave, or the acceptance of his services, was considered theft and punished by death. An ancient Sumerian law only condemned a man to restore head for head, or, if he possessed no slave, to pay twenty-five shekels of silver, if he had given asylum to a runaway slave for a month. The death penalty might be inflicted on a brigand, or upon a defaulter from military service, even if he had provided a substitute. The officer who tolerated the substitution incurred the same penalty. It was also pronounced against the governor, or prefect, who attacked the privileges of officers, the hostess of a tavern who sheltered rebels, the man who violated a young girl, or who tricked a surgeon into branding a slave with the unalienable mark. Thus, according to the Sumerian laws of Nisaba and Hani, the seducer of a girl, whose hand had been refused him, must die. In all these cases the law gives no indication of the sort of death to be inflicted upon the culprit. Sometimes it is more explicit. Drowning was specified for the tenant of a tavern who sold drinks above the legal price, refused payment in barley, or demanded a higher payment in silver; for the wife who, when her husband had been taken prisoner, despite the enjoyment of adequate means, had gone to live with another man; and for the bad housewife who wasted her husband's property and wanted to desert him. It had been decreed in the old Sumerian law in every case where the wife claimed a divorce. The same penalty was likewise prescribed for the adulteress and her accomplice, and for the father-in-law and bride who had incestuous relations; the pair were tied together and thrown into the water. The penalty of burning was inflicted upon a mother and son convicted of incest, a priestess who opened a tavern or entered one to drink there, and the man who took advantage of a fire to commit a theft. Impalement was the fate of the wife guilty of having her husband assassinated in order to contract a new marriage.

Finally, the death penalty resulted from the operation of the *lex talionis*, but only where the injury had been sustained by a person of quality. If a freeman, surety for a debt, perished in the creditor's house from blows or starvation, the creditor's son was condemned to death. If a freewoman had a miscarriage and died as a result of blows, the aggressor's daughter had to die. If a badly-built house collapsed and killed the owner and his son, the capital penalty was incurred by the architect or his son. Indirectly, death might result from the ordeal prescribed by two articles of the law : for cases where anyone believed himself the victim of a spell cast upon him, or where a wife was accused of adultery without being taken in the act.

The tribunal had to order the excision of the tongue of the child of parents abandoned to prostitution if he denied his adopted parents, and the putting out of his eyes if he forsook their house to return to father or mother. Amputation of the hand awaited a son who struck his father, or a careless surgeon who, in opening a sty with a bistoury, injured his client's eye, or who, without the master's knowledge and on his own responsibility, branded a slave with the unalienable mark, or the tenant farmer who stole grain or plants. Amputation of the breast was the fate of a wet nurse who, without the permission of the parents whose child she was suckling, took a second nurseling and let the first die through negligence. The slave who disputed his master's rights had his ear cut off. A Sumerian law prescribes the sale of the delinquent in this case. Anyone who struck a person of higher rank than his own might be condemned to receive in public as many as sixty lashes with an ox-hide whip.

Banishment was the sentence pronounced on a father who had intercourse with his own daughter.

There existed a whole scale of damages, ranging from three to thirty times the value of the object to be restored—three times for sums taken on deposit from a business agent; five times for what the unfaithful depositary had converted to his own use, or for a stolen object sold by the thief if the latter died before justice overtook him, and the purchaser could prove he had acted in good faith ; six times for money improperly claimed by an agent from his employer, ten times for an object stolen from a *mushkinu*, or animals fraudulently sold by a herdsman; twelve times the value of the object of the action had to be paid if the judge annulled a sentence previously pronounced by him, and thirty times the value of what had been stolen from a temple or the palace.

The tribunal had to estimate the damage done by brigands ; the city and the governor of the territory where the brigandage took place were responsible therefor. It would condemn the negligent cultivator to pay in proportion to the productivity of adjoining estates, and apply the various indemnities provided in the law in cases of accidents caused by animals and deliberate injuries when the victim was not a free man, and the *lex talionis* was therefore inoperative.

CHAPTER III

Economic Organization

1. LANDED PROPERTY

IN Sumer and Akkad, from the earliest times, property in land was vested in individuals, or in social groups. pre-Sargonic deeds of sales afford precious evidence for this. The temples had their fields and their orchards; the ishakku's wife and children their private lands. The little house of the poor man was not always immune from the greed of the rich, and his mother's plot was too often plundered by the priest. Already, apparently, the prince rewarded his faithful servants by grants of land, either in perpetuity, or simply in usufruct.

The deed of acquisition by king Manishtusu of various demesnes proves the existence of collective ownership side by side with private ownership. In it a farm is mentioned bounded by two canals, a tribe, and an individual; one of the blocks of land extended over more than 1350 hectares (3300 acres), another scarcely reached an area of 36 hectares (90 acres).

Hammurabi's Law distinguished between private possessions and *ilku* possessions. The latter, granted by the king by way of reward for public services, could be neither sold nor seized, nor mortgaged, nor transmitted on any terms whatsoever except to the male heir, and on condition of the fulfilment of the appropriate duties. The disposal of private property itself was subject to restriction in favour of the family. In principle it could only be alienated for debt. A married woman only enjoyed the usufruct of her dowry; the absolute ownership belonged to her children, and, in default of children, to her brothers. A priestess, or a prostitute, enjoyed more extensive rights if her father had specifically laid down in her tablet the right of disposal.

Every family probably had a right of pre-emption over property they had been obliged to alienate.

In the Kassite period some towns possessed great landed estates. It was the same among tribes who had settled in the ancient Sumer, near the shores of the Persian Gulf, as a result of the troubles provoked in Babylonia by the Hittite invasion. To reward services rendered to the State, to show gratitude to the gods, or to provide an appanage for

FIG. 10.   Kudurru
(Délégation en Perse, Louvre).

their children the kings used to buy estates from these cities or tribes. Not only did they have the usual proprietary titles established on clay tablets, but they wished to place the newly-granted territories more formally under the protection of the gods. On a great ovoid boulder, a stele of stone or terra-cotta, they had engraved religious emblems, the deed of donation and curses upon whoever should oppose their will. These documents, called *kudurrus* (boundary stones), which were once supposed to have been set up on the property itself to maintain the divine protection over it, were also called *narû* (stelæ) by the Babylonians, and seem to have been placed in the temples.[1]

The tribes just settled in the south of Babylonia had chiefs and administrators. They each occupied a more or less extensive territory, where rose their cities and villages. They owned part of the lands ; each town, each village and certain families had likewise a part. It was all divided into plots exploited by individuals, plots which ran into one

FIG. 11.   Kudurru
(Délégat.on en Perse, Louvre).

another without being merged ; for despite revolutions and invasions people still knew how to estimate and measure areas and define boundaries just as well as a thousand or fifteen hundred years earlier. Passing into the king's hands, the demesne acquired from the tribe became private property. The chief had agreed to the transfer in the name of the community, the capital value had been paid, the neighbours compensated if they had any claim to establish. This domain became exempt from any recovery by the tribe—

[1] Cf. **XXIII, CXXVII, LVII, LXI,** Figs. 10 and 11.

the vendors or their heirs—on any pretext whatsoever. All these stipulations are carefully enumerated.

The fief created by the king was granted in hereditary and absolute title, and not at all conditionally like the *ilku* properties of the previous epoch. The recipient remained subject to the charges and imposts with which the fief was encumbered, unless he obtained, as most commonly happened, a tablet of exemption.

Uncultivated lands were at the disposal of the first occupier ; they became the property of the man who had cleared them. King Melishipak gave his daughter Hunnubat-Nanaï an estate on the borders of the Land of the Sea, and he was at pains to declare the legality of his tenure on the grounds that he had cleared it, established on it an irrigation system and a reservoir, had made the land arable, and had founded three villages.[1]

Landed property was, in fact, subject to servitudes in the interests of the neighbours, especially for watering the lands. The governor had a right to pasturage, to firstfruits on the harvest and hay, and to requisition men, animals, and chariots, for the levy, maintenance of canals, fords, and roads. The exemptions granted by the king, in remitting these charges of public utility, give us detailed information about them. So on the *kudurru* of Melishipak, in favour of his daughter, we read : " Cattle small and great, impost, corvée, care of canals, channels, works on reservoirs, labour at ferries, levy of employees for the canal, equipment of chariots, mowing of hay and stubble, the royal impost whatever it be—the tablet of exemption of the villages he has sealed and has given it to her." To confirm his intention the king placed the estate under the protection of the gods soliciting their wrath against anyone who might wish " to take from these villages cattle, small or great, to subject their inhabitants to charges or levies on any royal impost whatever it be and however small." The same Melishipak, when he set apart the appanage of Marduk-apal-iddin, his son, is no less explicit as to the servitudes from which he exempted it.[2] " His franchise is thus established : on his land firstfruits and tithes must not be imposed ; to the levy, to labour, to defence against flood, to maintenance

[1] **XXIII**, vol. X, p. 87.   [2] **XXIII**, vol. II, p. 99.

and embanking of the royal canals, to protection of the
cities, Bît-sikkamidu and Damiq-Adad, in the companies
raised in the cities of the district of Ninâ-Agade, the people
of his domain must not be summoned. They have not to
work on the dam of the royal canal, to embank, to close, or
to clear out the bed of the canal ; a cultivator on his lands,
foreign or native alike, no governor of Bît-Pir-Shadurabu
from the domain shall make to go. Neither by royal order,
nor by order of the governor, nor by order of anyone at all,
on wood, grass, straw, barley, or any other crop, on chariot
and equipage, on ass and man, can any claim be made.
During a shortage of water in the canal connecting the
Rati-Anzanim and the canal of the royal district, on the
waters of the irrigation canal no claim can be made ; from
the channel of its reservoir water must not be drawn ; the
irrigation must not be divided in two ; another property
must not be watered or irrigated therefrom. Nor may the
grass on his land be cut ; on its borders must no one drive
the beasts of the king, or of the governor, nor make fodder
of its grass ; a way or a bridge, neither for the king nor for
the governor, have they to make, and any new levy which
in future the king or the governor may ordain, or any old
levy fallen into desuetude that may be revived, that levy
they need not perform at all."

The alluvial land which forms Tigris-Euphrates plains
is naturally fertile provided it be properly drained and
watered. The earliest inhabitants recognized this, and
there is scarcely an ishakku, of Lagash for instance, from
the old king Ur-Ninâ onwards, but boasts of having had
canals cut, and having bestowed much care on irrigation.
The works to which the creation of canals gave rise " pre-
suppose a system of knowledge and procedure constituting
engineering science, unless we suppose that they were constructed by successive advances, blindly, with repeated
rectifications in the course of execution which would have
required considerable time even with numerous unpaid
labourers, such as prisoners barely fed. We must then
admit that there were preliminary surveys, advance plans,
final plans involving the use of levelling instruments, and

of graphic methods plotting on a draught the results of the
measurements made on the land, and the proportions of
the work to be carried out." [1] Some plans of canals and
streams have come down to us from the pre-Sargonic epoch
—for instance, a fragment of a tablet on which was represented the canal Hummadimsha, cut by order of Eanatum,
and to which was attached a reservoir with a capacity
exceeding a thousand hectolitres (2200 gallons). This
reservoir was strengthened by Entemena, Eanatum's nephew,
who finished another canal connecting the two rivers, and
a little later by king Urukagina. The latter had the old
canal of Girsu, called " Ningirsu-at-Nippur-is-prince,"
restored ; a tablet gives details of the levies. The task
imposed upon the professional excavators was more imposing
than that of simple manual labours ; this canal was about
280 metres long, and was executed on a plan.

Utterly preoccupied with his pious labours and the reconstruction of temples, Gudea could make only incidental
allusion to his other works. He, however, cut the canal,
Ningirsu-Ushumgal, a local event commemorated in the
name of one of the years of his reign. He must have maintained in good order for navigation those which previously
existed ; it was by water that the transportation of building
materials, wood, stone, and metal, was always effected, and
to unload them he built a quay by a gate of the city. In
the court of Ningirsu the care of the canals, channels, and
watering machines was assigned to the cultivator of the
sacred territory.

Ur-Engur, king of Ur, cut the frontier canal, Nanna-gugal,
and "made its basin equal to the waters of the sea." A
tablet of this period contains the wages of women employed
in making a dam of reeds at the head of the canal. Sin-
idinnam of Larsa " cut the Tigris, the broad river, and
procured good water, unfailing, for his city and his land."

Hammurabi, having achieved the unity of the empire,
undertook important works. He cut the Nâr-Hammurabi,
" wealth of the people which brings abundant water to
Sumer and Akkad, converts its banks into cultivated fields,
heaps up the piles of grain, and furnishes perpetual water
to the people of Sumer and Akkad." The Nâr-Hammurabi

[1] **XCVII**, p. 428.

has not entirely vanished ; it began at the Euphrates, below Kish at the level of Borsippa, descended towards Umma, which it passed on the left, and after reaching Larsa turned towards the Persian Gulf. The royal orders show how the central power organized and used the levies. One day the king directs Sin-idinnam, governor of Larsa, " to call together the people who possess fields on the banks of the canal Damanum to clean it out. The cleaning of the canal Damanum must be finished by the end of the month." On another occasion he orders the same official to finish in three days the cleaning of the canal which runs to Uruk and had not been put in order as far as that city.

The exemptions granted by Melishipak bear witness to the maintenance of levies for the purpose of upkeep and embankment work under the Third Dynasty. Letters addressed to king Kudur-Ellil show how officials charged with water supply discharged their duties in the fourteenth century. An inspector denounced a prefect who had blocked a canal in such a way that if two estates could be irrigated from it there were twenty others absolutely parched whose crops had been lost. The prefect, however, defended himself, and claimed not to have neglected a single field.

In the Neo-Babylonian epoch, Nebuchadrezzar II connected the Tigris and Euphrates by the Median Wall, which was the bank of a canal, and finished at Babylon the supporting walls of the banks of the Arahtu commenced by his father.

The great canals, national undertakings, created in the first place to enrich and drain the land, were at the same time admirable waterways, but they required considerable upkeep because the ground was soft, the banks very friable. The waters of the Euphrates reach the latitude of Babylon charged with sand and clay, at present one kilogram per cubic metre at ordinary seasons, and as much as twenty-five kilograms at the flood.[1] Canals of minor importance and channels carried the waters to the edges of the fields and meadows ; there, from the pre-Sargonic period, they were drawn by means of elevating machines worked by oxen, or simply by pails operated by a lever. This apparatus, depicted in a scene of pastoral life on a cylinder-seal, is

[1] *Génie civil*, Mar. 10, 1906.

still in use not only in the East, but also in certain parts of France, notably in the Loire Valley between Angers and Nantes. Hammurabi provided against the theft of such an apparatus ; the thief was made to pay the injured owner five shekels in respect of an ox machine and only three shekels for a bucket-apparatus. In the first year of Darius II certain inhabitants of Nippur made an agreement under which four animals were needed for the irrigation of a certain estate.

The elevation of the water did not exceed four metres at the time of low water in the winter ; at that season fields are to-day given three waterings of two hundred cubic metres each per hectare (17,800 gallons per acre). Hammurabi's law provided against damage caused to someone else's field by a cultivator who kept his channel in bad repair. If he omitted to strengthen it and a breach developed, he must make restitution for any crop thus ruined. If he were not in a position to do this, he would be sold with all his belongings for money, and the injured neighbours would share the proceeds. Whoever forgot to replace the dam after having opened it to water his field, was likewise responsible for the flood spreading to adjoining fields, and had to make compensation in accordance with the average yield of the land ; if it were a question of a machine the rate was fixed at a gur of barley per gan of surface, almost $3\frac{1}{2}$ hectolitres per hectare ($3\frac{1}{5}$ bushels per acre).

Meadows required no care beyond watering them and cutting the hay. Asses, cattle, and sheep were let out to graze there. The herdsman normally received an annual wage of 8 gurs of barley (20·200 hectolitres, or $55\frac{1}{2}$ bushels). In the days of Hammurabi, if he lost a beast he had to replace it at his own expense. He would make the lease multiply according to agreements made with the owner ; but if he falsified the state of the stock, and sold any beast for his own profit, he was liable to pay ten times the value of what he had stolen ; if mischance befell the stable, it was for him to make good the loss at his own expense unless he exculpated himself by oath when the accident was caused by forces beyond his control. The stable, like most of the rustic buildings, was usually built of reeds, and the pastoral scenes engraved on the cylinder-seals offer many illustrations of it.

The fields of grain were tilled with ploughs drawn by oxen. An archaic cylinder reproduces a scene of cultivation. The ploughman holds the tail of the plough with both hands, men armed with staves and whips urge on the animals. More perfect ploughs were equipped with a drill. The rent of plough and oxen was fixed in Hammurabi's time at four gur of barley (more than 5 hectolitres, or 13¾ bushels) annually. The law made provision for accidents, which might happen either to the animal, or by its fault, and determined the compensation. In the pre-Sargonic epoch, the proportion of the harvest to the sowing, and the yield per hectare, can be estimated approximately from the data in tablets of the ishakku Lugalanda ; about 22 hecto-litres of barley were gathered from a hectare (22½ bushels per acre), sown with 42 litres or a little above 50 to 1.

In the period of Ur, the cultivator, the cattleman, and the herdsman were hired by the year ; as wages they received barley, wool, sometimes even silver or animals. Regulations existed for the cultivation. In respect of a priest's tenants, someone affirmed on oath that they had cultivated a field " with slaves and oxen," had been paid, and had presented their accounts regularly.

Under the law of Hammurabi a man who had taken a piece of land and had not made barley grow on it, was obliged to pay the owner in proportion to the yield on adjoining farms. If he had not cultivated it at all, he was compelled to clear it, sow it and surrender the whole harvest. If he had taken a lease for three years, to put under cultivation a piece of uncleared land, and had not kept his engagement, in the fourth year he would sow it, and must return the owner one gur per gan—about 7·16 hectolitres the hectare (8 bushels the acre). In the case of the destruction of the harvested crop by a storm, if the landlord had been paid, the whole loss would fall on the farmer ; if there were a share-farming agreement at the rate of one-half, or one-third, and the quota had not yet been paid over, the remnant of the harvest would be divided in the stipulated proportions.

The law gave protection to the small cultivator whose resources were too limited for the purchase of plant at the beginning of his exploitation. If he had an understanding with a neighbour for making the sowing, the owner could not touch him till after the harvest, and then received what was due to him. A cultivator who had borrowed at interest, and could not gather the harvest through circumstances beyond his control, such as a storm, or failure of water in the canals, was not obliged to pay any interest that year. A field might furthermore be mortgaged.

At the same period the cultivation of a farm was sometimes entrusted to a man engaged at an annual wage of 8 gur of barley, the rate paid to a herdsman. The owner supplied the capital. If the hired man was caught red-handed in theft of grain or plants, he was condemned to have his hands cut off; if he neglected the field work, hired the beasts to a third person, or stole the seed, he was obliged to pay 60 gur of barley in respect of every 100 gan of land (roughly 4·30 hectolitres per hectare, or 4¾ bushels per acre), and, if he was unable to meet the loss, he would remain tied to the soil " among the live stock."

Under the Achæmenids, as in the time of the First Dynasty, lands were often leased for three years, which presupposes the maintenance of the triennial rotation of crops. The rent was paid partly in money, partly in kind—wine, flour, beasts. Compensation was provided for the tenant if before the expiration of his lease he was turned out of his farm.

When harvest arrived it was cut and trodden by animals. Hammurabi fixed the rate for hire by the day of a threshing ox at 20 qa of barley (17 litres, or 30 pints), that of an ass at 10 qa. Only 1 qa was paid to the driver of ox or ass. An ox-wagon with driver was rated at 180 qa daily, the wagon by itself at 40 qa. As in France to-day, an agricultural labourer received different wages at different seasons— 6 grains of silver during the first five months in the year, 5 grains during the other seven.

Orchards formed a third species of landed property after meadows and plough land. As they were less extensive than grain fields they were measured with greater precision from the pre-Sargonic epoch onwards. Vegetables, especially onions, were grown on them and trees were planted. It was the same in the age of Agade, when plantations of onions are mentioned reaching an area of one gan (35·28 ares or 3⅓ roods).

Hammurabi fixed the owner's share, in respect of orchards in full bearing, at two-thirds; if the gardener carelessly let the productivity decline, he was obliged to pay in accordance with the normal yield. The lease of a field to be transformed into a garden was for five years—the first four for planting, in the fifth the yield was apportioned, and, by an old Sumerian custom, the owner was entitled to make two equal parts, leaving in the lot of the lessee any land left uncultivated. If the lessee had not produced any transformation, he had to pay at the rate of the normal yield for every year, and was condemned to put the land under cultivation. If he had received a piece of virgin land, he would likewise put it in order, but would give only one gur of barley per gan per year of the lease. Felling a tree in an orchard without the owner's knowledge involved, as in previous centuries, the payment of thirty shekels compensation. The harvest of a date plantation might be offered in advance for the liquidation of a debt, but the creditor was not obliged to take this risk. An orchard, like any other real property, was accepted as a pledge, and that would be so till the end of the Neo-Babylonian Empire.

Property, with buildings on it, was valued according to the area occupied; it was measured very accurately in the cities. The latter, at least in their origin, were almost exclusively places of cult and of refuge as well as markets. The bulk of the population lived in the country, often in wattle-and-daub huts, or even under tents; perhaps, as the Arabs do in that region to-day, people dug cellars lined with mats and reeds to afford them better shelter from the heat.

The very archaic houses, discovered among the ruins of Shuruppak, were formed of small rooms set round a rectangular court. That was the arrangement which we meet subsequently on architects' plans and in constructions of the New Empire. They might be built of bricks, and the roof was supported by beams. The doors and the bolts were not fixtures. That was intentional; given the rarity of wood they were articles of value which might be offered by themselves as securities, not be included in the sale of a house or belong to the tenant. Many houses must have been without them. The Babylonian house was usually all on one floor; it rarely boasted a second storey. Some-times it had a right of way over a neighbouring property; more often it opened directly on to the street.

At Lagash, in the pre-Sargonic period, the houses for sale had an area varying from $\frac{2}{3}$ to $1\frac{1}{2}$ sars (23·52 to 52·92 square metres, or 28 to 63$\frac{1}{3}$ square yards). In Hammurabi's time the average price was 15 shekels a sar; it might rise to 71 shekels, or fall even to 2 or 3. Built land in town was, on the average, worth 225 times as much as land under cereal crops; but in the country it was much less dear, and some granaries were only valued at one-sixth of a shekel the sar, two and a half times the value of the land.

Hammurabi's law fixed the fees of an architect at two shekels per sar. It saddled him with the responsibility for bad construction. He had to rebuild at his own expense a wall that collapsed, to replace furniture broken, or a slave killed thereby, and to pay with his own life for the death of the owner crushed in the ruins.

Property, with buildings on it, might be mortgaged,[1] and in the Neo-Babylonian epoch the creditor sometimes dwelt there himself, sometimes left the debtor the use of it. Under Nebuchadrezzar II,[2] a certain Shâpik-zêr mortgaged his house to Shulâ, who came to live there; the rent balanced the interest on the sum raised. But Shulâ, being in want of money in his turn, asked Nergal-uballit for 2 minæ 14 shekels, and as security handed over to him Shâpik-zêr's house; as he would continue to reside there, he would have to pay his creditor a rent equivalent to the interest on the borrowed money.

2. INDUSTRY; APPRENTICESHIP

From the earliest times a rudimentary organization existed, at least in the case of certain trades; at the epoch

[1] CX, 39.   [2] CLXI, Nbk. 123.

of Dungi, weaving was carried on under overseers appointed by the king.

The Code of Hammurabi regulated and fixed the wages of workmen employed by the day, and assigned them 4 or 5 grains of silver (16 to 20 centigrams, or $2\frac{1}{2}$ to 3 grains troy). It also determined the fees of the architect and the caulker, without forgetting to define their civil liabilities in the case of bad workmanship.

This law of Hammurabi is likewise the evidence for a system of apprenticeship towards the end of the third millennium. A man might take a child into his house to bring him up and teach him a trade. If he made a good workman of him, his natural parents, after agreeing to separation from their child, were no longer entitled to reclaim him ; but if the child had learnt nothing, he might return home.

In the Neo-Babylonian epoch, and under the Persian kings, a master sometimes apprenticed his slave to a craft. It meant losing the interest on a mina of silver, but the capital thus tied up might appreciate in value. The owner, therefore, took precautions against the first eventuality happening ; the instructor-workman would be obliged, if he neglected to teach his pupil his craft properly, to pay damages. As, on the other hand, he profited by the work performed by the apprentice, he had no claim to payment— at the most a present would be offered him by way of testimonial. In the seventh year of Cyrus, a slave baker had already had another slave as apprentice for nine months ; he was to keep him another six months, but if at the end of that time he had not given him adequate training, he would have to pay at the rate of 6 qa of barley per day for the whole period. Next year, Itti-Marduk-Balatu apprenticed a slave to Hashdaï, slave of Cambyses, the Heir Apparent, to learn the trade of a mason ; if the result were unsatisfactory, Hashdaï would pay a third of a mina of silver to Itti-Marduk-Balatu. In the same year a married couple bound one of their slaves for six years to learn service. In case of success, the instructor would receive as a present a garment worth four shekels ; but were his lessons unprofitable, he would pay 3 qa of barley a day for the whole period of six years. The result was not always

brilliant, and the instructor found himself obliged to pay
the compensation stipulated, but he did that without demur
when he had made sufficient profit from his pupil's services.
On the 20th Teshrit, in the second year of Cyrus, Nubtâ had
apprenticed Atkal-ana-Marduk to Bêl-etir for five years to
learn weaving ; the pupil brought one qa of food daily and
clothes with him. The weaver pledged himself to pay
damages at the rate of 6 qa per day if the instruction was
unsatisfactory, and the transaction was complicated by a
sum of 20 shekels of silver to be paid by whichever party
broke the agreement. On the 30th Ab, in the eighth year,
ten months after the expiration of the agreement, the slave
was still with the weaver, and the latter made a payment
of five shekels to Nubtâ.

3. TRADE

From pre-Sargonic times the rivers and canals were the
natural means of communication between the various
districts of Sumer and Akkad. The cities, moreover, were
for the most part planted along the banks of the Euphrates.
By water the early king, Ur-Ninâ, transported the timber
requisite for the construction of the temples of Lagash ;
Manishtushu had floated down the diorite obelisk on which
he inscribed the list of his land purchases ; and Gudea had
imported wood, stone, and precious metals. Archaic
cylinders bear pictures of boats. At the epoch of Ur there
were some with a capacity of 90 gur of barley, and they
were used for all sorts of freight—passengers, animals,
cereals, oil, flour, wood, and all sorts of materials. A voyage
from Lagash to Susa by canal took at least two months.
Hammurabi's law fixed the daily rent of a boat of 60 gur
burthen at one-sixteenth of a shekel, and that of a fast
boat at $2\frac{1}{2}$ grains. It awarded the boatman an annual wage
of 60 gur, valued the caulking of a boat of 60 gur burthen at
two shekels, and fixed the responsibility for the loss of the
vessel and its cargo. In the Neo-Babylonian epoch river
traffic had not been reduced in intensity. Under Nabonidus,
a shekel and a quarter of silver were paid for the hire of a
boat engaged to transport three oxen and thirty-four head
of small stock offered by the Heir Apparent to Shamash and
other gods at Sippar. The ordinary tariff had risen since

Hammurabi's time, and reached on an average a shekel a day ; a boat was sold for from twenty to thirty shekels.

We have no information about the establishment or maintenance of land routes in Babylonia. Convoys between the capital and the chief towns existed in the epoch of Agade ; in the days of the kings of Ur, numerous messengers travelled as far as Elam to carry the prince's orders. Perhaps they usually followed the towing-paths, or tracks traced across the plain. Besides, the necessity of importing from abroad a great number of primary materials not found in their country had long ago obliged the inhabitants of Babylonia to develop foreign trade, especially with Elam on the east, and with Asia Minor and the Mediterranean coasts to the north-west. They conducted this trade by commission contracts, or the appointment of proxies. If it was a question of finalizing a business deal, selling a house, recovering a debt, hiring a boat, borrowing barley, leasing a farm or a beast, when the principal could not attend in person, he chose a proxy, fixed in writing the extent of his competency with the authorization to execute the deed, and confirmed it on oath.

For trade in distant towns or foreign countries the business man formed a sort of share-partnership ; he entrusted sums of money to be employed profitably in business, or remitted merchandise to be sold to a commercial traveller who lent him his talents, his experience, and his credit.

A great expansion of trade with the north and west, consequent on the political expansion of a united Babylonia, coincided with the reign of Hammurabi. Thanks to its geographical position between Upper Asia and Hither Asia, at the point where the two rivers came close together, the new capital was the veritable centre of the commerce of the East. So the legislator devoted several articles of his law to the affairs of great merchants, and regulated the relations of employer and employed. Unfortunately, we have not got the first articles treating of the constitution of the partnership.

For the validity of the agreement a written document defining the exact duties of the agent and indicating precisely the money or merchandise at his disposal, the gratuitous advance to provide for the journey, must have been required. The employee was obliged to keep an exact account of his operations, and to note all profits realized. On his return he gave back the whole stock to the principal, obtained a receipt for it, and took the portion of the profits on which he had agreed before setting out. If, through negligence or incapacity, he made bad bargains, he had to make compensation by returning twice the sum confided to his care. If he could prove that he had made a loss, he would only restore the money entrusted to him, and if finally he had lost it through the insecurity of the roads or other causes beyond his control, he was absolved from all liability on certifying these facts on oath. Disputes between agent and employer were scarcely ever admitted without written proof. Had the traveller made a mistake to his own disadvantage in making up his accounts, if he had not exacted a receipt for the money expended, he could not secure reimbursement. In default of written proof, the person against whom the claim was made summoned the other to the temple in the presence of witnesses. The traveller convicted of owing money to the business man was condemned to pay three times the sum owed ; if it were the business man who was in default, he must pay his traveller six times what he had wrongly kept back.

The insecurity of the caravan routes was a reality, and in the fifteenth century the kings of Babylon complained of the molestations and murders to which their merchants were exposed in the parts of Syria subject to Egyptian control.

In the last centuries of the Babylonian monarchy a business man often associated himself with foreigners, especially Aramæans, whose language was spread throughout Babylonia, Palestine, Syria, and Asia Minor. The commercial traveller handled the business during the period fixed by his contract of engagement. He had to bring back at least the equivalent of the sum advanced him ; for he shouldered the losses alone ; if there was a profit, it was divided equally.

Even before the contract of share-partnership between a merchant and a traveller who took money or merchandise to employ profitably, the contract of partnership was known to Sumero-Akkadian civilization—at first in the form of the association of two or more persons to buy and cultivate a field—but the conditions governing the enterprise are not indicated.

We have to wait till the First Dynasty of Babylon to get more exact information. The partners did not necessarily contribute capital in money as the basis of their arrangement; often their aim was to borrow the sum needed for the projected operations by pledging themselves jointly to effect its repayment. On the dissolution of the partnership profits and losses were divided in the proportions agreed on at the time of its formation, and the liquidation would be universal, or, as the saying was, "from the wisp of straw to the gold." The declarations were made before the judicial authority, and if disputes arose between the partners, they were sent to the temple, where the defendant was obliged to take an oath to clear himself of the imputations cast upon him.

The holder of the common stock was further obliged to declare upon oath that he had hidden none of the assets of the partnership.

Here is a specimen of a partnership between two persons for purposes of general trade : [1] " Erib-Sin and Nur-Shamash have formed a partnership, have come to the temple, and have concluded their project. Silver, merchandise, male or female slave abroad or at home, they share them in common. Their project is realized—silver for silver, male or female slave, merchandise abroad or at home from mouth to interest brother will not dispute with brother. By Shamash Aia, Marduk and king Hammurabi have they sworn "? in the presence of seventeen witnesses.

In the Neo-Babylonian epoch, the formula was sometimes drawn up in quite general terms. Under Nabonidus we read, for instance : " Itti-Marduk-Balatu and Shâpik-zêr pool a mina of silver as the capital of a parnership. The result of their operations belongs to them jointly." Others specify all the business they may do " in town and in the country " as involved in the partnership. The same Itti-Marduk-Balatu, an important business man, made an

[1] CXXXII, p. 288.

agreement with Marduk-Shâpik-zêr, perhaps the same person as the Shâpik-zêr of the preceding contract, to employ together for gain five minæ of silver and some spices. Each of them would entrust the exploitation of the enterprise to one of their slaves ; the gains would be shared between the contracting parties, while the servants would be fed and clothed from the funds of the partnership, not by their respective masters.[1] Next year a similar covenant —it was agreed to put a mina of silver at the disposal of Marduk-Shâpik-zêr's slave, and Itti-Marduk-Balatu, on his part, would also supply one of his servants to make profitable use of this money.

A partnership contract was sometimes made for a short term, and sometimes it would be operative over several years, during which a provisional settlement would be made from time to time. When the day for final settlement came there was opportunity, as before, for the courts to intervene, and for declarations to be reinforced by tendering the oath. In 617 B.C., the eighth year of Nabopolassar, Nabu-kîn-aplu and his son, Nabu-bêlshunu, had gone into partnership with Shulâ and Mushezib-Bêl. Thirty-one years later, in the eighteenth year of Nebuchadrezzar II (586), they decided to wind it up. They settled their accounts before the courts, and divided up the fifteen shekels of silver paid by Nabu-kîn-aplu and his son. There was to be no rediscussion of the business and no fresh claims. The partnership was dissolved, and each would go his own way. The settlement was completed and, to prevent any difficulty in the future, the old tablets were destroyed. The gods were invoked to witness to the regularity of the liquidation, and each on withdrawing took with him the proof in writing.

4. SALE

Sale was a transfer of property for money or more rarely for barley. The deed which attested it must include three essential elements—an indication of the object sold, the names of the parties, and the price to be paid or the receipt for payment affected in ready money.

Some deeds of sale have come down from the very dawn of

---

[1] CLXI, Nbn. 199, 572, 653.

the historical period ; they had been executed in the ancient city of Shuruppak before the epoch of Ur-Ninâ, king of Lagash.[1] We find in them land valued at a price of $2\frac{1}{2}$ shekels of silver a gan ; structures annexed to the fields at 5 or 10 shekels of silver or even 10 shekels of copper. Such documents do not, any more than those of later date, give an absolutely accurate idea of the real value of the objects sold ; for account must be taken of the quality of the slaves, the condition of the houses, the situation of the lands, and even of the personal taste of the purchasers. A stone tablet, likewise archaic, gives a list of several estates purchased for silver and cash-down in the district of Uruk. Unfortunately the majority of the figures are mutilated, but the value of the gan works out at not less than six shekels.[2] At Lagash, in the reign of Enhegal, one of the predecessors of Ur-Ninâ, Lugalkigalla, high priest of Ningirsu, bought various properties ranging from 48 to 900 hectares ($118\frac{1}{2}$ to 2220 acres) in area, assuming the superficial measures to be the same as at later dates. He paid for them in copper, barley, wheat, and other fruits of the earth.

In the days of Entemena, a slave woman was handed over for 10 shekels of silver and 120 qa of barley ; another with her son for 20 shekels of silver, a gur of barley, and a jar of wine, while a male slave fetched 43 shekels. An ass was valued at 20 shekels and a pig at 4 or 5. A sar of land with buildings might be worth 15 or $22\frac{1}{2}$ shekels, according to its situation and the condition of the building. A gan of agricultural land fetched 2 gur of barley ; the appurtenances for its exploitation were paid for separately by a supplementary sum. The deed was executed in the presence of witnesses, members of the vendor's family and sometimes of the purchaser's, experts, scribes, men of business, and various officials who received presents. Assent was given on oath, and the impression of a seal-cylinder might serve to authenticate the document.

The practice of offering gifts on the occasion of a purchase of land was observed in the time of Manishtusu, king of Agade ; it was to remain in force after the fall of Babylon and, under the Achæmenids, the purchaser would add to the principal sum a garment " for the lady of the house." Man-

[1] CIV, Nos. 9–15.   [2] XIII, 38, p. 818.

ishtusu had the conditions of sale of various large estates ceded to him engraved on a diorite obelisk, together with the names of their former owners, the price paid, the charges on them, and their boundaries. A gan of land in the district of Agade was then valued in barley at 3½ gur, not including the necessary buildings, and a gur of barley was worth in turn a shekel of silver. An ass cost 20 shekels, often more than a male or female slave; for a married slave was exchanged for a shekel of silver and a sheep. A mina of wool cost a quarter of a shekel, oil a shekel the 10 qa pot. Silver was worth two hundred and forty times as much as copper.

In the days of the kings of Ur if a dispute arose about a sale, the judges tendered the purchaser the oath if he could not produce his tablet, and confirmed the deed. This was done in the reign of Gimil-Sin in the case of a plantation of twelve big date palms ceded before witnesses by a certain Lu-Nanna, who then repudiated the transaction.

Under the Amorite dynasty, before Hammurabi, the price of the object sold was not always indicated; the sale was as a rule made for ready money—the contract simply gave the receipt. Beginning with Hammurabi the price was stated and the supplements customary in earlier epochs seem to have disappeared for a while.

Warad-Sin and Bêli-rîm-ilê together bought an ox with the harness and paid " 8¼ shekels in the weights of Shamash " for it. The harness was to be at the disposal of either, and when they returned they would share out the money.[1]

The purchaser of a slave received a guarantee against inherent vices. Before the promulgation of Hammurabi's law the parties mutually agreed upon the period for which the guarantee held good and sometimes specifically extended it in perpetuity. Article 278 of the Code limited it to a month. The vendor was likewise responsible for the recapture of a slave who fled his new master's house, provided he was advised within three days. He further gave a guarantee against seizure—he had to meet any claim made in respect of that slave.

The deed of transfer of a house indicated its area, the adjoining properties, the vendor's name and that of the buyer, the price paid, the clause of irrevocability, the oath by the

[1] LIV, p. 196.

gods and the king, the list of witnesses and the date. The sale of a house property situated in the town of Sippar[1] at a street corner resulted in the following deed under Samsu-iluna. " Two sar, 4 gan of house property : next the house of Ili-awilim-rabi, son of Shamash-natsir, and next the street ; one end abutting on the street, the other on the house of Sin-idinnam ; from the hands of Ili-awilim-rabi, son of Shamash-natsir, Shamash-bani, son of Kishti-Ningizida hath bought. The full price, ⅔ mina and 9 shekels of silver hath he paid. The transaction is completed ; his heart is satisfied. Never shall the one make any claim against the other. In the names of Shamash, Aia, Marduk, and king Samsu-iluna have they sworn.—2 sar 4 gin ceded in possession." Then follow the names of twelve witnesses and the date.

The seller sometimes indicated in the deed the previous history of the property. He had to hand over the title-deeds or declare that they had been lost; in the latter case a pledge was given to transfer them to the purchaser if they were re-discovered. If the fixed property had undergone any change, attention was called thereto so as to avoid any error in inter-pretation.

At Dilbat deeds prior to the promulgation of Hammurabi's legislation contain references to a ceremony consecrating the irrevocability of the contract, as in France the extinction of the third light without a higher bid indicates the conclusion of the auction. This was the " passage of the *bukanu*." An ancient Sumerian usage, apparently going back to a period prior to written contracts, was to conclude the transaction by fixing a nail in the wall and under the Entemena, ishakku of Lagash, the wish was expressed that the claimant, if malice were found in his mouth, might have his teeth broken with a wedge.[2] The oath was taken in the name of the local god and the reigning king. Often the obligation rested upon the former owner to satisfy any claim that might be raised. Six contracts from this period indicate the area of the house, and at the same time the price of the transfer. Two structures of 2·081 and 47·04 square metres (2½ and 56¼ square yards) in area were valued at 3½ and 25 shekels respectively, 2 shekels the sar in the first case and 18¾ in the second. Yet they were situated not only in the same town, but also in the

---

[1] XCIX. [2] CV, No. 61.

F

same quarter. The first, it is true, was hemmed in among a group of other dwellings while the second opened directly on the chief market-place and possessed " a door and bar." The other four buildings were regarded as " houses with wells," the expression E-BUR-PAL designated them. The smallest occupied an area of 1·76 square metres ($2\frac{1}{10}$ square yards); this lot was valued at the highest price—$23\frac{1}{3}$ shekels the sar—but it adjoined the actual abode of the buyer, and that fact gave it an increased value. The others vary in size from 13·5 to 80·84 square metres ($16\frac{3}{4}$ to 37 square yards); they cost 0 shekels 814, 2 shekels 629, and 11 shekels 6, the sar. One of the deeds mentions the origin of the property ; the vendor brought with him as witness the very man from whom he had previously acquired it.

In the twentieth year of Ashurbanipal the sale of a house took place at Uruk, a house well built, with door-sashes, door, and bolt, fenced in and not opening directly on the street. The area is not stated : still, it was sold to a neighbouring householder for 1 mina 15 shekels of silver. It was " sold, received, paid for," no claim would be made ; the transaction would not be repudiated, neither party would sue the other. Precautions were taken against anyone—brother, children, parents—who might either raise a dispute himself or promote litigation. Executed before five witnesses, and sealed only by the vendor who marked the clay with his finger nail, this deed was drawn up according to the Assyrian formula.[1]

The most interesting contracts of sale from the Neo-Babylonian epoch are those concerning slaves. The servant is surrendered with a guarantee against flight, claim, the *arad-sharrutu*, and the *mâr-banutu*. When possible, the seller guards himself against actions by calling as witnesses the former owner and his heirs.

The *arad-sharrutu* was the king's service ; we do not know very accurately to whom it applied and what privileges it conferred.

The *mâr-banutu* was the status of a person descended from

[1] **XL**, p. 170.

a freeman or once enfranchised. The slave Barikiel,[1] bought
by the business man Itti-Marduk-Balatu in the seventh year
of Nabonidus, laid claim to this privilege. The case was
taken before the court. Unluckily for the petitioner he
had been sold in the thirty-fifth year of Nebuchadrezzar
for 28 shekels to Ahnuri ; four years later he belonged to
the woman Gaga ; then he had been given as a pledge for
a loan of 20 shekels, was included in the dowry of Nubta,
Gaga's daughter, and by an exchange passed into the hands
of Nubta's husband and son who once more put him on the
market. The tablets dealing with these various situations
were collected and read out. The judges invited the plaintiff
to expound his arguments. Obliged to admit the authenticity
of the documents arrayed against him, he confessed that he
had no right to claim the *mâr-banutu.*

As soon as the purchase money was paid the slave became
the property of his new master, and the risks of death or
gains by birth were taken to the latter. That was specified
in a deed of the seventh year of Cambyses. Itti-Marduk-
Balatu had resold to Habatsiru a slave woman and her two
children whom he had bought of him the previous year, but
for some reason or the other he had not surrendered them.
" The day that Habatsiru shall send his representatives to
Itti-Marduk-Balatu, the latter will give the slaves to the
representatives of Habatsiru at Babylon. The slaves who
die or are born among them belong to Habatsiru."[2]

5. EXCHANGE

Exchange is a convention, the origin of which is older than
sale and by which a person binds himself to transfer the ownership of an object to someone else on condition of receiving
another object. In Assyria, sale and exchange were contracts
subject to the same formula. In Babylonia, exchange was
treated separately. Under Cambyses, that same slave woman
and her two children, repurchased in the seventh year by their
former master, Habatsiru, had some time before been exchanged by Itti-Marduk-Balatu for a house. In the eighth
year of Cyrus, again, a man exchanged a slave he had just
bought for his wife's dowry.

[1] **CLXI,** Nbn. 42.   [2] **CXLIX,** vol. II, p. 40.

Very often the value of the objects exchanged was unequal, and the contractant favoured thereby had to pay an offset. We find an example at Dilbat[1] in the reign of Sin-muballit, with a penal clause against either party who should repudiate the transaction. "One third of a sar 2/60 of house BUR.PAL, next Nawiraïa's house and next Ana-ili's house, one end abutting on Nahil's house, the other on the great market— Marduk-muballit's house. A sar of house BUR-PAL, Adad-ilu's house next Lama ——'s house and next Adad-ilu's house: one end abutting on Warad-Urash' house the other on Eli——'s house—Adad-ilu's house. Adad-ilu and Marduk-muballit have exchanged house for house. Adad-ilu to Marduk-muballit has given 1⅓ shekels, 12 grains of silver as offset. Whoever dispute it, house for house shall give."

6. HIRE

Hire is a transaction whereby one person gives another the use of an object for a limited time in return for the payment of an agreed sum. Hammurabi's law provided for the hire of boats, beasts, granaries, houses, wagons, land, services, etc.

A plough ox was valued at 4 gur of barley per annum, a draft ox at only 3 gur: that was the price paid at Dilbat[2] before the promulgation of the Code, by one Huzalum, for an ox belonging to the domain of Shamash and his consort, Aïa. "An ox, an ox of Shamash and Aïa, Huzalum, son of Nahilum, for a year has hired : its rent for a year (is) 3 gur of barley; on the day of the harvest shall he measure it."

For treading the corn a day's hire of an ox was reckoned at 20 qa—a very high rate corresponding to 24 gur a year if we lose sight of the impossibility of imposing such work on the same animal for a whole year and the urgency of finishing the work quickly so as to put the crop under shelter. An ass was hired for 10 qa under the same circumstances, or without wagon, for half that sum. The hirer was responsible for accidents save those beyond his control. If by inadequate attention or by blows he injured the animal or rendered it unfit for work, he had to restore head for head ; injury to one eye halved the value of an ox or an ass, the breaking of a horn, amputation of the tail, injury to the head, involved the payment of only a quarter of its price.

The law distinguished three sorts of boat—the ferry boat, hired for 3 grains of silver per day ; the fast boat for 2½ grains, and the vessel of 60 gur burden for $\frac{1}{10}$ shekel. The boatman hired out his services by the year for an average wage of 6 gur of barley. A wagon with oxen team and driver was let for 180 qa of barley daily, the wagon alone for 40 qa.

The agricultural labourer, like the shepherd and cattle-herd was hired for an annual wage of 8 gur of barley ; the ox drover was paid at the rate of 6 gur : the day labourer earned 5 or 6 grains daily according to the season. The law provided also for the wages of manual workers : the carpenter's wage, 4 grains a day, is the only one that is certain. The hire of slaves was in vogue already among the ancient Sumerians. A man who had taken someone else's slave into his service became, by analogy with the case of beasts, responsible for the servant's flight, death, temporary or permanent incapacity, or even sickness ; the rate of hire was in principle fixed at 10 qa of barley a day.

Cultivable land was leased for a specific period, usually for three years, sometimes for only one. An example from Dilbat :[1] " 30 gan 70 sar of field situated in the parish of —— next Sin-ilu's field and Lite ——'s field ; 10 gan of the field Bâb-Adad, next Ibiq-Ishtar's field and Etil-pî ——'s field ; in all 13 gan 70 sar from the hands of Eli-erisha, daughter of Nahilum, Huzalum, son of Nahilum, this land to plant with sesame and barley, for a year has leased." Payment was made in kind at harvest time. Under Nebuchadrezzar II a plantation of date-palms was let for eleven years.[2] For four years the whole revenue of the land and trees went to the tenant ; for the next three years the owner received one-third, for the eighth to the eleventh only a quarter.[3] A barn was leased by the year ; an example comes from Dilbat. More commonly the harvest was garnered in a storehouse, and the fee was paid in proportion to the quantity. Hammurabi's law fixed the tariff at 5 qa per gur, or 1·66 per cent.

It contained also dispositions relative to the letting of houses ; only one of the articles survives. The tenant seems to have been obliged to pay in advance for the term. He

---

[1] **LIX**, No. 39.   [2] **CLX**, Nbk. 90.   [3] **LIX**, No. 28.

might be turned out before the end of his lease, receiving in return compensation. This right of revocation disappeared in the Neo-Babylonian epoch, but the advance payment was retained. In the first year of Cambyses a house was let for 5 shekels a year, payable in two equal amounts at the beginning of the year and in the seventh month. Tenants' repairs were specified and 10 minæ damages were to be paid by the contractant who should break the agreement.

7. LOAN

In every organized society it happens that one of the members finds himself under the necessity of turning to others and borrowing for a longer or shorter term, in money or in kind, what he needs in order to profit by his own industry or to meet his own needs. From the most remote antiquity down to the Persian Empire, Babylonian legislation on this subject had been extraordinarily stable. Besides the loan without interest with or without a penal clause especially for consumable commodities, it recognized loans at interest and fixed a maximum rate which remained practically unchanged for two thousand years. Interest was called *sibtu*, " growth, increase of capital," there was, therefore, opportunity for interest wherever the capital sum lent was subject to an increase, save, of course, in the case of *force majeure* duly proven.

The law of Hammurabi[1] consecrated a custom already established under the kings of Ur, and distinguished only two substances for lending—barley and silver. Taking " barley " in an extremely wide sense to designate any sort of grain and even any sort of crop (dates, for instance) which were all alike to the legislator, the rates of interest did not vary; a contract of the third year of Hammurabi relating to a loan of barley and dates is proof of this.

Barley was the most important medium of exchange in this eminently agricultural region where, with the most primitive methods of cultivation, a thirty to fortyfold return was obtained. It was also the staple diet of men and animals to such a degree that not only the wages of labourers, but the hire of plough animals and even the salaries of certain officials

---

[1] **XXXV**, vol. V, and **I**, vol. XIII.

were payable in barley. At the epoch of Ur the customary rate for a loan of barley was 33⅓ per cent per annum, i.e. a third of the principal. That rate was retained in Hammurabi's legislation. Later it was lowered, and in the Neo-Babylonian epoch, when loans in silver were becoming more common, it fell to the same rate as the latter. This at all epochs was fixed at 20 per cent per annum, or a fifth of the principal.

Still, there were cases, certainly very rare, in which a higher rate might be demanded. There is an example from the epoch of Ur and another in the Babylonian period in which the rate of interest on a sum of silver reached 25 per cent. Much more often the capitalist contented himself with a smaller return, and in that followed the example of the State which sometimes granted loans of money at 12 per cent, or of the temple administrators who demanded even less : the god Shamash of Sippar used to lend barley at 20 per cent, and money, a few years later, at one-sixteenth of the principal, or at least a third of the legal interest.

To secure the borrower against usurers, Hammurabi required the contract for a loan at interest to be drawn up in the presence of the official who from the Ur period had been charged with cognizance of deliveries of money, cereals, animals and commodities of all descriptions. Thereafter every contract written and sealed on a day when the control had not been working, would be null and void and the lender would lose all right to reclaim his property.

Before the institution of this legal injunction, the contracting parties often used to recognize that the payment had been made by a " just and upright man " ; before and after it they stipulated again and again that the weight and measure should be determined in accordance with the weights and standards kept in the king's palace or in the temples of the gods.

Despite the presence of an official, the contract might be so worded that the law was evaded and the rate of interest raised above the legal maximum. In that case the agreement would be voided. So soon as the overcharging was noticed, the creditor lost his title to the debt, but kept the interest he had received already ; the debtor on his side was out of the reach of any action for recovery.

Hammurabi's law made provision against the dishonest creditor who had had interest paid him, but disputed the payment with a view to doubling his profits. Unfortunately the sanction has not come down to us. He must in any case have had to execute a fresh tablet specifying the original debt and what remained to pay. When the dishonest creditor could not escape this obligation, he contrived to turn it to his own usurious ends ; he deducted the interest received quite properly, but took care on the new title-deed to add the balance of the interest to the principal and so made the borrower pay interest on the interest, in other words, he would draw a higher interest than the legal rate. In that case the penalty was the repayment of twice the sum wrongly received. If that was not a heavy penalty, the reason probably was that the legislator imputed carelessness to the borrower ; for it was his duty to verify the figures inscribed on the tablet and to resist the fraudulent manœuvres of which he was to be the victim.

The use of false weights and measures either in the delivery of the loan or on payment of the debt exposed the creditor to the voidance of his claim.

The debtor, thus protected against any dishonest practice on the part of the lender, obtained from the law certain facilities for the settlement of the account when it became impossible for him to make restitution in kind. Had he borrowed money and possessed none while he was the owner of some barley, the creditor would have to accept the barley, but he might exact interest at $33\frac{1}{3}$ per cent, the legal rate for barley, instead of at 20 per cent, the maximum for silver. If the debtor had neither silver nor barley, he might offer any other goods in his possession to escape debt slavery, and the lender was obliged to accept them if the proposition was made before witnesses. In the absence of any other mode of quittance there was room for a new contract. The two parties would discuss its terms ; it is no longer a loan at interest.

8. PLEDGES

The legislator did not mean to devote his care to the borrower only ; justice obliged him to secure to the lender the return of his capital and interest. He therefore allowed him to exact pledges or a surety.

The law of Hammurabi regulated the mortgaging of fields. Whoever received as a pledge possession of an unsown field to cultivate it, was entitled at harvest time to take the equivalent of the loan plus interest and the expenses of cultivation. Had he received a field under seed, he had no direct claim upon the crop ; the owner of the land was allowed to sell it before reimbursing his creditor. Other combinations might also be imagined. Under Samsu-iluna a priestess lent one of her colleagues the money for the purchase of a field, receiving in exchange an annual income and presents at certain festivals. The security was the field itself ; it would become the property of the lender to counterbalance the sum advanced if the obligations were not fulfilled.

The deposit of a pledge seems to have been very widespread in the Neo-Babylonian epoch. The creditor was sometimes paid the interest and even the capital by the use of the pledge assigned him. It was partly so in the case of Ina-tsilli-Bâbi-rabi, the baker, whom his father compelled to serve the lady Ahata to pay off a loan of 42 shekels of silver ; [1] he remained in servitude for ten years and his daily services were valued at 6 qa of barley towards the amortization of the debt. The law had been modified ; in the days of the First Dynasty the physical bondage could only have lasted three years ; now its duration was unlimited, unless redemption was possible.

Any property, real or personal, might be pledged—wife, children, slaves, fields, houses, credits, household utensils, etc. In the twenty-first year of Nebuchadrezzar II, Babia and Sha-Nanâ-shi his wife, having borrowed a mina of silver from Nabu-ban-ahi gave him as security " the door of the porter's lodge of the Salimu Gate." As in the days of the First Dynasty, wood was rare and a door was an object of value. However, they added to it " all their possessions in town and in the country " by a provision less usual than the pledging of a specific commodity on which no other creditor should have a claim before the final extinction of the debt.[2] Nabu-balatsu-iqbi acted in that way when he borrowed half a mina of silver from Gimillu at 20 per cent in the sixteenth year of Nabonidus ; he hypothecated his

[1] I, vol. XII, cf. p. 80 above.
[2] CLXI, Nbk. 129.

house and provided : " No other creditor shall have a claim
thereon until complete payment."

When a man contracted several successive loans from
the same money-lender, the latter took care to mention
on the new tablets the existence of the previous advances to
prevent confusion between them. Iddin-Marduk lent Nabu-
ah-iddin half a mina on the 9th of Siwan in the eighth year
of Nabonidus—" the note," he wrote, " of further money
to be received from Nabu-ah-iddin." Next year on the 24th
of Nisan he remitted him $\frac{4}{6}$ mina, $4\frac{2}{3}$ shekels of silver, and
specified that there were further earlier notes of hand without
forgetting the interest. On the 9th of Kislew in the same
year an advance of 45 gur of barley at 20 per cent was
granted. This time the creditor merely noted—" To that
are added the earlier receipts." [1]

Three contracts dated in the ninth year of Nabonidus show
how a security, which the creditor himself had used to
guarantee another loan, was in practice redeemed. Nabu-
tultabshî-lîshir had borrowed 35 shekels of silver from the
lady Bunanutum, and had given her as security a female
slave. Bunanutum and her husband, being in want of their
money, had asked Ina-Esagil-bêlit for 30 shekels and handed
the slave over to him. Nabu-tultabshî-lîshir sold three
servants, including the pledged slave-woman, to Iddin-
Marduk for 2 mina 50 shekels. On the 11th of Adar, Iddin-
Marduk directed his banker to pay Bunanutum 35 shekels,
who thereupon released the slave by repaying Ina-Esagil-
bêlit. On the 15th of Adar, Nabu-tultabshî-lîshir received
the balance of the purchase money, but gave a receipt for
the whole sum as his agent restored to him the tablet for
the loan granted by the lady Bunanutum.[2]

The security was not always handed over to the lender :
very often he would have no effective claim thereto till the
day when, failing to obtain repayment, he would secure the
permission of the tribunal to take possession of it. That
was the position of the door belonging to Babia. But if
the pledge was handed over, there was still room for an
agreement as to the profits the lender might draw therefrom
and the conditions of its use.

[1] CLXI, Nbk. 294, 325, 369.
[2] CLXI, Nbn. 390, 391, 395.

Sometimes it would serve to pay off the principal and interest : at the end of Ina-tsil-bâbi-rabi's service the whole interest was reckoned up and there was no annual amortization. Shâpik-zêr borrowed from Shulâ and pledged his house ; Shulâ came to live there. There was to be neither payment of rent by Shulâ nor payment of interest by Shâpik-zêr ; the rent was considered equivalent to the interest on the borrowed money. In the third year of Cyrus, Bêl-uballit put 1 mina 13 shekels of silver at the disposal of Nabu-zêr-iqishâ ; a slave was given him for the term of the loan to balance the interest. In the nineteenth year of Darius a field was pledged from which the creditor would get his interest while the debtor remained liable to make up the shortage in case of an insufficient crop.

Several debtors might pledge their joint credit. In the tenth year of Darius a married couple guaranteed a loan together and hypothecated all their property.

The pledge was transferable to a third person. The lady Bunanutum gave the female slave she had received from Nabu-tultabshî-lîshir to Ina-Esagil-bêlit. The tablet explains the real position of this slave, " Shalamdinni, slave of Nabu-tultabshî-lîshir, security of Bunanutum." Shulâ, contracting a loan with Nergal-uballit, gave him as security the house which he himself held from Shâpik-zêr and added the whole of his town and country property as well as a slave.

9. SURETIES

Often the pledge related to the interest on the loan and the principal was guaranteed by a surety.[1] Bêl-uballit was not content with the slave of Nabu-zêr-iqishâ : he required the guarantee of Mushallim-Marduk, and the latter pledged all his belongings for the repayment of the principal. At Dilbat in the twenty-sixth year of Darius another Mushallim-Marduk had borrowed the substantial sum of 10 minæ from the temple of Anu for a month. Suqai and Nabu-ballitsu became his sureties. If on the appointed day they brought Mushallim-Marduk and made him repay his debt, they would be released ; otherwise they themselves would be liable to make the payment on the stipulated terms.

[1] LX.

The guarantee might be conditional and take effect only in special circumstances, for instance, in case " of the feet of the debtor out of the hands of the creditor." By this legal phrase was understood the disappearance of the debtor, leaving the creditor powerless to seize his person. In the third year of Cyrus the woman Diditum went surety " for the feet of Nabu-zêr-lîshir out of the hands of Gimil-Shamash " : if he went away, she would pay the 35 gur of dates which formed the balance of his debt.

In the days of the First Dynasty it was the custom to provide a surety when an employee, having been engaged, did not have to take up his duties till a later date There is an example from Sippar under Samsu-iluna—" Sippar-lipîr of his own accord and at his own request, Imgur-Shamash in employment has engaged. His salary for a month, one shekel of silver, he has received. He will come and will not go away. Bond of the king (otherwise) he will pay this sum. His hand (his surety) is Idin-Dagan, son of Shamash-rabi."[1] If as a result Idin-Dagan was obliged to liberate Sippar-lipîr for not keeping his engagement, it would be said that he " withdrew his hand."[2] That expression alludes to the creditor's hand which would have seized that of the debtor to enslave him, and for which had been substituted that of surety who, in a symbolic ceremony, had struck the debtor on his hinder parts to put him under his protection.

The debtor who was unable to repay a loan might on his failure be reduced to slavery ; more often an agreement was made for the payment of an indemnity If he was at the mercy of several creditors and one of them had reduced him to slavery, the others were entitled to appeal to the courts ; if the parties belonged to different cities they must file their pleas with the court of Babylon. The insolvent debtor had, moreover, the right of substituting for himself his wife or children (Code 117) for a maximum period of three years, or a male or female slave (Code 118, 119), subject to the reservation that a female slave by whom he had had children might be redeemed. He was also allowed with the consent of his creditors to transfer his debts to his son, and once the deed was inscribed and accepted, they were no longer entitled to demand its revision.

[1] XCIX, No. 276.   [2] I, vol. XIV.

10. DEPOSIT

Deposit, the act whereby one person entrusted a movable object to another to take charge of it gratuitously and return it on the first demand, was regulated by Hammurabi's law as was loan. The deposit of crops was distinguished from that of any sort of object. For the warehousing of crops the legislator provided for the hire of the granary or magazine and fixed the rate at 5 qa per gur (1⅔ per cent), but the owner of the building was responsible for loss. In the case of anything else the law required the deposit to be accompanied by a tablet, executed at the time in the presence of witnesses, in which the depositor enumerated the obligations of the depositary. Third persons had no power without the authorization of the depositor to take possession of crops or other commodities placed on the deposit to reimburse themselves for any claim they had over him ; by so doing they would lose all title to their capital, and they would have to restore whatever they had appropriated. The depositary was responsible for the disappearance of an object placed on deposit, but an agreement might be made that he should use it and only return an equivalent amount either in the place of deposition or in any other appointed spot.

11. THE TEMPLE; TEMPORAL ADMINISTRATION

In Babylonia the temple was not only a place of worship and prayer, it was also an important organ of temporal administration. To feed the staff engaged in the service of the god, to maintain in repair buildings which fell into ruins in a generation or were devastated by enemies, enormous resources were needed. The god possessed lands where grain was harvested, where flocks and herds were pastured. In the towns he owned granaries and storehouses where likewise the offerings of princes and of the faithful, his share of the spoils after a victory, were heaped up, and buildings of all kinds. At Tello a granary of the Eninnu built by the old king, Ur-Ninâ, has been discovered, and from the epoch of Lugalanda a system of carefully kept accounts bears witness to an advanced hierarchical organization. They include lists of monthly payments to the servants of

Bau with a note of the stores from which the requisite barley had been taken, a register of the people of the goddess's estate—145 men and 31 women with a note of the portion accruing to each, names of the intermediaries, if the occasion arose, the anticipated payments, a roll of fishers to the number of forty-four, a list of wagons for the goddess' goods, the food of the beasts.[1] At the period of Ur, the temple of Enlil owned a great park, half an hour out of Nippur, whither the dues from towns and ishakkê flowed.[2] Later on, for instance, at Sippar, the temple treasury granted loans in money and cereals. Sometimes, when they were made to the poor or sick, these advances were free of interest, subject to the obligation of requiting the god when recovery or a return of fortune permitted the repayment of the debt.[3] The persons relieved vowed to make an offering on the day of their cure of the diseases from which they suffered. When the loan was given at interest, the temple seldom demanded the current rate ; most commonly it would be content with an income half or a third as large. Each temple seems to have been a seat of justice. It was at the gate that the priests heard the witnesses and pronounced sentence. When the civil or religious court could not secure written proof—if, for instance, a title-deed had been lost—the oath was tendered to one of the parties, usually the defendant, and this oath had as a rule to be sworn in the temple.

Many offices were hereditary, but they might be sold or leased. In Hammurabi's day the heir might find included in his inheritance certain temple revenues for eight or fifteen days each year or a priesthood for a limited period. A pashihu, whose function was to anoint with oil the divine images and the cult objects, sold his office and a field for 10 shekels of silver.

It was from these temples, in which princes were proud to fulfil sacred functions, that the high officials of the State were recruited. It was in the shadow of the temples that the schools which trained scribes were gathered, it is definitely to the clergy that writing and that collection of texts of all sorts which allow Babylonian civilization to be reconstituted were due.

[1] LXXVIII. [2] LXXIX; LXXXIII.
[3] XCIX, No. 76 ; I, vol. XIII, p. 202.

BOOK THREE

BELIEFS AND CRAFTS

CHAPTER I

RELIGION

1. THE GODS

IT is still hard to determine which elements in Sumero-Akkadian religion were originally due to the Semitic section of the population, and which belonged to the Sumerians. The principal dogmas were established and the ritual elaborated in its main lines by the beginning of history. In cult the Sumerian language was used, even after the disappearance of the race, and the same great gods had their sanctuaries in both regions, but according to tradition those of Sumer were the older, and the first of all to be raised was the Esagil at Eridu on the shores of the Persian Gulf.

The fundamental idea of any religion is the conception of one or more superior beings to whom humanity owes certain duties. The Sumero-Akkadians admitted the existence of a great number of deities who were all celestial beings, and the ideogram by which the idea of god was represented was the star, the proper meaning of which was " heaven," while the various stars were indicated by the same sign repeated three times. The supreme god, Anu, was denoted by one star alone—he was the god of the sky and the other gods formed the army of the sky, the host of the stars.

The Sumero-Akkadians had attributed to their deities the virtues and passions of humanity, had endowed them with the same mode of life, but raised them above mankind, by conferring immortality upon them and acknowledging them as good and merciful in all circumstances even when they were chastising humanity guilty and erring. There was no evil god—evil was caused in the world by perverse spirits, superior perhaps to men, but below the gods. No religious worship was paid to these genii ; people tried to combat them and to render them innocuous by magic practices.

Sumerians and Akkadians could not conceive of eternal being with no beginning. For them, at the origin of the universe nothing existed. In this nothing two humid principles were differentiated—one male, Apsu, the fresh-water ocean which surrounded the world, the other female,

FIG. 12.   Sumerian Deity (Niffer, University of
Pennsylvania Museum).

Tiamat, the sea. They gave birth to all beings. The *Poem of the Creation* opens thus :

> When the heaven above was not named,
> And the sea beneath had no name,
> Of Apsu primordial, their father,
> And of tumultuous Tiamat, the all-mother,
> The waters mingled in one.
> The rush-beds were not fixed ; the reed breaks were unseen.
> When no god had been named, when no fate was appointed,
> The gods they were created.[1]

The *Chaldæan Cosmogony*, inserted in an incantation, admits the same humid elements in the origin of things.

From the primordial pair sprang at first Lahmu and his consort, Lahamu, deities whose rôle was almost entirely obliterated. Then an indeterminate period elapsed and from the original pair Anshar and Kishar sprang : in their two

[1] **LVI**, pp. 3–5.

selves they represent the totality of heaven and earth. They gave birth to three other gods, the supreme triad of the Babylonian pantheon—Anu, Enlil, and Ea.

2. THE FIRST TRIAD

These three deities divided the universe between them ; for according to Semitic ideas no good could exist without having an owner. Anu, the supreme god, reigned in the heaven ; Enlil was lord of the atmosphere and the earth, Ea, called Enki in Sumerian, ruled the waters of the primordial ocean. Each of them had his own special path on the ecliptic and their dwellings were on the summit of the skies.[1]

Anu was regarded as the supreme god in the earliest historical times. In Akkad Dêr was his town; in Sumer he was honoured at Uruk in the E·Ana " abode of Anu " or " house of heaven," where the cult of his daughter, Ishtar, goddess of pleasure, supplanted his even before the time of the most archaic monuments. At Lagash, in the quarter of Girsu, the same substitution took place : there also was an E·Ana where, from the reign of Eanatum, the daughter of Anu was worshipped under the name of Ninni. Lugalzaggisi, king of Uruk, besought Enlil to present his prayer to Anu, and Gudea names him at the beginning of the imprecations formulated against whomsoever should violate his work. He was the first god to glorify the E-ninnu and " the king of the gods," a title which Ur-Engur likewise gives him. Hammurabi calls him " the supreme god " in the prologue to his laws. He inhabits the summit of the vault of heaven, " the heaven of Anu." His gate is guarded by two deities, Tammuz and Gizida, and before him " the sceptre, the diadem, the crown, and the commander's baton " were placed before the institution of terrestrial sovereignty. When the gods were in fear of the Deluge, they fled, climbed up into the heaven of Anu, crouched like a dog on the battlements, lay down and stayed there till they scented the sweet odour of the sacrifice.[2]

Although the highest of the gods, regarded as their father and the prototype of creation, Anu could not retain the supreme authority when Babylon had concentrated the power

[1] **CLVIII**, vol. I, p. 259 ; **LVI**, p. 179.
[2] **LVI**, pp. 111, 115, 155, 167.

in her hands and had subdued Sumer and Akkad to the
sceptre of her kings.

Theological speculation had to adapt the old myth to the
new political situation, and since nothing existed in this
world save by the order of the gods and the destinies which
they had decreed, the exaltation of the god of Babylon above
all other gods was the necessary counterpart to her elevation
above other towns. The word of Marduk became " like to
that of Anu," and the deposition of the latter was referred
to the beginning of time. Commanded by the old Anshar to
fight against the rebel Tiamat, Anu lacked the courage to
face her and turned back. Marduk, on the other hand,
became the champion and avenger of his brethen. At a
solemn banquet where they gave themselves over to drunken-
ness, they decreed to him a peerless destiny and proclaimed
him their king.

Enlil, lord of the earth, sometimes usurped the titles of
Anu and was called " father of the gods." It is so in an
inscription of Entemena and in the poem of Ea and Atarhasis.
His emblems, moreover, like Anu's, on Kassite *kudurrus* are
the throne and the tiara. He is above all the councillor of the
gods, and it was he who was the author of the Flood. So
when the angry Ishtar wished to prevent him sharing in the
sacrifice of Uta-napishtim, the Babylonian Noah, "let the
gods come to the sacrifice," cried she, " but let not Enlil
come ; for he hath not reflected, but hath made the Flood ;
as for my people he hath sent them to destruction." Ea
reproached him with the same deed, " O Thou, the wise one
of the gods, the hero ! Why, why hast thou not reflected
and hast caused the Flood ? " However, he fixed the fate
of Uta-napishtim and caused him to dwell " at the mouth of
the rivers." He was, in fact, the master of mortals and
entrusted them to princes to guide them into the ways of
justice. He is the god of Nippur, the sovereign of Sumer.[1]

The Semitic name of Ea, the third god in the supreme triad,
means " house of water," and his Sumerian name Enki,
" lord of the earth." His domain was the Apsu, " the abode
of knowledge," the waters which uphold and encircle the
earth. He was symbolized by an amphibious being, the goat-
fish. God of wisdom, he had created man by modelling a

[1] **CV**, pp. 62, 38, 286, 280, 212 ; **LVI**, pp. 133, 135, 103, 107.

lump of clay and animating it with his divine breath. It was he who at the time of the Flood had saved humanity from total destruction. He had revealed various industries to men, he gave understanding to princes, and aided priests in their sacred functions, especially in the magic rites for which was used holy water drawn from the basin of "Apsu" in the temple at Eridu.[1]

3. SECOND TRIAD

A second triad was formed of Sin, the moon-god, and his two children, Shamash, the sun-god, and Ishtar, the planet Venus.

Sin measured time, and it was for him to bring to an end in tears and sighs the days, months, and years of guilty kings. His symbol was the crescent moon. At Ur he was worshipped under the name of Nanna, and from his temple in Harran his cult was diffused throughout the Aramæan countries.

Shamash was above all the supreme judge whose children were Kittu and Mesharu, justice and right. He trampled iniquity under his feet and personally dictated equitable laws to Ur-Engur and Hammurabi. His symbol was a disc adorned with a star of four points separated by bundles of wavy rays. On engraved monuments—the cylinders of the epoch of Agade, the Code of Hammurabi, Nabu-alpa-iddin (ninth century)—he is characterized by flames sprouting from his shoulders.[2]

Ishtar, "the kindly," male as deity of the morn, female as goddess of the evening, was sometimes the daughter of Anu, sometimes the daughter of Sin, the goddess of war and the goddess of pleasure. At Uruk her cult supplanted that of her father. Her lovers were innumerable and she tried to seduce mortals. At Hallab she was the daughter of Sin and mistress of battles. At Agade and Sippar, under the name of Anunitum, she seemed to combine both characters, at least in the days of Nabonidus : for he calls her "the lady of combat who carries the quiver and the bow," and at the same time she made the omens at sunrise and sunset propitious for him. Her personality had absorbed the other goddesses ; her name was used in the singular to mean any one of them, and in the plural to denote them all collectively. Daughter of

---

[1] **CV,** pp. 389, 38, 66, 94.   [2] Cf. Fig. 7, p. 52.

Sin, her emblem was a star. Warrior goddess standing erect on one or two lions, she carried the quiver, in one hand she held a curved weapon, in the other a sceptre formed of a mace attached to two curved weapons surmounted with lions' heads.

4. MARDUK

All the forces of nature, all the powers of good had been deified by the Sumero-Akkadians. The number of deities in-

FIG. 13.   The god Marduk
(Babylon, Berlin Museum).

voked by them was substantial. Each town had its own ; every man was protected by a divine couple. Nevertheless, one of them was to excel the rest to such a degree that in the theological speculations of the Neo-Babylonian era the latter were regarded as appearances of him. His exaltation took place when the Amorite dynasty of Babylon finally united in a single realm the lands of Sumer and Akkad. Hammurabi then successfully laboured to place Marduk, the local god, in the first rank. New versions of the antique

legends were composed ; they were adapted to the contemporary situation. Enlil had enjoyed the title of Bêl, " lord,"
and from time immemorial had been the possessor of the
tablets of destiny. To rob him of them an episode from the
Creation of the World was invented : it was Marduk who had
vanquished Tiamat, chaos, and as a reward the gods had
granted him thenceforth the right of determining destinies.
That ceremony took place in future in the Du-azag of Babylon, at the New Year festival. Anu abandoned his powers
to Marduk. Ea, his father, granted him his own name—
" Let him be called Ea like me." Moreover, he possessed all
his wisdom : " My child," Ea had said to him, " what is there
that thou knowest not and what could I teach thee ? What
I know, thou knowest also." That is why he was, like his
father, the god's magician, the god of priesthood, the creator
of humanity. He was represented with large ears symbolizing
a great understanding, and armed with the bent weapon with
which he had overcome Tiamat. The monster he had subjugated was depicted at his feet. A lance was his symbol
on the *kudurrus* of the Kassite period and on Neo-Babylonian
seals.

Annually on New Year's Day the gods of Babylon and
Borsippa came to pay homage to him. A great procession
was marshalled on the Sacred Way. On its solemn march to
his temple, *Akiti*, and on the way back it halted at the Du-
azag. On the eighth and the eleventh days the gods assembled
there, greeted Marduk in awe, and knelt before him while the
fates were irrevocably fixed for the whole year. The suppression of these ceremonies in time of war or public misfortune
was a calamity specially mentioned in the city annals.

5. SOME OTHER DEITIES

Among the remaining deities, Inurta, the firstborn of
Enlil and his champion, was a warrior god, " wise in combat,
whose crushing force the countries of the earth cannot
support." He was identified with the " bêls " (lords) of
certain towns, and then his name was masked by that of the
place : at Lagash, in the quarter of Girsu, he was called
Ningirsu, " the lord of Girsu " ; at Susa, In-Shushinak, " the
Susian." He was assimilated also to other gods, to Zababa of

Kish and Urash of Dilbat. At least twenty different weapons were attributed to him; in his right hand he held the *shar-ur*, a bundle of maces and weapons with convex blades surmounted by a lion's head : on his shoulders often appear the forequarters of a lion and the same symbolic animal is found among the supports of his throne or even under his feet. Astrologists identified him with Betelgeux in Orion, and the constellation of Orion as a whole formed his army. The divine consort of Ningirsu, Bau, eldest daughter of Anu surnamed " the good woman," was mother of seven twin daughters. In the age of Hammurabi the wife of Inurta was called Ninkarrak ; in the time of the Kassites, Gula. Under both these names she was the goddess of medicine who dressed wounds made by the god and cured diseases.

The Egyptians revered the Nile ; the Greeks raised altars to the river-god ; the Sumero-Akkadians before them had also worshipped him and had chosen him in company with Gibil, the fire-god, " to judge the judgment of mankind." " When the great gods had dug him, they placed favours on his banks." They granted him the power of discerning the just and the unjust man. By the law of Hammurabi anyone accused of sorcery would be hurled into the divine river with whom rested the duty of revealing innocence or guilt. On cylinder-seals of the epoch of Agade he presides at the judgment, seated on a throne and holding in one hand a vase whence pour two streams in which fishes are swimming.

A goddess of the waters, Ninâ, daughter of Ea, was also worshipped. Her ideogram was a fish in the middle of a basin. She had a shrine at Lagash ; a suburb of the town was sacred to her. On certain festal days, when she went out with a procession, her sacred barque sailed about on the canal.

Adad, god of the atmosphere, was at once feared and respected. Was it not he who now dispensed beneficent rain and now inspired terror by his thunder-claps ? He was depicted clad in a short garment, standing on a bull armed with the thunder-bolt and brandishing a weapon over his head.

To Nisaba, sister of Ninâ, was attributed the growth of the great reeds, one of the sources of prosperity in the region. They were used for the construction of wicker shelters,

stools, tables, baskets, and as fuel. The stem suitably cut
served as a stylus for writing on the clay tablets, and even
the ashes could be used for the bleaching of linen. Goddess of
writing and the fruitfulness of the earth, Nisaba used to
sit on a pile of boughs ; she liked to let her hair fall in waves
over her shoulders whence sprouted reed-stems, and in her
hand she held an overflowing vase, the symbol of the pros-
perty she dispensed.

Several mythical heroes had been deified by the Sumero-
Akkadians. Some figure in the royal lists of prehistoric
times such as Dumuzi, the Tammuz of the Syrian peoples,
inscribed in the fourth place among the princes of the first
dynasty of Uruk. Son of Ningizida, grandson of Ninazu,
"the lord of divination by water," he became the consort of
Ereshkigal, the goddess of the underworld, after the love of
Ishtar, goddess of Uruk, had caused his destruction. The god
of graminaceous plants in general he was reborn every year
in the spring : "Tiny he lies in the vessel that sinks ; big
he lies in the harvest and rest there."

The prototype of the Greek Adonis, in the month of summer
sacred to him when the harvester had laid aside his sickle
and gathered the ears into sheaves, he died and descended
into the underworld. Then the women repeated the annual
lamentation decreed by Ishtar :

> "How long shall the seed be held captive ?
> How long shall his verdure lie in chains ?"

And the goddess set out for the country "from whose bourne
no traveller returns," to seek her lover and bring him back
to earth.

6. THE DEIFIED PRINCES

Numerous princes who have left us authentic documents,
had also enjoyed even in their lifetime the prerogatives of
divinity. The onomasticon of the reign of Manishtusu,
perhaps, gives evidence of this in the name, Sharru-kin-ili,
"Sargon is my god." Under Narâm-Sin proofs are multiplied ;
in inscriptions he is called "god of Agade" and "god of his
land." On the stele of victory he wears on his head the horned
tiara which the Kassite king, Agum-kakrine, was to call
"the diadem of domination, characteristic of divinity."

Later on pious foundations were established at Lagash for
the cult of the ishakku, Gudea. The kings of Ur had their
temple, and every year one month was consecrated to Dungi.
Hymns were composed in praise of them. Incense was
burnt before their statues. Sacrifices were offered to them.
From the days of the kings of Ur, it was not only by the gods,
it was also by the reigning king that people took the oath, an
essentially religious act.

7. THE TEMPLE

The god inhabited the temple with his wife, children, and
servants. The description of the sanctuary of Ningirsu at
Lagash, given by Gudea, unfortunately does not allow us to
attempt a reconstruction. The excavations have only
revealed one corner block and an entrance[1] resting on two
layers of sun-dried bricks separated by a layer of sand. The
corner was orientated to the west ; on the south-west side
the wall was plain, to the north-west it was ornamented with
doubly notched grooves, and about five metres from the
corner was a wide bay flanked on each side by three successive
projections. Not a trace of door-sockets nor any other
indication of a gate to close this entry was noted. Not far
away one of Gudea's predecessors, the ishakku Ur-Bau, had
also built a temple. Only the west corner of the platform
remains. Under it a copper statuette and a foundation-
tablet were discovered enclosed in an earthenware vase with
a base perforated by three holes.[2]

In 1923 the excavations by the Joint Expedition of the
British Museum and the Museum of the University of Pennsylvania brought to light the ruin of the temple of Nannar
at Ur. Originally built of sun-dried brick in the reign of
Ur-Engur, it was rebuilt with kiln-bricks a few centuries later
under Kudur-Mabug. In the centre of the south side rose
the sanctuary composed of an entrance hall and three long
rooms symmetrically arranged, two behind the hall and one on
either side. An outer corridor separated the sanctuary from
other chambers which may have been magazines.

In 1919 at a neighbouring site, Tell el 'Obeid, Dr. Hall
had discovered a structure, the foundation-tablet of which

---

[1] **LIV**, p. 18 and plan k ; cf. **XCVIII**, p. 396 and pl. 50.
[2] **XCVIII**, pp. 241, 400 ; **CV**, pp. 96 ff.

was recovered by the Joint Expedition in 1923. This building was a temple of the goddess Ninhursag, originally built by king A-an-ni-padda in the time of the First Dynasty of Ur. It rested on a platform, supported by a wall of baked plano-convex brick, access to which was given by a stairway. Upon this foundation A-an-ni-padda had erected a temple of sun-dried bricks of which only part of the external decoration, abandoned in its ruins, survives. Enough remains, however, to prove that the door was preceded by a pillared porch, probably flanked by mosaic columns and guarded by two life-sized copper lions. On this face a row of marvellously lifelike copper heifers, and of artificial flowers of clay crusted with mosaic occupied a ledge of the platform. The wall immediately behind them was faced with wooden panels overlaid with copper. Above this wainscoting ran a frieze of copper bulls and, still higher up, one or more rows of ex-quisite shell and limestone inlays depicting scenes of pastoral life in which the cow, the animal emblematic of Ninhursag, figured prominently.[1]

From the Neo-Babylonian epoch four temples survive all from the same town, Babylon,[2] and it has been possible to recover the complete plan of these.

The study of these remains shows that, if any rules sanctified by tradition existed, the architect still enjoyed great freedom in the arrangement of the several parts of each edifice. They were approximately rectangular structures orientated by the corners like those of Ur-Bau and Gudea. But while the ishakkê of Lagash had used baked bricks bonded with bitumen, Nabopolassar and his successors employed only sun-dried bricks. On the outside the walls were divided at equal distances by pilasters adorned with flutings, stepped in the temple of Ninmar, semicircular in the Esagil, elsewhere rectangular as in the Ezida of Borsippa ; such pilasters are not found in any civil monuments. One or more entrances with double gates, encased in bronze, resting on stone sockets and fastened by a bolt fitting a socket in the pavement, gave access to a central court. It, too, like the outer one, was embellished with pilasters becoming more elaborate near the

---

[1] *Antiquaries' Journal*, III, pp. 311 ff., V, pp. 1 ff., and IV, pp. 330 ff. ; cf. *Man*, XXV, 1.

[2] **CLVI**, Figs. 38, 114, 119, 137–139, 142, 143, 244–247.

gates, at the main entrance and in front of the sanctuary. The latter stood at the end of the court to the west in the Esagil, to the south-west in the Emah. The walls of the shrine of Marduk had been overlaid with gold, lapis, and marble by Nebuchadrezzar II.[1] The roof, formed of the finest cedars of Lebanon, was likewise covered with glittering gold. For Ishtar of Agade the walls were merely whitened with chalk ; the niche for the sacred image was covered with a solution of asphalt, with white bands near the edge, as were the main entrances. In the Emah the deity dwelt in a small building, the foundations of which have been preserved. The sanctuary, measuring 12 metres by 5, was preceded by an antechamber ; these two rooms each formed a sacristy. The idol could be seen from the court, but not from the street, because the entrance door and the vestibule were not on the axis of construction. In the temple of Inurta there was no antechamber, but on either side of the sanctuary stood another shrine. Around the court, the dimension of which varied from one monument to another—the Emah had a façade of 30 metres and a depth of 50, the Esagil formed a square of 60 metres either way—were arranged, sometimes grouped round subsidiary courts, rooms the destinations of which we cannot determine. In the Emah, moreover, two narrow corridors, ending in culs-de-sac, have been observed : in the Esagil a small shrine on the north side has been noted.

In the foundations of each temple it was customary to place prophylactic figures. Under the main gate of the Emah a bird, the symbol of the goddess, reposed in a niche ; under the pavement of Inurta's sanctuary the foundation-cylinder in the name of Nabopolassar.

No altar has been discovered inside the temples of Babylon. However, before the entry of the Emah an altar of sun-dried bricks was erected on a brick pavement. Another altar, likewise of sun-dried bricks and standing on a pavement, stood in front of the temple of Inurta. The sacrifices took place outside ; only the priests and the prince might enter the sanctuary into the presence of the god. Thus, on the testimony of Herodotus, " outside the sanctuary (of the Esagil) a golden altar and another very large one for the immolation of cattle are to be seen."[2]

---

[1] **XLIII,** pp. 124, 126.   [2] Herodotus, I, 183.

Beside the chief temples rose a massive structure formed of quadrangular prisms superimposed and getting smaller and smaller the higher up they were. This artificial mountain, called a *ziggurat*, was depicted on a *kudurru* of Merodach-baladan I. That recently excavated at Ur consisted of four stages which diminished in area upwards. In the middle of the top platform was doubtless a small shrine, now ruined. The lower stage, 9·75 metres high, was the work of Ur-Engur; the remaining three, 2·50, 2·30, and 4·00 metres high respectively, were built by Nabonidus. The ascent consisted of three staircases built by Ur-Engur, each composed of a hundred steps. One flight rose up at right angles to the face of the tower in the middle of the great north-east side ; the others began from opposite sides of the same face and met the first at the level of the second stage of the tower. The stages were not symmetrically arranged and their terraces varied in width. The shrine on top is said to have been faced with blue-glazed brick ; the topmost stage of the *ziggurat* had red walls, while the body of the structure was painted black with bitumen. These colours, viewed together with the whitewashed walls of the courtyard, constituted a colour scheme to which the ruins of Dûr-Sharrukin in Assyria offer analogies.[1]

The ziggurat of Babylon,[2] the Etemenanki, lay to the north of the temples described above. It was built of sun-dried bricks faced with baked bricks, forming pilasters found on two adjacent sides, which measured 91 metres in length. It is not so well preserved as those of Ur and Borsippa ; the ruins of the latter, still unexplored, rise more than 40 metres above the plain. At Babylon, only one storey and the three stairs, giving access to the first storey on the south, survive to-day. A tablet in the Louvre, dated in the eighty-third year of the Seleucids (229 B.C.),[3] gives the geometrical description of this monument and its outworks. The whole formed a rectangle 2190 feet long and 1200 feet wide. The main entrance to the east, on the Sacred Way, gave access to two successive terraces which preceded the square court, likewise terraced,

---

[1] *Antiquaries' Journal*, V, pp. 1 ff., and figures.
[2] **CLVI**, Fig. 119.
[3] *Mémoires de l'Academie des Inscriptions*, vol. XXXIX, 1913.

where the tower rose. The latter had a base of 600 feet square ; the next storey, the *kigal*, resting on the western side of the base, was only 300 feet long.[1] It contained several chapels—those on the east side dedicated to Marduk, Nabu, and Tashmetum ; those on the north to Ea and Nusku ; those on the south to Anu and Sin. In it, too, were to be seen the " house of the bed," the " house of the utensils," the " house of the thread," and a court surrounded by a wall pierced by four gates. In the centre of the *kigal* five superimposed stages supported a shrine which formed the crown of the edifice. Herodotus describes the Etemenanki thus as " a regular square, two stades wide in both directions. In the middle is seen a massive tower, a stade long and a stade wide. Above this tower rises another, and then yet another, and so on till eight towers in all may be counted. The ascent is made on the outside by means of a ramp winding round the consecutive stages. Almost in the middle of this ascent is a chamber and seats whereon those sit and rest who have set out to climb to the summit. In the topmost stage is a great sanctuary, and in this sanctuary a great bed richly adorned, beside which stands a golden table. No statue is to be seen there ; no one spends the night there, save a woman of the country selected from among all her companions by the god himself, according to the tale of the Chaldæans, who are priests of this god.[2] "

Nabopolassar, the founder of the Neo-Babylonian Empire, had undertaken the rebuilding of the Etemenanki at the behest of Marduk.[3] Like Gudea before him, he consulted oracles, he performed the purifications required. Like the ancient king Ur-Ninâ, he carried building material on his head while among the workmen ; the Heir Apparent carried clay to be made into bricks ; and his other son, Nabu-shum-lishir, wielded the shovel and the pick. Despite revolutions, the religious rites for the building of monuments for worship seem to have been handed down intact for more than twenty centuries.

Another instance of this spirit of tradition is to be seen in the difficulties which Nabonidus encountered when he wanted to restore the crown which Nabu-apal-idden had

---

[1] **CLV,** 106 metres.   [2] Herodotus, I, 181.
[3] **XLII,** pp. 60–62.

offered to Shamash of Sippar in the ninth century.[1] The
king desired to refashion it all in gold, but the elders averred
that no alteration of it was permissible. Thrice he consulted the oracles of Shamash and Adad, thrice they replied
in the negative. He turned to Marduk, but in the victim's
liver the soothsayers read the resolve of the gods to accept
no innovation. The prince obeyed, and had the crown
restored to its original state.

8. THE HIGH CLERGY

The prince was the high priest of his town's god, the
king, the high priest of the national god. Entemena was
high ishhakku of Ningirsu. Gudea himself offered sacrifices
and made libations. He observed the omens, and the god
issued his orders to him direct. It was he who purified the
city before the erection of the temple, who performed the
needful consecrations, and pronounced the seven benedic-
tions at the dedication. So, too, Lugalzaggisi, king of
Uruk, called himself also priest of Anu, the god of Uruk, and
after the conquest of Sumer, high ishakku of Enlil, the
god of Sumer : " in the sanctuaries of Sumer as ishakku of
the countries and at Uruk as priest, they (the gods) have
established him."

The high priests of the chief sanctuaries were important
personages whose positions were sought after by the sons of
princes. They were appointed by omens, and that event
was worthy of commemoration in the names of years. Thus,
in his father's reign, the son of Ur-Engur was chosen by
the deity as high priest of Innina (Ishtar) at Uruk ; two
years elapsed between the election and the enthronement.
Later on, under Gungunum, king of Larsa, there was to be
an interval of three years in the case of the high priest of
Shamash. From the earliest times there might be a college
of high priests attached to certain temples—a text of Gudea
bears witness to this.

A prince, deposed from his throne, did not disdain to
keep his religious functions. Ur-Ningirsu, son of Gudea,
remained priest of Anu and Ninâ when he was no longer
ishakku of Lagash.

[1] *Ibid.*, pp. 264–270.

Under the high priest (*en*, lord ; in Semitic, *enu*) were
ranged the various categories of priests described by the
general term *sangu* (Semitic, *shangu*) : it seems to have
been applied especially to the administrator of the temple,
but was nevertheless used of any person fulfilling sacred
functions.

9. THE FIRST CLASS OF THE CLERGY (MAGICIANS)

The priesthood was divided into three orders : the
magicians made the gods propitious and drove away demons,
the soothsayers foretold the future, the singers performed
the office of deacons. Some forty different functions are
known.

Fig. 14.   Balaggu (Louvre).

A priest of the first class bore the title of *mashmash*
(Akkadian, *ashipu*), but from the earliest times functions
had been divided, and he whose mission it was to appease
the hearts of the angry gods by psalms, was called *kalu*.[1]
On certain fixed days he repaired to the temple to offer
sacrifices, and to intone the sacred lamentations, accompanying himself on various instruments of percussion. He
used the *balaggu*, a big drum depicted on a vase fragment
of the Louvre,[2] and consecrated to the god Lumha, patron
of the *kalu*, when he chanted in honour of Enlil, or Ishtar,
one of those numerous poems which likewise bore the name

[1] I, vol. XVI, p. 121 ; **XX**, p. 53.
[2] I, vol. IX, pl. III.   See Fig. 14.

of *balaggu*. With the *shem*, or *halhallatu*, he accompanied
the *er-shem-ma*. Another of his instruments was the *lilissu*,
a copper kettle-drum covered with an ox-hide ; the rite
for the consecration of this instrument has been preserved
in a tablet from Warka, dating from the epoch of the
Seleucids.[1] Other tablets [2] contain formulæ to be recited
in course of the ceremony.

Among the *kalê*, the *kalamah*, or high *kalu*, was distinguished. The office seems to have been hereditary. A
number of functions had to be performed out of the sight
of profane eyes, but novices might be present and thus
receive initiation. Under certain exceptional circumstances
the *kalu* intervened. For instance, in the event of the
rebuilding of a ruined temple, when the soothsayer had
obtained a favourable omen, on a propitious day the *kalu*
prepared and offered during the night five sacrifices in
honour of the five gods, and chanted a lamentation and an
er-shem-ma. Then he offered three sacrifices—to the god
of the temple, to the goddess, his consort, and to the genius
of the temple. At dawn three more sacrifices—this time
to the great Bêls, Anu, Enlil, and Ea. The preparatory
ceremony ended with the chant, " When Anu, Enlil, and Ea
created heaven and earth," sung before the foundation-
brick of the old temple. The foundations of the new edifice
were then laid, and till the completion of the construction
the *kalu* would not cease to make offerings and lamentations.

His good offices were also needed on the occasion of dire
omens. If an earthquake announced an attack by the
enemy,[3] it was he who, after the purification of the king,
would offer by night sacrifices to the god and goddess of
the sovereign, and in the morning would sacrifice to the
gods Anu, Enlil, and Ea. Then, when the king had pros-
trated himself and had been shaved, he would take in a
vase *lahan-sahar*, the hair from the royal body, and would
go to leave it on the frontiers of the foe before making
lamentations, propitiatory *er-shem-ma*, in all the towns
under the mantel of the king. " If thou fulfillest these
obligations," declared the ritual, " the evil shall not approach
the king."

[1] I, vol. XVII, p. 55.   [2] *Ibid.*, p. 95.   [3] *Ibid.*, p. 87.

Besides the *kalu* another *ashipu* had the task of purifying
the sick and sinning, especially by means of incantations
and magic rites. He acted by virtue of the god Ea of Eridu,
or, later, when Babylon had won the hegemony, of Marduk,
Ea's son.

> The great lord, the god Ea, hath sent me ;
> He hath put his holy spell in place of my spell ;
> He hath put his holy mouth in place of my mouth ;
> He hath put his holy saliva in place of my saliva ;
> He hath put his holy prayer in place of my prayer.[1]

There were incantations for all circumstances and against
all evils—against evil spirits (*utukki limnuti*), the ghost
(*edimmu*), and the *labartu*. Against a sorcerer, the spell
maqlu (combustion), or *sharpu* (conflagration), so-called
because an image of the sorcerer was thrown into the fire,
was used. Headache, fever, and rheumatism were considered as real entities, and were supposed to disappear as
a result of magic operations. The *ashipu* made prayers to
the gods, offered them sacrifices, and poured libations.

10. THE SECOND CLASS OF THE CLERGY (SOOTHSAYERS)

The second class of the clergy was composed of the soothsayers. They were known at Lagash from the dawn of
history, and were divided into several groups according to
the various sorts of phenomena to be observed. In the time
of Ur-Ninâ the head soothsayer (*pa-azu*) invoked the god
Enki to obtain an oracle with reference to the construction
of the house of Girsu.[2] Under the predecessors of Urukagina,
if a man wished to drop oil on water to learn the will of the
gods, he had to pay five shekels of silver for the ishakku,
one shekel for the prime minister, and one shekel for the
soothsayer, *abkallu*, who devoted himself specially to lecanomancy.[3] At the same period other priests interpreted
dreams, the *ensi*, or observed various phenomena, the
igi-du. All bore the general appellation, *baru*.

Divination was applied not only to private affairs, but
also and above all to public business. No prince would
embark upon any important action without having taken

---

[1] **LVII**, p. 287.   [2] **CV**, p. 19.   [3] *Ibid.*, p. 89.

the advice of the deity, whether the latter manifested his
intention by some extraordinary or unexpected phenomena,
or, as more often happened, the enquirer solicited his intervention by seeking the divine will in the phenomena observed
by the soothsayer. Ammiditana, king of Babylon, consulted them in respect of a shipment of wheat.[1]

The functions of a soothsayer were hereditary. He was
" the progeny of a priest, sprung from a healthy priest."
He must be without blemish physically, and the science
which he possessed he had by tradition from Enmeduranki,
the seventh of the antediluvian kings [2] who had established
the priesthood. If, after centuries, he " clad him in a pure
garment," that was only because modifications had been
introduced into the ritual ; for originally he was stark
naked in the exercise of his office, as the archaic tablets from
Nippur and the seal cylinders show.

(a) Hepatoscopy, Lecanomancy

Divination took as its material all phenomena possible
and impossible. In the collections drawn up for the use of
soothsayers, men carefully noted down the events which
had happened after such or such a phenomenon, and which
it was believed would inevitably recur in the same circumstances. Further, hypotheses were invented, and by various
associations of ideas the fated outcome was deduced.

The livers of animals being regarded as the seat of life,
the examination of this organ would allow one to see there,
as in a mirror, the intentions of the god who had accepted
the offering of the animal sacrificed. Still, it was necessary
for the practice of hepatoscopy to choose an unblemished
animal, and to immolate it under the conditions prescribed
in the ritual, varying with the hours of the day. At dawn,
for instance, it was an ewe that the deity accepted most
readily. Before the god the soothsayer placed a brazier,
and on a table behind the brazier four pots of sesame-wine,
three dozen cakes, a mixture of butter and honey, and
finally salt. After sprinkling the brazier the priest grasped
the offerer by the hand and recited this prayer : " So and
so, thy servant, may he at morning's hour offer sacrifice !

---

[1] **CXXVI**, p. 159.　　　[2] **LVI**, p. 143.

G

May he present himself before thy august majesty. May he be pleasing to thy august majesty in virtue of this ewe, which is entirely composed of perfect flesh and perfect parts." The victim immolated, the share of the god was composed of the right leg, the kidneys, and a roast. A manual enumerated the signs which the soothsayer might discover on the liver, and determined which were favourable or unfavourable. Observations bearing upon events befalling the dynasty of Agade have survived, and the British Museum possesses a clay liver divided into fifty compartments, corresponding to as many different signs.

Lecanomancy was still easier. According to the position and form which a drop of oil let fall into a jar of water might take, the soothsayer without hesitation would tell whether the sick man, about whom he was consulted, would recover or die, whether the enterprise in view would succeed or would fail.

(b) Accidental Phenomena

But it is phenomena which one is not looking for which force themselves upon attention. They, too, could be auspicious or inauspicious. To this category belonged anomalies in the birth of children or animals, anomalies which were an omen for the house where they happened, and sometimes even for the city or the State. Because of a vague resemblance in the head, it would be said that a woman had brought forth a lion. That would suggest the idea of force and might, a propitious sign for house and land. Did the child's head call to mind the idea of an ass or a lamb, that was again a favourable sign; a dog or a serpent, a portent of ill-omen. The movements and acts of animals possessed prognostic value which might vary with the time and place of observation. A white dog entering the palace foretold a siege to the city. A bird of prey flying into the house heralded the death of the mistress of that house. Cockroaches boded ill for the house where they were met.

All the phenomena of the human body likewise gave rise to interpretations carefully handed down from age to age, and collected by Ashurbanipal in his great library at Nineveh.

(c) Dreams

The gods loved to communicate with pious men, and to announce events to them by means of dreams. When serious matters were at stake, the prince, or a seer, might obtain this favour by going to rest in the holy place. Thus, when Eanatum, ishakku of Lagash, was attacked unprepared by the men of Umma, who had invaded the Gu-edin of Ningirsu, he lay down in the temple of his god to learn by a dream what line of conduct he should pursue. Ningirsu stood by his head, and revealed that Babbar would march at his side, and promised him victory.[1]

It was in a dream that Gudea received the command to rebuild E-ninnu, the principal temple of Lagash.[2] " Gudea will sigh, saying : Come, let me speak ! These words may I utter ! I am the shepherd, the sovereignty hath been given me at the present. Something hath come unto me in the night watches ; its meaning I know not. May I be enabled to bear my dream to my mother ! May the prophetess, she who hath the knowledge of what appertaineth to me, may my goddess Ninâ, sister of Sirara-shum, reveal to me its import." He offered sacrifices to Ningirsu and to the goddess Gatumdug, then, after a fresh sacrifice, this time in honour of Ninâ, he addressed this prayer to her : " O Ninâ, O queen, O mistress of unfathomable decrees, queen who like Enlil fixest the fates, O my Ninâ, thy word is faithful and shineth most brightly. Thou art the prophetess of the gods. Thou art the queen of the countries. O mother interpretress of dreams, in the midst of my dream, a man whose stature matched the heavens, whose stature matched the earth, who, as to the tiara on his head, was a god, by whose side was the divine bird, Imgig, at whose feet was a hurricane, at whose right hand and his left hand a lion crouched, hath bidden me build my house. I have not recognized him. The sun rose from the earth. A woman— who was she not ? who was she ? . . . she held in her hand a pure stylus. She bore the tablet of the good star of the heavens. She held counsel in herself. A second man like unto a warrior . . . He held in his hand a tablet of lapis. He was laying down the plan of a temple. Before

[1] CV, p. 27.   [2] Ibid., pp. 137 ff.

me the pure pad was set. The pure mould was placed thereon. The brick of destiny in the mould was found. The sacred . . . set before me. . . . An ass was lying on the right hand of my king." To the ishakku his mother, Ninâ replied : " O my shepherd, thy dream, I, even I, will explain unto thee. As for the man whose stature matched the heavens, matched the earth, who as to his head was a god, at whose side was the divine bird, Imgig, at whose feet was a hurricane, at whose right hand and his left hand crouched a lion, it is my brother, Ningirsu. He commanded thee to build his house of the E-ninnu. The sun which rose before thee, it is thy god, Ningizida—like the sun he cometh from the earth. The young woman who . . . who held in her hand a pure stylus, who carried the tablet of the good star, who held counsel in herself, it is my sister, Nisaba. The pure star of the building of the temple she announced to thee. The second man who like unto a warrior . . . who held in his hand a tablet of lapis, it is Nindub—he . . . the plan of the temple. The pure pad set before thee, the mould placed thereon, the brick of destiny found in the mould, it is the sacred brick of the E-ninnu. As for the sacred . . . set before thee which . . . that meaneth that in order to build the temple, before thee no pleasure shall come. As for the ass which lay at the right hand of the king, it is thou ; in the E-ninnu like . . . thou liest on the earth." And after giving directions for the offering of certain presents to the god, she ended with these words : " Ningirsu . . . will reveal to thee the plan of the temple ; the warrior whose decrees are great, will bless thee."

Two thousand years later the last king of Babylon, Nabonidus, was also invited by a dream to rebuild a temple, the E-hulhul of Sin at Harran. The interpretation of the dreams was entrusted to a special priest, the *shâ'ilu*.

(d) Astrology, Atmospheric Phenomena

The gods manifested their will also in the movements of the stars. The astrologer read upon the starry vault what was going to happen upon earth. The moon-god, Sin, for instance, did not always appear at the beginning of the month. Sometimes he vanished on the twenty-seventh day and sometimes on the twenty-eighth ; sometimes he showed his crown in its full brilliance on the thirteenth or the four-teenth, sometimes on the fifteenth, and sometimes even on the sixteenth. Hence arose various interpretations referring to affairs of State which these phenomena directly concerned. It was the same with the manifestations of the sun-god, Shamash, of the goddess Ishtar (the planet Venus), of Marduk (the planet Jupiter), and of other stars. To them were attributed fortunate or adverse events that befell the land, military expeditions, invasions, the sickness or death of the prince, drought, flood, etc.

The atmospheric phenomena, storms, rains, lightnings, and earthquakes, were added as manifestations of the god Adad, lord of the hurricane.

11. THE PRIESTESSES

Sumero-Akkadian religion did not reserve sacred func-tions for men alone. Women might be priestesses, enchan-tresses, prophetesses, or singers. The mother of Sargon of Agade was a priestess according to one tradition. That of Gilgamesh used to interpret dreams, and it was through her that the hero learnt of the existence of Enkidu.[1] The Bibliothèque Nationale possesses the cylinder-seal of a high priestess of the god Adad.

Like the high priests, the high priestesses had to be appointed by omens. A year-name previous to the epoch of Ur gives evidence of the practice.[2] Twenty centuries later, Nabonidus, whose mother was a priestess of Sin at Harran, declared that, if he consecrated his daughter to the temple of Ur, he did it at the behest of the deity.[3] " As I was busied with his sanctuary and called upon his majesty, to the desire which he revealed to me I paid heed and I esteemed it most highly, I did not refuse him his desire, and I obeyed his behest. I raised to the office of priestess the daughter, offspring of my heart, and I called her name Bêl-shalti-Nanna since I made her enter the E-gipar." The E-gipar was a dwelling built upon a terrace planted with trees, reserved for the habitation of the high priest and the high priestess.

[1] **LIV,** No. 96.   [2] **CV,** p. 329.
[3] **I,** vol. XI, p. 144.

Among the reforms of Urukagina reference is made to the perquisites of the high priestess. Her Sumerian name, *nin-dingir-ra*, consort of the god, corresponds to the Semitic *entum*, the feminine of *enum* (Sumerian *en*), the name of the high priest. Her legal position was regulated by the law of Hammurabi, whether she were attached to the temple of Marduk or vowed to the service of some other god. Just as several high priests of the same god might exist under the authority of an arch-high priest, so, attached to the chief temples, there were veritable congregations of high priestesses recruited from the upper classes in society. The *sal-me* (consort of the god), the *qadishtum* (healthy), and the *zêr-mashitum*, were also priestesses. To the cult of Ishtar were also attached three classes of prostitutes who lived in the *gagum* under the oversight of an *ukkurtum*, as near the same temple there existed an establishment of men directed by a high priest called *ukkurum*.

The daughters of the high nobility did not despise subordinate employment in the divine cult. A witness to this is that granddaughter of Narâm-Sin, Lipush-iau, who was a lyre-player to the god Sin.[1] In the Kassite period upon a *kudurru*, unfortunately unfinished,[2] a woman bearing quiver and bow figures in a procession of priest-musicians and plays the tambourine. It is also apparently a woman who is beating a big drum in company with a young man on a religious scene from the epoch of Gudea.[3]

12. THE NECESSITY OF RELIGION

The origin of man was explained in various ways by the Sumero-Akkadians in theological or popular poems, but all agreed on one essential point : he had been fashioned by the deity from a lump of clay and created for the service of the gods. " To give the gods a dwelling to inhabit which should rejoice the heart, Marduk created humanity : Aruru produced with him the seed of humanity," declared the *Chaldœan Cosmogony*.[4] And in the *Poem of the Creation* the same god proposes to raise up man by kneading earth

[1] CV, p. 237.
[2] XXIII, vol. VII, p. 149. See Fig. 11, p. 103.
[3] I, vol. IX, pl. III. See Fig. 14, p. 150.
[4] LVI, p. 87.

with his own blood,[1] in order to establish the cult of the gods.

This creation was made in the image of the deity, and each god might share therein, since it was repeated as often as the fancy took them. The divine creator formed in his heart an "image of Anu," took earth, and informed it with this likeness. Aruru acted thus to produce Gilgamesh and the monster Enkidu. Ea, one of the gods to whom certain. primitive traditions attributed the appearance of man on the earth, created Asushunamir and Adapa in the same way. And, at the time of the Flood, Ishtar claimed to be the mother of men and cried, " Have I brought forth people that they, like the little fishes, should fill the sea ? " [2]

If mankind failed in its mission, the gods inflicted terrible punishments, such as floods which turn everything into mud, drought, famine, and pestilence. In all these catastrophies the god Ea showed himself always favourable, and endeavoured to save men.

13. MAN AND HIS GOD

Every human being was in dependence on a god, his guardian angel, and he called himself the " son " of that god. The princes of Lagash of the family of Ur-Ninâ were under the protection of one and the same deity, Dun-X. Urukagina claimed descent from Ninshubur, and his adversary, Lugalzaggisi, had the goddess Nisaba as his personal deity. Gudea expressly states that he was the son of Ningizida ; many a time he calls him his " god," and reveres him to quite a special degree. In the seventh century, Shamash-shum-ukîn, king of Babylon, carrying on the traditions of the third millennium, says in an incantation : " I, Shamash-shum-ukîn, son of his god, whose god is Marduk, whose goddess is Zarpanitum."

It is especially in the time of the Amorite dynasties of Isin and Babylon that we meet many allusions to this religious dogma in the lists of names. Names are compounded of ilî, " my god "—Ilî-duri, " My god is my fortress " : Ilî-amranni, " My god, behold me ! " ; Ilî-ishmeanni, " My god has heard my prayer " : Ilî-Amurrum,

---

[1] *Ibid.*, p. 64.   [2] *Ibid.*, p. 113.

" My god is Amurru " ; Ilîma-abi, " In sooth, my god is my
father " ;   Mannum-kima-ilî,   " Who   is   like   my   god ? "
Others contain the component *ilushu, ilishu,* " his god "—
Ilushu-abushu, " His god is his father " ; Ilushu-ibnishu,
" His god has created him " ; Ilushu-ibishu, " His god has
called him " ;   Sha-ilishu,   " Property   of his god," Gimil-
ilishu, " Gift of his god " ;   Apil-ilishu, Mâr-ilishu, " Son
of   his   god " ;   Mannum-balu-ilishu,   " Who   (can   exist)
without his god ? " Women's names likewise give evidence
of the same religious concept—Ilî-imdi, " My god is my
support," Ilî-awilim-rabi, " The husband's god is great."

The god took an interest in the man whose guardian he
was. He acted as intermediary between him and the other
deities. Urukagina ends some of his inscriptions with this
formula : " May his god, Ninshubur, for his life in the days
to come before Ningirsu prostrate himself ! " An analogous
formula is already to be met in the texts of Entemena, but
that prince most usually contents himself with ending his
legends by a simple reference to his protector—" His god is
Dun-X."

When Gudea had undertaken the reconstruction of the
E-ninnu, during the procession which preceded the making
of the first brick of the monument, Ningizida, his god, held
him by the hand. That is a rite of which the carved monuments give repeated illustrations. The cylinder-seal of the
famous ishakku,[1] presents an analogous scene, and if we
had any hesitation in recognizing the persons, one of the
stelae which he set up would banish all doubts ; on the very
figure of the prince his name is inscribed in a cartouche.[2]

At this epoch the subject engraved on a cylinder was usually
a ritual scene in which the owner of the seal is being led into
the presence of another deity by his god. Sometimes led
by the hand he himself raises the right hand to his mouth.
Sometimes he stands humbly, both hands clasped together,
and behind him a goddess intercedes on his behalf.[3] That is
because the man's god is his protector and intercessor before
other deities. So in the epoch of the First Dynasty of Babylon,
when the personal names provide evidence in such abundance
for the belief in a guardian god, the glyptic supplies con-
firmatory testimony. The pious Babylonian loved to have

[1] Fig. 31, p. 190.   [2] **CXLVII,** Fig. 368d.   [3] **LIV,** pp. 49, 57.

the names of his god and goddess engraved in the legend on
his cylinder, whether he describe himself as their servant or, in
self-effacement before the divinity, he omit all mention of his
own personality. And it would be a mistake to seek any
direct connexion between the text and the subject engraved
on the same stone ; that had not been the intention.[1] Adad
is the god of the thunder-bolt : Awil-Adad, his servant, has
it depicted. The god of the West is characterized by a curved
staff : he protects Zazum, who likewise has it figured on his
seal. But further, beside the warrior goddess, the names of
Enlil and Ninlil, that of Nergal, that of Bau are to be read.
The names of the god Shamash and of the goddess Aïa
appear from the period of Ur in front of the divine king
equally with those of Adad and Shala. They are found in the
epoch of the First Dynasty, not only accompanying the sun-
god, but also other deities, and these names are inscribed on
certain cylinders where the engraver has depicted the god
of the West. Then the custom of restricting the subject
began to spread under the last kings of the dynasty and
became very common under the Kassite rule. Only a single
personage making his prayer would be figured. But the
legend expanded and turned into a long inscription. That
has happened with two cylinders which bear a dedication to
Gula and the god of the West without any figure.[2] Elsewhere we read for example : " To Girra the great lord who
increaseth the grain, who multiplieth living beings, who
secureth an heir and a name to Mannum-balu-ilishu, son of
Iddin-Bêltu, servant of Girra and of the goddess of Agade," [3]
or again to Marduk, "sublime lord, god pitiful towards
Shamash-shipir, the servant who revereth him." [4]

14. FEAR OF THE GODS, PRAYER AND SACRIFICE

The first duty in religion was the fear of the deity. Hammurabi " feared the gods." Nebuchadrezzar II " with all
his faithful heart loves the fear of their divinity " and
trembles before their domination. Nabonidus " whose heart
is full of fear, keepeth the word of the gods." Yet according to

---

[1] *Ibid.*, Nos. 250, 256, 233, 227, 228, 226, 106, 116, 117, 118, 160, 148, 149,
203, 217, 221, 162, 289, 291, 295, 296, 288, 296.
[2] I, vol. XVI, pp. 6 and 89.
[3] **LV**, p. 298,   [4] **LXII**, No. 266.

Cyrus he was punished and deserted by Marduk " because he did not fear him."

The second duty of religion was prayer and sacrifice.

> Each day pay thy homage to thy god :
> Sacrifice, prayer, worthy incense.
> Before thy god have a pure heart :
> That is what is pleasing to the deity.
> Supplication, prayer and prostration,
> Thou shalt render every morning and he shall grant thee treasures.
> And thou shalt abundantly prosper thanks to thy god.
> In thy understanding consider the tablet :
> Fear brings forth good will :
> Sacrifice adds to life :
> Prayer delivers from sin.[1]

Sacrifice consisted in food offered to the deity and was accompanied by the burning of aromatic plants. Liquids were served by way of libation ; cylinders and engraved plaques show this. Lugalzaggisi of Uruk offered the offertory-bread and pure water to the god of Nippur. Gudea set up in the *ba-ga* his oblation-table, round which the gods of Lagash gathered. Hammurabi set pure dishes before the gods and Nebuchadrezzar II poured wine " like to the water of a river in quantity " upon the table of Marduk and Zarpanitum.

The manuals give the composition of the sacrifices differing according to the object in view. Here is that which the *bâru* offered at dawn on behalf of a pious votary of Shamash. He placed a brazier before each of the eight deities, Shamash, Adad, Marduk, Aya, Bunene, Kittu, Mesharru and the personal god of his client; on a table behind each brazier stood four pots of sesame-wine, three dozen loaves, a mixture of butter and honey, and finally salt. The priest, after having sprinkled the brazier before Shamash, took the offerer by the hand and pronounced this prayer. " So-and-so, thy servant, may he be permitted at the hour of morning to offer thee a sacrifice. May he raise the cedar and stand before thy august majesty. May he be pleasing to thy august majesty in virtue of this ewe which is composed entirely of perfect parts and of perfect forms."[2] The victim was slain and the god received his portion—the right leg, the kidneys, and a roast.

---

[1] **LXVII**, p. 21.   [2] *Ibid.*, p. 107.

The bleeding sacrifice was generally that of a sheep or a kid, and is frequently depicted on the engravings of the third millennium. The animal really represented the institutor of the offering.

> The lamb is the substitute for humanity :
> He hath given up a lamb for his life :
> He hath given up the lamb's head for the man's head :
> He hath given up the lamb's neck for the man's neck :
> He hath given up the lamb's stomach for the man's stomach.[1]

Other animals, however, might fulfil the same rôle. To expiate the faults of the sick man a hog would be sacrificed. " Divide the hog into six parts," said the manual, " and place them upon the sick man, make him pure with the blessed water of the apsu. Bring to him the brazier and the torch ! Place near the closed door twice seven loaves cooked under the ashes. Give the hog as his substitute ; give the flesh for his flesh, the blood for his blood, and let the demons accept them. The heart which thou shallest place on his pillow, give it instead his heart and let them accept it." [2]

The bloody sacrifices were carefully regulated. Gudea, after Lugal-ushumgal, fixed the number of fish, oxen, sheep, lambs, and horses to be immolated in the temples of Lagash in the name of the town on the occasion of the chief festivals of the year. Dungi imposed dues on the governors of the towns to assure the regularity of the monthly sacrifices in honour of Enlil, and Nabu-apal-iddin gives details for the future of offerings to Shamash in his cult-tablet of Sippar.[3]

The regular public sacrifices varied necessarily in accord- ance with the resources at the disposal of each temple. At Uruk,[4] in the temple of Anu, at some period two repasts consisting of drink, bread, fruit, and viands were served to the gods every morning, and two more every evening according to a document copied in the period of the Seleucids.

Anu's drink was presented in eighteen gold vases : four kinds of beer, pressed wine, and, in the morning only, milk in an alabaster vessel. He was served with thirty loaves

---

[1] **LXVII**, p. 274; **LIV**, No. 157.   [2] **LXVII**, p. 273.
[3] **LXVI**, p. 391.   [4] **CVII**.

each made of two litres (3½ pints) of flour—three-parts
barley flour to one part of wheaten—eight at each repast
in the morning and seven at each in the evening. Dates
from Babylonia and dates from Dilmun were presented on
a slice of bread soaked in oil; figs and raisins were added
thereto.

The other deities received smaller portions : Antu was
not entitled to wine ; Ishtar got twelve vases of drink and
Nana only ten. These three goddesses each received thirty
loaves like the god. Twelve were set before the divine
throne and the domestic god of the sanctuary, four before
the two tiaras, sixteen before the staged tower and its
domestic god.

For the principal dishes 21 rams, two years old, fed
on barley, 4 sheep fed on milk, 25 sheep of second quality,
2 bulls, one sucking calf, 8 lambs, 40 fowls of two different
species, 3 chickens, 7 ducks, 4 boars from the swamp,
3 *lurmu* eggs, and 3 ducks' eggs. The morning meals were
the most substantial: for breakfast, 18 sheep, one bull, and
the sucking calf; for luncheon, 6 sheep, the other bull, the
lambs, almost all the barn-yard animals, and the eggs. In
the evening for dinner, 10 sheep and 10 fowls ; for supper
only 10 sheep.

Individual ritual handbooks give details of the sacred
functions to be carried out on feast days. By putting together several fragmentary texts we can reconstruct the
greater part of the order of ceremonies during the *Akitu* of
Marduk, the most solemn festival at Babylon.[1]

On the second day of the month Nisan the *urigallu* (high
priest of the Ekua) rose two hours before the end of the night,
purified himself with river water, clad himself in a linen
vestment, entered the sanctuary of Marduk, and recited an
oraison. Then he opened the doors so that the enchanters,
kalê, and singers might carry out their duties as usual.
The same day various preparations were made, certain
objects were set before the gods. The next day the ceremony
of the last vigil was analogous to the foregoing. Three hours
after sunset three craftsmen and a weaver were summoned to
the temple to make images. These were to be seven fingers
high, adorned with precious stones, clad in red, girt about the

[1] CVII.

loins with a palm branch. One of cedar wood had to hold in
its right hand a serpent ; the other of tamarisk wood a
scorpion. Both would raise the right hand before Nabu on
his arrival at the E-hursagtila on the sixth day. They would
then be decapitated by a sword-bearer and thrown into a
brazier. From the beginning of the fabrication to the time
of their cremation, the workers appointed to fashion them
were fed on choice morsels picked from the sacrificial feasts.
The goldsmith was given a sheep's breast, the wood-carver a
leg, the weaver chops. A shoulder was set aside for the
third workman called *gurgurru* (metal engraver).

On the fourth day the secret ceremony included two
litanies, and commenced four hours before dawn. Two hours
after sunrise began the purification of the temple. An
enchanter sprinkled it with water drawn from the cistern of
the Euphrates and the cistern of the Tigris. He sounded
the brazen timbal, used a censor and a torch. He did not
enter the sanctuary of Marduk where the *urigallu* remained
shut up. He went next to the temple of Nabu and performed
the same rites there. He applied cedar oil to the door leaves
and rubbed the walls with the still warm body of a sheep,
the head of which the sword-bearer had just cut off. These
two men then went out into the country, one carrying the
animal's body, the other its head, and threw them into the
Euphrates. Made impure by contact with this victim, they
would stay outside the walls of the city for the duration of
the festival of the *Akiti*. The *urigallu* had remained shut in
the sanctuary to avoid contamination by the bare sight of
the purification of the temple. Shortly after the fourth hour
he came out and summoned the subordinate employees. The
" heaven of gold " was fetched from the treasury. The temple
of Nabu was veiled from the copings down to the foundations.
Subsequently the *urigallu* prepared a sacrifice before Marduk.
The golden table which was used was then carried to the
bank of the canal for the use of Nabu at the moment of his
landing.

The same day the king arrived, perhaps the god of Borsippa
accompanied him. He was conducted into the Esagil and
left alone in the main court. Then the *urigallu* came forth
from the sanctuary. He relieved the prince of his royal
insignia, the sceptre, the circle, the toothed sickle, and the

tiara, and went to deposit them on a seat before the image of
Marduk. He then returned to the prince, smote him on the
cheek, conducted him into the presence of the god, pulled his
ears, made him kneel down. Then the king recited a negative
confession.

" I have not sinned, O Lord of the lands, I have not been negligent with
    regard to thy majesty,
 I have not destroyed Babel, I have not ordered its dispersal,
 I have not shaken the Esagil, I have not forgotten its rites,
 I have not smitten clients on the cheek, I have not caused their
    humiliation,
 I have cared for Babel, I have not broken its walls."

The *urigallu* answered the king : " Be without fear . . .
Bêl will bless thee for ever, he will destroy thy enemies, he will
overthrow thy adversaries."

The king came forth from the sanctuary. The insignia
were restored to him. Once more the *urigallu* smote him
on the cheek. His tears must flow otherwise it will be an
evil omen ; the god was angry, a portent of hostilities, and
the end of the reign.

On the same day, shortly after sunset, the *urigallu* made a
bundle of forty reeds tied together by a palm branch, placed
them in a trench in the centre of the main court of the temple,
watered them with honey, cream, and oil. A white bull was
led thither to be immolated, and the king himself lighted the
faggot by means of a burning bough.

The seventh day of the same month was probably, as at
Uruk, reserved for final preparations for the procession and
the clothing of Marduk.

On the eighth day the god left his sanctuary. The privilege
of " taking his hand " to conduct him to the *Akiti* was
reserved for the king. In other cities where he enjoyed the
same prerogatives, the sovereign might send his robes to
represent him. At Babylon he had to come in person, otherwise the procession could not take place, and that was a
public calamity since the destinies of the year would not be
fixed.

On coming forth from his sanctuary, Marduk halted
" between the curtains " in a resting-place set up in the middle
of the main court. There were gathered in the order pre-

scribed for the ceremony the sacred emblems and gods
admitted to the cortège. The ritual had laid down the sacrifices to be offered, the chants to be sung. At the second
station, Marduk seated himself on a seat before a star whose
name is unknown to us. The third stopping-place was in the
Du-azag, the Sanctuary of Destinies. On quitting the Du-
azag the procession left the courts of the Esagil, debouched
upon the Sacred Way, turned northwards, passed through the
gate of Ishtar and reached the Euphrates. There the god
entered his boat to go and touch at the quay of the Arahtu and
thence to proceed to his *Akiti* called Ezur, " the Temple of
Prayers." He abode there till the eleventh day of the month
and then the procession traversed the same route in the
opposite direction. After a fresh halt at the Du-azag, Marduk
re-entered his sanctuary. Next day Nabu went home to
Borsippa.

15. SIN

To enjoy the favour of one's god was the source of all
good, to lose it became the beginning of troubles. The
divine protector was in some way responsible for the faults
committed by his protégé against the other gods, and had to
punish them. The scribe of Lagash who lamented the destruction of his city formally declares : " Sin on the part of
Urukagina, king of Girsu, there was none. As for Lugalzaggisi, ishakku of Umma, may his goddess Nisaba take that
sin upon her own head ! " [1] How would the angry deity
express his wrath ? In normal times he dwelt in the body of
his servant. When compelled to show his displeasure because
of sin, he withdrew his presence and immediately evil demons
came to occupy his place with their train of troubles and
sorrows. "He who hath no god, headache covereth him as
with a garment when he walketh in the street "; " he who
hath no guardian goddess, headache racketh his frame." [2]

To return to grace the demons would be banished by the
practice of magic, and the good-will of the god would be won
back by expiatory rites, sacrifices, purifications, and, above
all, prayer accompanied by ritual attitudes and gestures.
The " psalms of penitence " contain the confession of sin,

[1] CV, p. 93.
[2] XXIX, vol. XVII, pls. XIV and XIX.

witting or unwitting, and sometimes end in a hymn of
praise :—

Lord, my sins are many and my faults are grave.
My god, my sins are many and my faults are grave.
My goddess, my sins are many and my faults are grave.
O god, whom I know or whom I know not, my sins are many and my
    faults are grave.
O goddess, whom I know or whom I know not, my sins are many and
    my faults are grave.
Let the anger be assuaged in the heart of my lord.
The god whom I know or know not, let him be appeased !
The goddess whom I know or know not, let her be appeased.[1]

The faults which the faithful might commit are partly
revealed by the "negative confession." In this, after reference to sins against the gods, mention is made of sowers of
discord, liars, quarrelsome persons, merchants dishonest in
the quality or measure of their wares, and those who remove
boundary-stones, take their neighbours' goods, assault him,
or commit adultery.

16. RETRIBUTION

Every fault, however, was punished in this world ; just
retribution required that virtue should be rewarded here.
Man, created by the deity and for his service, had nothing
to expect beyond this life, and sooner or later he must leave
it to descend to the nether world from which there was no
returning. " When the gods created humanity," the nymph
Sabitu told Gilgamesh, " they set death as the portion of
mankind and kept life in their hands." The plant of life
which must be eaten for the attainment of immortality grew
in the Apsu. After a very painful journey Gilgamesh
reached it, but it was stolen from him by a serpent. Adapa
would have been no more in bondage to mortality had he
accepted the food and drink offered him by the god Anu,
but his destiny caused him to refuse it. Ishtar herself,
although immortal, could not have escaped from Hades
whither she had descended seeking her lover, had she not been
sprinkled with the waters of life.

So fearing death the Babylonian besought his gods to prolong his present life. That was the supreme aim of his prayer :

_____
[1] **LXVII**, p. 237.

that was one of the bases for his religion. Lugalzaggisi of
Uruk asked that life might be added to his life.[1] Gudea
begged for long days because of his pious works.[2] Arad-Sin
and Agum-kakrime desired " a destiny of life." Nebuchadrezzar II named the palace he built : " May Nebuchadrezzar
live ! May he live to an old age, the provider for the Esagil ! "
And Nabonidus addressed this prayer to the moon-god :
" Deliver me from sin against thy august majesty and grant
me a life of long days. For Bel-shar-utsur, the eldest son
sprung from heart, place fear of thy august majesty in his

Fig. 15.   Tombs at Lagash (after *Nouvelles fouilles de Tello*, p. 126).

heart. May he commit no sin. May he be saturated with the
fullness of virtue." [3]

17. AFTER DEATH

However long his existence had been, a day would yet come
when the Babylonian died. The living were careful to accord
him an honourable burial which varied with the circumstances
of the defunct, and was altered in the course of centuries.[4]
At Tell el 'Obeid, for instance, about 3000 B.C., the corpse
was just laid in a shallow trench and beside it were set vases,
arms, and ornaments. At Sippar, towards the end of the
third millennium, the dead was laid on his back in a rectangular

[1] XCIX, pp. 55 ff.   [2] CV, p. 175.
[3] XLIII, p. 253.   [4] CLVI, pp. 214, 265 ff.

brick cist and vessels of clay and vases of bronze were placed within his reach. Later the cist became oblong and the funeral furniture was made up of different objects—knives, weights, cornelian beads, kegs, arrows. . . . Still later the cist was replaced by two big earthenware jars. Food sacrifices were offered once a month to the departed, not so much to honour him as to avert his maleficence. Immediately after death, in fact, the shade of the defunct separated itself from his body and becoming a maleficent spirit called *edimmu*, it joined the ranks of the wicked *utukke*. It would get no rest as long as the corpse was unburied. " He whose corpse lies in the fields, his shade rests not in the earth. He whose shade has no one to care for it, dish scourings, scraps from the gutters he eats."[1]

So the supreme penalty was the privation of burial : " Let his corpse fall and find no tomb."[2]

So soon as the body had received the last dues, the *edimmu* descended into the " great earth " to the " house of darkness, abode of Nergal," " to the house whence whoso enters comes not out." According to the poem of *Ishtar's Descent into Hades*,[3] it was a place fenced about with seven walls each pierced by one gate. A profound gloom reigned there at all times, and the dead, "clad like birds in a garment of feathers," had dust for food and mud for drink! Nergal and Allatu, surnamed Ereshkigal, were sovereigns in that realm. Under their orders the demons of pestilence and diseases kept watch over the dead and usually prevented them from reascending to attack the living.

When Enkidu, the companion of Gilgamesh, saw himself in a dream transformed into a denizen of Hades, he found that lord and priest, magician and prophet, all sorts and conditions of men were gathered there without distinction.[4] When after his death Gilgamesh summoned him back to learn " the law of the land which he had seen," it was a revelation so painful for the living that it would make him weep. However, the sad lot of the departed was not the same for everyone. Some like old clothes were devoured by a worm ; others were full of dust. But there were some less hapless who rested on a couch and drank pure water, while those who

[1] LXVI, p. 315.
[3] *Ibid.*, p. 326.
[2] *Ibid.*, p. 397
[4] *Ibid.*, p. 215.

had fallen in battle were assisted by their parents and their
wives.[1]

The heavens, divided into dwellings reserved for the gods,
were not for any man. The hero of the Flood and his wife,
becoming immortal, were relegated to a distant island " at
the mouth of the rivers." Two men alone had ascended into
the heavens—Adapa of Eridu and Etana, king of Kish.[2]
Adapa, after breaking the wings of the south wind, had to
appear before Anu. On the advice of Ea he refused the food
and drink offered him. Anu, contrary to the anticipations
of the god of Eridu, had calmed his wrath. It was the food
and the waters of life. " Why hast thou not eaten ? " said
he, " why hast thou not drunken ? Thou will'st not live."
Etana, twelfth king of the first mythical dynasty after the
Flood, had also ascended into heaven with the intention of
stealing the royal insignia set out before Anu. On the
mountain to which he had gone to seek the " plant of child-
birth " to secure the happy delivery of his spouse, he became
acquainted with the eagle and the latter offered to carry
him up to heaven. The ascent took place to the amazement
of shepherds and their dogs.[3] After reaching the heaven of
Anu the eagle wished to mount up to the very throne of
Ishtar. Giddiness seized Etana, who in his fall carried his
steed with him. His *edimmu*, like that of all deified mortals,
was found among the dead in the nether world.[4]

[1] *Ibid.*, p. 325.   [2] *Ibid.*, pp. 148 and 162
[3] **LXV,** T. 97; **CXLVII,** Fig. 391.   [4] **LXVI,** p. 215.

CHAPTER II

THE ARTS

1. ARCHITECTURE

THE first dwellings of the inhabitants of Sumer and Akkad were tents or huts of reeds. As is the practice in those regions to-day, reeds were planted in a circle or in two parallel rows, and the stems, bent together, united to form a series of arches. Some scenes on cylinders furnish precious testimony to this. The land possessing no stone, the structures were finished off by a coat of adobe—clayey earth mixed with straw. It was soon noticed that in the summer heat the clay acquired solidity in the sun, and the idea was conceived of making it into cubes and letting them dry. These were sun-dried bricks. By placing them one upon the other before they were quite dry an admirable bonding was secured without mortar. The principle of the brick wall had been discovered. With sun-dried bricks square houses of small size were built and the roof was made of reeds covered with adobe resting on a frame of palm rafters. The invention of baked brick seems due to chance. In the hearth the brick became harder and more solid than when merely dried in the sun. It was set to bake by this rudimentary process, and later on men learnt to prepare bricks in a closed kiln.

The oldest bricks of king Ur-Ninâ at Tello, and others from Abu-Shahrein are rectangular and pillowed on one face. Later they are smooth. In official buildings they bear an inscription incised or stamped. Their dimensions at each epoch were fixed whether they were rectangular, square, triangular for the corners as at Muqayyar, or truncated arcs of a circle for pillars as at Tello. Their quality varied from one period to another. Those of Nebuchadrezzar at Babylon, square bricks with an edge of 31·5 cm., are perfectly cooked.

A last step forward was the invention of the enamel glaze which was largely used under the new empire for facing the palace walls. The Babylonians learnt this technique through Assyria.

Before the reign of Nebuchadrezzar II stone was only used for door-sockets in temples and public edifices. That luxury goes back to a remote antiquity. On the testimony of Herodotus and Diodorus a stone bridge had been thrown across the Euphrates at Babylon in the sixth century, but in point of fact stone can only have been used upon it to form the platform on each pile, and to support rafters of wood; the seven piles discovered are of baked brick.[1] Stone was employed at this epoch to pave the Sacred Way to Babylon, for the hanging gardens and for the north wall of the citadel.

A building—palace, temple, or private house—was always a rectangular parallelopiped, resting originally on a platform which put it out of reach of the flood. This platform, termed *temennu*, was formed of earth and rubbish between four walls of bricks, generally baked. To secure its permanence and avoid an accumulation of rain-water, drains were laid through it. In Sumer vertical ones have been found formed of an earthenware tube filled and surrounded with sherds and closed by a trap perforated with a grating on the level of the pavement. At Babylon, in the Neo-Babylonian city, there are big ones covered with a corbelled vault and small ones formed of two bricks arranged in a V and roofed by a third brick lying horizontally.

The houses were sometimes constructed entirely of baked bricks, and sometimes they rested on a few courses of such. The latter system, adopted at Babylon from the days of Hammurabi, was kept up till the fall of the empire. In the private quarters the houses had very flimsy walls and rarely boasted an upper room above the ground-floor. They were packed close together, scarcely leaving room for passages and alleys between them. However, building did not proceed at random. From the time of the First Dynasty there existed a plan for laying out the streets to which no equivalent can be detected in the old Sumerian towns. This plan, maintained for the future despite revolutions, made provision for main streets running north and south intersected at right angles by cross streets.

We do not know how the roofs were laid out. On all sites

[1] **CLVI**, p. 193.

the ruins of the ancient walls remain standing to a height of a
few feet only, and no indication of what was above has yet
come to light. Private persons must have utilized the palms
which grew in the region and covered the rafters with well-
stamped adobe. For public buildings from Ur-Ninâ's time
cedar logs, the wood of which is proof against decay, were
fetched from the mountains, especially Lebanon.

There can scarcely have been any openings beside the doors,
at the most some ventilators at the top of the walls. The
whole structure would not produce a handsome appearance.
So the walls were covered with a coloured wash which embellished them and protected them against the weather.

We have already seen the arrangements peculiar to
temples.[1] The palace of Nebuchadrezzar II at Babylon was
composed of buildings grouped round four main courts.
The throne room, 52 metres long by 17 metres wide, facing
north, was located in the third and largest court, and communicated with all the neighbouring structures. A vast
niche at the further end where the king sat, visible from the
court, was the only ornament in this chamber. Its walls
were 6 metres thick and painted white all over. The walls
of the court, on the other hand, were adorned with enamelled
bricks and the decorations, inspired by Hittite and Assyrian
art, consisted of yellow columns on an azure ground supporting a broad band studded with white roses with yellow
centres and blue lozenges outlined in yellow.[2] The private
apartments were preceded by a vestibule, access to which was
through two rooms; two circular pits have been found there.

At the north-east corner of the palace a huge structure
composed of fourteen vaulted rooms arranged in two rows
existed. As a pit and worked stones were found there we may
ask whether this was not the substructure of the hanging
gardens, one of the wonders of Antiquity. In any case, the
gardens were situated within the walls of the citadel according
to the Greek authors.

This citadel, of which the palace took up the greater part,
was, like the city, encircled by a double rampart. The

[1] See pp. 144 ff.   [2] Fig. 37, p. 193.

outer wall of Nebuchadrezzar's town was built of baked
bricks cemented with bitumen 7·81 metres thick. It was
reinforced on the outside in the moat and up to the ground-
level by a second wall 3·25 metres thick. The inner wall,
separated from the first by an interval of 11·25 metres, was
built of sun-dried bricks and was slightly less thick (7·12
metres), but it was equipped with towers at regular intervals
jutting out on both sides. This aggregation of defences was
2400 metres away from the Esagil, the temple Marduk, the
heart of the town. In the preceding century, under the
Assyrian domination, the city had covered a smaller area,
and its fortifications, 1400 metres from the sanctuary, had
consisted of a double rampart of sun-dried bricks, 6·50
metres wide, flanked by large towers alternating with
smaller ones. It is likely that the city was still smaller in
previous centuries, but its older defences have not been
discovered.

The Sumerian towns were also surrounded by walls of sun-
dried brick; traces of them have been discovered at Tello.

The finest monument at Babylon is the Gate of Ishtar,
reconstructed by Nebuchadrezzar II, near the citadel at
the point where the Sacred Way entered the old city. It
was composed of two structures of baked brick, each corresponding to one of the town walls, and each of which was
closed outside and inside by a door. A court separates
them, itself enclosed by two small walls. On the two lateral
sides the gate is flanked by a wing through which a passage
had likewise been driven. There were therefore three
distinct entries closed by eight gates.

The two central towers flanking the entry on the north-
west, the whole façade, the main passage, and the south-east
façade facing the town, are decorated with animals arranged
in tiers each representing a single species—the bull of Adad,
the dragon of Marduk. Six tiers are below what seems to
have been an ancient causeway of the Sacred Way; eight
below a causeway of baked brick; ten below the causeway
of Nebuchadrezzar paved with stone. The animals in the
first nine tiers are in relief, and composed of bricks not
enamelled. Above, there are two tiers of animals in enamelled

brick, not in relief, then two tiers where the bricks are enamelled and in relief.

It has been calculated that 575 figures went to make up these thirteen groups of animals ; 152 are still in position. They all, as far as possible, face persons entering the town.

By way of fresh fortifications at this gate, Nebuchadrezzar fenced the Sacred Way with a wall 7 metres thick, flanked

FIG. 16.   The Ishtar Gate at Babylon (after Koldeway, *Das wieder erstehende Babylon*, Fig. 24).

with towers between which enamelled lions in relief, to the number of sixty on each side, faced the city.

The Sacred Way is paved with broad slabs of limestone brought from Hit, on the Euphrates, between two borders of red breccia veined with white. The stones, cemented with asphalt, rest on a foundation of baked bricks covered with bitumen. The Way seems to have been reserved for pedestrians and religious processions. After following the peribolos of the *ziggurat* on the east, it turns at right angles, leaves the temple of Marduk on the left, reaches the Euphrates bridge, and again descends from north to south towards Borsippa.

The Babylonians seem to have intended to arrange their buildings with corners to the points of the compass. That allowed them to prevent any face being permanently sunless. They never built any edifice without performing certain rites, and under the wall or the pavement they contrived little cists where a commemorative inscription, accompanied by prophylactic figurines, and sometimes by amulets and other objects, was hidden. When a building had fallen into ruins and the gods had authorized its rebuilding, it was a duty to hunt for the old inscription, to sprinkle it with holy oil, and to replace it in the sub-soil of the new structure.

Artificial mounds were formed of rubbish and debris between walls of brick generally baked. Crude brick was carefully dried before use. In the dense pile numerous very narrow apertures were left to ensure the drying. In Assyria, where the material was used wet, none are found and no gap can be discovered.

The mortar was composed of asphalt mixed with clay or straw. A lime mortar was used under Nebuchadrezzar, asphalt alone for the Euphrates wall under Nabonidus, and clay mortar in Persian and Greek buildings.

The external decoration of the edifices consisted in mouldings of brick or pilasters, which served to break the monotony of the walls. The brickwork was everywhere hidden by a coat of chalk or asphalt, which protected it against the weather. It was probably not till the period of Assyrian domination that enamelled brick was introduced to enhance the splendour of this decoration, a finishing touch being given by elaborately wrought gates. Those of Gudea, in the E-ninnu at Lagash, were made of cedar covered with metal, like the later doors of the temples in Babylon restored by Nebuchadrezzar, or the leaves of the Gate of Ishtar adorned with copper. The latter, turned on bronze hinges, fitting into a threshold of the same metal, the reliefs on which were perhaps borrowed from Assyrian art.

2. SCULPTURE

The art of the Sumero-Akkadian sculpture had developed
down to the epoch of Gudea and the kings of Ur only to
fall into decadence with the accession of the First Dynasty
of Babylon, and to be replaced in the time of the Kassites
by a new style, the Mesopotamian art. The Sumero-
Akkadian aimed at representing nature. In his great
diorite statues, a trifle heavy, he succeeded in indicating
form in the muscles despite the hardness of the stone, and
he attempted to mark the folds of textiles. This is quite
lacking in the subsequent evolution of Babylonian art,
and constitutes for the high antiquity of the period the
most perfect representation of the human form.

Statues are rare. The Louvre possesses eight of diorite
once placed by Gudea in the temples of Lagash. All depict
the ishakku in an attitude of submission before the deity,
with his hands clasped together, either standing or sitting,
and sometimes holding on his knees the plan of the temple,
or a ruler and stylus. Unfortunately, all are decapitated,
and the separate heads found in the ruins do not fit them.
It has been possible to reconstitute one sitting statue of
the smallest size.[1] The head, with the neck rather easy,
almost undamaged, is shaven all over and covered with a
turban. The lips and cheeks are carefully modelled. But
we should not regard this work as the portrait of the prince ;
that was not the intention of the sculptor of Oriental antiquity, at least not before the Achæmenid epoch, for all his
figures were conventional. The careful indication of the
muscles, and the exact representation of the natural movement of the draperies is still more life-like in a little statue
of Ur-Ningirsu, son of Gudea, the masterpiece of Sumerian
statuary. It remained in fashion during the century of the
kings of Ur. But it was not primitive as a little statue
carved in marble of a king of Adab older than Gudea shows ;
his garment forms a sheath, not a muscle is indicated, the
eye sockets are empty, as in most of the archaic statues, and
the head is completely shaven.[2] The proper proportions
were not always observed. So a statue of Ur-Bau,[3] one of

---

[1] Fig. 5, p. 32.   [2] **XCVIII**, pl. 21, Fig. 4.
[3] *Ibid.*, pls. 7 and 8.

Gudea's predecessors, is disproportionately short, and in one archaic statuette [1] the total height is not four times that of the head alone.

The big statues are of hard stone, the statuettes more often in soft stone—limestone, alabaster, or onyx. Attempts were sometimes made to infuse life into them by an incrustation of stones of other colours or of metal. On the statue of the king of Adab the eyes were certainly inset. A female figure of grey limestone, belonging to the epoch of Gudea,

FIG. 17. Fragment of the Circular Bas-Relief
(Tello, Louvre).

wears on her wrists copper bracelets plated with gold. [2] Another in the same style is decked round the neck with a string of beads of cornelian, torquoise, and gilded copper. [3]

The series of bas-reliefs is more complete than that of sculptures in the round, and permits us to follow more successfully the technical development in the representation of the human form from the *Figure with the Feathers* [4] to the stelæ of Gudea. The Circular Bas-Relief, [5] the pictures of the family of Ur-Ninâ, [6] the Stele of the Vultures, [7] the bas-relief of Dudu, the stelæ of Sargon and Narâm-Sin, [8]

[1] *Ibid.*, pl. 1 *ter*, Fig. 3.   [2] **LXXI**, No. 108.   [3] *Ibid.*, No. 121.
[4] **XCVIII**, pl. 1 *bis*, Fig. 2.   [5] *Ibid.*, pl. 1 *bis*, Fig. 2 ; see Fig. 17.
[6] *Ibid.*, pl. 0 *bis*, Fig. 1 ; see Fig. 3, p. 23.
[7] *Ibid.*, pls. 3–4 *ter* ; see Fig. 8.   [8] See Fig. 4, p. 31.

illustrate the intermediate stages. The Stelæ of the Vultures, with its two faces, the one historical, the other mythical, divided into registers one above the other, shows a more liberal execution than the reliefs of Ur-Ninâ. In the monuments of Narâm-Sin, the artist has been able to utilize for the composition of his subject an irregular surface on which the king planted proudly occupies truly the first place.

The Sumerians, like the Hittites and Assyrians of later days, sometimes combined bas-relief and sculpture in the round in one and the same composition. Recent excavations have brought many archaic examples to light : a large relief in copper, measuring 2·44 by 1·07 metres, was discovered by H. R. Hall, at Tell el 'Obeid, in 1919. It

FIG. 18.   Mace-head of Gudea
(Tello, Louvre).

represents the man-headed eagle seizing two stags by the tails ; the heads of these stags stand out in high relief, and widely-branching antlers had been fixed by means of lead.

Representations of animals, as of the human figure, form a continuous series. Gudea had had life-sized lions carved, of which only fragments survive,[1] and a basin decorated with lions in profile.[2] A head and the hind-parts of the same animal, still of archaic workmanship, bear an inscription by Ur-Ninâ.[3] A comparison between the lion-mace of Mesilim [4] and that of Gudea [5] reveals the technical progress in the treatment of circular objects. Bovidæ are likewise numerous. On the bas-relief of Dudu a steer is lying down. On the Stele of the Vultures, a bull, doomed to sacrifice, is fastened to a stake. A heifer's head in limestone [6] gives an

[1] **XCVIII**, pl. 24.   [2] *Ibid.*, pl. 24.
[3] *Ibid.*, pl. 25 *bis*.   [4] *Ibid.*, pl. 1 *ter*, Fig. 2 ; see Fig. 2, p. 22.
[5] *Ibid.*, pl. 25 *bis*, Fig. 1 ; see Fig. 18.
[6] *Ibid.*, pl. 11 *ter*, Fig. 1 ; cf. p. 145 above.

idea of the methods of inlaying : the whites of the eyes are made of shell and the pupils have been cut out of bitumen.

Moreover, the Sumero-Akkadian was not content with representing real beings ; on the strength of more or less striking resemblances between men and animals, or anomalies observed in nature, he was very prone to invent hybrid creatures, some of which were handed on from age to age. The lion-headed eagle, for instance, emblem of the god Ningirsu, is common on monuments from Lagash. The human-headed bull, another hybrid, seems to spring directly

FIG. 19.   Libation-vase of Gudea
(Tello, Louvre).

from attempts to depict the bison.   On one of these animals carved in steatite, shell has been used to fill the hollows for the eyes except for the pupil which is missing.   This object, more recent than Gudea, and comparable to another design, firmer and without incrustation,[1] had its whole body flecked with trilobate plaques of shell.   So on the libation vases of the ishakku [2] the serpent-headed dragons are covered with incisions which were undoubtedly originally filled with some substance contrasting in colour with the ground. This dragon will become the emblem of Marduk of Babylon. It is just the same fantastic monster twenty centuries later in the days of Nebuchadrezzar II on the paintings and

[1] *Monuments Piot*, VII, pl. 1.   [2] Fig. 19.

reliefs at the Gate of Ishtar, with the same scaly body with
a lion's fore-paws and the hind-paws of a vulture, serpent's
tail and head surmounted by a crest of horns turned into
scrolls, and of feathers transformed into a pointed horn.
Only the wings have vanished, and are replaced by a spiky
ridge running down the length of the spine.[1]

The dog of Sumu-ilum, seventh king of the dynasty of
Larsa, about 2000 B.C., is still a very fine statuette,[2] but
soon after decadence in art corresponds to the establishment of political unity and the disappearance of the Sumerians as a people.   The bas-reliefs of Hammurabi are a
glaring illustration of the decline and, beginning with the

Fig. 20.   Dog of Sumu-ilu (Tello, Louvre).

Kassites, the carving of the *kudurrus*, gives evidence of the
deliberate abandonment of form in the striving after detail
of the person.   We still find, indeed, simple shawls, but they
do not form a drapery.   We note also the appearance of
fringed or embroidered robes on which a profusion of
rosettes, stylized versions of the sacred tree and animals, are
scattered about.   All these subjects exhibit the influence of
Hittite art, which perhaps reached Babylonia through the
mediation of Assyria.   The same luxury is found again in
the ninth century on the lapis *kunukku* engraved in honour
of the god Marduk by Marduk-zakir-shum [3] and on that of
the Louvre.[4]

[1] Fig. 36, p. 192.   [2] Fig. 20.
[3] Fig. 13, p. 140.   [4] **LXV**, pl. 93, A. 330.

3. METAL FIGURES

Not only in stone did the inhabitants of Babylonia seek material for their statues and bas-reliefs to embody gods, men, and animals. Very early they acquired skill in the use of metals, and especially copper. A life-size bull's horn, discovered at Tello,[1] was composed of copper leaf wrapped round a wooden core and fastened by little nails. The same procedure seems to have been applied to certain objects of larger dimensions, such as the palm-trees which Gungunum, king of Larsa, set up in the temple of Shamash in the second year of his reign (2263 B.C.). Later, he installed copper statues in various sanctuaries, and Sumu-ilum, his second successor, had copper lions fabricated. In the same period, besides a statue in cornelian and lapis ordered by Abi-sarê, mention is made of many a statue in precious metal; Sin-iqîsham (2173–2169) by himself manufactured eleven of silver and one of gold for the god Shamash. Warad-Sin introduced a gold effigy of his own father, Kudur-Mabug, into the same god's temple, and Rîm-Sin had one of Sin-idinnam, one of his predecessors, made for a temple at Adab. It is probable that these objects were not made of solid metal. Perhaps they were of copper or bronze covered with a layer of gold or silver. They have not been recovered and must have been destroyed, but from the excavations at Susa comes a small gold statue now in the Louvre.

Copper documents, on the other hand, are quite plentiful. Such are little solid figurines deposited under the foundations, often bearing an inscription and accompanied by a tablet commemorating the erection of the edifice. The oldest are busts of women with long wavy hair and a sharply-accentuated profile as in the bas-reliefs. The busts end in nails, and were stuck into the sub-soil in concentric circles in two spots under a structure older than Ur-Ninâ.[2] Under Ur-Ninâ himself,[3] and under his third successor, Entemena,[4] they were still female figures, in the latter case distinctly marked as genii by horns clearly visible on the forehead. In the reign of Ur-Bau the subject was varied It is now a kneeling god : he does not himself end in a point for

---

[1] **XCVIII**, pl. 45, Fig. 1. [2] *Ibid.*, pl. 1 *bis*.
[3] *Ibid.*, pl. 2 *ter*. [4] *Ibid.*, pl. 5 *bis*.

driving into the soil, but he holds with both hands an enormous stake and makes as if to implant it in the earth. This is the finest specimen of this series of monuments.[1] Under Gudea the same type will not attain such finished execution. Then basket-bearers erect on a stake begin to appear. Under Dungi and Bur-Sin they were women who are found again in the time of Rîm-Sin.

Sometimes representations of animals were substituted for these human figures. Gudea had bulls cast lying on a

Fig. 21. Prophylactic deity
(Tello, Louvre).

plinth which supported a huge nail. Under Dungi [2] the same subject was rendered much more happily.

Metal figures of larger size were cast hollow.[3] Two bull's heads are fine specimens from the pre-Sargonic epoch. As in certain stone statues, the eyes were inlaid ; in this instance they are of mother-of-pearl with pupils of lapis lazuli. A bronze bull [4] of unknown origin, inlaid with silver and standing on a plinth, bears witness to the persistence of the Sumero-Akkadian style. According to his inscriptions Nebuchadrezzar II set up brazen bulls and dragons at the Gate of Ishtar. Not one of them has been discovered : the very fragments have vanished.

[1] **LXV,** pl. 8 *bis.*   [2] *Ibid.,* pl. 28.
[3] *Ibid.,* pl. 5 *ter*   [4] *Monuments Piot,* VII, pl. 1.

Sculpture in stone or metal, or even on earth dried in the sun—such as the reliefs from the Gate of Ishtar—springs from modelling in clay. From the pre-Sargonic epoch there existed besides models, figurines, stamped in a mould in one piece, the reverse of which has been hand modelled [1]— naked or clothed goddesses, gods with the tiara on their heads. The epoch of Gudea provides numerous specimens the moulds for which had been carefully prepared. They include : gods, the hero Gilgamesh, the kid-bearer, clothed goddesses, and in particular the goddess making the gesture of intercession. These figurines persist till the Greco-Persian period, and the types of the naked goddess are multiplied more than the rest.[2] In the foundation deposits

Fig. 22. Engraved shell
(Tello, Louvre).

of Neo-Babylonian temples a terra-cotta figurine of Paps-ukal is generally to be found.

4. ENGRAVING

Engraving on shells goes back to a very early age. From the columella of certain shells small plaques or curved slices were taken, and it is possibly from the use of shells that the employment of cylindrical seals arose. Just as on very archaic cylinder-seals, so on a fragment of shell we find the lion-headed eagle pouncing upon a bull to devour it.[3] On a fragment of a bowl another theme common in gylptic, the struggle of a lion and a bull in which some personage interferes, recalls the style of the mace-head of

[1] **XCVIII**, pl. 39.   [2] **LII**.   [3] **XCVIII**, pl. 46, cf. Figs. 22–23.

H

Mesilim.[1] A provision-bearer is likewise older than Ur-Ninâ, judging by his *kaunakes* loin-cloth with a single row of tassels.

Other objects cut out were 'destined for use as inlays, such as a frisking kid or a broken torso carefully pierced

FIG. 23.   Engraved shell
(Tello, Louvre).

between breast and arms. But the masterpiece of shell-work from this remote epoch is a lion's head barely 24 millimetres across, sculptured in the round with the eyes inlaid and pupils of lapis lazuli.[2]

FIG. 24.   Silver vase of Entemena
(Tello, Louvre).

Mother-of-pearl-gradually replaced shell, and the engraving on this brittle material was reduced to purely linear tracing.[3] Engraving on metal is represented by a colossal lance,

[1] **XCVIII**, pl. 46.   [2] *Ibid.*, pl. 46.   [3] *Ibid.*, pl. 271.

on which a king of Agade has had a lion depicted,[1] and by
the silver vase of Entemena.[2] The body is adorned with
four lion-headed eagles, which link alternately lions and
stags, then again lions, and finally wild goats. These four
groups are independent, and each lion is biting the stag
or the wild goat of the neighbouring scene. Above the
band which borders the field seven heifers are lying one
behind the other, and each raises one of his fore-hoofs. The
engraving is carefully executed ; the lines very sharp and
uniform. The animals in profile are faithfully rendered,
while the full-face heads of the eagle and the lions do not
possess the same character and, as on the cylinders of this
epoch, the artist did not succeed in giving them a semblance
of truth.

5. CYLINDER-SEALS

Engraving on stone had been practised from the archaic
epoch : the ruins of Nippur and Lagash have preserved
some examples of it on large-sized plaques. But it was
developed above all on the cylindrical seals employed down
to the Persian epoch for the authentication of documents.
Thousands of these stones are now in museums and private
collections, some derived from methodical excavations, a
large number thrown on the market by native diggers.
They are classified in well-defined chronological periods,
and that even independently of their artistic quality, sometimes by means of legends engraved on them, sometimes
by comparison with impressions on dated tablets. The
subjects are not indeed different from those presented in
sculpture, but owing to their very diffusion over a large
number of private objects they illustrate the popular taste
at each epoch. The choice of stones itself is often characteristic. Before the kings of Agade the columellæ of certain
shells, limestone, prase and lapis lazuli were most popular.
Marble was already rare by the epoch of Agade ; steatite,
serpentine, and hæmatite were beginning to make their
appearance. Hæmatite was still dominant under Gudea
and the kings of Ur and their engravers continued to use
serpentine and lapis lazuli ; they were experimenting with
some kinds of jaspis and rock-crystal. Hæmatite still held

---

[1] *Ibid.*, pl. 5 *ter.*   [2] *Ibid.*, pls. 43–43b.

the first place under the Amorite dynasty of Babylon, but in time of the Kassites jaspis was in more general use and agate began to come in. Chalcedony was the most widely used stone in the sixth century, especially for flat seals, while ivory, hyalin quartz, jaspis and agate were used by the Persian gem-cutters.

The most archaic epoch is distinguished by a series of geometric patterns [1] derived from the conventionalization of representations of objects, animals, and human figures, and in addition, a scattering of animals coarsely engraved by the drill. Man was handled in the same fashion : his figure was still like a bird's beak if the artist used the drill, like a lozenge if he was working with the graver. Cylinders [2]

Fig. 25.   Archaic seal (Louvre).   Fig. 26.   Cylinder not developed (Bibliothèque Nationale, No. 74).

were still rare ; the flat seal carved in the form of animals with the round eyes, hollow and probably inlaid, [3] was preferred. Then the battles of animals, either amongst one another or against heroes such as Gilgamesh and his loyal comrade Enkidu, appear.

A dozen themes cluster definitely around the name of Lugalanda, ishakku of Lagash, of whom the impressions of three different seals have been discovered. [4]

Under the reign of Narâm-Sin and Shargalisharri, the battles of Gilgamesh and Enkidu with the lion and the bull continue. One of the cylinders from Tello, bearing the divine name of [d]Ninin, is particularly remarkable for the depth of the engraving and modelling of the figures. [5] This

[1] Fig. 27.   [2] Fig. 26.   [3] Fig. 25.
[4] Fig. 29.   [5] Fig. 28,

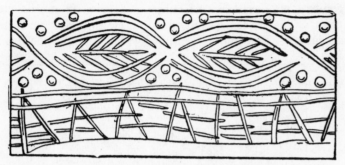

FIG. 27. Archaic cylinder (Tello, Louvre, 4).

FIG. 28. Cylinder of the epoch of Agade (Louvre, Tello, 83).

FIG. 29. Cylinder of Lugalanda, ishakku of Lagash
(Collection Allotte de la Fuye).

is the finest period of glyptic, and the artist expends much ingenuity on variations of subjects derived from the chief myths. The series of Shamash, the sun-god and high justiciary, is the most highly developed; the deities of

Fɪɢ 30.   Myth of Zu ; epoch of Agade (Bibliothèque Nationale, No. 74).

agriculture, the judgment of Zu,[1] who had tried to steal the tablets of destiny, the myth of Etana carried up to heaven by an eagle, and the enchanted tree, are handled, however, in an uneven manner.

In the time of Gudea and the kings of Ur, religious scenes were preferred in which a human being was put in touch

Fɪɢ. 31.   Cylinder of Gudea, ishakku of Lagash (Tello, Louvre, 108).

with a divinity by the mediation of his protecting god. Examples of it are extremely numerous, and hardly any scenes deserve special notice. The seal of Gudea himself [2] is, however, distinguished by its technique, and by the composition of the subject with its well-characterized gods and a serpent-headed dragon the minutest details of which, despite the smallness of its figure, are as clearly marked as

[1] Fig. 30.   [2] Fig. 31.

on the ishakku's libation vase. Some cylinders do not
belong to this series, but, as in the previous centuries,
depict the conflict of a hero with wild beasts.

FIG. 32.   Kassite cylinder (Louvre, A. 600).

It will be still the same under the kings of the First Dynasty
of Babylon. Gilgamesh is always popular, he remains the
vigorous hero always ready for battle, and in company with

FIG. 33.   Neo-Babylonian cylinder (Louvre, A. 770).

Enkidu he sometimes assumes the task of presenting the
kid to the deity, especially Shamash. Another god now
appears for the first time clad in a short garment with a

FIG. 34.   Form of a Neo-   FIG. 35.   Neo-Babylonian seal
Babylonian seal (Louvre).   (Louvre, A. 759).

turban on his head, and armed with a mace. He seems to
be Amurru, god of the West. Adad, rarely Marduk, warrior
goddesses and the naked goddess complete the repertoire of
the period.

Under the Kassites the subject was very often reduced to a single person, or a few divine symbols. The legend becomes the central feature. It is generally an invocation to a deity to beg aid, protection, and long life for the seal's owner, his faithful servant.[1]

During the Assyrian domination, Babylonian glyptic scarcely put out any characteristic products. It allowed itself to be induced to replace the cylinder by the flat seal [2] of small size, and already adopted the scenes characteristic of the Neo-Babylonian and Achæmenid period—a priest

FIG. 36.   Marduk's dragon, on the Ishtar Gate (after Koldeway, *Das wieder erstehende Babylon*).

standing in prayer with hand upraised before an altar on which are set sacred emblems.[3]

The decline in glyptic had not been arrested since the epoch of Agade.   For the quest for original and artistic compositions had been substituted from the days of the kings of Ur the manufacture of standardized seals often hastily executed by artisans and reduced, especially in the sixth century, to mere outlines.

6. ENAMELLED BRICK

The Babylonians of the New Empire, as we have remarked already, employed enamelled bricks for the decoration of public edifices. That was the chief use they made of colour

[1] Fig. 32.   [2] Fig. 34.   [3] Fig. 35, cf. Fig. 33.

in decoration apart from the inlaying of statues and bas-reliefs. The walls of the Gate of Ishtar are decorated with fantastic animals, the bull of Adad, the dragon of Marduk, nine rows of which stand out in relief on the building-bricks. Above are two tiers of similar animals in enamelled bricks, in turn surmounted by two more rows of bricks carved and enamelled. The blue ground was obtained from powdered lapis lazuli, as in the eighth century in Assyria at the palace of Sargon. The bulls stand out in yellow with green horns and hoofs, the brush of the tail and the mane being blue. Marduk's dragon is white ; his horn, his forked tongue,

Fig. 37. Decoration on the outer walls of the throne-room in the palace of Nebuchadrezzar II at Babylon (after Koldeway, *Das wieder erstehende Babylon*).

the lion's claws of his fore-feet, and the talons of his hind-feet are tinted yellow. The hinder-feet are composed of a glazed paste which is sometimes coloured by the neighbouring enamel. The technique of these bricks has recently been rediscovered.[1] It seems to have been borrowed from the Assyrians, who had themselves possibly acquired it from the Hittites. It passed on to Persia, where Darius employed it in the decoration of the palace of Susa. The choice of colours and their use are certainly borrowings from Assyria, and the themes themselves are sometimes imitations of Hittite art ; for instance, on the outer walls of the throne-room, where yellow columns capped by a double

[1] Bigot, *Reconstruction des frises du Palais de Darius*, 1913.

capital of blue volutes surmounted by a white rose with
yellow centre stand on a deep blue ground. That is a
motive previously known in Asia Minor, whence it had
likewise passed over into Cypriote art.

7. COSTUME

In the figured monuments of all periods gods are distinguished from men only by their head-dress—a cap adorned
with horns whose points meet in front and in pairs. Save
for some very rare exceptions in the case of secondary
deities their images are exclusively anthropomorphic. To
distinguish between them they are identified by the arms
which they hold in their hands, by emblems above their
shoulders, or by animals on which they set their feet. Later,
their images were replaced by symbols based on their
mythological characters, their qualities, and certain traditions. Anu was the master of the gods ; his symbol will be
the horned tiara, the divine insignia *par excellence*, resting
upon a throne. Marduk had won the power by his contest
with Tiamat ; a defeated dragon lies at his feet, and his
symbol is a spear. Nabu, the god of the scribes, is represented by a stylus or a bird. Shamash, the sun-god, is
surrounded with flames, and Nisaba, goddess of vegetation,
appears in the midst of reeds.

The representation of naked figures is rare. Such are
deities engaged in conflict, a priest pouring a libation, some
secondary persons on the glyptic scenes, and a goddess of
fertility, especially in the clay figurines and on the cylinders
of Hammurabi's dynasty. The hero Gilgamesh on archaic
intaglios generally has his body encircled with a girdle,
the end of which hangs down the leg. In the epoch of
Agade certain gods, or genii, are clad merely in a piece of
stuff passed between the legs and held in place by a girdle.
The oldest costume of the Sumerians and Akkadians consisted essentially of a shawl wrapped round the loins like a
skirt and hanging almost to the knees. This shawl was in
one piece and generally fringed with threads or the web
forms projecting tassels sticking out in regular rows. This
then is the fabric called by the Greeks *kaunakes*, which in
the days of Aristophanes was woven at Ecbatana. On the

oldest monuments the gods are thus clad. It was also the
dress of the ancient king of Lagash, Ur-Ninâ. Soon a
second garment draped over the left shoulder was added ;
such is the dress of king Eanatum on the Stele of the
Vultures. By new advances the shawl grew in size and
covered the whole body. Fastened below the armpits, it
enveloped the left arm and the free end passed under the
right arm. This was the dress of gods and men in the time
of Sargon of Agade. It was that of Gudea and Hammurabi.
The Kassites adopted the tunic with long tight sleeves.
They wore shawls of fringed fabric, or woven in several
colours,[1] the use of which was very ancient ; for the looms
of the kings of Ur provided the princes with pieces of stuff
of considerable weight, in which wools of varied tints were
harmoniously mingled. About 1000 B.C. in the royal costume textiles appear the patterns—rosettes, sacred trees,
genii, and animals—on which have been borrowed from Hittite art, either directly (for Hittite influence had made
itself felt as far as the ranges bordering Iran) or through
the mediation of Assyria, where the same motives were
likewise reproduced. The robe of private persons remained
plain, of one piece and generally fringed. Gilgamesh
hardly ever wears any head-dress. Men of the epoch
of Ur-Ninâ sometimes wear a trellised tiara resembling
the *kalathos* of the Greeks, then about Gudea's period
appears the turban which will be the head-dress of Hammurabi. The gods, bearded, wear long hair bunched in a
knot on the neck, double at first and later simple, but always
carefully dressed. The goddess has sometimes hanging
tresses and sometimes a chignon supported by a fillet. The
oldest heroes wear the beard and have long locks. Those of
Gilgamesh are always divided by an impeccable parting,
and form a triple row of ringlets on either side of his head.
Akurgal, son of Ur-Ninâ, is once depicted with shaven head
and once with a bunch of hair on the neck. Narâm-Sin is
bearded on his Stele of Victory. Gudea and his contemporaries at Lagash have generally a smooth visage and
shaven head like the persons on the *kudurru* of Marduk-
balatsu-iqbi [2] at a later date. The Neo-Babylonian priests
will wear wigs fastened by a diadem. Sumerian and

[1] **CXXVII**, pl. LXXIV   [2] *Ibid.*, pl. XCVI.

Akkadian women took special pains over their coiffure, adjusted it in various fashions, and kept it in place by ribbons, fillets, or a scarf, one of the ends of which, fixed by fringes, itself formed a narrow fillet.

Men and women, generally barefooted in the primitive period, wore sandals on their feet by the epoch of Agade. Their necks were decked with strings of shells, engraved stones or amulets ; their arms were encircled with massive bracelets.

8. FURNITURE

Furniture consisted of beds, various chairs, and household utensils. Inventories bear witness to a large number of seats of various forms. The figured monuments allow us to recognize some of them, from the simple stool on which Gudea is seated, to the carved throne of the deity on the cylinder of Hashhamer, a contemporary of Bur-Sin, king of Ur. Cube-shaped panelled seats, at the epoch of Agade, stools covered with *kaunakes* in the time of Dungi, chairs and arm-chairs of different models are also depicted.

Fig. 38.   Painted vase (Tello, Louvre).

Vases were made of stone, clay, or even metal. They were manufactured of copper and also of more precious metals. Such is the silver vase of Entemena at the beginning of the third millennium, decorated with fine engraving and mounted on a copper stand.[1] Stone vases were a great luxury ; for the most part they were reserved for the temples and quite often bear a dedication.[2]

[1] See Fig. 24, p. 186.   [2] **XCIX**, p. 261.

The clay vases, some hand-made, some thrown on the wheel, are sometimes covered with paintings. This practice was current in Susiana, where through two long and distinct archaic periods the artists devoted their ingenuity to varying the patterns.[1] The types there in use are reducible to three—a conical drinking-cup, a bowl with perforated lugs for containing food, and a jar for the conservation and transport of liquids. Till recently, only very rare specimens of painted pottery had been found on Sumerian territory (Fig. 38). The new English excavations at Eridu, Ur, and Tell el 'Obeid have proved that at the period of Ur-Ninâ and before, ceramic decoration in the Euphrates Valley passed through a development parallel to that observed at Susa. Both at Tell el 'Obeid and at Eridu the bowls are carinated, and this form, absent from Susa, recurs in Egypt among diorite vases of the Third and Fourth Dynasties.[2]

[1] **XXIII**, vol. XIII; cf. **CIX**, p. 349.
[2] Hall, **XVI**, vol. VII (1922), p. 299.

CHAPTER III

LETTERS AND SCIENCE

1. THE SCRIBES

THE general term "contract" has been improperly applied to all instruments of various periods which create an obligation sanctioned in law or custom. The use of written agreements was very widespread, and most acts of civil life purporting to create an engagement or obligation had no legal value unless they were founded on a written document.

The cuneiform script includes several hundred signs, and formed in itself a science only to be mastered slowly and with difficulty. However, at all epochs there was a great number of scribes, male and female, and some of them attained to the highest dignities. Lugal-ushumgal, under Narâm-Sin and Ur-Abba, in the days of the kings of Ur, became ishakkê of Lagash. Ashurbanipal, king of Assyria, boasts of having become a master in writing.

Schools existed where lessons were given in reading, and in tracing on clay the elements of the script's signs. That of Sippar [1] was in the first millennium the most famous for the antiquity of the texts preserved in its archives. A number of tablets from the century of Hammurabi, models and copies, illustrate the method of instruction—first reading and writing simple signs, with a study of their various phonetic values ; then the pupils' initiation into the use consecutively of groups of signs, of ideograms, and then of current formulæ. He was next given instruction in grammar in the guise of paradigms—declensions and conjugations. Finally, he finished his education with mathematics—the four rules, weights and measures, money values.

From the beginning the scribes felt the need of drawing up aids to memory, collections of signs, words, or phrases.

[1] **XCIX,** p. 33.

An archaic tablet gathers together the compounds of *ka* and *sag* ; another, dating from the epoch of Agade, contains the signs in which *gal* appears ; a third gives the names òf a certain number of unguents, and so collects the expressions compounded with *shim*.[1]

The scribe took pride in his science. To know how to read and write was a title to equality with a temple administrator or a judge. No one forgot to mention it in his deeds, and the distinction would be engraved on cylinder-seals. In Lugalanda's reign a special scribe was attached to the establishment of his wife, princess Barnamtara ; his seal bears the legend : " Eniggal, scribe of the House of the Wife." After the reforms of Urukagina, when properties improperly secularized were returned to the gods, he replaced that legend by "Eniggal, scribe of the House of Bau." It was in the shadow of the temples that scribes were trained. So they gradually came to form a special caste attached to the administrators of sanctuaries, and in the Neo-Babylonian period the two functions were nearly always confused in some towns, notably Sippar. There, the *shangu* (temple administrator) is frequently mentioned on tablets, while the title *dupsharru* (scribe) appears very rarely.

The preparation of tablets required fine clay kneaded for a long time and formed into biscuits the size, and colour, and shape of which varied with the time and place.

The oldest tablets of Lagash, earlier than Ur-Ninâ, are of unbaked clay and round. Others, quite as archaic and likewise rounded, but baked, come from Shuruppak ; the obverse of these is flat, the reverse pillowed. Under Lugalanda and Urukagina of Lagash, the shape has not varied, but the tablets are baked. Less than half a century later a considerable change has taken place. The documents contemporary with the kings of Agade are sharply differentiated from the foregoing : the clay is unbaked, and save for texts relating to the survey the tablets assume the rectangular shape which they are to keep for the future.

On the still damp clay the scribe traced out signs with a triangular prism-shaped stylus. He held it slanting and

[1] **XXIII**, vol. XIV, pp. 87–89.

pressed lightly. The corner made a stroke, the base of the
prism left a more or less deep impression, and the joint
effect was a figure resembling a wedge or nail. Hence
the name cuneiform applied by moderns to the Sumero-
Akkadian script. This shape for the components of the
signs is due to the use of the stylus and clay. Later on it
was adapted to inscriptions on stone, but in the primitive
periods it is not met on hard substances on which only
simple strokes are observable.

Down to the age of the kings of Ur two systems of ciphers
were used for numerals, some formed of wedges, like the
other signs in the script, others composed of circles and
figures derived from circles. They were obtained by use of
a cylindrical stylus, stamped perpendicularly or obliquely
on to the tablet. This practice fell into desuetude in the
second half of the third millennium, and thereafter the
scribe only used the triangular stylus.

This instrument did not allow of the drawing of curved
lines. All the signs must be composed of straight lines,
vertical, horizontal, or oblique, and the circles of the original
figures became squares, or lozenges. All the horizontal
wedges of a given sign were usually made before the oblique,
or vertical wedges, which often intersect them, but each
sign was completed before passing on to the next ; for the
latter sometimes overlaps upon its predecessor. But when
we speak of vertical or horizontal wedges, that means,
according to our modern way of reading, fixed by the
arrangement of the text on stone monuments, beginning
with the Kassite period. The signs were arranged in vertical
lines in earlier ages—on the Code of Hammurabi, the Obelisk
of Manishtusu, or the Stele of the Vultures. On tablets
the scribe probably traced all the wedges from the top to
the bottom, and turned the tablet round through an angle
of about ninety degrees from right to left and from left to
right; all the elements of the signs, in fact, resemble one
another exactly, and if, for instance, the stylus leant one
way in making the horizontal wedges, just the same pecu-
liarity is found in the tracing of the vertical wedges.

The script changed from century to century, and even
from town to town within a given epoch it was not absolutely the same. Each school had its own traditions and

methods ; in the days of the kings of Ur, for example, that
of Umma was clearly distinguished from that of Lagash,
a neighbouring town.

Writing on clay with a triangular stylus has distorted
the original hieroglyphics, and it is difficult to recognize
them. Yet some documents take us back to an epoch when
the object was still represented in its natural shape. On a
tablet, of which the British Museum possesses some fragments, an Assyrian scribe has collected the oldest forms
known to him side by side with the signs current in the
reign of Ashurbanipal.[1] On a stone tablet coming from
Umma,[2] appears a beaked vase with conical base covered
by a piece of stuff ; another similar vase is resting on a
support. The ideographic sign for " lord " and " fortress,"
the transformation of which can be followed down to the
last days of the Babylonian Empire, is represented on the
same stone and on an amulet in the Louvre by a rectangular structure flanked by a tower. The foot, again, on it
has a shape which can still be recognized in later writing.
Further, several kinds of vases, the comb, the harp, the
bow, the arrow, branches and flowers, can be distinguished.

It was the same in Elam, where a peculiar script, sprung
from the same root, developed independently of the evolution observed in Sumer and Akkad. The excavations at
Susa have yielded archaic signs, among which many a
primitive hieroglyph can be recognized.[3]

Prior to the kings of Agade, and later on tablets of large
dimensions, the text was arranged in columns divided into
compartments. In the age of Lugalanda and Urukagina
the scribes of Lagash, after filling the obverse from left to
right, turned the tablet over and went on writing on the
reverse from right to left ; the first compartment of the
reverse thus comes next to the last compartment on the
front. The summary of the document did not immediately
follow the full text, but began at the top of the left column
on the reverse, and went on in the neighbouring columns
if necessary. Beginning with epoch of Agade on the account
tablets, a blank space separates the various items of the
reckoning from the several totals. Under the First Dynasty

---

[1] **LXXXVII**, vol. I, p. 727.   [2] **XXIII**, vol. II, p. 130.
[3] **XXIII**, vol. VI.

of Babylon the employment of lines between the columns of the writing tended to disappear. Still, it remained to mark off, sometimes the list of witnesses, sometimes the dates, sometimes the total. Still later, parallel lines were ruled along the long side of the tablet, and the text was divided into sections indicated by blanks.

Documents authenticated by seal impressions are very numerous. The scribe generally mentioned them in the text. Before the First Dynasty of Babylon the cylinder was sometimes rolled over the whole surface of the tablet, or sometimes only the legend giving the name, profession, and ancestry of its owner ; this operation preceded the inscription of the text. From the Babylonian hegemony onward, in contracts, the majority of the witnesses affixed their seals near those of the contracting parties, preferably on the edges of the instruments. As these seals were often uninscribed, the name of the person to whom it belonged was written-in by the scribe near the imprint. Local customs were handed down by the schools : at Nippur, in the case of certain deeds, a special matrix was manufactured, on which the names of the contracting parties was inscribed. Under the New Empire the seal-impressions, sometimes on the edges, sometimes in the blanks between the several sections of the text, were affixed after the redaction of the instrument.

These precautions appeared insufficient to ensure the protection of the document and prevent its falsification. From the pre-Sargonic period, in the case of important tablets, care was taken to powder them with dry clay, and to insert them in a clay envelope on which the text was repeated, and which most usually served by itself to receive the seal-impressions.[1] If a dispute arose, in case the parties denied the authenticity of the document, the envelope would be broken open, and no one could suspect the tablet within it.

The use of clay envelopes was applied also to official or private correspondence, at least in the epoch of Agade, but they were apparently often replaced by a piece of stuff to which was attached a small lump of clay. The latter bore

[1] **LX**, pls. 112 ff.

a seal-impression, and fulfilled the function of the modern lead tags.

The tablet finished, a copy of it was supplied to everyone who had an interest in possessing one, and quite often another was deposited in the archives of the temple or the palace. The archivist sorted them into baskets carefully labelled. The labels were also of clay. In the reign of Lugalanda they resembled tablets. One bears the following text : " Basket for tablets (of what) the fishers of the sea and the fresh-water fishers have brought. Barnamtara, wife of Lugalanda, ishakku of Lagash : year 2." Later, they assumed the shape of perforated olives, through which a string passed. According to a methodical classification by subjects in the period of Ur, the archivist collected in one basket the judgments pronounced by such and such a group of magistrates, or the offerings made to the temple or gods on festal occasions, payments to mercenaries year by year, with a note of the responsible official, the wages in barley and in wool of the workers in the royal weaving establishment, or the lists of barley delivered for sowing or for consumption, and so on for all branches of social activity.[1]

Letters from one city to another were despatched in sealed baskets. A lump of clay was affixed to the knot in the string tying the basket, and was stamped with the seal of the sender and the name of the addressee. To this custom we are indebted for our knowledge of a number of fine specimens of the glyptic of the Agade period.

Under the New Empire, the Aramaic tongue developed in Babylonia. The exiles brought from Syria possessed a system of writing infinitely simpler and more practicable than the cuneiform script. It had only just been adopted, but in the eighth century it had become a general practice to employ Aramaic in many circumstances, to use it often on the margin of cuneiform tablets, to give a summary of the document. This was the work of scribes versed in both tongues. It is valuable in more than one respect, and allows us to determine the pronunciation of certain letters in the Babylonian speech of this epoch.

[1] **XXIV**, Nos. 810, 695, 713, 651, 7911, etc.

2. LITERATURE

The Sumerian and Babylonian scribes were not content with drawing up tablets of accounts or contracts. The princes caused them to mention the chief acts of their reigns on door-sockets, building-bricks, stone tablets, and stelæ. They transcribed laws, copied legends, ritual formulæ, prayers, incantations, and there are some of their works which are interesting even from the point of view of literary composition alone.

Here is the beginning of the simple Sumerian narrative, in which Entemena relates the quarrels of Lagash with her neighbour-town, Umma.

"At the veridical word of Enlil, king of the countries, father of the gods, Ningirsu (god of Lagash) and Shara (god of Umma) made a delimitation. Mesilim, king of Kish, at the voice of his goddess Kadi, in its place set up a stele. Ush, ishakku of Umma, in accordance with ambitious designs acted. He removed the stele and came into the plain of Lagash. At the just word of Ningirsu, warrior of Enlil, with Umma a combat took place. At the voice of Enlil the great (divine) net overthrew the foe ; (funerary) mounds in the plains in their place were heaped up. Eana-tum, ishakku of Lagash, grandsire of Entemena, ishakku of Lagash, made a delimitation ; from the great river he drew a ditch into Gu-edin. On this ditch he inscribed a stele ; he restored the stele of Mesilim ; he did not invade the plain of Umma."

After relating how he himself had dictated a peace to the enemy who had again invaded the territory of Lagash, he ends with these curses : " When to ravish the land under their hands the men of Umma shall cross the frontier-ditch of the Ningirsu and the frontier-ditch of Ninâ, whether it be the men of Umma or the men of other countries, may Enlil destroy them utterly, may the great net of Ningirsu defeat them, may his sublime hand, his sublime foot from on high fall (upon them), may the soldiers of his city be full of rage, and may fury be in all hearts in the bosom of his city." [1] Thus with curses finish numerous texts in which

[1] **XCIII**, p. 63.

kings mention their institutions, their buildings, or their decisions. Such is the conclusion of the tablet on which a scribe of Lagash has written this truly touching lament on the destruction of his town in the days of Urukagina : [1]

" The men of Umma the e-ki . . . have set on fire ; the antasurra they have set on fire ; the silver and precious stones they have carried off thence. The palace of tirash they have put to the sword ; the abzu-banda they have put to the sword ; the shrine of Enlil and the shrine of Babbar they have put to the sword ; the ahush they have put to the sword ; the silver and precious stones they have carried off thence. The e-babbar they have put to the sword ; the silver and precious stones they have carried off thence. The gikana of Ninmah of the sacred wood they have put to the sword ; the silver and precious stones they have carried off thence. . . ."

The litany goes on without omitting a single sanctuary without forgetting even the sacred field of Ningirsu from which the grain had been stolen. In the face of such a disaster the pious citizens of Lagash could only express this wish :

" The men of Umma, because they have laid Lagash waste, a sin against Ningirsu have committed ; the might which has come to them, from them shall be withdrawn. Sin on the part of Urukagina, king of Girsu, there was none. As for Lugalzaggisi, ishakku of Umma, let his goddess Nisaba take that sin on her own head ! "

The *Poem of the Creation*, composed for the exaltation of Marduk, the god of Babylon, aims at showing how that god won the first place by his battle with Tiamat.

Tiamat, the sea, and Apsu, the ocean, had from their mingled waters begotten all the gods. Dissatisfied with their creation they decided, on the advice of Mummu, their firstborn, to destroy it. Ea, god of wisdom, was apprised of their plot ; Apsu and Mummu were made prisoners. Then Tiamat to avenge them, created a crowd of monsters against whom the gods Anu and Ea in turn hesitated to do battle. Marduk, called in by Anshar, had demanded exaltation by the assembly of the gods before agreeing to undertake their defence. Anshar sent Gaga, his messenger,

[1] *Ibid.*, p. 91.

to summon first of all the oldest deities, Lahmu and
Lahamu : [1]

> He went, Gaga, he set out on his journey
> And before Lahmu and Lahamu, both his fathers,
> He humbled himself, he kissed the ground before them,
> He prostrated himself, then rose and spake :

> " Anshar your child hath sent me,
> He hath revealed to me the command of his heart,
> Even this : Tiamat, our mother, hath conceived hatred against us,
> She assembleth a band, she stormeth in fury.
> They turned to her the gods altogether,
> Even those you created, beside her do march.
> They curse the day, with Tiamat they advance,
> They are furious, they plot without rest by night or by day,
> They get ready for battle, they devastate, they rage,
> They form up a phalanx, they organise battle.
> The mother of the whole, the creatrix of all things
> Hath collected her matchless arms, hath brought forth huge serpents
> Sharp of fang, without pity in slaughter ;
> With poison for blood hath she imbued their bodies.
> She hath clothed with terror the horrible dragons ;
> With brilliance she hath filled them, she hath given them a lofty mien ;
> Whoever beholds them will perish with terror.
> Their body ariseth, none can withstand their attack.
> She hath caused the serpents to rise, the monstrous reptiles, and the
>   Lahamu,
> The storm monsters, the furious dogs and the scorpion-men,
> The powerful hurricanes, the fish-men, and the monsters
> Who bear pitiless arms, who fear not the combat."

After reporting that Qingu was at the head of this army,
the messenger continues in the name of Anshar :

> " I have sent Anu, but he hath not had the power to approach her,
> Ea was afraid and turned him back.
> Marduk hath risen, wise among gods, your offspring,
> To march against Tiamat his heart hath impelled him.
> To me hath he spoken the word of his mouth :
> ' If I, your avenger,
> Must enchain Tiamat and cause you to live,
> Call an assembly, exalt, proclaim my destiny.
> In the Upshukina sit ye together with joy,
> Let the word of my mouth, as ye do, decree fates !

[1] **LVI,** p. 37.

Let all that I do, be changeless in future !
Lest it change, lest it flinch, the word of my lips,
Haste ye, swiftly determine for him your fate
That he may go, may attack Tiamat, your dread foe ! ' ' "

They heard, Lahmu and Lahamu, they cried aloud ;
The Igigi[1] all together wept bitter tears
" In fear of what foe hath the Ocean come forth
We know not the work of Tiamat."

They gathered, they went
The great gods altogether, they who fixed fate,
They came before Anshar, they filled . . .
They embraced one another in the assembly . . .
They conversed together, they sat at the feast,
The sweet wine changed their . . .
With drinking they reached intoxication, their bodies waxed joyful,
They shouted much, their hearts were exalted ;
For Marduk, their avenger, decreed they destiny.

The combat ended, when Marduk the victor had announced his intention of kneading clay with his blood to
raise up Man ; the gods assemble again and proclaim his
" fifty names." [2]

We cannot pass over in silence the narratives of the
Flood. The one from which the following extracts are
taken forms part of the *Poem of Gilgamesh ;* in it Uta-
Napishtim, the Babylonian Noah, reveals to the king of
Uruk how he had earned immortality. At the command
of the god Ea he had built a ship :

" What I had," said he, " I loaded thereon, the whole harvest of life
I caused to embark within the vessel ; all my family and relations,
The beasts of the field, the cattle of the field, the craftsmen, I made
    them all embark.
I entered the vessel and closed the door
To guide the vessel, to Puzur-Enlil, the boatman,
I entrusted the structure with its contents.

When the young dawn gleamed forth,
From the foundations of heaven a black cloud arose.
Adad[3] roared in it :
Nabu[4] and the king[5] march in front :

[1] The gods of the skies.   [2] **LIV,** p. 109.
[3] God of the hurricane.   [4] Herald of the gods
        [5] The god Marduk.

They come, the heralds, by mountain and field ;
Nergal[1] seizeth the mast
He goeth, Inurta[2] he leadeth on the attack ;
The annunaki[3] have brought their torches
With their light they enveloped the lands ;
The tumult of Adad ascends to the skies ;
All that is bright, is turned into darkness. . . .

The brother seeth his brother no more,
The folk of the skies no longer can recognize each other.
The gods feared the flood,
They fled, they clomb into the heavens of Anu.
The gods crouched, like a dog on a wall, they lay down. . . .

For six days and nights
Wind and flood marched on, the hurricane subdued the land.
When the seventh day dawned, the hurricane was abated, the flood
Which had waged war like an army ;
The sea was stilled, the ill wind was calmed, the flood ceased.

I beheld the sea : its voice was silent,
And all mankind was turned into mud !
As high as the roofs reached the swamp !
I opened the window and light fell on my cheek,
I made for shore and stayed seated ; I wept :
Over my cheeks flowed my tears.
I beheld the world, the horizon of sea ;
Twelve (measures) away an island emerged.
Unto mount Nitsir[4] came the vessel.
Mount Nitsir held the vessel and let it not budge. . . .

When the seventh day came,
I sent forth a dove, I released it ;
It went, the dove, it came back :
As there was no place it came back.
I sent forth a swallow, I released it,
It went, the swallow, it came back :
As there was no place, it came back.
I sent forth a crow, I released it,
It went, the crow, and beheld the subsidence of the waters :
It eats, it splashes about, it caws, it comes not back.
I sent them forth to the four winds, I poured a libation.
I set an offering on top of the mountain.
I set fourteen adagurru-pots,

---

[1] God of war.   [2] Infernal spirits.
[3] God of the nether-world.
[4] Between the Tigris and the Lesser Zab.

Under them I spread reeds, cedar, and myrtle——
The gods scented its savour,
The gods scented the sweet savour,
Like flies, the gods gathered above the sacrifice.

In the myth of Etana, one of the kings earlier than the historical period, a graceful fable—that of the eagle and the snake—is to be found. The eagle had formed the wicked plan of eating the snake's young, and despite the sage advice of one of his more prudent children, he put his project into execution. The snake complained to Shamash, the god of justice.[1]

When he had heard the prayer of the serpent,
Shamash opened his mouth and said to the serpent :
" Go thy way ! reach the mountain :
I will catch thee a buffalo.
Open his entrails and pierce his stomach !
Take up thy abode in his stomach !
Every kind of bird from heaven will descend
To eat the flesh of the buffalo.
The eagle will descend with them and
What it knoweth not . . .
It will seek the entry to the flesh, in the . . . it will flutter around,
In the secret place of the heart, it will dream.
When it entereth the interior, do thou seize it by the wings.
Cut off its wings, its wing-feathers, its talons,
Tear it and cast it into a ditch. . . .
The death of hunger and thirst let it die ! . . ."

The serpent obeyed, and ensconced himself in the stomach of the buffalo.

Every sort of bird from the sky descended and ate of the flesh.
If the eagle knew his misfortune,
With the little birds he would not eat the flesh !

The eagle opened his mouth and said to his young :
" Come, let us go down and eat this buffalo's flesh ! "
A tiny youngling, very understanding, spake a word to the eagle its
        father :
" Descend not, my father, haply within this buffalo a serpent lieth
        hidden ! "

The eagle too spake a word within himself ;

[1] **LVI**, p. 167.

He understood them not, he did not understand the reflection of his
   youngling ;
He descended, he perched him upon the buffalo.
The eagle considered the flesh, he thought of what was before and behind
   him.
He repeated the process ; he considered the flesh, he thought of what
   was before and behind him.
In the . . . he fluttered around, in the secret place of his heart he
   dreamed.
When he entered, the serpent seized him by his wings. . . .

The eagle opened his mouth and said unto the serpent :
" Have pity on me and, as to a bridegroom, will I give thee a dowry ! "
The serpent opened his mouth and said unto the eagle :
" If I let thee go, how shall I answer to Shamash, the exalted ?
Thy punishment will return upon me,
The punishment which I, even I, inflict upon thee."
He cut off his wings, his wing-feathers, his talons ;
He tore him, he cast him into a trench,
That he might die the death of hunger and thirst.

The problem of good and evil on earth did not fail to
attract the attention of the Babylonians. Suffering comes
upon the righteous and spares the wicked. Faced with
this experience the pious man, faithful to his duties, asks
why he has been smitten : [1]

Scarcely had I come to life than I have already passed the appointed
   time,
I have turned back : it is evil, still more evil !
My oppression hath increased, I have not found my right !
I have cried to my god and he hath not shown his face ;
I have invoked my goddess, her head is not even raised.
The prophet by divination hath not determined my future.
The sorcerer by a sacrifice hath not made my judgment bright,
I have spoken with the necromancer, but he hath not opened my under-
   standing,
The wizard with his magic passes hath not unbound the wrath of which
   I am the object.

What various happenings in the world !
I have looked behind me ; evil is on my trail.
As if to my god I had not offered sacrifice regularly,
And as if at the feast my goddess had been forgotten,
As if my face were not bowed and as if my adoration had not been seen,
Like to him in whose mouth prayers and supplications have ceased,

[1] **XLIII,** p. 375.

For whom the divine day is ended, the new moon is dead,
Who hath lain on his side, despised their images,
Who hath not taught his people fear and veneration,
Who hath made no mention of his god, devoured the food for him designed,
Who hath abandoned his goddess, brought not the writing,
Who hath been an oppressor, who hath forgotten his master,
Who hath taken in vain the word of his mighty god, to him am I likened.

Every day the persecutor pursueth me,
At night he alloweth me not a moment for breath.
Through agitation my sinews are loosened,
My strength cast down, I see an ill omen
On my bed, brought to nought like an ox,
I am covered with the excrement of my body like a sheep.
My sick muscles have put the magician to the torture,
And by the omens which befall me, the prophet hath been lead astray.
The enchanter has not lightened my sickness,
And the prophet hath not put an end to my infirmity,
My god hath not come to my aid, he hath not taken my hand.
My goddess hath not taken pity upon me, she hath not walked at my side.
The tomb is opened, my dwelling hath been taken in possession.
Without my dying the lamentation over me is finished ;
All my land hath said : " How he is destroyed ! "
My foe hath heard it, his lips have smiled,
The message of joy hath been brought him, his heart hath waxed glad.

The process of composition scarcely varied across the ages. Lugalzaggisi, king of Uruk in the twenty-ninth century, recalls at the beginning of his Sumerian inscriptions the blessings of the gods upon him. Nabonidus, the last king of the Neo-Babylonian Empire in the sixth century, used similar formulæ.

The first expresses himself as follows : [1]

" When Enlil, king of the countries, to Lugal-zaggisi, king of Uruk, king of the Land, priest of Anu, prophet of Nisaba, regarded with a favouring eye by Anu, king of the countries, high ishakku of Enlil, endowed with understanding by Enki, whose name hath been uttered by Babbar, chief minister of Enzu, shakkanakku of Babbar, provider for Innina, child of Nisaba, fed on the sacred milk of Nin-harsag, man of the god Mes, priest of Uruk . . . pupil of Nin-a-

[1] **CV**, p. 219.

BU-ha-DU, lady of Uruk, very high abarraku of the gods, when Enlil, king of the countries, to Lugal-zaggisi the kingship of the Land had given, when before the Land he had made him prosper, when to his power the countries he had subdued, and when from the rising to the setting of the sun he had conquered all, upon that day. . . ."

And the second asserts : [1]

"When Marduk, the lord of the gods, the sublime, the master of the universe, created the prince, called him Nabonidus, king devoted to worship, to exercise the power, raised his head above all kings, at his word the great gods rejoice because of his royalty ; Anu and Enlil granted him for ever the throne, the diadem, the sceptre, and the crosier, the royal insignia ; Ea, creator of all things, made him perfect in wisdom ; Bêlit-ile, the creatrix of the universe, completed his frame ; Nabu, watcher of the world, granted him intellect ; Sin, the son of the Prince, contemplated his form ; Shamash, the light of the gods, made him shepherd of his flock, and placed his subjects under his orders ; Ira, the great, the mighty among gods, granted him strength ; Zababa, the exalted, made him perfect in vigour ; Nusku, the formidable, adorned him with the royal glory ; to regulate revelation, to take decisions and determine the future, he turned towards his guardian spirit ; the great gods summoned him to his aid that he might carry out his command."

The continuation of the text is a good example of Babylonian historical inscriptions : [2]

"Nabonidus, king of Babylon, sublime prince, prudent shepherd, who reveres the great gods, pious lieutenant who pays heed to the revelations of the gods, who every day busies himself with the ritual of the gods and goddesses, son of Nabu-balatsu-iqbi, sage prince, I, since Marduk, the great lord, appointed my father to the post of sovereign, and Nabu, son of the Prince, magnified my royal name, I repeat every day my reverence for their majesty, I busy myself continually with what may be pleasing to them, I multiply my care for the Esagil, [3] and the Ezida. [4] I present before them the best of all my beautiful things, I busy myself with the offering which must not cease ; in their

---

[1] I, vol. XI, p. 113.   [2] I, vol. XI, p. 114.
[3] The temple of Marduk.   [4] The temple of Nabu.

honour I erect their sanctuaries, their great towns, I magnify their name in the speech of all mortals.

" For Shamash, the great judge, the sublime god, master of Sippar, the Ebara, pure sanctuary, the *temen* of which he had not caused any king before me to see, Shamash, the great lord waited for me to make it, and I laid its foundations on the *temen* of Narâm-Sin.

" Of the wall Ugal-amaru, the wall of Kutha, I raised the pinnacle. The wall Melam-kurkura-dula, the wall of Kish, I caused it to tower up like a mountain. For Urash, mighty lord, I remade afresh, just as before, the peaceful festal mansion. Of the city . . . between Babylon and Borsippa, I raised the pinnacle with asphalt and baked bricks, and I caused Nanâ, the princely goddess, to enter her sanctuary.

" For Sin, the great lord who dwells in the E-kis-shirgal which lies in Ur, I put the crown to his appointed offerings, and I made his optional offerings magnificent. As I was busied with his sanctuary and called on his majesty, to the desire which he signified to me I showed my respect, and I paid special heed thereto, I did not refuse his command and I obeyed his order : I raised to be priestess the daughter, offspring of my heart, and called her Bêl-shalti-Nanna since I caused her to enter the E-gipar.[1]

" To busy myself with the cities of all the great gods my heart led me. Then for Lugal-marada, the sublime warrior, the resplendent hero, who is perfect in strength, the hurricane whose assault none can resist, he who deluges hostile lands, who ravages the lands of the foe, who dwells in his temple, the E-igi-kalama, who is my lord, him I exalted and his car, vehicle of his majesty, emblem of his courage which ravages the land of the foe, which is adapted for battle, the which car since ancient times no king before me had remade, the stones of its decoration and its gear were noticed in the foundations of the E-igi-kalama ; this car I rebuilt anew, I embellished it highly with pure silver, with shining gold, and with precious stones. Then I presented it before him. The E-igi-kalama, his temple which a former king had made and the head whereof he had raised, but the ramparts whereof he had not encircled with a supporting wall nor had consolidated the

---

[1] Dwelling of the high priestess of Ur.

guard-wall, his sanctuary was in ruins and the threshold-stones thereof were no longer joined. Its heaps of crumbling earth I took away ; its ancient *temen* I examined and I re-placed its foundation on its *temen* ; I constructed its rampart and consolidated its guard-wall, I remade afresh and raised higher its summit—O Lugal-marada, magnificent lord, mighty warrior, when thou enterest with joy this temple and when thou regardest all the pure works that I have accomplished, repeat every day what is favourable to me before Marduk, king of heaven and earth ; may the days of my life be prolonged, may I be crowned with many offspring ; drive back my foes with thy furious arms, destroy the totality of my adversaries ! "

3. EPISTOLATORY CORRESPONDENCE

Written communication seems to have been in use from the earliest times. The letter was written on a tablet, usually baked, enclosed in a clay envelope; no one could read it without breaking the seals which provided a safeguard against indiscretions. Sometimes people were content with wrapping it in a piece of stuff to which was affixed a piece of clay bearing the imprint of the sender's seal.

The oldest letter preserved seems to be a message relating to an Elamite invasion of Sumerian soil.[1] It is addressed to Enetarzi, the future ishakku of Lagash. Lu-enna, his correspondent, informs him that he had routed the enemy, enumerates the spoil, and probably what falls to the portion of the ishakku whose name unfortunately is irretrievably lost, to the *abarakku* and to the goddess Ninmar.

" What Lu-enna, sangu (administrator) of Ninmar sends him, to Enetarzi, sangu of Ningirsu, say : 600 Elamites, outside Lagash, booty to Elam have carried off. Lu-enna, *sangu* [of Ninmar, with the Elamites] hath fought. The Elamites he hath put to rout. 540 Elamites [*he hath slain or made prisoners* (?)]. Ur-Bau, craftsman of Niglunutum, the chief-founder, has taken charge of : 5 minæ of pure silver, 20 ——, 5 royal robes, 16 minæ of wool of sheep for eating ——, to ——, ishakku of Lagash, his *portion ;* to Enanatum-sibzid (the *abarakku*, his *portion*). Let the —— to Ninmar

[1] LIV, p. 52.

be taken ! 5th (year)." Here is another letter written in the time of Lugalanda :[1] " Referring to 660 ewes and lambs, 24 bulls and cows, 16 asses, that Gubi sends him, to Lugalmu say : The scribe has fixed the despatch. Let him inform him ! 4th (year)."

The formula, " What X sends him, to Y say," recalls the period when the message was entrusted verbally to the messenger. It is addressed to the scribe who will communicate to the addressee the contents of the document ; for the majority of the Sumero-Akkadians could not read and had of necessity to invoke the good offices of educated people. In the period of Agade this formula underwent a slight modification,[2] but remained in general use whatever the rank or quality of the addressee : " What Luba, the *nubanda* (superintendent), sends him, to my king say." It was sometimes abbreviated : " To my king what Enniglula sends him." In the days of the kings of Ur the first part, containing the name of the sender, disappeared and there only remained : " To So-and-so say."

Beginning with the First Dynasty of Babylon a number of letters exist, some referring to affairs of State, others to private matters. The former are not, like official inscriptions, designed for posterity, but they aim at securing the settlement of cases, communication of an order or of reports. Consequently they afford excellent evidence of usages, manners, customs, and events. Thus the correspondence of Hammurabi with Sin-idinnam, governor of Larsa, shows how the central power concerned itself with the administration of the realm, paid attention to the least details, and organized the direction of all affairs at Babylon. The unity of the empire had at least been realized, and the king uses it, and uses it successfully, to endow with stability all the machinery which he had created or transformed. The wealth of the temples was very great and their administrators enjoyed a large influence. Hammurabi had account given him of the revenues and interested himself in the restoration, rebuilding, and decoration of sanctuaries. When large public works were on foot, he looked after the engagement and wages of the workmen. Some questions which had formerly been settled by

[1] I, vol. XI, p. 65.   [2] XXIV, Nos. 1058, 1170, 1261.

the local authorities were now decided by the central agencies. The calendar belongs to that class. Once each city had decided whether the current year should comprise twelve months or thirteen ; there had rarely been an agreement between neighbouring princes, and each acted as his own fancy dictated. Hereafter there was one calculation made for the whole empire, and the king determined by his own sovereign authority when it was necessary to add a month to the current year. Thus Hammurabi warned Sin-idinnam in one of his letters that it was time to reckon in that year a second Elul. Not only was he at pains to collect decisions of justice, to define jurisprudence, to rectify certain abuses, but he also took the principal cases into his own hands, heard appeals, and directed the provincial judges. A case of corruption was detected at Durgurguri. He ordered an enquiry and directed that the guilty should be sent to Babylon so that he could punish them in person. " To Sin-idinnam say : thus speaketh Hammurabi : Shumma-Ilu-la-ilu speaketh thus, thus saith he : ' At Durgurguri there has been corruption. The people who have let themselves be corrupted and the witnesses cognizant of the case are here.' Thus said he. Behold, I send thee Shumma-Ilu-la-ilu himself. . . . On receipt of this letter hold an enquiry. If there be corruption, take the silver or whatever has been given as a bribe, put it under seal, and send it to me. The people who have let themselves be corrupted and the witnesses cognizant of the case whom Shumma-Ilu-la-ilu shall discover, send them to me."[1] Ea-lu-bani had been dispossessed of a field. He presented his title of ownership to the king and the latter ordered its restitution.[2] A citizen of Nippur complained that grain deposited in a granary had been abstracted. The king enjoined Sin-idinnam to settle this business :[3] " To Sin-idinnam say : thus speaketh Hammurabi : Thummumu hath informed me thus and said : ' I have deposited 70 gur of barley in a granary at Unabu ; Awil-ili hath opened the granary and taken the barley.' Behold, I send thee Thummumu himself. Go seek Awil-ili. See what he hath to say. The barley belonging to Thummumu that Awil-ili hath taken, make him restore it to Thummumu." Ilushi-iqîsh[4] had leant thirty

---

[1] **CXXVI**, No. 11.   [2] *Ibid.*, No. 76.
[3] *Ibid.*, No. 12.   [4] *Ibid.*, No. 24.

gur of barley to Sin-mâgir and had taken a receipt for it, but for three years he had demanded repayment in vain. The king had seen the receipt; there was therefore no need for an enquiry and in this case the king settled the difficulty himself: " Make Sin-mâgir give up the barley and the interest," wrote he to the governor, " and give them to Ilushi-iqîsh."

The tax collectors were in no hurry to send in their accounts. They were farmers-general who paid a fixed sum to the Treasury and recovered at their own risk and charge the taxes due in the district for which they had contracted. Shêp-Sin had made himself notorious for his want of promptitude in paying the fee for the privilege. One day the king had had him bidden put his affairs in order.[1] Another time he fell back upon the pretext of the difficulty of collecting the money due to a certain temple.[2] At last Hammurabi grew angry and wrote to Sin-idinnam:[3] " Concerning chief-collector Shêm-Sin I have written to thee: ' Send him with the 1800 gur of sesame and 19 minæ of silver owed by him as well as chief-collector Sin-mushtal with the 1800 gur of sesame and 7 minæ of silver owed by him. Send them to Babylon.' But thou hast replied that these chief-collectors had said: ' Lo, it is harvest-time: after the harvest we will go.' Thus have they said and thou hast informed me. Now the harvest is over. So soon as thou seest this tablet which I address to thee, send to Babylon Shêp-Sin, the chief-collector, with the 1800 gur of sesame and 19 minæ of silver owed by him and Sin-mushtal, the chief-collector with the 1800 gur of sesame and 7 minæ of silver owed by him; with them thy loyal guard. And let them come to present themselves before me with all their wealth." Other officials sometimes incurred grave reproaches and were likewise sent to the king. That happened to Etil-pî-Marduk by reason of his usurious practices.[4] An ishakku under his orders asked to be transferred to service under another chief,[5] and a certain shepherd complained because he had imposed the levy on exempt herdsmen.[6] The maintenance of canals was one of the most important works not only for the watering of the lands and their drainage, but also for commercial relations. The

---

[1] *Ibid.*, No. 16.   [2] *Ibid.*, No. 30.   [3] *Ibid.*, No. 33.
[4] *Ibid.*, Nos. 18, 30, 73.   [5] *Ibid.*, No. 38.   [6] *Ibid.*, No. 3.

I

dwellers on their banks were subject to levies for compulsory labour under the control of the governors. The king did not disdain to give orders to call them out and impose on them the task of cleaning the channels within a limited time.[1] One day he learnt that the clearing of a certain canal had not been finished and he directed its completion within three days.[2] The king's flocks and herds and his private landed estates were the subject of numerous letters. He received reports about them and sent officers of his household to superintend the shepherds. He had occasion to summon to the palace as many as forty-seven shepherds to get inform- ation first hand. He was engaged with the sheep-shearing, the crops of dates and cereals, the supplies of timber, etc. During an expedition to Emutbal, a province bordering on Elam, the royal troops had captured the goddesses of that land and had carried them off to Babylon. According to the religious ideas at the time these divine prisoners had to be treated with respect and installed in the temples of Babylonian gods until the day when, becoming friendly to the conquerors, they would be permitted to return to their sanctuaries so as to facilitate the peaceful conquest of the territory subject to their jurisdiction. Hammurabi wrote to Sin-idinnam about them :[3] " Embark at once the goddesses on a processional (barque) ; send them to Babylon. Let the *hieroduloi* (temple prostitutes) come with them. For the entertainment of the goddesses, load the barque with food, drink, small cattle, equipage and the supply for the *hieroduloi* till its arrival at Babylon. Appoint people to tow the barque and let the goddesses come without hindrance to Babylon. Let them not delay, but come promptly to Babylon." We do not know what results followed this letter ; another, likewise to the governor of Larsa, ordered the return of the same deities to their temples : " Say to Sin-idinnam : Thus speaketh Hammurabi : The goddesses of Emutbal who are under thy charge, the troops of Inuhsamar shall escort to thee under good guard. When they have reached thee, join these troops to thine and establish these goddesses in their sanctuaries again."[4]

Lalu complained to Samsu-iluna, Hammurabi's successor,

[1] **CXXVI**, No. 26.
[2] *Ibid.*, No. 5.
[3] *Ibid.*, No. 34.
[4] *Ibid.*, No. 45.

of a governor who had claimed rights over the harvest of an
ilku property and had seized the crop. The tablet was at
the palace; the plaintiff is, in fact, the owner of the usufruct
of this gan of land. Word was sent to Sin-idinnam[1] to conduct
an enquiry, and if the governor had granted a mortgage on
this piece of land to censure him. At this period a regulation
concerning fishing was in force and each district reserved to
itself certain rights over its territory in compensation for the
labour involved in the maintenance and clearing of the canals.
Samsu-iluna, having received a complaint, gave the following
order :[2] "To Sin-idinnam, Kâr-Sippar and the judges of
Sippar, say : Thus speaketh Samsu-iluna : I am reminded
that the fishers' boats descend to the districts of Rabî and
Shamkâni and catch fish there. I send an officer of the
'Gate of the Palace'; when he reaches thee recall the fishers'
boats which have been to catch fish in the districts of Râbi
and Shamkâni and do not let it happen any more that the
fishers' boats descend to the districts of Râbi and Shamkâni."

A letter of Ammi-ditana preserved in the Louvre[3] attests
the practice of paying the dead a monthly cult. "To
Shumma-ilum, son of Iddin-Marduk, say : Thus speaketh
Ammi-ditana : The milk and butter for the funerary offerings
of the month are wanting. So soon as thou seest this my
tablet, let thy intendant take 30 cows and 60 qa of butter ;
let him come to Babylon. Until the funerary offerings be
completed let him bring milk ! Let him not delay, promptly
let him come ! "

Another letter from Samsu-ditana[4] reveals the conditions of
extreme insecurity during the last days of the First Dynasty :
"'Referring to what you have written me namely : The grain
which grows in the territory of Sippar-ia'rurum, it is not
proper to leave it in the fields at the mercy of the enemy's
soldiers. Will our master please give the order that instruc-
tions be sent us to open the gate of Shamash and transport
this grain into the city.' That is what you have written to
me. The grain, the tillage of the city, being entirely harvested, immediately open the gate of Shamash, and until
the grain, the tillage of the city, be entered therein, cause

[1] *Ibid.*, No. 6.   [2] *Ibid.*, No. 80.
[3] **XXX**, p. 160.   [4] *Ibid.*, p. 161.

the judges to sit ; let them not neglect to have the gate
guarded ! "

Letters between private persons treat of personal affairs
and often remain obscure because we know nothing beyond
what the tablet itself tells us. The drafting is often extremely
concise and the text bristling with allusions to facts known
to the addressee of which we for our part are ignorant.

A farmer whose stock had been raided by the enemy, asks
his master to supply him with a cow ; he sends him 5 shekels
of silver and promises to pay the balance when he has received
the cow. " To my master, say : Thus speaketh Ibgatum,
thy servant : As thou hast heard, master, the enemy has
taken away my cattle. Never before have I written to thee ;
now I cause a letter to be carried to thee, master. Send me,
master, a young cow. I will weigh out and send thee 5
shekels of silver, master. . . . With Ili-iqisham, my brother,
let the young cow come. And I, that my master may consent
without delay and may send me the young cow, I shall immediately weigh out and send 15 shekels of silver to thee, O
master."

Erîb-Sin and Ibni-Nabu were partners in a business ven-
ture. The former has asked the latter to pay fourteen
shekels to a certain Shamash-bêl-ilâni, and the latter tells
him in reply to take them out of the sum of two-thirds of a
mina of silver previously sent to the person named Warad-
ilishu :[1] " As concerning Warad-ilishu, son of Ibni-Dibbara, I
have sent him two-thirds of a mina of silver and the receipt
of that has been acknowledged in writing in the presence of
my witnesses. He has gone to Assyria. He has not paid the
money to Shamaiatu. Shamaiatu and I met at Dagana and
we had a discussion on this topic. 'I have sent thee,' said I,
'the money by means of Warad-ilishu.' 'If Warad-ilishu,'
replied he, ' has paid the money, may he . . .' And as
concerning what thou has written about the fourteen shekels
of Shamash-bêl-ilâni, I have not paid him the money. Catch
Warad-ilishu and make him weigh out the silver with interest
more or less ; from this sum take the fourteen shekels and
send me the balance."

[1] CXXXII, p. 334.

A man cast into prison five months before complains of
his wretchedness and begs his master to have means of
subsistance transmitted to him.[1] " Send me either half a
mina of silver or two minæ of wool for my use. Let Mâr-
abulli not be sent empty-handed : if he come empty-handed,
the dogs will devour me. As thou, O my master, and all the
people of Sippar and Babylon know, I am not in prison for
brigandage nor for house-breaking. Thou, O my master, hast
sent me with oil across the river. The Sutæans have attacked
me and I have been imprisoned. Say a word in my favour to
the familiars of the king's *abarakku*. Send me somewhat lest
I die in the house of wretchedness. Send me one qa of oil and
5 qa of salt. What thou hast sent me heretofore, has not
been given me."

The excavations at Nippur have introduced us to the letters
addressed to the Kassite kings and to the correspondence
between officials in the fifteenth and fourteenth centuries. An
anonymous note shows that the system of accounts for temples
and large estates had remained just as elaborate as at the
beginning.[2] " Thus saith thy father : Turn thy face, be
kind, and send as soon as possible the report to the ' master
of barley ' in order that I may be able to send in my own
report. . . ." It was a question of the accounts of various
granaries or silos in the charge of a single official ; each
guardian had to give a list of commodities to allow the
summary list to be drawn up which would be despatched to
the superior authority. The terms " father " and " mother "
in the sense of " superior " and " brother," meaning " col-
league, friend, or equal," were already beginning to appear ;
in the epistolatory style of the New Empire they were regularly
employed. Another complains of a mistake : he had asked
for pots and been sent straw.[3] The lady Inbi-Airi writes to
the head-guardian of the stores of the temple at Nippur and
orders him to pay out a certain quantity of barley : " To
Innani say : Thus speaketh Inbi-Airi : Give Idin-Nergal
3 gur of barley. Do not deal with me in an unfriendly spirit,
but, as I have told him, let him take and bring away this
barley. The securities for the people, send them to Sin-
issahra. To Dini, daughter of Abîa, send 4 gur of barley."

[1] *Ibid.*, p. 331.   [2] **XXXII**, vol. XVII, 76.   [3] *Ibid.*, 45.

As in the time of the First Dynasty the king often adjudicated on cases in person. " To Awil-Marduk say : Thus speaketh the king, thus saith he to Awil-Marduk : Errish-nâdin-shum, son of Appanâi, who hath slandered Hanibi, Damgu, son of —— who hath slandered Sin ——, bring him before me ! "[1] This Awil-Marduk was chief of police at Nippur in the reign of Shagarakti-Shuriash (about 1270 B.C.). Imgurum begins a report to Burnaburiash about the affairs under his care in these terms : " Thy servant Imgurum. Into the presence of my master may I come ! Greeting to the house of my master." He then describes the state of the work on various buildings in hand, some of unbaked brick, other of kiln brick. He then notes the non-receipt of wool from Bêl-usâtum, gives details of the division of what he has received, requests the king to send some since he has no means of procuring any at Dur-Kurigalzu, and declares that he " finds no pleasure in his office." He ends by asking for the release of the weavers held prisoners at Pân-Bali ; he had already spoken to the king and had written three times to him on this question without obtaining a reply. Another person named Kalbu[2] calls himself humble as the dust and loving servant of his king. He begins his letter with this compliment : " To my master, glorious in splendour, of celestial origin, strong, mighty, wise, light of his brethren, who shines like the dawn, escort of mighty and terrible lords, aliment of his people, table of the nobles, hero of his clan, to whom Anu, Enlil, Ea, and Bêlit-ilê have granted a fief of grace and of integrity, to my master, say : thus speaketh Kalbu, dust and servant who loves thee." This courtier was governor of Mannu-gir-Rammân. His district had been devastated by " the rain of heaven and the waves of the abyss." The floods had destroyed the gates and annihilated a flock of two-year old ewes. Nothing remained to feed the inhabitants. And after treating of other affairs he concludes by soliciting an immediate reply.

At the same epoch the priceless collection of the Tell el-Amarna Letters casts a flood of light on the policy of the eastern empires and of Egypt in Canaan and Amurru, regions always coveted by their mighty neighbours because they were not only rich countries, but traversed by the only commercial

[1] **XXXII**, 75. [1] *Ibid.*, 24.

route running from Babylonia, Assyria, and the Hittite realm to the Empire of the Pharaohs. The letter of Hattusil, king of the Hittites, to Kadashman-Enlil, king of Babylon,[1] is no less precious for the information it gives on the relations of the two lands.

A Babylonian letter of the seventh century, written by an Assyrian king, directs a search for ancient documents, copies of which he wanted for his library. It gives a vivid glimpse of the methods adopted by Ashurbanipal in building up the large collection of texts assembled by him in his palace at Nineveh. " The king's commands to Shadunu. I am well : may thy heart be glad ! The day you read my tablet, take Shumâ, son of Shumukîn, Bêl-etir, his brother, Aplâ, son of Arkat-ilâni, and the artisans of Borsippa whom you know for thy service and seek out all the tablets that are in their houses and all the tablets that are deposited in the Ezida and the tablets of (?) amulets of the king, of the rivers, of the (?) conflagrations, of the month of Nisan, the . . . of the (?) rivers, of the calculation of days, four (?) amulets of the pillow of the king's bed and of the king's . . . the arm *eru* of the king's bed ; the incantation ' Ea and Marduk the wisdom which they accomplish, the meeting . . .'; the narratives of battle all that there be with their very big tablets all such as there are ; (the series) ' let not (the evil) Ash-mê-gi approach the man going forth to battle (or) entering into the palace '; the ritual texts, the upliftings of hands, the inscriptions on stone and those that are good for my royal majesty ; (the series of) the purification of the whole city (?), ' for anguish and dire need,' all such as there are in the palace and the precious tablets in your (personal) apartments which do not exist in Assyria, seek (them) out and send (them) to me. Instantly have I written to the intendant and the officer ; in thy magazine shall you place them. No one may refuse you a tablet. And if there exist some tablet and ritual texts about which I have not written to you and which you regard as good for my palace, select, take, and send (them) to me." [2]

[1] Cf. p. 48 above.   [2] **LXXXV**, p. 19.

4. WEIGHTS AND MEASURES

Among the statues of Gudea preserved in the Louvre are
two in which the ishakku, seated, holds on his knees a tablet
on which rests a graduated ruler. It is the only standard we
possess for estimating the measures of length used in the third
millennium. One specimen is complete. The two extreme
notches are 26·45 centimetres apart : one scale is divided
into sixteen equal parts, four of which are subdivided into
two, three, four, five, or six parts ; the other scale likewise
comprises sixteen equal divisions of which two are divided
into twelfths and eighteenths. The statues are a little less
than natural size, and it is questionable whether the ruler
represents a real measure or whether it is reduced and only
represents a scale.[1] Other data, notably the sizes of the building bricks, allows us to regard the divisions as each equal
to a fraction of the unit of length adopted at this epoch.
This subdivision can only be the " finger," the thirtieth part of
the " measure " or cubit in use at Lagash in the pre-Sargonic
period. The cubit is approximately equal to 49·5 centimetres.[2]

The fractions of the cubit of 30 fingers are the " measure "
or foot of 20 fingers, the " open hand " of 15 fingers, " mason's
hand " of 10 fingers, and, finally, the finger. Its multiples
are the " reed " of 6 cubits, the " pole " of 12 cubits, the
" tsubban " of 60 cubits, and the surveyor's cord of 120
cubits. The accompanying table gives the evaluation of these
measures in terms of the metric system.

Finger	=		0·0165	metres	($\frac{2}{3}$ ins.)
Surveyor's cord	=120	cubits	59·4000	,,	(65 yds.)
Mason's hand	= 10	fingers	0·165	,,	($6\frac{1}{2}$ ins.)
Open hand	= 15	,,	0·2475	,,	($9\frac{3}{4}$,,)
Foot	= 20	,,	0·330	,,	(13 ,,)
Cubit	= 30	,,	0·495	,,	($19\frac{1}{2}$,,)
Reed	= 6	cubits	2·97	,,	($3\frac{1}{4}$ yds.)
Pole	= 12	,,	5·94	,,	($6\frac{1}{2}$,,)
Half-cord	= 60	,,	29·70	,,	($32\frac{1}{2}$,,)
League	=180	cords	10692·00	,,	(6·65 miles)

---

[1] **XCVIII**, pl. 15.　　　　[2] **V**, vol. XVIII, No. 3.

Beginning with the Third Dynasty of Babylon we become aware of a third measure or cubit : 45 fingers. It was called the " itinerary measure " or great cubit, and corresponds approximately to $\frac{3}{4}$ metres.[1] It has been possible to check these data by comparing the dimensions of the ziggurat of Babylon, given on a tablet of the Seleucid period, with the actual measurements made of the ruins of the monument at the moment of its discovery.

The unit of area in the third millennium was the *sar* or " rood," a square with a side of one " pole." Its subdivisions are the " sixtieth " and the " barley corn " which is a third of a sixtieth. Its multiples were the *gan* or " field " of 100 " roods," and the *bur* of 18 *gan*. On this data the corresponding modern measures are :

Barley corn	= 0·196 centiares	= (2·1 square feet)
Sixtieth	= 0·588 ,,	= ($6\frac{1}{3}$ square feet)
" Rood "	=35·2836 ,,	= ($33\frac{1}{2}$ square yards)
" Acre "	=35·2836 ares	= ($\frac{7}{8}$ acre)
Bur	= 6·351048 hectares	= ($15\frac{3}{4}$ acres)

With the Kassites a new measure of area appears, corresponding to the new measure of length. Just as there was a great cubit corresponding to the pace of ·75 metres, two-thirds of the ordinary cubit, so lands were sometimes surveyed in " *gan* measured by the great cubit " : this *gan* or field which persisted till the fall of Babylon concurrently with the old *gan* measured 17·465 square metres. It is to the other *gan* as 9 is to 4. The unit measure for volumes was the twelfth of the cubic cubit, which is equivalent to 8·42 decilitres. Its subdivisions was the *gin* or " sixtieth."[2]

The basic unit in measures of capacity was the *qa*, $\frac{1}{144}$ cubic cubit or about 8·42 decilitres ($1\frac{1}{2}$ pints). For liquids there was a division, the *gin* or sixtieth, very frequently mentioned at Lagash in the period of Ur in determining the quantities of oil supplied for the entertainment of travelling officials beside another measure, the *agum ;* this seems to have equalled 5 *gin* or $\frac{1}{12}$ *qa*. The multiples are the " little pot " of 5 *qa ;* the *nigin* of 10 *qa ;* the *dug* or " pot " of 20 *qa* in the pre-Sargonic epoch—the pot equalled 30 *qa* in the time

[1] I, vol. XV, p. 59.   [2] *Ibid.*, vol. VI, p. 75.

of the Dynasty of Agade—the *sadug* of " amphora " of 30 *qa* ;
the double amphora and the *adapa* of 300 *qa*.

From the time of Lugalanda and Urukagina dry measures
of 6, 36, 72, and 144 *qa* were known. The last named was
called the *gur saggal*, and it too had a multiple containing it
3600 times. It lasted in use till the Ur period, but at the same
time there existed another measure, the *gur* of 300 *qa* (252·6
litres, 55½ gals.), later called the *gur* of Agade or royal *gur*.
It continued in use till the time of the Third Dynasty, and
was then replaced by the *gur* of 180 *qa* (about 151·56 litres or
33⅓ gals.).

The unit of weight was the mina, the weight of $\frac{1}{240}$ cubic
cubit of water and not of a *qa* which was the $\frac{1}{144}$. The mina
was divided into 60 shekels, while 60 minæ made up a talent.
A certain number of Babylonian, Assyrian, and Elamite
weights are in existence : they have enabled us to fix the
value of the mina at about 505 grammes (16⅛ oz.). In the
third millennium the mina was divided into 60 shekels, the
shekel into 180 grains. Three grains formed a little shekel ;
60 a minette ; 90 a half-mina and 120 a double minette.
Hence the following table :

Grain	0·046 grammes	(¾ grain)
Little shekel	0·140 ,,	(2·1 grains)
Minette	2·805 ,,	(43⅓ grains)
Half shekel	4·208 ,,	(65 grains)
Double minette	5·611 ,,	(⅕ ounce)
Shekel	8·416 ,,	($\frac{3}{10}$ ounce)
Mina	505·00 ,,	(1 ℔. ¼ ounce)
Talent	30·505 kilos	(67⅓ pounds)

In the Neo-Babylonian period the shekel was divided into
⅔, ½, ⅓, ¼, ⅕, ⅙, ⅛, $\frac{1}{10}$, $\frac{1}{12}$, and $\frac{1}{24}$; the last-named weight, the
obol, was equivalent to 35 centigrammes.

The circumference of the circle was divided by the Sumero-
Akkadians into 360 degrees of 60 minutes each, and this
division has persisted despite its incompatibility with the
metric system, and does not seem likely to yield to the division
into grades for many years to come.

How did the ancient Sumerians come to invent their
sexagesimal system of numeration ? The names of the

numbers themselves give us the answer. At first they considered the five fingers of the hand and counted : *ash* (1), *min* (2), *esh* (3), *limmu* (4), *i, ia* (5). The number 5 being conspicuously inadequate they developed this notation by adding on the first four. That gives *ash* (iash, 6), *imin* (i-min, 7), *ussu* (? i-esh, 8), and *ilimmu* (i-limmu, 9), and for the two groups of five they invented a new name of which they made a new and higher unit the decade *u* (10), twice which, the score, was called *nish* (20). With these two names for the decades they made compounds to denote four multiples : *ushu* (ush-u, 3 decades, 30), *nimin* (nish-min, 2 score, 40), *ninu* (nin-u, 2 score plus 1 decade, 50), and for sixty they adopted a new name *gesh.*

The higher units were the square, the cube, and the fourth power of 60. Sixty squared was called " sare " (3600): 60^4 (12,960,000) was the " great sare," or the " great intangible sare."

The figures were at first stamped on the tablets by means of two styles circular at the base, of different sectional diameter. By pressing the smaller circle obliquely on to the clay a more or less elongated semicircle was produced which represented unity. Two and three were formed by repeating this unit on the same line, and then, beginning with 4, the figures were arranged in two rows to facilitate reading. When 9 was reached they preferred to write 10–1, the minus sign being denoted by a right angle turned towards the figure to be subtracted. This sign was very freely used to avoid confusion and simplify the writing. Thus 7 is found written 10–3, and the sum of 56 shekels of silver is denoted by " 3 minæ — 4 shekels."

The numeral for decades was obtained with the same stylus held perpendicularly and not slanting, so that a complete circle was obtained. The decades after 3 were arranged in two rows like the units.

The higher unity, the sixty, only differed from the numeral 1 by its greater size ; it was formed by the application of the big stylus. The sign for ten sixties was made up of the semicircle representing 60 with the little circle 10 inscribed within or intersecting its edge. The *sare,* sixty squared, was traced with the big stylus and formed a complete circle. To indicate a decade of *sares* (36,000), the little circle was impressed in the middle of the big one, and the same figure intersected by four strokes grouped to form a double X denoted the cube of 60.

Very early fractional symbols were invented ; the sign for unity turned through 90 degrees to the right was bisected by a stroke to denote the fraction $\frac{1}{2}$, or accompanied by an angle to represent $\frac{1}{3}$. For fractions higher than $\frac{1}{2}$, the expressions, $igi - 3 - gal$ ($= \frac{1}{3}$), $igi - 4 - gal$ ($= \frac{1}{4}$), $igi - 5 - gal$ ($= \frac{1}{5}$), and so on, were generally employed.

To denote areas the *gan*, or " acre," was represented by unity ; 6 *gan*, equalling 600 *sares*, or " roods," by the numeral 10 ; 10 *bur* by the same numeral cut by four lines like an X ; 60 *bur* were indicated by the big circle, 600 *bur* by the little circle inside the big one, and 3600 *bur* by this same figure intersected by an X of four strokes.

With the *gur* as a measure of capacity, the numerals of ordinary counting—1, 10, 60, 600—were used. The unit lying on its right side denoted a fifth of a *gur*, and might be repeated as many as four times ; the same figure cut by from one to five strokes represented from one to five-thirtieths of a *gur* respectively.

By the time of Lugalanda, the scribe did not always use the stylus with a circular section for making numerals ; he sometimes used the triangular stylus with which the other signs were traced ; then he obtained slanting wedges instead of circles, and erect wedges instead of semicircles.

The two systems persisted side by side till the age of the kings of Ur, then the curvilinear system disappeared and only the cuneiform system remained. In texts in which they are simultaneously used, it is not apparently due to chance, or the caprice of the scribe. " One of the two was usual for such and such a kind of counting, but it was replaced by the other when it was desired to draw distinctions assisting the clearness of the text, exactly as we use italic characters with the same object." [1]

The survey seems to have been an established institution long before Lugalanda and Urukagina presided over the destinies of Lagash. The people drew up numbered plans, and could calculate the area of the most irregular spaces. The Sumerians had formulæ for finding the areas of triangles, trapezes, and irregular four-sided figures; in the case of polygons with a larger number of sides, they drew an auxiliary figure, more readily measurable, and added to its area those outside it.

The surveyor's linear unit was the reed of six cubits, a reed 2·97 metres long. In measuring fields, any length less than one reed was ignored, and usually areas under a quarter of a *gan* were omitted too; the possible error could not exceed 4·50 *ares* (504 square yards). In the case of lands cultivated as gardens, owing to their higher value and smaller size, the unit of area was the *sare*, the hundredth of a *gan;* only fractions less than half a *sare* were ignored, and the limit of error was nine centiares (10¾ square yards). Finally, for building land, the reed was too rough a measure, and it was replaced by the cubit, and the areas were computed correct to a sixtieth of a *sare*, equal to 58 square decimetres (6¼ square feet).

Manishtusu, king of Agade, had various purchases of large estates engraved on an obelisk. Of these the largest contained 3834 *gan*, or more than 1352 hectares (3095 acres); in some cases the boundaries are mentioned, but more often they are omitted. No particulars are given about the determination of the areas, it is simply noted that the surveyors received presents. [2]

The excavations at Tello have brought to light a number of survey-documents, from the epoch of Agade to that of Ur. [3] Some give in detail the calculations for arriving at the area of fields: length of the sides of auxiliary figure, portions to be added or subtracted, the actual area of the land to be measured. On others plans are given of houses,

---

[1] **I,** vol. XII, p. 121.   [2] **XXIII,** vol. II.
[3] **CIV,** pls. 63–68 and 150.

cities, lands divided into plots, or lands traversed by canals. The unit of measure was no longer the reed of 6 cubits, but the " pole " of 12 cubits, the square of which was exactly a *sare* (30·28 centiares, or 33½ square yards), the hundredth of a *gan*. Thus, on a single tablet from Agade,[1] we find for two pieces of land following data :

20 front (double)　180 side (double)　field of 2 *bur*
17 front (double)　180 side (double)　field of 1 *bur*, *gan*

Now $20 \times 180 = 3600 = 60^2$, and on the other side of the equation, 2 *bur* = 3600 *sares ;* the unit of length is therefore the side of a *sare*, that is a " pole." For the second plot, as in the pre-Sargonic epoch, the area of less than a quarter of a *gan* was neglected, since the product of 17 " poles " by 180 " poles " equals 3060 square " poles," or *sares*, i.e. 1⅔ *gur*, ½ *gan*, and 10 *sares*.

The use of numbered plans was not abandoned in the age of Hammurabi.[2] Building lands were measured correctly to $\frac{1}{240}$ *sare*, or ·147 metres (5⅔ inches).

The Kassite kings introduced innovations into the measurement of lands, or strictly speaking into the form of the deeds. While Manishtusu purchased a piece of land of an area of a definite number of *gan*, the value of which was first reckoned in barley and then converted into money, Kashtiliashu, Nazimaruttash, and the other princes of their dynasty, had properties transferred the extent of which was calculated in *gurs* of barley, the *gur* being estimated at thirty *qa* the great cubit. This small quantity of grain apparently represents conventionally the quantity sown.

This new method of estimating lands persisted till the end of the Neo-Babylonian Empire, though the proportions varied.

The Kassites likewise introduced a new method of reckoning the stock of bricks. From the epoch of Agade the practice had been to measure the side of the stack. The scribe noted its height, length, and breadth. Under the Third Dynasty computation by units began, and this was still the rule under Nabonidus and Artaxerxes I.

[1] **XXIV**, No. 2923.　　　[2] **XCIX, LIX.**

5. MONEY

The Babylonians had no money strictly speaking till the Persian domination. In the earliest times barley was the medium for all transactions. Before the third millennium ingots of copper and silver had been added, and consequently barley and silver were two standards to which the value of everything might be referred.

Their relations varied ; so conventions or customs were imposed for the settlement of certain accounts with one currency or the other, and not with either indifferently. Thus, in the age of Hammurabi, the salaries of royal officials, like the wages of agricultural labourers, were reckoned in barley, and artisans—caulkers, brickmakers, masons, carpenters—were paid in silver like architects or doctors.

It would be interesting to follow the changes in value of the chief articles of commerce from the beginning to the end of the empire, but the data are insufficient, and do not permit of the establishment of any statistics.

Sin-gashid, king of Uruk, praying that his reign might be an unbroken series of years of plenty,[1] expressed the wish that it might be possible to obtain three *gur* of barley, twelve minæ of wool, ten minæ of copper, or thirty *qa* of oil for a shekel of silver. That would have made silver worth six hundred times its weight of copper, or seven hundred and twenty times its weight of wool. In reality prices were higher. Thus in the time of Ammiditana and Ammizaduga, wool was worth twice as much, and oil fetched three times the price mentioned. The value of barley varied during the year and sometimes doubled itself. Under Ammizaduga, it fetched $1\frac{2}{3}$ shekels the *gur* in the fourth month, while at the end of the year, just before harvest, its price rose above 3 shekels.

The value of gold is given in some texts from different epochs : it was worth eight times as much as silver in the epoch of Agade, reached the proportion of ten to one in the eighth year of Bur-Sin, and six to one in Hammurabi's thirty-fifth year, to rise again to twelve to one in the eleventh. year of Nabonidus.

[1] **CV**, p. 315.

6. THE CALENDAR

After the day which nature imposes on all men, the first measure of time to be adopted by the Sumero-Akkadians was the lunar month. Its beginning was regulated by the appearance of the crescent moon in the sky, and it lasted till the next appearance. This empirical method is still in use in Musulman countries to determine the end of the fast of Ramadan, and it was thus that the Jews, till about A.D. 360, when their present calendar was composed, used to determine the beginning of Nisan, the month of the Passover. The new moon, the full moon, and the disappearance of the crescent gave the signal for religious ceremonies. On the two first dates sacrifices were offered in the palace, the last was a day of mourning and desolation.

It was soon judged necessary to take account of a longer period, and attempts were made to find a fixed number of months to coincide with the cycle of the seasons. But there is no common measure between the phases of the moon and the solar year; the realization of an universally accepted civil year had to await the centralization of power in a single hand.

In the pre-Sargonic period the names of the months varied from town to town; at Lagash, at least twenty-five were counted. In the days of the kings of Agade a reform was introduced, or at least some of the names were changed. The kings of Ur did not succeed in imposing an uniform system of nomenclature on their whole empire. Each city still had its own special mode of computation. Even the beginning of the year was variable, and the intercalation of extra months in a different order, without any rule, often caused fresh confusion in the calendars. Can we be surprised at this state of affairs four thousand years ago, when in Europe at the present day in Constantinople Westerners, Greeks, Armenians, Mohammedans, and Jews are still all using different almanacks in a single town?

The selection of the years, in which thirteen months instead of twelve should be reckoned, was made in an empirical manner. Sometimes even one month was intercalated after the sixth, and another was counted after the twelfth, producing a year of fourteen months. At Drehem, in the fifty-fourth year of Dungi, as many as three supplementary months have been noted.[1] Hammurabi included among his reforms that of the calendar.[2] He made it his prerogative to decide personally, when the time had come for replacing the ordinary year, by an intercalary year,[3] and he imposed the same month names on his whole empire.

But no modification was made in the practice established since the kings of Agade whereby each year was designated by an important event anticipated in the course of the year, such as the erection of a statue, the dedication of a temple, the cutting of a canal, or, at a later date, a king's accession, the defeat of a hostile land, a high priest's election. This usage itself marked an advance on the computations of the pre-Sargonic epoch, when people indicated on a tablet by a bare ordinal numeral the number of years of the reigning prince, and when they were content with such formulæ as this : " In that time Entemena was ishakku and Enlitarzi sangu of Ningirsu."

The Kassites simplified the calculation of the years by establishing for each reign an indefinite series starting with the first year after the accession. Their method persisted till the Seleucids, who introduced their own era into Babylonia, where it was still observed under the Arsacids.

7. MEDICINE, ASTRONOMY

Babylonian medicine was purely empirical, and played a less important rôle than magic rites in the cure of disease. When the patient was restless in bed, the maleficent influences of evil spirits within him and around him were detected,[4] and it was the business of the conjurer to drive them away. However, the doctor also played a part. For the ophthalmia, so common in those regions, he applied to the eyes an ointment composed of plants cooked in grease, or a decoction of copper-ore in beer. The pharmacopœia made use of all sorts of ingredients from the mineral, vegetable, or animal kingdoms, and gazelle's dung was not the most disgusting.

[1] **I,** vol. XVII, p. 208.   [2] **I,** vol. XVII, p. 211.   [3] Cf. p. 232 above.
[4] **XCVI,** No. 122 ; **LXV,** A. 831 ; **I,** vol. XVII.

Certain doctors enjoyed a high reputation. Ur-Lugal-edina, whose seal is in the Louvre,[1] was one of the notables of Lagash in the time of Ur-Ningirsu, son of Gudea. In the second millennium the Hittite kings asked the king of Babylon to send them doctors when they, or members of their families, were attacked by serious sickness. The law of Hammurabi ignores them, but it fixes the fees of surgeons according to the client's station, and for any professional fault it imposes very severe sanctions guided by the same considerations.

A text of the fifth century, a sort of introduction to astronomical studies, shows how very rudimentary the science still was at that epoch. The stars and constellations, to the number of seventy-one, are divided in it into three groups, over each of which ruled one of the three great gods of the supreme triad : thirty-three are allotted to Enlil, twenty-three to Anu, and fifty to Ea. A second table gives the heliacal rising of certain important stars. The salaries of the observers is also indicated : 4 minæ per day and 2 minæ per night from the 15th of Tammuz to the 15th of Tebet, 2 minæ per day and 4 minæ per night for the remaining months. A third list includes the simultaneous heliacal risings and settings of fifty-five stars. Another gives the intervals in days between the heliacal risings of sixteen important stars. Among other notes were the time during which certain phenomena were observed at the rising or setting of the stars, fourteen stars of Ellil to be used for controlling observations on the heliacal risings and settings, and the stars and constellations scattered along the moon's course. From observation of the heavens the Babylonian sought above all omens.

8. GEOGRAPHY

He was no less interested in picturing to himself the real configuration of the earth on which he dwelt. This people, who in the earliest times had gone so far with the survey of rural property, also sketched maps of cities and canals

[1] **LXV**, T. 98.

sometimes grouped in a series. A single map of the world has come down to us. The universe is represented by a circle, from whose circumference triangles of varying area project. The circular crown stands for the " bitter river," or Oceanus, which encircles the world wherein Babylonian influence is felt. The city of Babylon itself is marked below and to the right of the centre. Then round the circumference on the inside are ranged reading downwards on the right a city, Assyria, the region of Dêr, the Bit-Yakîn ; the latter region, the most southerly, is separated from Babylon by a band of swamps. Among the lands situated beyond the ocean is one in the north, " where the sun is not seen." Should we admit that the Babylonians had some knowledge of the polar regions ? Or is it not wiser to recall that in the *Epic of Gilgamesh* the hero in his journey to the ends of the earth—probably to the north-west—follows the nocturnal path of the sun in the mountains of Mashu—" the gloom there is dense and there is no light " —in a stretch which he covered in ten double-hours ? [1] The tablet on which this map is drawn bears a copy of an ancient text relating to the campaigns of Sargon of Agade in the Taurus region. [2]

To make up for the almost entire lack of accurate geographical maps, lists were compiled showing, for instance, the distances between two points, or the regions to be traversed to get from one spot to another, or even the bare names of cities, temples, and canals in a given region.

Babylonian scribes had never applied themselves to the compilation of a didactic treatise on any of the disciplines of the mind. Abstraction was utterly incomprehensible to them, and they were content to group in accordance with arbitrary rules individual facts and concrete instances in greater or less number. This is the principle on which geographical and mathematical tablets and divinatory texts, as well as codes of law, were composed. In teaching and in literature the same procedure ruled. Moreover, as in all primitive societies, an idea which had caught its inventor's fancy was repeated as often as possible and in the same terms in the single work. It was then reproduced

---

[1] **LXVI**, pp. 275–277.   [2] **XLI**, *fasc.* 6, p. 92.

indefinitely in subsequent centuries, and the rules of composition in each style were handed down almost unchanged from the beginnings of Sumer and Akkad till after the collapse of the Neo-Babylonian Empire.

To such sources Assyria turned every century for the training of her scribes. The very zeal of the Sargonids for the development of letters and science at the apogee of the Ninevite Empire was often satisfied by having copies of old Babylonian documents made for deposition in their library at Nineveh.

SECOND PART

ASSYRIAN CIVILIZATION

BOOK ONE

HISTORICAL OUTLINE

ASSYRIA lies to the north of Babylonia. It begins with the high plain of Mesopotamia, a little above the junction of the Adhem with the Tigris, and occupies the middle part of the basin of that river as far as the Kurnib. On the east the middle course of the Great Zâb and the spurs of the Zagros separate it from the Kassites. Northward, Mount Masios serves as a frontier. To the west it does not reach the Habur or the Euphrates. This land of triangular outline does not possess the geographical unity of Babylonia. The western part in Mesopotamia is a vast undulating plateau, from which rise some chalky hills ; in the eastern section, beyond the Tigris, are numerous wooded hills and valleys whence flow important streams, the Kurnib, the two Zâbs, and the Adhem, a region rich in metals and fertile in cereals and fruit. On the east the Zagros forms a natural frontier, with its abrupt chains through which only two or three passes, and those impassable during part of the year, exist. On the north, terrace is piled on terrace, buttressing the Armenian massif. To the south the alluvial plain is inhabited by the Babylonians. Only on the west is there no natural boundary, and it is mainly in that direction that the Assyrian power will extend its conquests to the Mediterranean and Egypt. The area of Assyria has been compared by Rawlinson to that of Great Britain, while the extent of Babylonia would be roughly the same as that of Denmark.[1]

In the ruins of Assur, the first capital of Assyria, the oldest documents discovered under a temple of Ishtar are sculptures analogous to the Sumerian, a statue of a seated man, unfortunately mutilated and headless, and an erect statue with great empty eye-sockets and shaven head, but

[1] **XIX**, 1914, No. 54.

wearing a beard on the chin, contrary to the Sumerian usage. The chance of excavation has brought to light at Kala-tepe, near Kara-Eyuk, a mound lying eighteen kilometres north-east of Cæsarea in Cappadocia, some tablets written in Semitic containing theophorous names, compounds of Ashur—Itti-Ashur, Tâba-Ashur, Ashur-malik, Ashur-muttabil. That in this region far away from Assyria

FIG. 39.   Statue found among the ruins of Assur
(Berlin Museum).

there were votaries of Ashur in the twenty-fourth century before the Christian era, has been put beyond the possibility of doubt, since the publication [1] of a tablet belonging to this series bearing on its envelope the impression of a Sumerian cylinder in the name of a servant of Ibi-Sin, the last of the kings of Ur.

This seal is decorated with subjects likewise borrowed from the Sumerian glyptic of that epoch, but treated in an

[1] I, vol. VIII, p. 142.

utterly different style. Already in it we can usually detect
the tendency which was to prevail in Mesopotamian art—
to neglect the modelling of the figures in order to concen-
trate on the external decoration. And in products of this
class, side by side with details suggested by local cults and
customs, the habit is coming into fashion of engraving
the legend in the sense in which it is to be read directly
on the cylinder itself. The texts disclose a civilization
already highly developed outside the sphere of Sumero-
Akkadian culture. They reveal dispositions and characteristic formulæ which recur in Assyria down to the fall of
Nineveh. Thus, on the envelopes, the seals affixed to
authenticate the document are first mentioned, but here
the witnesses apply their seals close to that of the bond-
holder ; at Nineveh, in the days of the Sargonids, these
witnesses were merely mentioned at the end of the agreement.
The years again are denoted, as in Assyria, by eponyms,
and not by notable events, as was the custom in Sumer
and Akkad ; but we cannot yet decide whether the eponym
is the same as in Assyria. Very probably a regular trade
in various textiles, and in metals extracted from the mines
of the Bulgar Dagh, was conducted with Assur. The
caravans went down the Euphrates as far as the junction
of the Habur, and crossed the land of Hana. The culture
of the latter region was exposed to the same influences,
and there the textile industry engaged a large proportion
of the population, just as it did later on.[1]

This group in Asia Minor, these evidences of Sumerian
civilization discovered at Assur, prove that in the twenty-
fifth century the Assyrians already formed a distinct people
in relations with the Sumero-Akkadians. They experienced
influence from the latter, but yet already manifested quite
distinctly a peculiar individuality. Their origin is still
unknown ; they seem to have been spread over a vast area
in the third millennium, from which they may have been
driven back into Assyria proper by the Aryans. Their own
country even must have been occupied by Mitannians, at
least in the region round Nineveh ; east of that town, in
the neighbourhood of the Kerkuk, we find in the second

---

[1] Cf. Contenau, *Trente tablettes cappadociennes* ; S. Smith, *Cappadocian
Tablets in the British Museum.*

millennium some Aryan worshippers of Teshub, one of the
Hittite gods, and the tendency is to connect with the same
race the Kassites settled in the Zagros.

The oldest prince from whom a written document has
come down to us was called Zarikum (*circa* 2400 B.C.). He
was a contemporary and tributary of Bur-Sin, king of Ur.
Before him we hear of Ushpia, to whom the construction
of the fortifications is attributed, and Kikkia, founder of
the temple of Ashur. Irikapkapu, again, was an early
prince ; Adad-Nirari III says that he was king before the
reign of Sulilu, but Sulilu himself is scarcely known from
other sources.

About 2250 B.C. Puzur-Ashir I appears, and beginning
from that moment the list of Assyrian kings continues
almost uninterruptedly till the end of the empire.

Sumu-abum, founder of the First Dynasty of Babylon,
was attacked by Ilushuma of Assur, and seems to have
been defeated ; for the battle is not known to us from any
Babylonian document. This Ilushuma built a temple for
the goddess Ishtar. His son and successor, Erishum, rebuilt
the sanctuary of the national god first erected by Ushpia,
and cut a canal at the foot of the *ziggurat*. His son, Ikunum,
restored the walls of the city, and dedicated a temple to
Ninkigal, probably at Nineveh. Sargon I, who succeeded
him, restored a shrine of Ishtar. Shamshi-Adad I (2123–
2081) was the contemporary and vassal of Hammurabi.
A Babylonian garrison was installed at Assur, and the
Assyrian prince, either by design or of necessity, aided his
overlord in his war with the princes of Larsa. On a deed,
preserved in the University of Pennsylvania Museum, the oath-
formula contains the name of Shamshi-Adad side by side
with that of Hammurabi. The same name recurs also in
the legends of several cylinders in pure Babylonian style.[1]

Thereafter almost unrelieved darkness covers events till
the fifteenth century. Thothmes III of Egypt, in the
twenty-third year of his reign, received an Assyrian embassy,
bringing him three blocks of lapis lazuli and other precious
stones. The Tell el-Amarna letters reveal the international
situation at the end of that century, and the documents

[1] **LIV**, p. XXXVI, note 1.

unearthed at Boghaz-Keui, the site of the ancient Hittite capital, add valuable sidelights. Amenhotep III was occupying the throne of Egypt. The Syrian coast subject to Egypt was divided into two territories, Canaan in the south, Amurru in the north. The immediate neighbour of Amurru was the Hittite realm, extending in Asia Minor across the Taurus, and eastward reaching the Euphrates' bend. There it touched the realm of Mitanni, limited in its turn on the east by Assyria which it had subjugated. The origin of the Hittites and Mitannians is unknown. The latter worshipped Indra, Varuna, and Mithra. They had long played an important rôle in history. The Hittites had invaded Mesopotamia in the twentieth century, captured Babylon, and put an end to the First Dynasty of that city (1925 B.C.). At the epoch of Amenhotep III, their king was called Shubbiluliuma. The ruler of Mitanni, Dushratta, was brother-in-law to the Pharaoh, to whom he had given one of his sisters in marriage. He had been attacked by the Hittites, had successfully repulsed them, and from the booty had set aside a chariot and horses for the king of Egypt, and some pectoral ornaments for the queen, his sister. His power extended to Nineveh, the goddess whereof, revered by Babylonians and Assyrians under the name of Ishtar, seems to have been originally a Mitannian deity. In the previous reign she had made a journey to Egypt, and had retained the most pleasing recollections of the hearty welcome she had received there. She proposed to return thither, and caused the king of Mitanni to announce it.

On one occasion Pharaoh offered Dushratta twenty talents of gold. Ashur-uballit, king of Assyria (*circa* 1370), showed himself jealous, and immediately asked why the same favour had not been shown him. Burnaburiash of Babylon laid claim to suzerainty over Assyria and, hearing of the message sent by Ashur-uballit, complained and protested that the Assyrians, " his subjects," had no right to treat direct with Pharaoh. In reality, all these peoples were disputing the mastery over the Syrian coast, which was their common market, and the strongest of them were the Hittites. They fomented rivalries among the Amorite princes, and endeavoured to detach them from Egypt. They succeeded in controlling the Orontes Valley, but

Amenhotep III sent an army and restored order. Shubbiluliuma took vengeance on Dushratta, harried the frontiers
of Mitanni, then returned to Syria and captured Aleppo.

Amenhotep IV, who had just ascended the throne of
Egypt, does not appear to have worried about the civil
wars raging all through Syria. An Amorite prince, Aziru,
enlarged his own power after a victorious campaign, but
recognized the overlordship of Pharaoh and came to Egypt
to do homage to him. Shubbiluliuma regarded him as a
traitor, attacked and defeated him, seized Syria, and reduced
the Egyptian influence to zero. A revolution broke out in
Mitanni, Dushratta was slain ; his son, Mattiuzza, succeeded
him, and made an alliance with the Hittite king ; but the
old king's nephew, Sutarna, seized the throne and expelled
his cousin, who took refuge at the Hittite court. Assyria
immediately hurried to ravage Mitanni. Shubbiluliuma
betrothed his daughter to Mattiuzza, and restored him to
his rights, but treated him as a vassal. Mursil soon occupied
the Hittite throne, and inherited a great empire extending
eastward to the Assyrian frontier, and southward to Carmel
and Galilee. Defeated by Seti I, near Qadesh, on the
Orontes, and again by Rameses II, he died, and his two
sons, Muttalu and then Hattusil, beheld their power melting
away, till the day that the latter saw himself obliged to
make peace in the twenty-first year of Rameses II (*circa*
1279 B.C.). Soon Egypt in her turn fell into decadence,
and Babylonia lost all influence. That was the moment
chosen by the Hebrews for settling in Canaan, and by bands
of Aramæans for filtering across the frontiers of Assyria and
Babylonia.

Ashur-uballit had to restore the capital, the walls of
which had been recently destroyed, presumably as the
result of a siege. He also had to rebuild a temple at Nineveh.
He fought against the Shubarî, to the north-west of his
kingdom, and enlarged his territory. In Babylonia he
intervened against the Kassite faction who had assassinated
his grandson, Kara-indash II, and secured the throne for
his other grandson, Kurigalzu III. His son, Ellil-nirari
(*circa* 1345), advanced the frontiers of his realm at the
expense of the real Kassite land, and after making a heca-

tomb of Babylonians at Sugagi, he extorted fresh territory from his nephew, Kurigalzu.[1]

Arik-dên-ili (*circa* 1335) conducted at least five victorious campaigns, one of them to the Habur, in the direction of Harran. He brought back thence rich spoils of flocks and herds.

Adad-nirari I (*circa* 1330–1290) informs us about the campaigns of his predecessors. He himself had to fight against the Lullumê on the east, and in the south against Babylon, on whom he imposed a rectification of frontiers. He restored the royal palace and other structures, both at Assur and Nineveh. Shalmaneser I (*circa* 1290–1260), his son, continued the policy of conquest. He made three campaigns in the district of Diarbekir. He defeated Sattuara, king of Hannirabbat, the old Mitanni, who had allied himself with the Hittites and the Aramæan Ahlamê, and established his domination as far as Carchemish, on the Euphrates. The Lullumê on the east were likewise compelled to pay tribute. Having extended the influence of Assyria over the whole of Mesopotamia, Shalmaneser resolved to move the political capital of his realm. Assur lay on the right bank of the Tigris, below the confluence of the Upper Zab ; Shalmaneser chose the site of Kalah, on the left bank, a little above the same junction. In his reign the temple of Ashur was destroyed, apparently by an earthquake, as well as the temple of Ishtar of Nineveh.

His son, Tukulti-Inurta I (*circa* 1260–1240), in the first year of his reign, conquered the lands on the north and north-east, Qutu and Shubari. Then he pillaged and subdued the regions to the north-west as far as Commagene. A coalition was formed against him in Naïri, in the environs of Lake Van. The petty kings of that country were forced to acknowledge his supremacy and pay him tribute. Then he turned against Babylon, where he reigned seven years, and extended his conquests as far as the Persian Gulf. He built a new city, named it after himself, Kar-Tukulti-Inurta, supplied it with water by a canal, built a temple to Ashur, and constructed a palace there. It was there that he fell the victim to an assassin's hand in a rising fomented by his own son, Ashur-nâdin-apla I.

[1] Cf, pp. 47–8, ff, above,

For more than a century the history of Assyria is barely known. The statue of Marduk had been restored to Babylon.[1] Ashur-dân I, the fourth successor of Ashur-nâdin-apla, reconquered the Zab district, which he had had to surrender to Babylonia, and invaded the latter country, whence he brought home rich spoils. About Mutakkil-Nusku we know nothing. Ashur-rêsh-ish I, a warrior (*circa* 1135–1115), warred victoriously with the Ahlamê, the Lullumê, and the Qutê, against whom his predecessors had had to fight so often ; he also triumphed over Nebuchadrezzar I of Babylon. He rebuilt, or restored, the temples of Ashur and Ishtar.

With Tiglath-pileser I, son of Ashur-rêsh-ishi (*circa* 1115–1110), Assyria proceeds to extend her domination right to the Mediterranean.

The inscription on prisms, four copies of which he had deposited in the foundations of the temple of Anu and Adad at Assur, recounts the campaigns of the first five years of his reign. First of all he attacked the Moskians, inhabiting the mountains north of Commagene ; once in the days of Tukulti-Inurta they had paid tribute to Assyria, but for sixty years they had won back complete independence. Twenty thousand men, under the command of five kings, had come down into Commagene. The Assyrian gathered his troops together, crossed the Kashiari hills above Nisibis, poured down upon Commagene, and took six thousand prisoners and an immense booty. He cut off the heads of the slain, and decked the battlements of the cities with these gruesome trophies. Commagene being conquered, was annexed to the empire. In the following year, at the command of Ashur, while his troops were making raids in Kurdistan, the king advanced towards the mountains of Armenia, into the "impenetrable forests which no king had yet explored." In this broken country chariots could not be used, and the advance had to be carried out with infantry only. Kurhie and Haria were laid waste, their gods carried away in captivity, their inhabitants driven into exile, all their property confiscated, and their cities given to the flames. Then followed the war with the land of Naïri. Twenty-three petty kings tried to defend their

[1] Cf. p. 49 above.

territory. They were defeated, and pursued as far as Lake Van ; they had to accept the protectorate of Assur, give their sons as hostages, and provide as tribute twelve hundred horses and two thousand head of cattle.

In the fifth year of his reign, " after fixing a propitious day by the guidance of a dream," Tiglath-pileser set out from Assur, descended to the land of Suhi and, going up the Euphrates, destroyed the Aram of the Two Rivers occupied by the Ahlamê. He reached Carchemish (Jerabis), a Hittite fortress on the Euphrates, crossed the river, and subdued the land of Mutsru, extending from the Taurus to the Anti-Taurus. The conquering progress advanced to the land of Amurru. The king hunted buffalo at the foot of Lebanon, embarked on a vessel from Arvad (Ruad), and slew a shark in the Mediterranean. Only the coast became tributary to Assyria, which did not yet dare to attack the Aramæan kingdoms of Tsôbâ and Damascus, nor even the principalities of Tyre and Sidon, which had reorganized themselves in their independence.

Five years after his accession Tiglath-pileser could boast of having conquered forty-two peoples with their kings.

His immediate successors were incapable of holding together such a vast empire. For two centuries the remoter tributaries shook off the yoke one after the other.

At Assur, Tiglath-pileser rebuilt the temple of Anu and Adad, erected by Shamshi-Adad six and a half centuries earlier, and destroyed in the reign of Ashur-dân, who had made plans for its reconstruction, but had not been able to carry out his project. He restored the other temples of Assyria and the royal palaces, rebuilt the walls of the towns, and imported from the conquered lands horses, asses, cattle and, for the royal hunts, veritable herds of wild animals. He had plants, unknown in Assyria, sought out to be cultivated in the Crown parks and domains.

In the second period of his reign Tiglath-pileser twice made war upon Babylon. His son, Ashur-bêl-kala, made peace, and married the Babylonian king's daughter. Ashur-râbi II could not prevent the Aramæans from retaking the cities of Pitru and Mutkînu. His fourth successor, Adad-nirâri II (*circa* 910–890), began the resurrection of Assyria. He waged a victorious war with Babylonia, and then made an alliance with that country. His son, Tukulti-Inurta II, was a great conqueror (890–884); every year he made a campaign, and composed a journal of his march. That of his last year shows him setting out from Assur, descending the course of the Tartar to the arid desert, then reaching the Tigris, passing on to Dur-Karigalzu and Sippar, going up the Euphrates, back to the Habur, and pursuing his way through the Bît-Hallupi, Shadikani, and Nisibis to the Moskian lands.

FIG. 40.   Stele of Ashur-nâtsir-apla II

Ashur-nâtsir-apla II (884–860), son of Tukulti-Inurta, is one of the Assyrian princes who have left most inscriptions and carved monuments. In the ruins of his palace at Kalah, in the temple of Inurta, on bas-reliefs, on an obelisk, on his statue, on an altar, everywhere, his legends are to be found. The restorer of Kalah, he populated it with prisoners brought from the regions conquered by his arms, and led thither the waters of the Zab by a canal, the banks of which were planted with trees.

In his first campaign he attacked Kurdistan, conquered Kirhi, north of Kashiari, and heaped up in a pyramid the skulls of his enemies. In the autumn of the same year he invaded Commagene, and there received tribute from the Moskians. But Bît-Hallupi had rebelled against its Assyrian governor. The king hastened thither with his troops, captured the usurper and other rebels, had one or two of them put to death, and draped with their skins a monument set up before the city gates ; their headless carcases were impaled, and their heads hung like a crown round the monument. The pretender, carried off to Nineveh, was flayed alive, and his skin was nailed to the city wall.

In 883 B.C., after receiving at Nineveh the presents from the Ilu-ibni, governor of Suhi, he learnt that the Assyrian colony, planted at Halziluha, had revolted. He set out to restore order and, passing the source of the Subnat, he set up his stele beside those of Tiglath-pileser I and Tukulti-Inurta I. He traversed Kashiari and reached Kinabu, the centre of the resistance. The viceroy, taken alive, was skinned, and his skin stretched on the city wall of Damdamusa. Tushha, in Nirbu, was rebuilt ; a palace was raised there, and a royal stele set up. The old Assyrian colonists, reduced by hunger, had fled to Shuprî ; they were settled in that town which was annexed to the royal domain. The whole of Nirbu submitted ; the Bit-Zamani, Shuprî, Nirdum, Urume, and all Naïri came to do homage.

In 881 B.C. a revolt and hostile coalition in the Zagros ; the rebels had blockaded the Babite pass by a rampart. This pass was forced, a hundred and fifty towns and villages were destroyed. In 880 the king returned to Zamua for the third time. The next year he entered Commagene, dedicated a palace at Tulili, and received tribute. He traversed the pass of Ishtarâte and halted at Kibalki. The inhabitants of Kirhi having fled, he pursued them into their mountains, and cut off the hands of all he caught alive. In Naïri he destroyed two hundred and fifty villages. On his return he crossed the Tigris, went down stream as far as the Euphrates, and met the prince of Suhi, an ally of the king of Babylon, who sallied forth to give battle. This prince was defeated, his town captured, and the Babylonian general taken prisoner. Hardly had he returned to Kalah

K

when the Assyrian king learnt of a fresh revolt in Suhi, Hindânu, and Laqê. He traversed in the opposite direction the route once taken by Tukulti-Inurta II, defeated the coalition, and built a town on either bank of the river, Kar-Ashur-natsîr-apla on one side and Nibarti-Ashur on the other.

In 877 B.C. he took march for Carchemish. Sangar, king of the Hittites, made haste to bring him rich presents and offer him hostages. After fording the Euphrates they entered the land of Pattina, whose king, Lubarna, offered an escort, furniture, arms, slaves, precious metals, and animals. The army crossed the Orontes and the Sangura (Saruj); the land of Luhuti, south of Hamath, on the left bank of the Orontes, was conquered. The king proceeded to the Mediterranean and, following the ancient rite of the Sumero-Akkadian princes, washed his hands in the sea and offered sacrifices. Though continuing his westward march, he was content with the tribute from Tyre, Sidon, Byblos, Mahallata, Maitsi, Amurru, and Arvad, and was prudent enough to postpone for the moment a conflict with the mighty kingdom of Damascus.

On his return from this expedition he had cedars felled in the Amanus to provide wood for the construction of Kalah (Nimrud), where he had established his capital. This town, the old summer seat of his predecessors, was rebuilt. The old palace, raised long ago by Shalmaneser I, was pulled down and replaced by a more monumental edifice. A statue of the king in the round and a monolithic stele have been discovered there. The painted bas-reliefs with which the walls were faced allow us to study the Assyrian art of the ninth century, to follow the king to war or to the chase, to watch hostile princes paying homage, and to catch a vivid glimpse of many details of Assyrian life.

Shalmaneser III (859–824), his son, was a warrior. In a reign of thirty-five years he led thirty-two campaigns. No sooner had he come to the throne than he went to Syria to receive the tribute of Tyre and Sidon. In the succeeding years he consolidated his power in Urartu and Naïri. In 854 B.C. he returned to Syria and invaded the kingdom of Hamath, whose king, Irhulêni, was supported by a powerful coalition. Its head was Adad-idri of Damascus, who put into the field 1200 chariots, 12,000 horsemen, 20,000 foot soldiers. Ahab, king of Israel, son-in-law of the king of Sidon, had sent 2000 chariots and 10,000 men. Qué and Mutsru, regions of Cilicia, renowned for their horses, had only sent infantry; four cities of Phœnicia and the Ammonite Ba'sa had given their contingent. An Arab king had mobilized a thousand camels. Tyre and Sidon held aloof from the revolt, and prudently continued to pay their tribute.

The battle was fought at Qarqar, near the Orontes. According to the Assyrian account the plain was too small for the fall of the bodies, and the vast earth was insufficient for their inhumation. The bed of the Orontes was choked with a bank of corpses like a bridge. In reality the issue was indecisive ; Shalmaneser did not dare, or was unable, to take advantage of the success of which he boasts. After a sail on the open sea, he retired to Assyria.

In 853 B.C. he carried war towards the sources of the Tigris, and into the country round Lake Van. Twice he made his way into Babylonia (852, 851) to support Marduk-shum-iddin, against whom his brother, Marduk-bêl-ushâte, had raised the standard of revolt. In 850 a raid was made upon Sangar, king of Carchemish, and Aramê, king of Arnê, at the foot of Mount Amanus. In the next year came a second campaign to the land of Hamath, and a battle against the king of Damascus and his confederates, who were still fighting three years later (846). However, on Adad-idri's death, an usurper, Hazael, seized the throne of Damascus. Ahab, too, had disappeared, and the league dissolved. When the Assyrian king returned to the charge in 842, Hazael faced him alone. He had entrenched himself on the Sanir, at the entry to Coele Syria, but he could not withstand the assault and retired to Damascus. The Assyrian army wasted the surrounding country, ravaged Haurân, and returned to encamp at the mouth of the Nahr-el-Kelb, whither Tyre, Sidon, and Israel brought their tribute.

The principal pictorial monuments of the reign are an obelisk decorated with reliefs and some plaques of hammered bronze found in the ruins of the summer-palace built at Imgur-Ellil (Balawât).

Its closing years were darkened by the revolt of the king's eldest son, Ashur-danin-apla, who attracted to his side most of the cities in Assyria. It had lasted four years when Shalmaneser died (824). His younger son, Shamshi-Adad V, had to continue the struggle for a further two years before bringing it to a triumphal conclusion. It was also necessary to undertake hostilities against Naïri, where he conducted three campaigns. He interfered, moreover, in Babylonia and

Fig. 41. Tribute brought by Jehu, king of Israel (Obelisk of Shalmaneser II, British Museum).

routed Marduk-balâtsu-iqbi at Dur-Papsukal. Later he defeated and carried off captive Bau-ahê-iddin, Marduk-balâtsu-iqbi's successor. The name of his wife, Sammuramat, whose stele has been discovered at Assur, is still famous in the Greek form, Semiramis. During this reign the Assyrian power underwent a brief eclipse ; intestine strife had weakened it, and when the king laid down the frontiers of his empire he dare not push them west of the Euphrates.

Adad-nirari III, his son (810–782 B.C.), embraced within them not only all the conquests of Shalmaneser III, but extended them from the Persian Gulf and the borders of Elam to the Desert of Egypt. To the east and north the advance was negligible. The Medes were beginning to be restless and Urartu, vanquished by Shalmaneser in 829 and by Shamshi-Adad in 819 B.C., would not accept defeat, but took advantage of every opportunity to try and win back independence.

Shalmaneser IV (782–772) warred against the Aramæans, who were endeavouring to expand into Mesopotamia. He conducted six campaigns in Urartu, one in the direction of Mount Amanus, and two others, against Damascus (773) and the city of Hazrak (772) respectively.

Ashur-dân III (772–754 B.C.) continued the struggle with the Aramæans (769), sent an expedition to Media in 766, and against Hazrak in the following year. Pestilence stalked through Assyria ; an eclipse of the sun took place in Simannu (763), it was enough to make men think of a punishment from heaven. Assur revolted ; many another town followed her example. Only ten years after his first expedition against Hazrak could the king return against that town.

For the first four years of Adad-nirari IV (754–746) there were no wars. Then in 749 and 748 B.C. he was at war with Namri beyond the Lesser Zab. In 746 B.C. Kalah revolted ; Tiglath-pileser III, who was perhaps one of the king's brothers, met the insurgents, and the next year placed the crown on his own head. He was a very great prince (745–727). He raised Assyria above all her neighbours and established her supreme without a rival. Assuming the crown on the 13th of Aiaru, 745 B.C., he attacked Nabonassar of Babylon in the autumn of that year, pillaged one or two towns in Akkad, and carried off their gods into captivity. On the death of Nabonassar he took advantage of the civil war to return to Akkad, " take the hand of Bêl," and make himself " king of Sumer and Akkad, king of the four regions " under the name of Pulu (729).

The Aramæans had seized the opportunity offered by the momentary decline of Assyria to spread into Mesopotamia. Tiglath-pileser knew no less than thirty-five tribes of them " settled on the banks of the Tigris, the Euphrates, the Surappu, and as far as the Uknu (Kerkha), on the shores of the Lower Sea."

He made four campaigns against the city of Arpad and interfered in the internal affairs of Iôdi in order to restore to the throne the Carian Panammu II, whose father had been put to death by an usurper. Commagene, Damascus, Tyre and Sidon, Byblos, Que, Carchemish, Hamath, Gurgum, Melid, other cities in Cilicia and Melitene, and finally Zabibe, queen of Saba in Arabia, presented tribute to him.

Inaugurating a new method of conquest, Tiglath-pileser III deported the inhabitants of the devastated regions and often replaced the vanquished kings by Assyrian governors. In Hamath on the coast he settled people brought from Lullumu in the Zagros, and from Naïri near Lake Van.

In 737 B.C. there was a war in the east against the Medes, in 735 a fresh expansion westward, a campaign in Philistia, the sack of Gaza, and the establishment of Hoshea on the throne of Israel. In 733 and 732 wars with Damascus. The Arabs who dwelt " on the bounds of the lands of the west " vied with one another in hastily sending for the first time gold, silver, camels, and perfumes : they came from Teima, Saba, Badana in the land of Madian, and many other cities.

A revolt against his creature, Hoshea, required his intervention in Israel. At Askalon he confirmed in power Rukibtu, whose father had just abdicated and, as the price of his intervention, he took away part of his principality. He set up a governor over the Arabs themselves.

On his death Tiglath-pileser left to his son an empire wider and more strongly organized than any before it.

Shalmaneser V (727–722) reigned six years. At Babylon he was known by the name of Ululaï. Since the campaign of 783 B.C. he had been a governor of Phœnicia ; when he returned thence to Assur, Tyre revolted. He was obliged to revisit the shores of the Mediterranean and to go south to receive Hoshea's tribute. Soon the king of Israel was conspiring with Egypt, and the Assyrian army besieged his capital, Samaria, for three years.

THE SARGONIDS

Shalmaneser died in the tenth month of 722 B.C., and a few days later Sargon II (722–705), of unknown origin, ascended the throne of Assyria. Before the end of the year Samaria succumbed. Following the system inaugurated by Tiglath-pileser III, the Israelites were deported, some into the district of Harran, some to the banks of the Habur, some finally to Media. They were replaced by Aramæans from the region of Hamath, and to these were added Arabs in 715 and the people of Kutha and Babylon in 709.

At the beginning of 721 B.C. Babylon rebelled. The Aramæan, Merodach-Baladan II of Bît-Yakîn, seized the power and reigned twelve years. He made an alliance with Humbanigash, king of Elam, who beat the Assyrians at Dêr.

Meanwhile Egypt was growing alarmed at the advance of Assyria on the Mediterranean coast. Sib'u, the commander-in-chief of Pharaoh's armies, who at the beginning of the reign had been negotiating with Hoshea of Israel, succeeded in getting together a league guided by Yaü-bi°di, king of Hamath. Arpad, Simirra, Damascus, and Samaria lent it their support. As in the time of Shalmaneser III, the battle was fought at Qarqar. Yaü-bi°di was taken prisoner and flayed alive. Hamath was settled with Assyrians under the command of a general.

The coalition reformed further south ; Sib'u put himself at the head and brought the king of Gaza with him. Sargon attacked them ; they retreated on Rapihi (Raphia) on the frontier of Egypt. Under the pressure of the Assyrians Sib'u fled ; the king of Gaza was carried off to Assyria a prisoner.

In the north of the empire an ambitious chief of Urartu, Ursa I, had been trying for ten years to hatch plots. At his instigation in 719 B.C. Mitatti of Zikartu had seized two cities, and that without striking a blow. They were recaptured and destroyed by fire ; their inhabitants were deported to Syria. On the west, under the same influence, the king of the Moschi, Midas, son of the Phrygian Gordius, caused trouble. In 717 B.C. Pisiris, the Hittite king of Carchemish, was deposed ; his city became an Assyrian colony. In the following years fresh campaigns were undertaken in Urartu ; in 716 devastation of the territory between Lakes Van and Urmia ; in 715 a new raid ; in 714 the final campaign ending with the death of Ursa.

Sargon turned once more upon Cilicia, Tabal, and Musku ; in 713 B.C. he extended his dominions as far as the Halys, and imported thence stone, metals, and precious woods for the construction of Dur-Sharrukîn, the new town he founded east of Nineveh on the site of the village of Maganuba.

The year 711 was marked by an expedition to Philistia. The king of Ashdod had rebelled and, under Egyptian influence, had sought to stir up the Philistines, Jews, Edomites, and Moabites to revolt. He had been dethroned, but the people refused to accept the new king imposed by Assyria. Gath and the two Ashdods were conquered and annexed to the empire under the charge of governors-general. Sargon then attempted to reconquer Babylonia. The tribe of Gambulu submitted on the first assault ; others ranged themselves along the Kerkha, where they were blockaded and forced to surrender. A demonstration was made on the frontiers of Elam, and Merodach-baladan fled. The priests of Babylon opened the gates of the city to the victor ; at the beginning of 709 B.C. the king of Assyria " took the hand of Bêl," and became the legitimate sovereign of Babylon. The region of the Lower Euphrates pacified, exiles from the Hittite countries and Commagene were settled there. Blockhouses were established all along the frontier of Elam.

For the first time the king of Dilmun on the Persian Gulf sent tribute, as did Midas, now finally vanquished. From the island of Cyprus seven kings dispatched gifts and gave permission for the erection of a stele at Citium (Larnaka), on which Sargon had his royal portrait engraved with the symbols of the high gods of Babylon and Assyria.

In 708 Commagene was reduced to an Assyrian province under the control of a governor provided with considerable military forces. In the next year, after a journey in the south of Chaldæa, Sargon formally opened the palace and city of Dur-Sharrukîn. He was not destined to enjoy it for long. In the first months of 705 B.C. he died a violent death.

Sargon had perfected the system of organization instituted by Tiglath-pileser. Not only had he deported vanquished peoples and mingled their various races, but he had initiated a new method of fusion and domination by settling Assyrians permanently in the conquered cities. Still the peculiar vitality of the transplanted populations continued to assert itself, and his successors would have to fight to maintain the cohesion of the whole.

Sargon created the library of Nineveh. He encouraged trade by the establishment of new markets and agriculture by the creation of reservoirs and canals. His palace of Dur-

Sharrukîn was adorned with bas-reliefs, which it is interesting to compare with those in the palace of Ashur-natsir-apla. The subjects treated are often the same, but the technique has changed; the personages have become bigger than natural size, and the relief is accentuated. The bronze lion, chained like a watch-dog at the gates of this palace, is one of the finest specimens of Assyrian art.[1]

Scarcely had Sennacherib (705–681 B.C.), son of Sargon, ascended the throne, when a pretender seized the power at Babylon. Merodach-baladan sallied forth from his swamp, chased the pretender for the next month (703), and reigned for nine months. As before, he leaned upon Elamite forces for support. As soon as the king of Assyria marched out to attack him, he gathered together his army near Kish, three leagues from his capital. Conquering and welcomed in triumph into Babylon, the Assyrian installed there as viceroy, Bêl-ibni, a Babylonian educated at his court (703–700). Next he spent a whole year in destroying the Aramæan tribes of the Lower Euphrates, among whom Arabs had been filtering in and had already become numerous at Uruk and Nippur in Sumer, and at Kish and Kutha in Akkad. He turned again against the Aramæans of Mesopotamia and deported more than two thousand of them, made a raid upon the Kassites, extended the powers of the governor of Arapha over them, and completed his work in the east by some demonstrations on the frontier of the Medes.

In the west the king of Tyre had been unable to tolerate the submission to Assyria of the Cypriote princes, once his tributaries and clients of his city. He had sent troops to recapture Citium, the city where Sargon had had his stele set up. In 701 B.C. Sennacherib raised a strong army and marched against Tyre. Sidon, Acre, and the other cities of the coast attempted no resistance, but opened their gates to the Assyrians. The king of Tyre fled to Cyprus, where he was to die; the citizens organized the defence of the town, which remained inviolate. Phœnicia, organized as a province, beheld herself subject to tribute.

In Canaan Egypt was ever fomenting disorder. Zedekiah of Ascalon was the moving spirit in the plot; Joppa, Ekron and Jerusalem followed his lead. Zedekiah was defeated and

[1] Fig. 53, p. 332.

taken prisoner ; the territory of Joppa was pillaged. But the princes of the Delta and Pharaoh sent help. A great battle was fought in the plain south of Ekron. The Assyrian came out victorious, captured the city and hanged the corpses of the principal rebels from the walls. He then turned upon Judæa, seized forty-six walled villages and laid siege to Jerusalem. The garrison of the city grew mutinous ; king Hezekiah, obliged to sue for terms, pledged himself to a tribute of thirty talents of gold and ten times that weight of silver ; he saw himself, moreover, obliged to submit to a reduction of territory.

On his return to Assyria, Sennacherib was constrained to march against Bêl-ibni, king of Babylon, who had proved unfaithful to his oath. He pursued the Chaldæan Mushêzib-Marduk, who had proclaimed his independence, and Merodach-baladan II, who abandoned the Bît-Yakîn, took ship and fled to Nagiti-raqqi. Bêl-ibni, having been carried off to captivity, Ashur-nâdin-shumi, son of the Assyrian king, was set upon the throne of Babylon (700–693).

In 699 B.C. there was a campaign in Kurdistan and the region west of Lake Van. In 698 an army went to reduce Cilicia, the governor whereof had raised the standard of revolt. He was taken prisoner, brought to Nineveh, and flayed alive. In 695 an expedition was made to the land of Tabal.

The year 694 B.C. was marked by a quite new military operation. Resolved to pursue Merodach-baladan by sea to Elam, Sennacherib yet had no fleet. He had one built, partly at Kar-Shulmanu-asharidu (Birejik) on the Euphrates, partly at Nineveh on the Tigris. The work lasted a whole year. The workmen were Tyrians, Sidonians, and Cypriotes. The vessels from Nineveh sailed down stream as far as Opis, whence they were transported overland to the canal Arahtu, by which they reached the Euphrates. The muster took place at Bâb-Salimeti, and the whole fleet sailed with the wind towards the mouth of the Ulæus. Merodach-baladan was defeated, his warriors were carried into captivity with the Elamite troops, who had supported him. Halludush, king of Elam, at once took the field and invaded Babylonia. The inhabitants rebelled against Ashur-nâdin-shumi, delivered him over to the enemy, and proclaimed a certain Nergal-shêzib king. The Assyrian army returned, spread carnage everywhere, and captured Nergal-shêzib near Nippur. Mushêzib-Marduk reappeared and made an alliance with Elam.

At the end of 693 the Assyrian king endeavoured to profit by a revolution in Elam, in which Kutur-Nahhunte had dethroned Halludush. At first the Elamites retreated into the mountains, but at the beginning of 692 rain and snow fell so copiously that the Assyrian army was compelled to beat a retreat. Shortly afterwards Kutur-Nahhunte died, and his younger brother, Ummanigash, succeeded him. At the request of the king of Babylon he sent troops against Assyria. A great battle was fought at Halule, not far from the junction of the Turnat with the Tigris. It was indecisive (690).

In the same year, Sennacherib imposed his yoke on some Arab tribes, whose troops fled in the direction of Adummatu (El-Jôl), at the entrance to Nefud, " a place of thirst where there was neither food nor drink." The king of Assyria skirted the edge of the desert as far as the Egyptian frontier and pitched his camp at Lachish, whence he sent messengers to Hezekiah, king of Judah. Taharqu, king of Ethiopia, hastened to the scene. The Assyrian army prepared for battle. Already exhausted by the privations endured in the desert region, it was rapidly decimated by a plague spread by rats ; the king had to renounce his plans for battle and gave the order for retreat.

At Babylon, Mushêzib-Marduk was causing further unrest. Sennacherib resolved to make an end of him. The city was taken, razed to the ground, set on fire, and flooded. Eight years later, on the 20th of Tebet, 681 B.C., the king was slain at prayer in a temple by his son, Arab-Malkat, and by Nabu-shar-utsur, the eponym of the year.

Sennacherib had restored Nineveh, deserted by Sargon, furnished it with an ample supply of drinking-water, and built a palace there adorned with bas-reliefs in which upper rows of panels and a much more painstaking application to detail begin to appear. He had enlarged the library founded by his father and introduced into Assyria a number of new plants and trees.

Arad-Malkat did not enjoy the fruits of his parricide. As he was planning to proclaim himself king, his brother, Esarhaddon (681–668 B.C.), assembled his own partisans, gave battle, defeated him, and had himself crowned forty-two days after the death of Sennacherib.

Son of a Babylonian woman, he proposed to raise anew on its ruins, the wrecked capital. Nabu-zêr-kênu-lishir, son of Merodach-baladan II, was already trying to make capital out of the change of sovereign. He stirred up the Land of the Sea to revolt and came to besiege Ur. He was defeated and forced to flee to Elam, where Hummanaldash II (681–675) put him to death. His brother, Na'id-Marduk, immediately submitted.

In Syria, Pharaoh was trying to recover his influence. At his instigation Abdi-Milkutti, king of Sidon, revolted. A first campaign ended in the sack of the city ; in 676 B.C. he would be captured and his head cut off and carried to Nineveh. Sanduarri, king of Sis in Cilicia, who had been in league with him, met the same fate. The people were deported en masse ; Sidon was replaced by a new city, Kar-Ashur-aha-iddin, under an Assyrian governor and peopled by Chaldæans taken prisoner in the first year of the reign.

In Babylonia the Aramæans, especially the tribe of Bît-Dakuri, had plotted fresh intrigues, and had actually persuaded Hummanaldash to lend them tangible support. The Elamite army seized Sippar, but, on the sudden death of the king, his successor, Urtaku, did not continue hostilities.

Esarhaddon wished to carry on the secular conflict with Egypt, and to penetrate into the Delta, whither no Assyrian army had yet advanced. He forced his way as far as the River of Egypt (Wâdi-el-Arish) (675), but found himself summoned home to face a coalition of Aryans, Scyths, and Medes, who were threatening the northern and eastern frontiers of the empire. Coming from the continent of Europe, two groups of Scythians, the Ashkuzaï and the Cimmerians, had been defeated by Sargon (720). The Cimmerians had then slipped away westward and settled in the basins of the Araxes and the Halys. The Ashkuzaï had taken up their abode near the Mannæans, not far from Lake Van. Esarhaddon attacked Teushpâ, the Cimmerian chief, and drove him into Asia Minor. He beat the Ashkuzaï in alliance with the Mannæans.

The Assyrian army was again dispatched against Egypt, not by the route through Syria, but by the desert way that

Sennacherib had already followed. On their advance they subdued some Arab tribes whose petty kings were executed. Scarcely had the army reached the Syrian desert than it had to return to meet the Elamites and the Medes (673). The Gambulu took Assyria's side against Elam, and the kings

Fig. 42. Stele of Esarhaddon (Sinjerli, Berlin Museum).

of the Medes, hunted to the very foot of Demavand, had to submit and pay tribute.

In the whole of Syria, and even in Cyprus, levies were called out to transport to Nineveh the materials needed for the building of a new palace. Ba'al, king of Tyre, had sworn a solemn treaty with Assyria ; that did not prevent him from plotting with Taharqu, king of Ethiopia. His city was blockaded at the beginning of 671 B.C., and the Assyrian army passed on southward to Rapihi (Tell-Rifah), whither the Arabs brought camels for the crossing of the desert. For the first time the army made its way into Egypt. In fifteen days it went down as far as Memphis, fighting continuous actions en route. On the 22nd of Tammuz (July), after half a day's resistance, the city surrendered. Taharqu had fled south ; his wife, his women, and his sons were made prisoners. In the conquered towns the old princes were re-established in their dignities, but Assyrian lieutenants and scribes were attached to their courts.

In Assyria the rumblings of revolution were audible. In 670 B.C. the king slew at arms many of his nobles who would not accept without a murmur the choice of Ashurbanipal, Esarhaddon's younger son, as heir apparent to the Assyrian crown, while only the throne of Babylon was allotted to his elder son, Shamash-shum-ukîn.

Next year fresh intervention was needed in Egypt, where Taharqu had reappeared and retaken Memphis. Esarhaddon took the field, but soon, laid low by sickness, he died on the 10th of Marheshwan (October–November), 669 B.C.

Ashurbanipal (669–626) ordered the commander-in-chief to continue the march and assemble all the forces of the vassal countries he passed through. Taharqu's army was beaten near Karbanit in the Delta, and the Assyrians marched up the Nile Valley as far as Thebes. The land was re-organized, but no sooner had the troops regained Syria than three kings of the Delta conspired to make themselves independent. The whole of Lower Egypt was again invaded; Saïs, Mendes, and Tanis were sacked. On the death of Taharqu (666), his nephew Tandamane (Tanut-Amon), captured Thebes and Unu (Heliopolis) and marched upon Memphis, where the Assyrian police forces were concentrated. The Ninevite army reached the scene, drove the Ethiopian southward, pressed him into Nubia, and gave the city of Thebes over to plunder. Among the trophies of victory it carried home two obelisks.

One result of this campaign was the pacification of Syria, where no king dare conspire any more. The renown of Ashurbanipal was bruited abroad throughout Asia Minor. Gyges of Lydia sent an embassy to him and solicited his aid in the struggle with the Cimmerians, who were threatening his realm. While Lydia fought these Aryans, Assyria was to attack their allies, the Mannæans and Medes (*circa* 660), who had succeeded in combining under a single chief.

Shamash-shum-ukîn asked his brother for aid against the Elamites who, with the connivance of the Gambulæans, had descended upon Babylonia. Urtaku, their king, was defeated and died (661). An usurper, Teumman, seized the throne and demanded the surrender of the Elamite princes who had sought refuge at Nineveh. This caused a fresh war. Teumman was defeated at Tulliz, south of Susa ; his head was carried off as a trophy. Elam was divided into two kingdoms, where two sons of Urtaku, Humbanigash II and Tammaritu, were enthroned.

War was to be rekindled by the action of Shamash-shum-ukîn. About 652 B.C. this prince made a coalition against his brother which was joined by all the princes of Chaldæa. Humbanigash gave his adherence to it ; the mountain people followed his lead. Westward it reached through Arabia to the Sinai peninsula and Syria. Its suppression was prompt and stern. Babylon was put to fire and sword. Shamash-shum-ukîn shut himself up in his own palace, kindled a great fire there and perished in the flames. Chaldæa was parcelled out among Assyrian governors (648).

In Elam, Tammaritu had dethroned his brother and joined the Babylonian party too. An usurper, Indabigash, supplanted him, and was himself soon displaced by Ummanaldasi, then by Umbahabua. The Assyrian army marched upon Susa and restored Tammaritu. Ummanaldasi was not slow to emerge again, and a fresh insurrection ended in the sack and destruction of Susa (640). Not even the dead were respected ; their bones were carried off to Assyria, and their shades deprived of rest by the abolition of the funerary offerings. In Egypt, Psammetichus had tried to form a league, and had received reinforcements from Gyges, the Lydian. The cuneiform records are silent about the suppression of this revolt ; they only mention the death of Gyges in a conflict with the Cimmerians, and the message sent by his son to the Assyrian king to acknowledge his vassalage.

Several expeditions were undertaken against the Arabs.

Immediately after the capture of Babylon a first raid had reached Nabatene, whose king had humbly made a seeming submission. A return was soon necessary, and the Arabs endeavoured to entice the Assyrian host into the desert, but it took the camps of the Atar-samâin and of the men of Kedar. Uate, son of Bir-Dadda, once crowned by the Assyrians, made good his escape ; he was pursued. Pestilence and famine stalked abroad among the Arabs, who betrayed their king and surrendered him to the foe. Carried off to Nineveh, he was fastened by his lower jaw to a dog's chain, and exposed at the east gate of the city.

Assyria had reached its apogee. The empire was wider than it had ever been ; Nineveh was surfeited with wealth ; captive princes had dragged Ashurbanipal's car as he went up into the temple to return thanks to the deity for making him ever victorious. In the library, founded by Sargon, the most important documents of Babylonian and Assyrian literature had been collected ; the ceremonial halls of the palaces were adorned with reliefs, some of which are artistic masterpieces.

The narrative of the *Annals* breaks off in the year 636 B.C. No account whatever is to be found in them of the conflict which, in less than thirty years, was destined to bring to the dust this colossal empire.

To the east, on the table-land of Iran, a power had grown up which would invade the territory of Ashur, lay siege to Nineveh, and wipe it off the face of the earth for ever. Come perhaps from Europe across the Caucasus, the Medes and the Persians had settled there in the south and north respectively. In the ninth century the Assyrians came into conflict with the Median tribes for the first time ; in the following century Sargon had deported some to Syria and replaced them by Samaritans and other conquered peoples. In his reign a certain Daïaukku, the Deioces of the Greeks, had succeeded in uniting several of these tribes, had himself proclaimed king, and chose Ecbatana as his capital. Fravartis (Phraortes, *circa* 647–625) succeeded him, annexed some small neighbour states, and triumphed over the Persians, whose king, Teispes, had taken advantage of the destruction of Susa to seize part of Elam, and have himself proclaimed king of Anshan. The Mede then attacked Assyria, but was left upon the field of battle with most of his warriors.

Cyaxares, his son, reorganized the army after the Assyrian model and, when he entered the field again, the Assyrian generals were conquered and Nineveh was besieged. But then a new ethnic group took part in the conflict, the Scyths, who, coming from Europe, had been for over a century in relations with Assyria. They attacked the Medes in the rear, beat them north of Lake Urmia, ravaged their territory, then fell upon Assyria, burned Kalah and Assur, and destroyed everything in their wake.

Ashurbanipal had died in 625–624 B.C., and two of his sons had occupied the throne in turn, not without conflicts with pretenders. The second, Sin-shar-utsur, only extended his sway outside Assyria over a few Babylonian cities that had remained loyal. The Chaldæan, Nabopolassar, governor of Babylon, had been proclaimed king, and promptly made an alliance with the Medes. The latter besieged Nineveh with the help of the Babylonians and the Scythians. The city was taken and destroyed by fire and flood (612). An Assyrian army was reformed then at Harran, where a new king, Ashur-uballit, was proclaimed. He had the support of the Egyptians who had become the allies of the Assyrians some years previously, through fear of the Median peril. Attacked in 610 B.C. by Nabonassar, who was joined by the Scyths, Ashur-uballit was compelled to abandon Harran and crossed the Euphrates. He came back in 609, at the head of an Egyptian army and met his final defeat.[1] The Assyrian Empire was crushed for ever. And the peoples, delivered from her yoke, echoed the words of the Hebrew prophet : " All that hear the bruit of thee shall clap their hands over thee ; for upon whom hath not thy wickedness passed continually ? "[2]

[1] CXIV.   [2] Nahum iii, 19.

CHRONOLOGICAL TABLE OF ASSYRIAN PRINCES AND SYNCHRONISMS WITH RULERS OF SUMER AND AKKAD

The sign .. precedes the names of Assyrian princes whose inscriptions are extant.

A stroke — indicates a synchronism.

Ushpia ⎱ Order unknown,
Kikia ⎰ cited by later kings
Iri-kapkapu
Sulilu ?
..Zarikum   c. 2400 B.C.—Bur-Sin, king of Ur

1.	Puzur-Ashir I	**1st Dynasty of Babylon.**	
2...	Shalim-Ahum		
3...	Ilushuma I	c. 2220—1. Sumu-abum 2225–2212 B.C.	
4...	Erishum I	c. 2200—2. Sumu-la-ilum 2212–2176	
5...	Ikunum	3. Zabium 2175–2162	
6.	Sargon I		
7.	Puzur-Ashir II	4. Abil-sin 2161–2144	
8.	Ahi-Ashir	5. Sin-muballit 2143–2124	
9.	Rîm-Sin	6. Hammurabi 2123–2081	
10.	Ilushuma II		
11.	Erishum II		**2nd Dynasty**
12.	Shamshi-Adad I		
13.	Ishme-Dagan I	7. Samsu-iluna 2080–2043	—Iluma-ilum
14.	——ashshat	8. Abêshu 2042–2015	Itti-ili-nibi
15.	Rimush	9. Ammiditana 2014–1978	Dâmiq-ilishu
16.	Adasi	10. Ammizaduga 1977–1957	
17.	Bêl-bâni	11. Samsu-ditana 1956–1925	Ishkibal
18.	Shabaia		Shushshi
19.	Sharma-Adad I		Gulkishar
20.	Gizil-Sin		——ren
21.	Zimzaia		Peshdagal-daramash
22.	Lulaia		Adarakalana
23.	Pân-Ninua		Ekurulana
24.	Sharma-Adad II	**3rd Dynasty**	Melamkurkura
25.	Erishum III		Ea-gâmil
26.	Shamshi-Adad	1. Gandash c. 1761–1747	
		2. Agum I c. 1745–1724	
		3. Kashtiliash I c. 1723–1702	
		4. Abirattash c. 1701–1694	
		5. Kashtiliash II	
		6. Tazzigurumash	
		7. Harbashipak	
		8. ——	
		9. Agum II	
27.	Ishme-Dagan II	10. Kurigalzu I	
28.	Shamshi-Adad III	11. Melishipak	
29.	——		
30.	Puzur-Ashir III	12. Nazimaruttash I	
31.	Enlil-hâtsir I		
32.	Nur-ili		
33.	Ishme-Dagan III		
34...	Ashir-nirâri I	13. Burnaburiash I	
35...	Puzir-Ashir IV	—	
36.	Enlil-nâtsir II	14. Kashtiliash III	
37.	Ashir-râbi I	15. Agum III	
38.	Ashir-nirâri II		

	3RD DYNASTY	EGYPT
39. Ashir-bêl-nishêshu	16. Kara-indash I	—Amenhotep III.
		c. 1413–1377 B.C.
40. Ashir-rîm-nishêshu	17. Kurigalzu II	
41...Ashur-nâdin-ahi	—18. Kadashman-Ellil I	
42...Erîba-Adad	—19. Burnaburiash II	—Amenhotep IV.
		c. 1376–1361
43...Ashur-uballit	—20. Kara-indash II	
	—21. Kadashman-Harbe I	B.C.
	Nazibugash, usurper	
	—22. Kurigalzu III	23 years c. 1357–1335
44...Ellil-nirâri	—	
45...Arik-dên-ili		
46...Adad-nirâri I	—	
	—23. Nazi-maruttash II	26 years c. 1334–1309
	—24. Kadashman-Turgu	17 „ c. 1308–1292
47...Shalmaneser I	—25. Kadashman-Ellil II	6 „ c. 1291–1286
	26. Kudur-Ellil	9 „ c. 1285–1277
48...Tukulti-Inurta I	27. Shagarakti-Shuriash	13 „ c. 1276–1264
	28. Kashtiliash III	8 „ c. 1263–1256
	29. Ellil-nâdin-shum	1½ „ c. 1255–1254
	30. Kadashman-Harbe II	1½ „ c. 1254–1253
	31. Adad-shum-iddin	6 „ c. 1252–1247
49...Ashur-nâdin-apla I		
50...Ashur-nirâri III	—32. Adad-shum-utsur	30 „ c. 1246–1217
6 years		
51. Ellil-kudur-utsur		
5 years		
52. Inurta-apal-Ekur I	33. Melishipak II	15 „ c. 1216–1202
	34. Merodach-baladan I	13 „ c. 1201–1187
53. Ashur-dân I	—35. Zababa-shum-iddin	1 year c. 1188
	36. Ellil-nadin-ahê	3 years c. 1187–1185

	4TH DYNASTY	
54. Inurti-tukulti-Ashur	1. Marduk-shapik-zêrim	17 years c. 1184–1168
55. Mutakil-Nusku	2. Inurta-nadin-shumi	6 „ c. 1168–1162
56...Ashur-rêsh-ishi I	— 3. Nebuchadrezzar I	
	— 4. Ellil-nadin-apli	
57. Tiglath-pileser I	— 5. Marduk-nadin-ahê	
58. Inurta-apal-Ekur II	6. Itti-Marduk-balâti	
59. Ashur-bêl-kala I	— 7. Marduk-shapik-zêr-mâtim	
	— 8. Adad-apal-iddin	22 years c. 1095–1074
60. Ellil-râbi		
61. Ashur-bêl-kala II	9. Marduk-ahê	1½ „ c. 1073
	10. Marduk-zêr	12 „ c. 1072–1061
	11. Marduk-shum-libur	8 „ c. 1060–1053

	5TH DYNASTY	
62. Eribâ——	1. Shimmash-Shipak	18 years c. 1052–1035
63. Shamshi-Adad IV	2. Ea-mukin-shumi	5 m'ths c. 1035
64. Ashur-nâtsir-apla I	3. Kashdu-nadin-ahê	3 years c. 1034–1032
19 years		

	6TH DYNASTY	
65. Shalmaneser II 12 years	1. Ulmash-shakîn-shumı	17 years c. 1031–1015
66. Ashur-nirâri IV 6 „	2. Inurta-kudur-utsur	3 „ c. 1014–1012
67. Ashur-râbi II	3. Shiriqtu-Shuqamuna	3 m'ths c. 1012

	7TH DYNASTY	
68...Ashur-rêsh-ishi II	Mâr-biti-apal-utsur	6 years c. 1011–1006

	8TH DYNASTY	B.C.
69...Tiglath-pileser II	— 1. Nabu-mukîn-apli 36 years	c. 1005–970
	— 2. Inurta-kudur-utsur II	c. 970
	— 3. Mâr-bîti-ahi-iddin	c. 970–946
70...Ashur-dân II	— 4. Shamash-mudammiq	c. 940–905
71...Adad-nirâri II		
910–890 B.C.		
	— 5. Nabu-shum-ukîn	c. 905–885
72...Tukulti-Inurta II		
890–884		
	— 6. Nabu-apla-iddin	c. 885–852
73...Ashur-nâtsir-apla II		
884–859		
74...Shalmaneser III		
859–824		
	7. Marduk-zakir-shum	c. 852–822
Ashur-danin-apla,		
usurper		
75...Shamshi-Adad V		
824–810		
	8 Marduk-balâtsu-iqbi	c. 822–794
76...Adad-nirâri III		
810–782		
	9. Bau-ahê-iddin	
	10. Marduk-bêl- ——	
	11. Marduk-apal-utsur	
77. Shalmaneser IV	12 Erîba-Marduk	c. 782–762
782–772		
78. Ashur-dân III 772–754	9TH DYNASTY	
	1. Nabu-shum-ishkun II	c. 761–748
79. Adad-nirâri IV 754–746		
	2. Nabonassar	748–734
80...Tiglath-pileser III		
745–727	3. Nabu-nadin-zêr	734–732
	4. Nabu-shum-ukîn II	732
	10TH DYNASTY	
	1. Nabu-ukîn-zêr	732–729
	2. Pulu	729–727
81...Shalmaneser V	— 3. Ululaï	727–722
727–722		
82...Sargon II 722–705	4. Merodach-baladan II	721–710
	— 5. Sargon	709–705
83...Sennacherib 705–681—	6. Sennacherib	705–703
	7. Marduk-zâkin-shum	703
	8. Merodach-baladan II	703
	9. Bêl-ibni	703–700
	10. Ashur-nâdin-shumi	700–694
	11. Nergal-shêzib	694–693
	12. Mushezil-Marduk	693–689
	13. Sennacherib	689–681
84...Esarhaddon 681–669	—14. Esarhaddon	681–669
85...Ashurbanipal	—15. Shamash-shum-ukîn	668–648
669–626		
	16. Kandalanu	648–626
86...Ashur-êtil-iliani 626–	—17. Ashur-êtil-iliâni	626–
	11TH DYNASTY	
	1. Nabopolassar	625–604
87. Sin-shum-lishir	—18. Sin-shum-lishir	
88...Sin-shar-ishkun 606	—19. Sin-shar-ishkun	606

BOOK TWO

THE INSTITUTIONS

CHAPTER I

THE STATE AND THE FAMILY

1. THE STATE

THE view of the State was the same as in Babylonia. The god Ashur was the true master of the land and the city which bore his name. The king of Assyria was his vicegerent, and would not embark upon any important enterprise without receiving his command and rendering account to him; on his return from every campaign, for instance, the king rendered him a detailed report, a veritable campaign diary and history of the successes achieved. If Tiglath-pileser I attacked Commagene, it was only because " it had withheld its tribute and presents to the god Ashur." And the same prince says in another place of the defeated people : " I have subdued them to Ashur, my master . . . I have counted them among the subjects of Ashur, my master."

As on the Babylonian view, every town was the abode of deities. Sargon makes reference to " the gods who dwell in Kalah," " the gods and goddesses who dwell in Sumer and Akkad," and, after the destruction of Babylon, Esar-haddon declares : " The gods and goddesses who dwelt there ascended into heaven, while the people who dwelt there were sent under the yoke and fettered."

At the head of the social hierarchy the king, the queen, and the heir apparent each had their own houses with numerous officials. The king was eponym of the year following his accession.

The *turtan*, or commander-in-chief, gave his name to the next year; then the commandant of the palace, the chief cup-bearer, and a score of other officials succeeded to this honour in turn. The Sargonids surrounded themselves with a whole host of familiars—a keeper of the seal, a master of ceremonies, a major-domo, a chief-keeper of the keys, a chief cup-bearer, a chief master of the stables, a chief physician, assisted by an auxiliary physician and the king's personal physician, a scribe of the palace and a scribe of the harem, a scribe for Aramaic letters and a scribe for Egyptian letters, an inspector of the palace, a captain of the palace, a commander of the guard, a palace gardener, an inspector of the harem, a chief of the flocks, a head-baker, a chief eunuch, a sword-bearer, a sceptre-bearer, a head-goldsmith, a director of music, a head-fuller, a head-weaver, a head-keeper of the main gate, etc.

The queen dowager and the queen had their staff of scribes, a keeper of the seal, a head-messenger, weavers, etc.

The heir apparent, like the king, possessed a military house and a civil house. He was guided by a tutor and surrounded by priests, men of business, and inspectors.

The people were divided into two classes, men of free status and slaves.

As in Babylonia, the family was held in such high esteem in Assyria that it was customary to treat a family of slaves as an unitary whole, and not an aggregate of individuals. If a slave were to be sold, he would not be alienated by himself, but the bargain would also cover at the same time his wife, his boys and girls, his widowed mother, and a young brother, if the latter were still in tutelage in the eyes of the law. In 684 B.C. Ululaï purchased for six minæ of silver from Nabu-erîba the slave, " Kandalanu, his three sons, his wife, his two daughters, his brother, and this brother's three children." Kikinnânu sold a man and his mother to Shumma-ilâni. Iakar-ahê was handed over with his daughter. We find mentioned together in one and the same deed —a man, his wife and daughter; a man, wife and their three sons; two couples; and an isolated slave.[1]

---

[1] **CXXXI**, Nos. 230, 236, 245, 246.

Though, in the majority of cases, the slave's companion is designated by the vague term " woman," she is sometimes also called " wife " ; both expressions occur simultaneously in the deed just cited. The master himself often chose the slaves whom he wished to mate. Kakkullânu purchased for half a mina of silver the girl Abi-dalâli, and gave her to his slave Ululaï as wife ; on another occasion the same person carried through a similar transaction for the benefit of his slave Tarhunazi. Monogamy was the rule in such marriages as among free persons. However, cases of bigamy perhaps existed ; in a contract of 680 B.C., relating to the sale of seven persons, a slave is transferred with his two women and his children.[1]

A slave could not bestow his name upon his children ; each slave was known by his proper name alone, without mention of the father.

As in Babylonia, the slave might own real and personal property, and possess fields, a garden, a house and slaves of his own. He might transact business, buy and sell, borrow or be a witness, like a free man, and he, too, possessed a seal wherewith to authenticate documents. During the eponymy of Marduk-shar-utsur, a slave of Adad-rimâni was the vendor of a woman who belonged to him ; he transferred her to Abdunu, son of Kakkulânu, that important man of business whose name so often figures in contracts of Ashurbanipal's reign, and the content of the tablet does not differ in the least from analogous contracts negotiated between free men. Another slave sold a garden in 669 B.C. In 679 Nabu-tarits, slave of Tsapânu, acknowledged the receipt of 210 minæ of bronze from Shangu-ishtar by the affixation of his seal.[2]

Contracts in which slaves are mentioned among the witnesses are common. A slave, with two others dependent on him, was present at the execution of a deed dated 709 B.C. In a document already noted, because of the very special penalties threatened against anyone who might bring an action for the cancellation of the agreement, at least eleven of the witnesses were slaves of great persons of State. The act was drawn up " in the presence of Bagagi, of Bâbilaï, of Urdu, of Ashur-Kassum, in all four,

---

[1] *Ibid.*, Nos. 309, 308, 229.   [2] *Ibid.*, Nos. 311, 366, 161.

slaves of the governor of the palace ; in the presence of
Lukimama, of Sharru-iqbi, of Halmusu, in all three slaves
of the high commissary of provisions ; in the presence of
Ili-balatsu-iqbi and Kinani-Ishtar, in all two slaves of the
keeper of the seal ; in the presence of Tsil-Adad, slave of
the rab-karmani ; in the presence of Akru, the publican of
Nineveh, of Ashur-ahê-utsur, of Ashurai, of Ardi-Ishtar,
slave of . . . of Shumma-ilâni . . ." [1]

An important class of slaves was composed of the serfs
bound to the soil. When the property to which they belonged
changed hands, they were included in the deed of sale, and
as a rule designated by families. In 668 B.C. Milki-nûri
purchased a farm from Nabu-shêzib " just as it stands
with its tilled fields, its gardens, its personnel." Shumu-
ilâni bought fifty *imêr* of land, with 10,000 fruit-trees, a
house, " Hashana, his four sons and his wife, the woman
Dangî, her son and her daughter, nine persons in all." Sometimes the people were taken over without any guarantee ;
Milki-nûri seems to have acted so. Sometimes the purchaser
reserved his rights : in a sale authorized by Dujaua and
his father, a clause providing against epilepsy or any claim
has been inserted. If a property was mortgaged, the serfs
would be handed over at the same time, and were restored
as soon as the repayment of the loan had been effected.
The lady Addati, in 614, received as a guarantee for two
minæ of silver, not only a piece of land of twelve *imer*, but
also the two families who cultivated it—one composed of
five persons, the other of a childless couple. [2]

A slave could sometimes rise to high office : in 683 B.C.
a slave of the queen's house was inspector of cities.

2. THE ARMY

Almost every year, in the month of Tammuz, " which the
lord of science, the god Nin-igi-azag, has inscribed on the
ancient tablet as the season for the assembling of armies
and the pitching of camps," [3] the king of Assyria took the
field. Still, he never did so without consulting the gods
by medium of the soothsayers who studied the entrails of

[1] **CLIV**, 113 ; **XXX**, 464.   [2] **CXXXI**, Nos. 472, 422, 429, 58, 447.
[3] **XXV**, vol. III, p. 3 (translation by Thureau-Dangin).

victims, received the divine command in dreams, or were versed in the lore of the stars. The prefects of frontier towns had sent spies into the territories that it was proposed to attack, and their reports allowed the king to reckon on almost certain success.

The army was ready to march under the command of the *turtan,* the highest of all the court dignitaries, when the king did not put himself personally at the head of his troops. Sargon describes in detail the composition of such an army in 714, in the letter wherein he gives the god Ashur his account of his eighth campaign.[1] He has held a review of it, and then comes its arrival before Simirria, of which he gives a poetic description. It is " a great peak which rises like a lance-head, which towers over the mountains, the abode of Bêlit-ilê, the head whereof supporteth the sky on high, the root of which beneath reacheth to the centre of Hades, which, without like a fish's spine, leaveth no passage on the one side nor on the other, of which the ascent is difficult before and behind, on the flanks whereof chasms and precipices gape, the view whereof inspireth awe, which, for the ascent of chariots or the mettle of steeds, is not propitious, the ways whereof are hard of passage for infantry. By reason of the enlargement of the understanding, and the inward inspiration wherewith Ea and Bêlit-ilê have endowed me, who have extended my legs to abase the hostile lands, with strong picks of bronze had I equipped my foot soldiers : they made the rocks of the high mountains to fly in splinters like a mason's stone ; they made smooth the way. I took the head of my troops ; the chariots, the cavalry, the fighters who go at my side, like to bold eagles I made them fly over this (mountain). The men of toil, the sappers, I made to follow ; the camels, the draft-asses, like wild goats bred on the mountain, bounded over its summit. I caused the heavy troops of Ashur to climb its perilous slopes happily ; on the summit of this mount, I entrenched my camp." According to the continuation of the narrative the infantry were armed, some with the bow, some with the lance and shield ; sappers and pioneers were equipped with axe and pick. There were hardly any siege engines ; we shall meet them in other circumstances.

[1] *Ibid.,* p. 7.

According to the bas-reliefs which adorned the lower part of the walls in the palaces, the Assyrian heavy infantry wore a conical helmet equipped with side pieces to protect the ears; the bust and the upper part of the arms were covered with a cuirass formed of scolloped scales worn over the tunic. A pair of trousers and high laced boots completed their accoutrement. The heavy infantry was made up of two bodies of troops—archers and pikemen—both armed with a short sword for close fighting. The latter carried a long lance and a shield, either of metal, round and convex, or of wicker rounded at the top and straight lower down; the archers had a bow and a quiver slung diagonally across the back.

The light infantry also included archers and pikemen. The archers were not clothed in a cuirass and the pikemen wore a helmet, the peak of which curved backwards, and carried a small wicker shield.

Cavalry scarcely appears before the reign of Sargon. Its equipment resembled that of the infantry, the armament being almost identical, but the bow was shorter and the lance longer; the shield was almost entirely absent. The earliest knights sat their horses without saddle, and were accompanied by a servant similarly mounted, to guide their steeds during the action. Later on, in the time of Ashurbanipal, the animal was covered with trappings, and as a result of progress in equestrian skill the servant disappeared.

The war-chariot, mounted on high massive wheels, was formed of a body resting immediately on the axle. The panels were adorned with paintings and inlays. The pole was heavy; its end turned up, and was decked with a flower, or an animal's head. To it was attached a band of stuff, or cords, to unite the pole to the body and diminish the weight of the yoke. The use of shafts was unknown; two horses were therefore needed to draw each chariot; one or two others were often added as outspanners. The harness was light, and sometimes supplemented by trappings. Three men rode on the vehicle—on the left the driver to guide it, then the warrior armed with lance or bow, and a servant to cover the other two with a shield.[1] The company's standard was attached to one of these chariots; it

[1] **CXXXVI,** I, pl. 28.

was a long staff surmounted by a wheel, within which were
set sacred animals, or the image of a god.[1]

The chief episodes in each war were depicted on the bas-
reliefs of the royal palace. Here, for instance, we have
the siege of a fortified town in mountainous country, on
the bank of a river. This city, in accordance with its
importance, is represented by a simple postern between two
towers, and a double line of fortifications, or even a triple
series of walls. The mountain, as in Sumerian art, is symbolized by a scale pattern, and if the region be wooded a

FIG. 43.   Siege of a fortified city (Palace of Sargon, after Botta,
Monuments de Ninive).

few trees will be grouped about the field. A watercourse,
according to the same tradition, was indicated by undula-
tions and volutes, among which fishes are swimming. The
besieged are represented by one or more figures, whose
busts project from each tower.[2]

Ashur-natsir-apla, before a town, riding in his chariot
drawn by armoured steeds, is attacking a foeman. The
chariot of the vanquished opponent is overturned ; one of
the horses stumbles and falls ; the driver, pierced by an
arrow, is collapsing forwards ; the warrior sinks backwards
under the wheels of the royal car.[3] The god Ashur, above
the king, is taking a hand in the combat. On the ground
the plants trampled under the horses' hoofs are symbols of
the ruined crops and hay. In a little wood single combats
are in progress, from which the Assyrian always comes out
victorious. On another level a warrior, armed with a sword
and protected by a rattan shield, is transfixing a foeman,
who is sinking down and is being helped by a comrade.

[1] *Ibid.*, I, pl. 14.   [2] Fig. 43.   [3] Fig. 44.

However, the monarch has alighted from his chariot [1] and fights among the infantry. The besiegers are grouped in pairs : one shoots with the bow, the other guards him with his shield. Sappers, clad in coats of mail, are attacking the base of a wall with their picks, and beginning to undermine it. At another point a battering-ram, enclosed under a shield-like roof of wattling, is shaking the wall and causing enormous blocks to fall therefrom. The defenders are trying to catch the engine with a huge chain, to shake it, to separate it from the roofing. The besiegers, on their side, cling on to the ram with hooks to keep possession of it.

Fig. 44. Ashur-natsir-apla attacking a fortified city (after Layard, *The Monuments of Nineveh*, vol. I, pl. 13).

A tower on wheels has been brought up close to the ramparts, and from its summit archers are shooting arrows. The enemy reply with blazing darts and endeavour to set fire to the engine. Some defenders are falling from the top of the walls into the void. The civil population, represented by two women, is overcome with despair ; one is tearing her hair, while the other stretches out her hands to beg for mercy.

The assault is at last delivered.[2] The Assyrians have brought up ladders ; the garrison have exhausted all their arrows and have only stones left to hand. The king continues to shoot under cover of a shield while a sapper, having succeeded in breaching the wall, slips through to be among the first to enter the beleaguered town.

[1] **CXXXVI**, I, pls. 17, 19.   [2] *Ibid* , pl. 20.

The conquest is over, the Assyrian victorious. What will be his conduct now ? Tiglath-pileser had reduced the Moschians to sue for terms, a people formerly subject to Tukulti-Inurta who had regained freedom for some sixty years ; he beheaded the corpses to crown with heads the crumbling battlements, destroyed the palaces, burned the villages, carried off women and children into captivity, seized the deities, took all the goods he could lay hands on, consecrated part of them to the gods of Assyria, kept part for himself and left the rest to his soldiers. If the enemy asked for mercy, he would impose an annual tribute on them all the more grievous because their land had been utterly devastated.

Tukulti-Inurta burned cities, fired the crops and fruit trees. Ashur-natsir-apla cut off the heads of the slain and made pyramids thereof. Merciless to those who had rebelled against his yoke, he flayed them alive and hung their skins like a curtain on the city walls ; others were immured alive in masonry ; others, again, were impaled along the battlements. A relief in his palace[1] depicts the return from a successful expedition : the Assyrian chariots enter at a tranquil gait, scribes count the heads of the enemy and musicians with harps celebrate the triumph. The eagle who accompanies the victorious army in the pursuit of the foe[2] takes a share of the spoil, and is carrying off in his talons the head of one of the vanquished. In 879 B.C. the king boasts of cutting off the hands of two hundred prisoners who had fallen into his hand alive. " Over the ruins," he declares, " my shadow rested ; in the gratification of my wrath, I find contentment." He, too, carried off to Assyria the conquered deities. On a bas-relief four groups of porters are carrying images of the thunder-god and three goddesses :[3] one goddess is in her shrine ; another sitting, crowned with the horned tiara, holds a ring in each hand, the third, seated on her throne, is characterized by a lance-head and a ring. Captives and booty are depicted elsewhere.[4] The king's officers advance in pairs, their hands crossed as a sign of respect according to an usage laid down long before by the Sumero-Akkadians. Behind them a young chief drives in the prisoners. In front comes

---

[1] *Ibid.*, pl. 22.   [2] *Ibid.*, pl. 14.
[3] *Ibid.*, pl. 65.   [4] *Ibid.*, pl. 24.

a chief with a noose round his neck. A warrior grasps him
by the hair with his right hand and pushes him. Three other
captives with arms bound behind them and fastened together
with ropes are led by a soldier armed with the bow who holds
a rod over them. The booty is dispersed in the foreground—
vessels, dishes, cauldrons, horns, ingots of metal, and pieces
of stuff.

Shalmaneser II, son of Ashur-natsir-apla, was no less cruel.
He trampled on Urartu " like a wild bull," and reduced its
cities to heaps of ruins. He, too, heaped up pyramids of
skulls, and impaled the vanquished, burnt villages, rooted
up the crops, cut down the fruit trees, gave himself up
to rejoicings in the enemy's abode, broke open his treasuries,
and plundered them and did not depart without giving
to the flames everything which could not be taken away.
On the bronze reliefs of Balawat the prisoners taken at Sugunia,
a city of Urartu, defile before him, naked, their hands pinioned
behind their backs, their necks made fast in wooden collars.
Near another town of the same region the defenders are
impaled, the heads of the vanquished piled up, the Assyrian
warriors engaged in felling the trees.

Shamshi-Adad was perhaps less inhuman. Though he delivered cities to the flames after plundering them, he does not
boast of slaughtering the people who fell into his hands. He
was content with deporting them to Assyria, reducing them
to slavery, and dividing them among his soldiers.

Tiglath-pileser III, who ascended the throne in 745 B.C.,
loves to refer to the utter destruction of conquered cities
razed to the level of the surrounding soil. He, too, had the
trees felled and the chief rebels impaled. However, he
initiated a new system of colonization ; he deported the
inhabitants of conquered regions into other corners of the
empire and tried in this way to create a single people out
of the fusion of all races. He installed governors in the newly
conquered cities which he spared and placed new settlers
under their jurisdiction.

So acted Sargon. At the beginning of his reign he had
captured Samaria, the capital of the kingdom of Israel, which
had been besieged for three years by the Assyrian armies.
The majority of the inhabitants were driven off to the frontiers
of Media and replaced by people brought from North Syria

whose colony was later to be reinforced by Elamites, Arabs and Babylonians.   In each individual case he followed a deliberate policy and made the best use of the situation either by confirming as his vassal a native prince of the conquered region, or by installing one of his officers as governor. But where he did not think it possible to ensure his rule by other means, he did not hesitate to sow the seeds of fear and destroy everything.   He ravaged the crops, cut down the trees, and burned the villages.   The narrative of his eighth

FIG. 45.   Death of Teumman, king of Elam (After Layard, *The Monuments of Nineveh*, vol. I).

campaign gives evidence of the ruins that cumbered his wake :[1] " Seven fenced cities with thirty neighbouring villages lying at the foot of the Ubandia Mountains, I overthrew the whole thereof and levelled them to the earth ; the rafters of their roofs I consumed with fire, I turned into flames ; the storehouses where grain was heaped up, I opened : their immense stores of grain I gave to my troops to eat.   The harvest (the means of) subsistence for its people and the hay (which ensured), the existence of their cattle I set alight like a beacon.   I laid waste the region ; their plantations I cut

[1] **XXV**, vol. III, pp. 43–45.

down ; the forest I laid low. I piled up all the trunks thereof ; with fire I consumed them." After taking the fortress of Uaiais he " beat the warriors to death before the gate like lambs."[1] At the moment of return to Assyria he decided on a raid against the city of Mutsatsir. The king made good his escape, but his wife, his sons, and his daughters fell into the hands of the Assyrians together with rich booty. A bas-relief in the palace of Dur-Sharrukîn[2] shows the temple of the god Haldia and soldiers loaded with the spoils thereof : shields adorned with the head of a grinning dog, craters for libations, and the statue of a cow suckling her calf carved on stone, are among the objects described in the conqueror's list.[3]

Sennacherib did not hesitate to impale vanquished chiefs and reduce to ashes conquered towns. He rejoiced in making the smoke of the conflagration ascend to heaven as a sacrifice pleasing to the gods. And when he had defeated the coalition of Shuzubu with the Elamites, he mutilated the soldiers who fell into his hands in order to wrest away the bracelets they wore.

Esarhaddon cut off the heads of Abdi-Milkutti, king of Sidon, and Sanduarri, his ally. But he did not, like the other kings, revel in describing massacres, pillages, and conflagrations in his *Annals*. Son of a Babylonian princess, he seemed more humane and showed on all occasions greater clemency.

His son, Ashurbanipal, on the contrary, was second to none in cruelty. He beheaded the vanquished, slit their lips and sent them thus disfigured to Assyria to gratify the morbid curiosity of his subjects. At Babylon he presided over a gruesome massacre designed for " the appeasement of the gods' hearts " : some victims had their tongues cut out ; the limbs of others were torn off to be thrown as food to the dogs, wolves, swine, fowls of the air, and fishes of the canals. After the taking of Susa the army was given up for more than a month to ravaging the surrounding region. All the wealth accumulated by the kings of Elam was parcelled out between the temples and the warriors ; the monarch had the tombs of the old kings desecrated and carried off their bones

---

[1] **XXV**, p. 47.   [2] **XLIX**, vol. II, pl. 148.
[3] **XXV**, vol. III, pp. 59–63.

so as to rob their shades of rest for ever. After every victorious campaign a triumphal re-entry into the capital, accompanied by hymns and music, was staged. At the conclusion of the eighth expedition Dunanu of Gambulu appears in the procession carrying on his neck the head of Teumman, king of Elam, which is then to be exposed at one of the gates of Nineveh as evidence of Ashur's might ; on a bas-relief it figures again, hanging from one of the trees in the garden where the king is resting with his queen. Dunanu himself was taken to Arbela, had his tongue torn out and his skin stripped off ; brought to Nineveh thus skinned, he was led to the place of slaughter and immolated " like a lamb."

3. THE FAMILY

Marriage among people of free status was in Assyria as in Babylonia a modified monogamy, but the family there constituted a less firmly organized cell.

A young girl was under the absolute control of her father and could not marry without his consent, even though she were in service with someone as the surety for a debt. On her father's death it was her brothers' business to release her and find her a dowry. Failing to do that within a specified time, they lost all claim upon her, and the creditor might enfranchise her and marry her. The father's right was such that a girl might be given in marriage to a man who had forcibly outraged her, if such were the father's pleasure.[1]

Betrothal consisted of a ceremony in which the bridegroom elect poured perfumes on the maiden's head and presented gifts in the shape of jewels, various objects, and provisions. From this moment the bride elect belonged to the household of her father-in-law. If before the marriage her fiancé died or disappeared, she did not regain her liberty, but was handed over to whomsoever among her brothers-in-law of marriageable age it was thought well to give her. If her father-in-law were deceased and she had no brothers-in-law, she would have to espouse one of the grandsons if any were marriageable, but if none of them had yet reached the legal age which was ten, and then only, her father could give her in marriage to another family provided he gave back all

[1] CI, Laws 49, 56.

L

the betrothal gifts save such as were designed for consumption.
The betrothal might still be broken off with the same consequences, if one of the fiancé's brothers happened to die
leaving a wife whom the father forced the bridegroom elect
to wed.[1]

That under the Sargonids marriage by purchase was
sometimes the usage is shown by the following deed drawn
up just like one for the sale of a slave :[2]

" Seal of Nabu-rîhtu-utsur, son of Ahartishe, the *hasa*
in the hands of Ardi-Ishtar of the village of fullers ; seal
of Tebêtaï, his son ; seal of Silim-Adad, his son ; the masters
of their sister delivered.

"Ninlil-hatsina, sister of Nabu-rîhtu-utsur, the lady
Nihtêsharaü for the price of sixteen shekels of silver has purchased for Tsihâ her son for to be his wife ; she has taken her
away. She is the wife of Tsihâ. The money has been paid
in full. Whoever in the future at any time at all shall arise
and dispute it, be it Nabu-rîhtu-utsur or his children or his
grandchildren or his collateral relations or their children or
his tutor or anyone that is his, who shall bring an action
or institute proceedings against the lady Nihtêsharaü, her
children, or her grandchildren, that man shall pay ten minæ
of silver. If he begin the action, he may not profit therefrom.

" Sahpiamu the boatman, Bêl-shum-iddin, son of Ili-udan-
ninani, Ishdi-Ninlil, son of Atî the fuller, in all three ' follow-
ers ' of the woman. For claim of service, seizure, debts,
Karmeuni is surety.

" In the presence of Ahartishe, of Nabnîtu, of Ardi-Nanaï,
of Putum-hêshe, of Hashbabnushi, of Bêl-shar-utsur, . . .

" The 1st of Elul, eponomy of Ashur-mâtu-tuqqin.

" In the presence of Nur-Shamash, of Putu-Païti, of Atê, of
Nabu-Nâdin-ahê, the scribe."[3]

Sometimes the married woman remained under the paternal
roof ; at others she went to live with her husband. In the
first case the husband " set a *dumaki* on her "—a contribution
towards the regular expenses of the household. He might
also set aside a *nudunnu* or dowry for her, in which case she
became jointly answerable for the debts or obligations of

[1] CI, 23, 24, 44, 32, 31.
[2] CXXXI, Nos. 324, 307, 67, 137, 190, 232, 242, 245; CLIV, No. 655.
[3] CXXXI, No. 307.

her husband. Finally, he might give her a *tirhatu*, which would remain her own property in case of divorce ; such a woman's father-in-law might add thereto a *zubullu*—a present of "lead, silver, gold, and comestibles." When, on the other hand, the wife went to live with her husband, her dowry (*shirqu*), what she brought from her father's house, and what her father-in-law had presented to her, was all guaranteed to her children ; her brothers-in-law had no claim on such possessions.[1]

A married woman of free birth was not allowed to go out into the streets without covering her head with a veil, at least at a certain period in the second millennium. Her daughters also wore head-dresses prescribed by custom ; by this means they were distinguished from temple prostitutes, harlots, and slaves. A concubine (*esirtu*) was not entitled to wear the veil ; if her husband wished to raise her to the position of wife, he had to veil her in the presence of five or six witnesses and declare : " This is my wife ! "[2]

Towards the end of the second millennium a married woman might not engage in any business not directed by her husband, her sons, or one of his brothers-in-law. She might not receive anything by way of a loan from a person outside the family circle. The man who did business with her was a criminal, even if he swore that he was unaware that she was married. In the former case the husband received two minæ of lead ; in the latter the accused was thrown into the water without being bound, and if he did not drown, he underwent the same penalty as the husband might decide to inflict on his spouse.[3] In the period of the Sargonids a wife possessed a more extensive civil personality. However, she figures in deeds much more rarely than in Babylonia. In 692 B.C. Amat-Su'la, wife of Bêl-duri, was the proprietress together with two men of an undivided house in the city of Nineveh, and sold it without the intervention of her husband. A mother bought a girl to be her son's bride ; another sold her daughter to the lady Ahi-talli. The latter granted a loan in money or barley ; the former redeemed a field. She might buy or sell slaves and figures among litigants.

Adultery on the part of a wife was severely punished. The

---

[1] CI, Laws 28, 33, 31, 32.
[2] *Ibid.*, 41, 42.   [3] *Ibid.*, 22, 23.

wife of a free man outraged by a male in a public place was
not guilty, but her assailant, if convicted, must be condemned
to death. If a woman had deceived her husband and had
herself visited the domicile of her paramour, both would be
put to death. Had she had illicit relations with a man in a
brothel or public place, her husband would inflict chastise-
ment upon her ; the lover would suffer the same penalty
if he were aware of her condition, but could not be touched
if he believed her unmarried. In the case of a guilty couple
being caught in the act, the husband's anger was condoned
if he immediately put the two to death ; if he arraigned them
before the court or haled them off to the palace, it was incum-
bent on him to prove the charge. If he condemned his wife to
death, the man would meet a like fate ; if he had his wife's
nose cut off, her accomplice would be castrated and disfigured ; finally the husband might exercise clemency and
pardon the pair. A flirtation with a married woman involved
unpleasantness only for her ; if it degenerated into adultery,
the woman and her paramour must both undergo the same
punishment.[1]

When the adultery was committed in the dwelling of
another married woman, the law drew a distinction according
as to whether the wife had yielded herself or had been the
victim of force. In the first eventuality the wife, her accomplice and the procuress suffered the same penalty imposed
by the husband ; in the alternative the man and the procuress were condemned to death, but the wife was not punished if she had reported the facts to her husband.[2]

It seems, further, to be adultery that is dealt with in the
following article.[3] Here the case is considered of the freeman's wife who leaves the conjugal roof and adopts the habit
of visiting the domicile of another married woman. If the
master of the house she frequents be unaware that she is
married, when the wife is retaken, the ears of the woman who
has given her asylum will be cut off, but her husband may
ransom her by paying three talents and thirty shekels of
lead ; this indemnity would be multiplied by three if he were
aware of the station of the person coming to his house.
If there be a dispute between the two husbands, resort is

---

[1] **CI,** Laws 12 to 15.   [2] *Ibid.,* Law 24.
[3] *Ibid.,* Law 25.

had to the ordeal : both are thrown into the river. If the master of the refuge return, he will pay the triple indemnity; if it be the husband, he can inflict punishment on his wife.

To tell a man in cold blood that his wife has been unchaste and not to be able to prove it by witnesses, exposed one to the risk of being bound and thrown into the Tigris. If the reproach had been uttered in a quarrel in public, that was an extenuating circumstance ; the slanderer would receive fifty strokes of the rod, would do a month's forced labour in the royal levy, pay a talent of lead and undergo a mutilation. The same punishment awaited anyone who charged another with unnatural practices without being able to offer proofs.[1]

Abortion was a crime punishable in all cases under the Assyrian law. A woman convicted of having employed such devices on herself was cursed and condemned to the punishment of the stake ; had she died before the intervention of justice, she was deprived of burial. A man convicted of having struck a freeman's daughter and thus caused a miscarriage, had to pay two talents of lead, receive fifty strokes of the rod, and do a month's labour for the Crown. In the case of a freeman's wife in her first pregnancy, the assailant paid two talents of lead. If the husband of the injured woman had no other child or if such woman died, the attacker would be killed. In all cases he had " to replace the living being," however little pregnancy might be advanced. In the case of a prostitute the aggressor received blow for blow, and he had again " to replace the living being."[2]

Besides the legitimate wife the law allowed one or more concubines called *esirtu*. When she accompanied her mistress in the street, the *esirtu* covered her head with a veil ; in all other circumstances she had to dress as a servant unless raised to the status of wife when her lord had himself veiled her in the presence of five or six witnesses. A concubine's children had no claim to the paternal heritage if there were children of the veiled wife.[3]

---

[1] *Ibid.*, Laws 17–19.   [2] *Ibid.*, Laws 21, 52–54.
[3] *Ibid.*, Laws 41–42.

A married woman regained her liberty if her husband divorced her, if he were absent or missing for more than five years, and almost always when he died.

No legal restriction seems to have been imposed on divorce. The husband was not even obliged to give anything to the wife he put away, when she had lived with him, and it seems that the property brought to the household by her would remain at the disposal of her sons. If she lived with her father the husband would take back the *dumaki*, but abandon the *tirhatu*.[1]

Absence prolonged beyond five years was a ground for the annulment of the marriage, particularly when the wife enjoyed no private income and had no sons to provide for her needs. She had a tablet of widowhood given her and, after five years, went to live with the husband of her choice. If later on the first husband returned and could justify his absence as due to circumstances beyond his control, he might recommence conjugal life provided always that he procured a substitute for his wife to the second husband.[2]

It was the same with a man sent abroad on the king's service. If his wife had not waited the five full years before remarrying, the second marriage was null; the children born of such a union became in law sons and heirs of the first husband upon his return to Assyria.

When a man fell into the hands of the enemy, his spouse had to await him for two years, even if she had neither son nor father-in-law to provide for her needs. If she belonged to the retinue of the palace, she would be fed in return for her labour. If she were a woman of the people, she would appeal to the tribunal to cause the city magistrates to assign her a cottage on a strip of land to cultivate for two years. Her rights would be determined in writing and, at the end of the two years, she would be given a tablet of widowhood allowing her to contract a fresh alliance. If later on the vanished husband returned to the country, he might recover his wife, but had no claim over the children of the second union ; as to the plot of ground assigned to his wife for her support, if such a man did not rejoin the king's army, he would pay for it on the terms stipulated and become its owner. When the husband did not return, the woman's

---

[1] **CI**, Laws 30, 39.   [2] *Ibid.*, Law 37.

land reverted to the city and her second mate could not keep it.

Her partner's death did not always set a wife at liberty. In certain circumstances she had to marry her father-in-law, or one of her brothers-in-law who was already engaged but not married, or even one of her stepsons born of a different union. After her husband's death a widow might live with her sons and, if her lord had left her nothing in writing, they owed her sustenance. If she were the wife of a second marriage and had no children she would be supported by the sons of the first marriage, but if she had children of her own and the offspring of the first union did not want to take charge of her, she would serve her own sons in return for food.[1]

When a widow took a second husband, if he came to live with her, all that he brought became the property of his wife ; if it were the widow who entered her new lord's abode, she surrendered to him the ownership of all possessions brought with her to the household. If her duties were not then specified in a tablet, after two years of conjugal life she might not be put away. Sons of the first marriage reared in the second husband's establishment still belonged to their father's family, and were entitled to their share in his estate, unless they had received a tablet of adoption severing them from their former family and including them in their stepfather's lineage.[2]

A married man might lose his wife through the application of the *lex talionis*. If, for example, he had violated a maiden, the father of such maiden would take the assailant's wife, deliver her to outrage, and not return her to her husband.[3]

The family was constituted as in Babylonia, under the rule of a single head—the father or, on his death, the eldest son—and when the children were minors and fatherless, the mother fulfilled the functions of guardian. Still, there were profound differences. The legislation of Hammurabi of Babylon in the twentieth century B.C. gives evidence of quite extensive personal rights, while the customs ruling in the period of the Sargonids take us back to a less de-

---

[1] *Ibid.*, Laws 31, 34, 47.   [2] *Ibid.*, Laws 36, 35, 29.
[3] *Ibid.*, Law 56.

veloped stage of social evolution, at which the head of the family had absolute power to sell his children, perhaps even to put them to death.

In 694 Aplaïa bought Zunbu's son for two minæ of silver, with a guarantee against epilepsy ; in 687 the lady Ahi-talli, paid half a mina to the lady Daliâ for her daughter Ana-abi-dalati. In 668 Mannu-kî-Arbaïlu sold his sister Bilikutu to the lady Zarpî, with a clause relating to epilepsy and claims, and not omitting penal provisions against anyone who went back upon the bargain in the name of the vendor —payment of ten times the money expended, offerings of ten minæ of silver and one mina of gold to the god Inurta. In these various deeds the head of the family acts as " master of the child sold," following a formula identical with that for all other sales. No one gives any reason for the alienation ; it is otherwise in the case where Ishdi-Ashur delivers up his sister Ahât-abisha to Zabdi in the eponymy of Ashur-duru-utsur to acquit a debt.[1]

The right of selling a child involved that of giving it as a pledge. The father might also devote it to the service of the temple. An equerry, Mannu-dîq, offered his son Nabu-shârik-napishti to the god Inurta of Kalah " for the life of Ashurbanipal, king of Assyria." [2] The penal clauses take the form of imprecations : the donor begs the deity to smite with his pitiless arm whoever may divert the child from his service, Adad to reduce him to beggary, other gods to bring him to ruin. Still more worthy of notice is the case of a temple prostitute's son, consecrated to the service of the same deity by his mother's family. Apparently as in Babylonia, women attached to the temple service could not have legitimate offspring. In the case before us, the child does not belong to his mother Râ'imtu, but rather to his two uncles and two other men whose relationship is not clear. These four persons, " the masters of the child vowed to Inurta of Kalah," have brought him up ; they offer him to the god for service and levies, and beg the god to listen favourably to the prayers of him who respects their resolution, but to reject those of him who attempts to thwart it.

[1] **CXXXI**, Nos. 201, 687, 208, 86.
[2] *Ibid.*, No. 641.

Adoption gave rise to a contract whereby, as in Babylon, the adopted son obtained in his new family all the rights of a lawful descendant, even though children might subsequently be born to his foster-father. In the eponymy of Sha-Nabu-shu, Sinqi-Ishtar and his wife Ra'imtu accepted his little boy Ashur-tsabâtsu-iqbi from Nabu-nâ'id "to make him their child," and specified that, even though they might later have as many as seven heirs, Ashur-tsabâtsu-iqbi would always be regarded as the eldest.[1] It was not a question of the purchase of the boy, but only of his transfer to adoptive parents. Among the penal clauses directed against Nabu-nâ'id, or whoever of his family might repudiate the bargain, in addition to offerings to the gods—a mina of gold and a mina of silver to Ninlil, two white horses for Ashur—it was laid down that the eldest heir of the disputant should be burned in honour of Adad, and that the latter should make good the tenfold indemnity provided in the deeds of sale.

The property of a family might be partitioned on the father's death, but sometimes it remained undivided among the sons. A concubine's children had no claim on it, if there existed one or more sons by the wife, and probably they could not be adopted. If they were the only offspring, they divided the whole inheritance between them.

A father, in his lifetime, might grant to one or other of his sons who wished to set up house on his own an advance on his inheritance, either in whole or in part. Thus, in the seventh century, in the eponymy of Upaq-ana-Arbaïlu, Tebetaï gave his son Adad-uballit some slaves, cattle, and land, and made provision for his admission to the succession to the extent of one-eighth.[2] In similar circumstances a Babylonian would have lost all claim to any share in the patrimony.

On the death of a man whose wife lived under her paternal roof, the *dumaki* became the property of the sons ; if there were no children, and the partition of the inheritance had not been effected with the brothers, this *dumaki* fell to them without their having to take the oath, or undergo an ordeal : it was enough for them to prove their title. If lastly, having

[1] **XVIII,** vol. VI, col. 198.   [2] **II,** 1898, p. 202.

no sons, the deceased had already received his share of his paternal estate, the *dumaki* became the wife's property.[1]

Possessions brought by a wife, who entered her husband's household, and whatever she then received from her father-in-law, belonged to her sons. In no case could her brothers-in-law claim them.[2]

---

[1] **CI**, Laws 26, 27.   [2] *Ibid.*, Law 30.

CHAPTER II

LEGISLATION

NO collection of laws comparable in scope to the Code of Hammurabi has been found in Assyria. Just as in Babylonia there existed tablets on each of which the legislation dealing with a specific subject was inscribed. From the ruins of Assur one of these documents, written in the later half of the second millennium, has been retrieved almost undamaged. It gathers into some fifty articles the penalties awaiting certain delinquents, particularly if a freeman's wife had been smitten or outraged. Another tablet of the same epoch, unfortunately broken, deals with rural law. A third, in a still worse state of preservation, contains decisions relating to theft and groups therewith mercantilism.[1] From the closing years of the monarchy Ashurbanipal's library furnishes a certain number of documents, an analysis of which gives us a glimpse of what the legislation may then have been.

Towards the end of the second millennium a single judge presided in the court, whereas in Babylonia there were usually several to try each case. For certain crimes, or misdemeanours, even reference to the judge was not requisite. At least, a man who had suffered injury was sometimes competent to apply the law, or moderate its rigour : the husband of an adulteress had, in many cases, to determine himself the suitable penalty, or to admit extenuating circumstances.

The code normally demanded proof of the offence. As for the penalties to be inflicted on the guilty, it provided for death, mutilation, fining, flogging, and compulsory labour in the royal levy for a longer or shorter term.

A thief was punished by a fine, fifty strokes of the rod,

[1] CI.

and a certain number of days' compulsory labour. Under the Sargonids, a certain Ahu-lamashshi, having stolen a bull, was sent to prison till he should be in a position to make restitution. A slave, who had robbed other slaves, was handed over to the master of the latter until he could redeem himself. In 680, for taking three hundred sheep belonging to the Heir Apparent, and killing the shepherds, Hani was condemned to restore the stock, and to pay two talents of bronze per man ; he was given as a pledge, together with his slaves and all that belonged to him, till complete restitution was made.[1]

Whoever had received a deposit in the country was considered a thief if anything was missing therefrom as a result of his negligence. Similar treatment was accorded to the trader, if he had exaggerated the price of the wares he had for sale ; if the transaction had been conducted in writing, the scribe himself had to be punished. A married woman who had entered a temple and was convicted of appropriating anything there, was condemned to infamous penalties.[2]

A wife, who had misappropriated property belonging to the conjugal household, and transferred it to a third person, was very severely punished. If the husband were dead or dying, she would be killed as well as her accomplice ; if the husband were in good health, it was left to him to select the punishment to inflict. When the sale had been made in favour of a slave of either sex, the husband might cut off the ears of wife and purchaser ; in any case, he had to treat both alike.

If a married woman committed a theft involving more than five minæ of lead against another person, the husband might come to an arrangement with the victim, restore to him the stolen object, and cut off his wife's ears ; on the other hand, he might fail to come to terms with the injured party, who then seized the woman to cut off her nose.

In the case of a clandestine deposit made by a wife in the country, the buyer was treated as a thief.

Assyrian law punished with severity blows and wounds, at least when a married woman was the aggressor or the victim. She who laid hands on a man might be sentenced

---

[1] **CXXXI**, No. 1601.   [2] *Ibid.*, No. 161.

to pay thirty minæ of lead and receive twenty strokes of the rod. If, in a quarrel, she broke a man's testicle, one of her fingers would be amputated ; if both testicles were affected, or, if the surgeon in attending to the injured vessel damaged the other too, the woman shouldered the whole responsibility, and was condemned to amputation of the breasts. Convicted of striking a married woman, one became liable to lose a finger. The *lex talionis* was applicable to the murderer, but perhaps not in all cases ; unfortunately, the article referring to this subject is damaged. In the time of the Sargonids, to escape capital punishment, a murderer might wipe out the blood guilt by giving the son of the deceased a slave and his family, " otherwise he shall himself be sacrificed at the tomb of the slain." And when Silim-ili was found guilty of several murders, the eleven persons who were entitled to redress sealed a tablet before witnesses. " Tsiri," they declared, " is the master of the dead persons slain by Silim-ili. Before them—his wife, his brother, his son—whoever he be who riseth up—shall replace the deceased." [1]

We have no judicial decisions, only private documents relating to cases. In one, a borrower is granted a stay of proceedings while he brings witnesses and proves by their statements that he has actually repaid his creditor, otherwise he will have to pay principal and interest. In another, a slave woman is responsible for the death of a maid-servant : her surety will have to make good the loss if she herself be not in a position to do so within a fixed time. [2]

Two persons had had difficulties about a house. They came to an agreement and now there is no more room for disputes. They establish the fact by a deed before witnesses, and agree to pay damages rising to ten minæ of silver if either of them attacks the other. [3]

Shamash-natsir had reduced a wife and her son to slavery for debts, and had seized their property—fifty *imêr* of barley, an irrigating machine, an ox, and twelve and a half minæ of silver ; the debtors make an agreement with him to give him three slaves in addition. [4]

[1] CXXXI, Nos. 321, 166.   [2] Ibid., Nos. 101, 166.
[3] CLIV, No. 650.   [4] Ibid., No. 655.

CHAPTER III

ECONOMIC ORGANIZATION

1. LANDED PROPERTY

LANDED property in Assyria, as in Babylonia, falls under the three heads of fields and farms, gardens and orchards, and building land.

The farms, sometimes very large, were not valued by area, but by the quantity of barley requisite for sowing them, and the quality of the soil was distinguished according as to whether eight, nine, or ten *qa* of grain were needed per unit of area. The farm included not only arable land and pasture, but also gardens and buildings. The serfs attached to the soil formed part of the property, and passed with it from one proprietor to another, or were at the same time given as pledges to guarantee a loan.

A farm might belong undivided to several persons. In 687 B.C. Ribâte lent twenty-five shekels to three men, and received as a pledge two fields with a spring. In the eponymy of Sharru-nâ'id, Muttaqin-Ashur and Ashur-rêsh-ishi jointly borrowed seventeen shekels, and then in return gave the lender the use of a piece of land. In the eponymy of Upâqu-ana-Arbaïlu, two other persons, who do not appear to have had any family connection, possessed an estate in common.[1]

Leases were apparently for two years; the rotation was biennial : the land was called *mêrishu* (plantation) one year and *karabhu* the next. A lease was taken for " three *mêrishê* and three *karabhê*," and a pledge given for a like period corresponding to six consecutive years : " for three *mêrishê*, for three *karabhê*, for six years in all, he shall have the use of the field." A longer term might be considered ; in 678 an agreement was made for eight years. In this case it was a question of a field of six *imêr*, the security for a mina

---

[1] **CXXXI**, Nos. 624, 88, 628.

of silver, and it might be recovered in return for repayment of the sum lent, when the *mêrishê* were over ; since the *mêrishê* were the years of the largest harvest, the creditor would be at a disadvantage if he renounced the profit on them. However, judging from this text, the whole farm was not cultivated in the same way at the moment the deed was executed ; two-thirds were in *mêrishu* and one-third in *karabhu*. This provision, relating to leases, is different from the Babylonian, where the rotation was usually triennial.[1]

A rural proprietary estate was called sometimes after its owner at the time, sometimes by a special name, very often " the mother of such and such a place," meaning probably the first establishment in the said place—the mother of the *kudurru*, the mother of the village Dunni, the mother of the Aramæan farm, the mother of Chaldæans. In the deeds of sale, and often in the constitution of a pledge, the boundaries were defined by the enumeration of neighbours, border roads, streams, or canals. The vendor impressed his seal or his nail. The various structures were enumerated, the number of slaves attached to the soil, and the names of the more important among them. For a hundred days the buyer might formulate a claim if one of the serfs was attacked by epilepsy.[2]

Rural law, in the latter half of the second millennium, was governed by a series of royal decisions, some of which have been unearthed among the ruins of Assur.

The division of land among heirs was not always made in equal proportions ; in certain cases the eldest was allowed to take two-thirds—one-third selected, the other assigned by lot. The part forfeited by a man who had extinguished " a living being," might be claimed by " the master of such living being " if the latter considered the compensation adequate, and did not insist on the culprit's death. In this article of the law, " living being " seems to mean any human being, whether born or merely conceived in the womb, for the same term recurs in the provisions relating to the suppression of abortion.[3]

---

[1] **CXXXI**, Nos. 70, 622, 623, 8384.
[2] *Ibid.*, Nos. 373, 622, 391, 382, 443.
[3] **CI**, Laws I, II,

The city of Assur possessed rural properties which, under certain circumstances, were loaned, or came into the possession of individuals. From time to time titles were subjected to a review.

Three times a month an official, the *nashi*, made a proclamation in the town. All who had any claims to make in support of or against the possession of such and such an estate by So-and-so, son of So-and-so, were invited to appear that same day armed with their tablets before an arbitral tribunal composed of a representative of the king, assisted by the city scribe, the *nashi* himself, some governors, the burgomaster, and three notables. When the case was called each party presented his arguments and handed in his tablets for scrutiny. The decision, immediately set down in writing, was communicated to the litigants in course of the session. If, in respect of a given piece of land, no one put in an appearance at any one of three sittings, the tenant of that block lost all his rights, and the land was put up to auction through the town-crier.[1]

To enlarge your own estate, at the expense of adjoining farms, entailed severe penalties. A man, convicted of having displaced the main boundary of his field, would be condemned to give up three times the area of the stolen land, to receive a hundred strokes of the rod, to do a month's labour on Royal works, and often to amputation of a finger besides.

For the smaller boundary the penalty was analogous, but the beating was reduced by half the number of blows, and the mutilation replaced by a fine of a talent of lead. Digging a runnel on someone else's land was punished by thirty strokes and twenty days' compulsory labour. For fencing in a bit of land belonging to a neighbour and starting to build on it, the penalty was fifty strokes of the rod, a month's compulsory labour, confiscation of the bricks, and payment for the land at thrice its value. If an orchard were planted on the land of another, two possibilities were distinguished. If the owner lived near by, he was presumed to have given his consent, and merely received an equal block of land as compensation; if he lived far away, the work had been done against his wishes, and on his return he would take possession of the orchard.[2]

[1] **CI**, Law VI.   [2] *Ibid.*, Laws VII, IX, XII, and XIII.

Water rights have been in all countries, and in all ages, causes of fraudulent dealings among neighbours on the land. In principle, Assyrian law permitted understandings for the use of irrigation waters and rain-water. If such agreement could not be reached, it left it to the more industrious agriculturalist to appeal to the court, to have rights assigned to him and certified in writing.[1]

Various burdens in kind, by way of levies or of public services, cumbered rural possessions.

When the king wanted to reward a loyal servant of the empire for his zeal, and to grant him a farm, he usually specified the exemptions such appanage enjoyed. Adadnirâri had given Qanuni, Abu-lâmu, and Mannu-kî-abi some lands in the village of Managuba, and limited the tithes due to the god Ashur and the goddess Bau to ten *imêr* of grain. When Sargon decided to acquire this village and build the city of Dur-Sharrukîn upon the site, he exchanged these properties for others with Mannu-kî-abi, who was still alive, and the children of the two other men. He exempted them from the tax in barley and requisitions for fodder. He went even further, and freed them from their obligations towards the god Ashur; but to compensate the deity, and avoid infraction of the foundations of his predecessors, he assigned him a field of 15 *imêr* to balance his loss.

When Ashurbanipal desired to show his appreciation of the good and brave Bultha, he granted him a tablet of exemption for his fields and gardens : " No tax in barley shall be exacted thereon ; no fodder requisitioned ; no beast from flock or herd shall be taken as firstfruits ; his fields and gardens shall support no tax, levy, or recruiting of men ; they are free of all charges for rights of wharfage or passage. . . ."

These various obligations do not reappear in private documents, but it is not possible to determine the exact system of taxation in force, nor to define under what conditions it applied. In the eponymy of Shin-shar-utsur the property of Abu-erîba's son paid a tithe of the cereal crops, and had to supply a quarter of its hay to the royal cavalry. In vague

[1] CI, Law XVII.

terms the estate of Ardi-Ishtar and Ardi-Ashur was liable to
" requisitioning of fodder and the levying of a tax in grain " ;
on the other hand, in 682 B.C., Qurdini-Ishtar-lâmur's
orchard was exempt from the tax in grain and the rate for
the village. The last quoted text shows that " tax in grain "
must be understood in a quite general sense of all dues in
kind according to the several sorts of cultivation.

In the deed wherein a father set apart as the personal
property of his daughter a house and some slaves, he invoked
the curse of the god against anyone who " should levy the
king's tribute " on this property which presumably enjoyed
exemptions laid down in an older document.[1]

2. AGREEMENTS

The documents illustrating Assyrian private life known
up-to-date mostly come from the palace archives of Ashurbanipal, and are preserved in the British Museum. For the
most part they belong to the age of the Sargonids and cover
a period of a hundred years. From them information is to
be derived about the family, slavery, the constitution of
property, loans at interest, the law about pledges, the
operations of sale and exchange, the hire of services, and
penal legislation at the moment of the highest development
of Assyrian civilization.

Private agreements usually begin with a mention of the
seals of the persons who bind themselves. These seals,
either cylinders or flat stamps, were alone impressed on the
tablet by the principal himself or, where that was impossible,
by an accredited representative who would be specifically
mentioned so as to avoid any subsequent difficulty. It was
not the custom as in Babylonia or in the Cappadocian tablets
of the third millennium to exhibit the witnesses' seals.

When the contracting party had neither a cylinder nor a
stamp-seal, he used his thumb and dug his nail into the clay.
Reciprocal agreements seem to have been far from common.
Even in an exchange only one of the parties affixed his seal ;
he was considered the vendor while the other played the part
of purchaser. Very often the tablet expressly refers to a gift
of silver received for the application of the seal or nail. Thus,

[1] **CXXXI**, Nos. 652, 660, 809, 647, 623, 622, 370, 619.

in 713 B.C., in a sale of slaves delivered for 180 minæ of bronze, the remark is added : " four minæ of bronze for the nail."[1]

The text of the document, drawn up in impersonal phraseology, was followed by the list of witnesses and the date by the eponymy. The scribe did not always write in his own name ; if he did, it was at the end of the list of witnesses generally with the additional note—" the scribe who holds the tablet " or " the scribe who holds the document."[2]

3. SALE

In Assyria sales were always for silver, lead, or bronze paid cash down. If the vendor did not receive the total price of the object, he nevertheless gave a receipt and received a note of hand for the balance. The deed began with a note of the impression of the vendor's seal or nail together with a reference to the object of the contract. This object was then specified in detail together with the price, the name of the buyer, and the certificate of entry into possession. The scribe attests the payment and repeats that the object offered for sale has been bought and taken. The business is over and there is no further room for discussion. Penalties were provided against anyone who should contest it. The deed ended with the list of witnesses and the date.

" Seal of Daïan-kurban, master of the house sold. Three shops with a court including a door in Nineveh next Naharau, next Nabua, next Kumâ, Dira . . . has bought from Daïankurban for thirty shekels of silver ; he has taken them. The money has been given in full. These houses are bought (and) taken. No going-back, litigation, claiming. Whoever contests it, shall pay ten minæ of silver."

In the case of houses the deed did not give the surface area of the land as in Babylonia ; sometimes, however, it gave the measurements of the sides. It is accordingly difficult to estimate the value of building land. Some houses went for half a mina, others fetched as much as 12 minæ. Besides, even were the necessary data forthcoming, a fresh difficulty would arise. The scribe distinguished several kinds of structures—*bît akulli, bît qâtâti, bît ripitu, atru, butsê,*

---

[1] **CXXXI**, Nos. 307, 318, 393, 409, 452, 248.
[2] *Ibid.*, Nos. 412, 1141.

qaqqir, tabriu—the nature of which escapes us (shops, storehouses and so on perhaps) and the value of which did not depend solely on the space occupied. The existence of wells, cisterns, balconies, or doors was mentioned. As in Babylonia, doors were apparently deliberately not made as fixtures, and were as likely to belong to the tenant as to the landlord. The sale was agreed to in terms of silver or sometimes of bronze. A deed in which the principal sum was 32 shekels of silver mentions " a shekel of silver for the seal." The penalties provided against the seller or any one of his family who might bring a suit against the buyer or his heirs at law, usually were damages amounting sometimes to ten times the value of the house, and an offering to be paid to the temple of Ishtar of Nineveh or more rarely some other deity. This offering might mount up to 10 minæ of silver or gold.[1]

Fruit or vegetable gardens were sold like building land. The phrasing of the contract was identical: So-and-so buys a little orchard of thirty-five trees, another man purchases a plantation of six thousand for 10 minæ of silver. Usually no indication is given of the size of the land. It was thought sufficient to remark that it was in good condition, or was transferred just as it was. In the eponymy of Tsalmu-sharru-iqbi, Kulkulânu bought a fruit orchard, to which two slaves are attached, and paid 3 silver minæ therefor. The transaction must have been important; there were ten witnesses from the village to which the property belonged, and ten from a neighbouring village. Not only did the vendor render himself liable to pay tenfold if he went back upon his word, but he would have, in addition, to pay a talent of silver and 5 minæ of gold to the temple of Ishtar at Arbela. The buildings, serfs, and springs, or fountains, were enumerated in the description of the tract alienated.[2]

Arable land was not valued by its superficial area, but according to the quantity of grain requisite for sowing it, as was also the practice in Babylonia at the same epoch. Care was also taken to indicate its relation to the current measures of 10, 9, or 8 *qa*. The serfs attached to the soil were included in the transaction, sometimes also the birds.

[1] CXXXI, Nos. 356, 413, 354, 325, 330, 349, 357.
[2] *Ibid.*, Nos. 446, 468.

The existence of buildings or gardens was attested. Shummu-ilâni bought a field of 50 *imêr*, 10,000 trees in fruit, buildings, and nine slaves, in the village of Ti'i, for 6 minæ of silver. Some estates were very large. Ishtar-duri, one of the officers of the queen-dowager in the reign of Ashurbanipal, bought one on which there were no less than thirty-one slaves, and paid 58½ minæ for it. One of the king's officers acquired the whole village of Musina in the district of Arpad. He paid 17½ minæ, but there were only 1500 fruit trees and six persons in it. The penal clauses in this deed are rather remarkable. Anyone who contested the transaction in the name of the vendor would have to offer two white horses to the god Ashur, four colts to Nergal, two talents of silver, and a talent of gold to Ishtar of Nineveh, not to mention the damages reckoned at ten times the value of the property.[1]

The sale of a slave, treated like that of real property, included, however, a double clause of revocability analogous to that in the Code of Hammurabi. As in Babylonia, epilepsy was a defect that voided the sale ; the Assyrian buyer was allowed a hundred days in which to ascertain its existence, and have the deed of purchase annulled. A Babylonian of Hammurabi's time was only given a month ; after that interval it was presumed that the disease was newly contracted. As far as claims were concerned, there were no limits ; at least, the formula indicates in a very vague fashion that the seller must meet them "all the days, all the years." In 713 B.C. a family, consisting of father, mother, and five children, changed hands for 180 minæ of lead. Whoever commenced proceedings in contestation had to pay 10 minæ of silver to the god Inurta of Kalah, and a talent of lead to the governor of his city, quite apart from the tenfold damages to the buyer. As in a document cited above, a present for the seal is mentioned. In the case before us the seller had no seal, but for the imprint of his nail he received 4 minæ of lead, a little more than 2 per cent of the purchase price proper. A weaver skilled in the working of many-coloured stuffs was bought for 1½ minæ for the service of the temple of Inurta at

[1] **CXXXI**, Nos. 621, 622, 473, 443, 431, 422, 428, 471, 464, 429.

Kalah. In the case of difficulties about it, anyone who disputed the deed of sale would pay 10 minæ of silver and a certain quantity of gold to the temple, apart from the usual damages. A man was worth 20, 30, or 32 shekels of silver, 50 or 100 minæ of bronze, but sometimes even 1 mina 7 shekels of silver. An ass-driver fetched 1½ minæ of silver —as much as the weaver. A female slave changed hands at 9 shekels, or 32 ; she might fetch as much as 2 minæ.[1]

We have described the penalties against the vendor or the member of his family who went back upon the bargain ; it is not unprofitable to dwell a little longer on the point. The deed by which he pledged himself was on his side a solemn pact which bound him, not only to the buyer, but also to the deity. It included a sort of oath, at least tacitly, and the breach of the agreement became an act of perjury— a sin. This idea is formally expressed in a number of texts by the phrase " the gods are masters of his suit," which was narrowed down to " Ashur is master of his suit." That is why the culprit had to give them satisfaction, either in his own person, or in that of his children, or in his goods. It was the same with the king, because the king enjoyed the privileges of divinity : " the oath by the king is truly the master of his suit." When Aplâ made the purchase of a farm and four slaves in 698, anyone who contested it against him, or his children, must eat a certain amount of the belly of an ox with the excrement, and drink " the blood of cedar." [2] That is not an isolated example. The same formula recurs in a sale of slaves, or a sale of land. Another contract adds the obligation of eating a certain amount of a prickly plant until the tongue was perfectly raw and perforated. The fierce gods were yet more exacting, and sometimes demanded human sacrifices. The same Aplâ has it mentioned in one deed that the eldest daughter of the contestant shall be burnt with 20 qa of cedar wood in honour of the goddess Bêlit-tsêri. In selling three slaves, the lady Mannu-kî-Allâ required the same guarantee : " his eldest son, or his eldest daughter, shall be burnt in honour of Bêlit-tsêri with an imêr of excellent spices." The god Adad was no less cruel : to give him satisfaction,

---

[1] **CXXXI,** Nos. 248, 354, 642, 177, 180, 186, 196–199, 315 ; **CLIV,** Nos. 505, 506.   [2] An essence extracted from cedar wood.

burning awaited the eldest son of the heirs of Nabu-na'id, or his legal representative, who should bring an action to reclaim a child adopted by Sinki-Ishtar and his wife Ra'imtu.

The sacrifice of white horses was also a punishment inflicted on the contestant to the advantage of the gods. He would have to vow two or four to Ashur, Sin, or Ishtar. Often he would add four foals for Nergal, god of Hades. In the sale of slaves, reference is made to a bow for the god Inurta of Kalah. Still more frequently the clause obliges the repudiator to pay a specific sum of money to the treasury of a god, Ishtar of Nineveh, Inurta of Kalah, Apil-Addu of Kannu, Adad of Dur-Ellil, Sin of Harran. We find $1\frac{1}{2}$ minæ of silver and a half mina of gold to Ninlil prescribed in a deed of adoption, 10 minæ of silver and 10 of gold to the same goddess in 679, 20 minæ of silver in a sale of slaves valued at 2 minæ, a talent of silver and 10 minæ of gold, or elsewhere just a talent of lead. Another person will give this same sum of a talent of lead to a representative of the Government, apart from, and in addition to, what he has to pay to the gods.[1]

There was likewise room for compensation, or damages, against the opposing party—here, again, nearly always ten times the value of the disputed object; in one particular case, in which a piece of land was valued at 80 minæ of bronze, he would have to pay the price a hundredfold.[2]

However, one might make provision for the subsequent reclaiming of the object sold, and decide that the transaction should be annulled, but that would still entail expense for the man who went back upon his contract; he would be permitted to recover his house, his field, his garden, or his slave on the same terms as if he had given them as pledges, but only on condition of paying an indemnity, and sometimes of compensating the deity besides. In 687 B.C. a woman was bought for a talent of bronze. "No law-suits, no disputes. Whoever, in the future, at any time at all, shall arise (and say) 'the woman I redeem,' he shall give a mina of silver and take the woman." Six years later analogous conditions and a repayment of 2 minæ were

---

[1] **CXXXI**, Nos. 315, 163, 161, 318, 476, 473, 474, 244, 436, 481, 474, 310, 215, 350, 471, 326, 263, 262, 316, 161, 282, 283, 247, 523, 498, 326, 417, 248, 554; **CLIV**, Nos. 505, 506, 41. [2] *Ibid.*, No. 350.

prescribed for the recovery of a woman valued at 90 shekels. But, as a general rule, every contract of sale was final. The most usual formula provided that if the vendor or any member of his family went to law he would gain nothing ; according to another formula, the judge should not be allowed to hear the claim, and a third promised a non-suit.[1]

4. EXCHANGE

An exchange did not, as in Babylonia, form a special type of contract ; it was treated as a deed of sale. In the eponymy of Sin-shar-utsur, three persons who jointly owned the male slave, Ishtar-dur-qâli, exchanged him for a female slave belonging to Kakkulânu. We should expect to find, at the beginning of the contract, some mention of the seals of both contracting parties. Not in the least ; only the masters of Ishtar-dur-qâli affix their seals, as they alone undertake an obligation : " Seal of Nabu-ahu-utsur, seal of Ahuni, in all two sons of Nargî, seal of Ahu-nuri, son of Sîli, in all three men, owners of the man surrendered in exchange for a woman." And just as in a deed of sale the text goes on : " Ishtar-dur-qâli, the slave of these men, Kakkulânu, the *rab-kitsir*, has purchased from these men in exchange for his slave-woman Tuliha ; he has bought him and taken him. No going back, law-suit or claiming. Whoever in the future may arise and commit violence, be it Nabu-ahur-utsur, Ahuni, Ahu-nuri, their children, their grandchildren, their collaterals, their collaterals' children, or anyone belonging to them, who may bring a lawsuit or a claim against Kakkulânu, his children, or his grandchildren, Ashur, Shamash, Bêl, and Nabu are masters of his suit : he shall give 10 minæ of silver." Then follow the names of eleven witnesses and the date.[2]

Another tablet, although sadly mutilated, is no less instructive. It deals with three slaves exchanged for a good horse. They are " purchased, taken." The scribe adds the current formula for contracts of sale : " the money is paid in full." But, of course, there is no question here of any money at all, even as off-set, and the phrase is merely conventional.

---

[1] **CLIV**, Nos. 453, 218, 213.　　　　[2] *Ibid.*, Nos. 318, 252.

5. LOAN

A loan was scarcely ever granted in Assyria without the lender exacting real and immediate guarantees—a substantial pledge which passed into his control at once, and which he would very often retain without any further formalities if his money were not restored to him. In Babylonia, on the other hand, it was generally at the maturity of the loan that a creditor was permitted to prove his title to the goods given him as guarantee of repayment. There, too, loans were chiefly in barley; in the country round Nineveh it was more often a question of silver or bronze, the current money; sometimes, however, of grain, oil, or stock.

Loans free of interest for a short term were to be had in the seventh century. In 693 B.C. Arbâ received a sum of 17 minæ from Indibi, on the 9th of Ab, and promised " to repay the money in Tishri according to the principal ; if he does not pay, the monthly interest shall be 2 shekels per mina," or 40 per cent per annum. This very high rate is perhaps to be regarded as a penalty upon the debtor who had failed to keep to his agreement. In Babylonia the current interest was 20 per cent, but it is impossible to discover the usual rate in Assyria, because the deeds very rarely mention the interest. In one, 30 per cent occurs, in another the charge on a sum belonging to the temple of Arbela was 25 per cent. The interest was reckoned by the month or by the year. In 667 B.C. Nergal-shar-utsur lent 5 minæ, and this sum " grows by 5 shekels of silver every month "—that is 20 per cent. In 668, Sukâ had borrowed 3 minæ of silver : " by 6 shekels that increases monthly " (40 per cent). If the loan was free of interest, in case the debtor did not repay it after the expiry of the term agreed upon, the principal thereafter bore interest at rates of 40 per cent, 100 per cent, or even 141 per cent. For 50 per cent the usual phrase was " it increases by the half of its shekels " ; 33 and 25 per cent were expressed in similar terms : " it increases by its third or its quarter." That some customary rate of interest was recognized cannot be doubted ; in some cases we find vague references, such as

" the money increases," or, " if he does not repay the
principal, it is bigger." [1]

For advances in grain the interest was commonly 50 per
cent, once 30 per cent. In Babylonia it had formerly been
33 per cent, and had gradually sunk to the level of silver at
20 per cent. " Five *imêr* of barley, belonging to the heir
apparent, in the hand of Taquni the second, placed at the
disposal of Hamathuthu, of the village of Handuate. The
barley increases by 50 *qa* the *imêr.*" The same rate was
applied to loans without interest, when repayment was not
effected within the stipulated period. [2]

Kitsir-Ashur advanced 10 shekels of silver : it was the
price of a certain quantity of hay to be delivered. If the
hay were not delivered under the appointed conditions, the
money would bear interest at cent per cent. Similarly,
Shumma-ilâni, on 21 Ab, put 6 *imêr* of good oil at the disposal
of Ashur-bêl-utsur ; they had to be restored in the next
month, or, as in the last case, the interest would be equal to
the principal. In these two examples, one a sale with
advance payment, the other a loan without interest, the
interest clause is at the same time a penal clause, and cannot
be used in estimating the usual rate. [3]

When the borrower found himself unable to restore the
object lent in kind, or its equivalent, provision was often
made as to what he should pay. In the month of Tebet,
683 B.C., Mannu-kî-Nînua put 250 *qa* of wine at the disposal
of Uttâma, to be returned in the month of Aiaru ; " if he
does not give it, he will have to pay according to the market
price of Nineveh." So acted Silim-Ashur, in an analogous
position, in 675. In 674, Danâ gave Ili-mukîn-ahi and
Adad-apal-iddin the use of two dromedaries. They had to
return them on the 1st of Marsheshwan, or pay 6 minæ
of silver. If they were not in a position to do so, they would
pay interest. On other occasions " the value of contestation " was specified, meaning ten times the price of the
object not returned. An agreement might also be made as
to the place of delivery, and, in case of delay, for another
place. Nabu-dûri lent 30 *imêr* of barley to Tebêtai,
Maganitsi's charioteer, on condition of its return in Mar-

---

[1] CLIV, Nos. 78, 87, 27, 28, 271, 18, 258.
[2] *Ibid.,* Nos. 131, 129, 148.   [3] *Ibid.,* No. 151.

sheshwan ; if he delivered it later, he would have to bring it to Nineveh.[1]

6. PLEDGES

The pledge demanded by the creditor was a piece of real or personal property ; often it consisted of a farm, with the serfs attached to the soil. The current formula is given in the following deed : " Two minæ of silver after the mina of Carchemish belonging to Addati, the governor's wife, at the disposal of . . . —ia, assistant to the inspector of cities. In place of the 2 minæ, an estate of 12 *imêr*, a field which is in the country of the city of Assur, Qurdi-Adad, his wife, his three sons, Kandilânu, his wife, in all seven persons and 12 *imêr*, to the use of Addati are taken. So soon as he give the silver, the people and the field he shall take back." Then follow the witnesses' names and the date.

In this particular case, and in many others, the creditor entered into occupation of the field, which served as pledge ; its yield would balance the interest. That was more explicitly stated in other contracts. Thus, in return for 12 shekels, Mâr-sharri-bêl-ahê acquired and occupied a property of 2 *imêr* 20 *qa* by the 9 *qa* measure (i.e. it would take 9 *qa* of barley to sow the unit of land measurement) : " He shall have its yield every year." When Sin-kutsurani, the borrower, restored the money, he would recover possession of his field. Such a provision involved a certain risk for the lender, and was not always put into practice. The temple of Arbela lent two people a sum of 17 shekels at the rate of 25 per cent. The temple administrator was to exploit a plot of land given as a pledge, and would collect the harvest ; if the return exceeded the interest, the borrowers would enjoy the surplus, but they had to make good any shortage. When a house served as a pledge, if the lender went to live there, the rent was treated as the equivalent of the interest on the money on loan ; if he did not live in it, his debtor was bound to pay the interest agreed upon. A slave converted into a pledge rendered services to the creditor ; the value of such services was to be deducted from and might equal the interest. Thus, in 668 B.C., for a loan of 3 minæ, it was agreed that this money should

[1] CLIV, Nos. 127, 122–124.

bear no interest, since two slaves were placed at the disposal
of the creditor till the day of repayment. The risks of death
or flight were borne by the owner, and not the creditor;
Mushkinuba, who lent 30 shekels of silver to Nabu-nâdin-
ahi, in the eponymy of Nabu-shar-ahêshu, expressly specifies
this. Often it was the same in respect to the guarantee
against epilepsy. A provision might also be inserted that
the money loaned should be recoverable immediately if
the pledge happened to be missing.[1]

7. SURETIES

Like the Babylonian an Assyrian might pledge his wife,
his sons, or his daughters. The creditor had no right to
shave or mutilate such persons; he would become liable
to have his ears slit. A free girl, put out to service with
him, could not be given in marriage without her father's
consent. If the latter were dead, her brothers must undertake the duty of redeeming her within a short period, otherwise the creditor might himself liberate her and give her in
marriage.[2]

The sale of persons or animals, given as pledges, was
forbidden, and constituted a grave offence.[3]

As in Babylonia, but perhaps more seldom, a surety used
to be chosen in Assyria. Kitsir-Ashur did so, not in a loan-
transaction, but in respect of an advance of money granted
to three persons who were to supply him with hay. One of
them undertook responsibility for its full delivery, and
would meet the damages if the time limits fixed were not
observed. In 680 B.C. Danâ demanded a surety for the
restitution of seventy-two ewes lent for a month to Simannu,
in the month of Ab. A loan contract might also provide
for the intervention of a third party, who became the true
debtor and sealed the deed with his own seal. In 670 10
shekels were placed at the disposal of Mînu-ahti-ana-ili for
twenty days; he borrowed them to do a favour to Pudupiati, who did not inspire Silim-Ashur with sufficient confidence. "If Pudupiati give the money to Mînu-ahti-ana-
ili for Silim-Ashur (it is well); if Pudupiati do not give the
money, himself shall he (Mînu-ahti-ana-ili) pay it."[4]

---

[1] CLIV, Nos. 65, 67, 68.   [2] CI, Law 45
[3] Ibid., Laws B, C, D,   [4] CXXXI, Nos. 151, 119, 99.

BOOK THREE

BELIEFS AND CRAFTS

CHAPTER I

RELIGION

IN its essence Assyrian religion did not differ from the Babylonian. The cult was inspired by the hoary traditions of Sippar, Uruk, and Babylon, and the dogma was only modified to fit the peculiar genius of a warrior race. In any case, religion did not exercise such an exclusive influence on this military civilization ; that is particularly noticeable in the decorations of the palaces, where everything was planned to exhibit, not religious sentiment, but the glory of the ruling prince.

The supreme god Ashur (the well-wisher) gave his name to the first capital and the whole country. In the twenty-fifth century he had many votaries and took the first place among the gods honoured in the district of Cæsarea in Cappadocia. He was identified with Anshar, who, according to the Babylonian Poem of the Creation, was earlier than Anu, the god of the sky. He was king of the whole universe of gods, creator of the heaven of Anu, and of the infernal regions. Like Marduk, in the eyes of the Babylonians, he was also the creator of humanity, and a cosmogony was composed in his honour. A warrior-god, he claimed to subdue all men to his yoke ; for, from all eternity, Marduk " had granted him the gods of the four regions to honour him so that none might escape." [1] He was represented by a stretched bow ready to let fly an arrow in the middle of a winged disc, borrowed from Hittite symbolism. His consort was the Assyrian Ishtar, often named Bêlit (the sovereign).

[1] **XXV**, vol. II, Fig. 315.

After Ashur, Ishtar occupied the most prominent place
in the Assyrian pantheon, at least as far as warlike expeditions were concerned ; for she, too, was a warrior. Ashur-
rêsh-ishi calls her " the heroine of combats, she who spares
not the enemies of Ashur." And Ashurbanipal relates that
she had been seen in a dream with two quivers, one on the
right and one on the left shoulder, grasping a bow in one
hand and unsheathing a sharp sword, just as she was depicted
on cylinder-seals. Three goddesses worshipped under this
name had temples at Kalah, Nineveh, and Arbela respectively.

The gods Sin, Shamash, Adad, Bêl-Marduk, Nabu,
Inurta, Nergal, and Nusku are those most frequently
mentioned in historical texts, and most gladly invoked with
Ashur and Ishtar by the kings.

Assyrian temples were built on the model of the Sumero-
Akkadian sanctuaries, but the same technical differences
were observable in their structure as in civil architecture.
In the grounds of the more important shrines, just as in
Babylon, Ur, or Borsippa, the Assyrians built a *ziggurat,* or
staged tower—the last transformation of what had been
originally the emblem of the god. Ruins of them have been
found at Dur-Sharrukîn and at Assur.

The priesthood included the same orders, and the same
division into three classes of priests was observed, according
to the respective functions of those who purified men and
inanimate objects by magic rites and prayer, who read the
gods' will in the book of Nature, and who fulfilled the
subordinate rôle of singers and servers. The priestesses
seem to have been less numerous than in Akkad ; the texts
do not mention them so often.

The prince, the representative of the gods on earth, chosen
by them to exercise regal power, had a threefold mission
to fulfil—to preserve justice and maintain the right, preventing the oppression of the weak by the strong ; to subdue
to Ashur the peoples who did not yet revere him, and to
chastise those who betrayed their oaths of allegiance to
him ; and, finally, to officiate as priest himself, and that as
much on his return from the chase as in the most solemn

ceremonies of the cult. The bas-reliefs in the palaces include scenes in which the king is making libations in honour of Ishtar over the bodies of lions transfixed by his arrows.

The part played by the priests, who interpreted omens, was enormously important. In their libraries they possessed the Babylonian rituals, and constantly added thereto the results of their own observations. For every event of

Fig. 46. Image of the god Nabu about 800 B.C. (British Museum).

public or private life their good offices were invoked, and on momentous occasions the consultations were multiplied. At the moment of setting out against Mutsatsir. Sargon learnt that the stars of Nabu and Marduk were heading for a house in the heavens which betokened the ascendance of his arms; the old Sin had given favourable signs signifying the capture of power, and Shamash had inscribed on the entrails reliable omens meaning that he would march at the king's side. The gods revealed themselves by the most simple means. Ashurbanipal consulted Nabu; a breath answered him on behalf of the god : " Fear nought ;

I shall grant thee a long life." It was most often by dreams that the deity manifested his goodwill towards mortals. Ishtar often communicated in this way to comfort Ashurbanipal at critical moments. On one night even the dream was collective, and needed no priests for its interpretation. In the pursuit of the Elamites the Assyrian army had reached the banks of the Idide, beyond which the foe was entrenched. The current was swift and fierce, and no ford could be found. The most valiant warriors feared to cross the torrent. During their sleep, Ishtar of Arbela appeared to the soldiers and heartened them with these words : " I will march before Ashurbanipal, the king that my hands have made." Confidence revived, and the next day the crossing took place without incident.

As in Babylonia, divine worship consisted of public or private prayers, offerings, and sacrifices.

The chief festival of each deity was likewise an *akitu*, a procession during which the statue of the deity was escorted to a temple, called itself an *akitu*, situated outside the town. The *akitu* of Ashur, called *Akit tseri*, has been discovered two hundred metres beyond the city wall.

The *akitu* of Ishtar of Nineveh was celebrated in the month of Tebet, that of her namesake of Arbela in the month of Ab. In 655 B.C. Ashurbanipal was present at the latter. On the homeward journey he himself guided the car on which the image of the goddess was set, and made a triumphal entry into the city in the midst of the acclamations of the multitude. Some prisoners loaded with chains, Dunanu and Samgunu, princes of Gambulu, preceded him, and the head of Teumman, king of Elam, was exhibited to the people.

The royal inscriptions are full of prayers. Tiglath-pileser I begs Anu and Adad to turn towards him with constancy. " May they love the elevation of my hands and hear my fervent prayers ; may they grant my governorship abundant rains, years of fatness and prosperity. May they bring me safe and sound out of the combat and the din of battle. May they subdue beneath my feet the whole of the regions which are hostile to me, of the regions, princes, and kings who are my adversaries. May they bestow their gracious

blessing upon me and upon my priestly posterity. May
they establish for ever firm as a mountain my priesthood
before Ashur and their godhead."

Sargon did not begin the war with Ursa, king of Urartu,
without lifting his hands to Ashur and beseeching him
" to compass the defeat (of his enemy) in the midst of the
combat, the recoil on his head of the insolence of his mouth,
and the payment by him of the penalty."

Esarhaddon gave vent to this wish : " May the gods
who aid me, behold my pious works with gladness. May
their constant hearts bless my kingship. May my priestly
posterity be enduring, even unto the last day like the foundation of the Esagil and of Babylon. May the kingship be
welcome to the multitude of the people like the plant of
life, and may I lead them into pastures of justice and right."

The same Esarhaddon invited Ashur, Ishtar of Nineveh,
and all the gods of Assyria to the palace to offer sacrifices
and present gifts to them. So, too, on a propitious day in a
month of good omen had Sargon invited Ashur and the
other deities, offered them presents of gold and silver, and
" made their souls exultant."

The offerings to the gods were very varied. On his return
from each campaign the king set aside part of the spoils
for the maintenance or restoration of the sanctuaries, the
enrichment of the treasuries. Tiglath-pileser I offered the
gods of the conquered territories to Adad. Sennacherib
dedicated pious foundations in commemoration of his
victory over Babylon. Ashurbanipal, on his return from
Elam, after sacking Susa, sent the best of the slaves and
the pick of the spoils to the gods of Assyria. The private
citizens would donate to them lands and all sorts of commodities, or consecrate slaves, or even their own children
to their service.

The taking of the oath was sometimes accompanied by a
sacrifice, and the victim was identified with the party who
called the gods to witness to the veracity of his words.
As in Babylonia no abrupt line of demarcation separated
religion from magic. When Ashur-nirari was making a
treaty with Mati'ilu, prince of Arpad, a wether was immolated and the sacrificer declared : " This head is not the
head of the wether ; it is the head of Mati'ilu, the head of

M

his children, of his great men, of the people of his land. . . .
This right loin is not the loin of the wether ; it is the loin
of Mati'ilu, the loin of his children, his great men, the people
of his land. . . ." And they prayed that the fate of the
wether might befall Mati'ilu if he transgressed his oath.

Sacrifice, combined with magic rites, was employed on
many occasions in private life. Thus the purification of a
woman whose husband was failing in marks of affection
required, together with a sacrifice, an incantation addressed
to Ishtar. In course of the ceremony a braid with fourteen
knots made of hemp, wool, and " branch fillet of gazelle "
was laid upon her lap.[1]

As in Babylonia the fear of the gods was the very foundation of religion. Adad-shum-utsur, describing the happy
beginnings of Ashurbanipal's reign, wrote : " The gods are
well disposed ; the fear of god is great ; the temples are
rich," and the king himself says : " In the presence of the
sanctuaries of the high gods I am awed."

The violation of the precepts of religious duty involved
the punishment, sometimes even the death of the culprits.
Ashurbanipal punished public failures to fulfil this duty.
He tore out the tongues of the soldiers of Akkad who had
revolted against Ashur. And Sennacherib states : " At the
command of my Ashur, Kudur-Nahhunte, king of Elam,
completed not nine months, but died suddenly a premature
death."

Religious virtue, on the other hand, was rewarded by a
long life in this world ; life beyond the grave promised the
Assyrian no more than the Babylonian any sort of reward
for good or evil deeds, and justice required an adequate
sanction. Tiglath-pileser I asserts such a recompense in
the case of Ashur-dân, one of his predecessors. " His conduct and the oblation of sacrifice were pleasing to the high
gods, so that he attained old age and grey hairs." Ashur-
natsir-apla offers an altar " in order that the life of his
soul may be long, that his days may be numerous." And
Ashurbanipal says to the deities whose temples he had
restored : " To me who fear thy great godhead, grant a
life of long days, the joy of the heart, and that walking in
thy temple may make my feet old."

[1] I, vol. XVIII.

Of tombs of the Assyrian kings only five have been found, all at Assur close to the palace. They were vaulted subterranean chambers, lined with kiln bricks and closed by massive stone doors. Inside them lay great stone sarcophagi. Unfortunately, these tombs had been plundered in antiquity; the bodies and all funeral furniture had disappeared. But it has been possible to restore the inscriptions on three sarcophagi giving the names of Ashur-bêl-kala I, son of Tiglath-pileser I, Ashur-natsir-apla II, and Shamshi-Adad V.

CHAPTER II

THE ARTS

1. ARCHITECTURE

NO sooner did he ascend the throne than an Assyrian king was seized with the impulse to abandon a palace, on all the walls of which throughout the State apartments were to be seen reliefs and inscriptions extolling the bravery and commemorating the great deeds of his predecessor. The new king desired to erect a monument to his own glory, and to have the principal episodes of his own reign depicted there. The custom of arranging these sculptures in the form of plinths has saved a great number from destruction. When the walls collapsed, the upper part came to choke the rooms and courts without destroying the plan and co-ordination of the several elements.

The Assyrian palaces are all alike, if not in detail, at least in the general outline of their arrangement. That of Dur-Sharrukîn, built in the closing years of the eighth century, is at present the best known. Botta and Place have described its discovery, and illustrated it with very careful plates on which they show the results as at the several stages of the excavation. Perrot and Chipiez have devoted an excellent description to it, accompanied by a reconstruction a little different from what Thomas had imagined. The city of Dur-Sharrukîn and the palace were built at the same time. They only enjoyed an ephemeral existence; the chief construction underwent no alteration. Sargon had chosen as their site the village of Maganuba, on the Khaussar, some 15 kilometres north-east of Nineveh. He enclosed the city with a rectangular fortification wall. He erected his own dwelling on a platform level with the walls astride the north-east rampart, where a spur, flanked with towers identical with those of the fortification, projected into the country, and another spur-wall to the interior of the city.

The space occupied by this platform was about 10 hectares (24¾ acres), and was made up of two rectangles, the long sides of which coincided ; the smaller, on the outer side, measured 35,550 metres square (7·9 acres) and the other 60,916 (15 acres). The palace contained more than 200 rooms. Botta explored 40 of them and Place 186. They were grouped into three distinct blocks of buildings, in which reception-halls or domestic apartments and the temple could be recognized. On the side nearest the town rose a spacious façade pierced by three monumental gates flanked by square towers. The central and main entry was guarded by three pairs of winged bulls and colossal figures of Gilgamesh strangling a lion, and ornamented all round the arch with polychrome enamelled bricks ; the other two had each a pair of winged bulls as guardians. This gate gave access to the private apartments, arranged round three sides of a square court, the dimensions of which are roughly equal to those of the court of the Louvre. From the inside of this court one might pass into the other two blocks of buildings, the temple and the reception-halls which had no direct intercommunication. The way of ascent on to the terrace, 14 metres above the level of the plain, presents a problem to which the excavations have revealed no key. Neither in the direction of the country, nor on the side facing the town, has a trace of a stairway or ramp been found. The reconstructions of Thomas and Perrot and Chipiez are sheer conjectures, but, wherever they were placed, ways of access were indubitably required to allow chariots and fat stock to reach the store-houses for equipment and provisions, and to facilitate the coming and going of the huge retinue attached to the palace.

Reaching the great court of the domestic quarter, the visitor was faced by a high wall pierced by a single door which led to the reception-rooms. On the right numerous chambers grouped round smaller courts served as kitchens, bakeries, stables, etc. ; in this quarter even closets have been found. On the left were stores for provisions, utensils, bricks, metals, and various sorts of booty, mutually independent and each provided with a lodging for the custodian. In the middle of these structures a passage led to the temple and bifurcated to pass between high walls to the staged

tower and the rear parts of the monument. In front of the
block of reception-rooms extended a large court, the area
of which was about half that of the court of the domestic
quarter. It was very likely reached from without, on the
north-east, on the side of the fortification-wall; but that
part of the monument is utterly ruined, and no trace of
gates survives. These apartments were composed of sixty
rooms, grouped around various courts and divided into
two perfectly distinct blocks. The one constitutes what

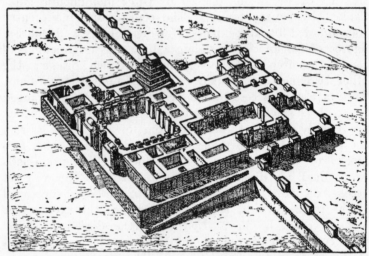

FIG. 47.   Palace of Sargon at Dur Sharrukîn; bird's-eye view
(After Perrot and Chipiez *Histoire de l'Art*).

Place has called the sculptural section—that is, the whole
series of ceremonial halls; the other, less ornate, was the
quarter of the offices and the chancellary.

The entry was so placed as to prevent any direct view
from without. First, one entered a small court whence
a narrow gallery, 45 metres long, led to the central
court, the most sumptuous spot in the whole palace. On
penetrating to this space, which measured 976 metres
square, the visitor found before him three beautiful vaulted
doorways and two others on either side giving access to the
seven main reception-rooms, all adorned with sculptured
slabs and enamelled brick. The court itself was decorated
in the same style, and the principal doors were defended

by winged bulls. The high plinths were uniformly divided into two fields. The upper space was covered with a long inscription, repeated in several of the halls. In one part the events of the reign are related in chronological order ; these are the *Annals*. In another, on the other hand, grouped geographically, the prominent deeds of the first fifteen campaigns form the king's *Fasti*. On the lower part the carved and painted bas-reliefs tell graphically what the texts inscribed above them narrate.

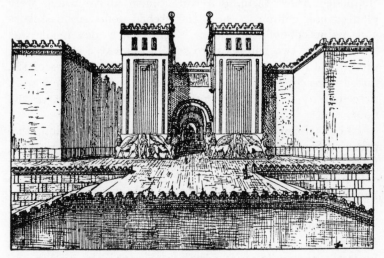

Fig. 48.   Palace of Sargon ; detail of the façade, viewed from the town side.

The materials used did not allow the architect to give the halls the dimensions he would have wished ; he made them all uniformly 32 metres long by 8 metres broad.

The offices of the chancellary were narrower. They were forty-nine rooms, clustered about five courts, and their walls were rarely adorned with sculptures, but were faced with painted stucco or frescoes.

Before leaving this quarter, let us note to the north-west of the entrance-court a large building, richly decorated, which included notably eight large reception-rooms.

South-west of the great court of the domestic quarter rose the temple. You first made your way into a court through an entrance which opened directly on to the domestic quarter, and by bend followed the rear wall of the reception-rooms, or else by a second entrance on the façade facing the city with a corridor turning sharply at right angles. The buildings formed three apartments, identical in plan and absolutely separated from one another ; the decoration in them was simple, and was most usually limited to a white stucco facing with a black plinth. Of the three courts, round which the structures were placed, one was remarkable for the luxury of its ornamentation. It was adorned with enamelled brick, forming a wide plinth above which were planted half columns. Near the arched doors stood statues and palms of gilded bronze. The brick pavement was traversed by two bands of crossed and elevated slabs, which united the corners and led to four chambers. Three of the latter were ceremonial rooms with a niche in the back wall, preceded by a postament raised 60 centimetres above the floor.

The platform of the palace supported, in addition, two other edifices on the south-east side. First came a *ziggurat*, four storeys of which, each showing traces of a different colouring, survive, and then an isolated building, now in ruins, built of limestone blocks adorned with basalt reliefs—scenes of the chase, of war, and of tribute.

The problem set the architect of the palace was this : to assemble together three groups of buildings which must have the very minimum of relations with one another and the outside world, and further, to constitute sub-groups under the same conditions, yet taking into account the requirements of work for the huge retinue attached to the palace. He solved it by an ingenious system of courts only connected by indispensable corridors, and assembled around each of them the several rooms requisite for a definite service. The heart of his system was the great court of the domestic quarter, which communicated directly with the outside on the one hand, and with the two remaining groups on the other.[1]

The type of ornamentation for the walls and gates had been imposed upon him by tradition from the last two centuries of the monarchy. The models were provided, for instance, in the palace of Sargon, in that of Ashur-nâtsir-

[1] **XCIII**, vol. II, p. 121.

apla at Kalah, which he himself restored and decorated with reliefs extolling his own exploits and in that of Ashur-etil-ilâni, Ashurbanipal's successor. This last was left unfinished, and its chambers of small size are adorned with roughly executed paintings. The tradition in question did not come from Babylonia ; the Assyrians had borrowed it from the Hittites, whose palaces, erected in the second millennium, also exhibit sculptured decoration on plinths, but of less height. Moreover, the king himself, like Tiglath-pileser before him, alludes to this influence and declares that he, too, has constructed a building in Hittite style, called *hilâni* in the speech of Amurru.

It has been asked why, in a country where gypsum is not rare, the chief edifices should be built of brick. It was not mere tradition, since stone was used to an extent unparalleled in Babylonia, even when the latter had in turn experienced Assyrian influence. May it not be rather, as Perrot has suggested, because the heavy work could be rapidly carried out by prisoners of war, so that the architects would thus find themselves in a position to satisfy the impatient demands of their sovereign ?

As in Babylonia the principal structures rested on a platform ; it was not needed in Assyria as a protection against flood, but it gave a more imposing character to the structural whole.

For the walls crude brick has been used before being completely dried, so that the successive courses might unite together without the employment of mortar. For the vaults fully dried material was employed, and the interspaces filled with clay.

Sargon had stone used to support the terrace of his palace. Walls 14 metres high rested on a foundation of 2·50 metres, and were crowned with a parapet 1·50 metres high. The stretcher blocks at the base measured 2·70 by 2 by 2 metres, and their weight exceeded 23 tons. The bondstones, only half as long, were 3 metres thick. The diminution in thickness progressed regularly to the summit, where bondstones and stretchers were both a metre less than at the base. The batter was entirely on the inside, to counterbalance the pressure of the earth, while the wall was absolutely perpendicular on the outside. No mortar bounded the blocks, which were carefully dressed save where they were in contact with the crude brick; on this side they were left rough to facilitate adherence.

For the fortification walls of the city, stone was not used in the same fashion. It only formed a revetment, 1·10 metres high, in which the facing stones, 24 metres apart, were carefully dressed and joined without mortar; the interspace was filled with unhewn blocks, levelled on top to receive the first layer of sun-dried bricks.

Even in the palace, stone was used for facings of walls, flag stones, and the capitals of columns.

Asphalt is met under the pavements and at the bottom of drains. In both cases the architect's aim apparently was to prevent the infiltration of water. The pavements

Fig. 49.   Plinth decoration of a passage in the palace of Dur-Sharrukin
(After Botta, *Monuments de Ninive*).

were, moreover, sloped towards the drain-traps, cut out of stone, from which the water flowed through a terra-cotta funnel down to the sewers of brick resting on an asphalt bedding. They, in their turn, ran towards main conduits, the bottoms of which were formed of large flags resting on asphalt.

No vault has been found in place, but in the debris in the middle of the rooms fragments of arched blocks have been discerned, sometimes quite large and covered with stucco on the lower face; the vaults of the rooms seem to have been surmounted with terraces, judging by the volume of the debris.

The vault was likewise used for the main sewers, in the shape either of the pointed ogive, formed on each side of four trapezoidal bricks of different shapes, bonded alter-

na tely between each pair of courses by clay or by a ninth
brick, or of the pointed alternating with the semicircular
arch. At Kalah the same process of ogival construction
was used side by side with channels of rectangular section,
roofed with simple flat slabs.

The palaces are too ruined for it to be possible to determine
how the chambers were lighted ; even when by chance the
wall of a room still reaches a height of 7 metres (which
is exceptional) no traces of windows have been found. The
bays for the doors were wide. At Khorsabad they are never
less than 2 metres wide, and most commonly 3 metres,
while the height ranges from 4 to 6 metres. That was
not enough to give an adequate illumination in the halls.
Still, the rare representations of houses do not depict any

Fig. 49 (*continued*). Plinth-decoration of a passage in the palace of
Dur-Sharrukin (After Botta, *Monuments de Ninive*).

opening in the walls except, occasionally, ventilators near
the top. Probably tubular terra-cotta frames, about a foot
in diameter, were used since the position of such objects
in the heaps of debris seems to show that they had fallen
with the vaults, or else a gallery was left under the roof,
as in the houses of Kurdistan to-day.

On the bas-reliefs the doors were arched over, or, less
often, rectangular. In the latter case a lintel of wood,
stone, or metal was required. The palace of Sargon has
yielded an example in limestone, ornamented with winged
dragons rampant, grouped on either side of a vase.

The sills were usually of stone in the ceremonial halls.
The Louvre possesses a fine model from Nineveh,[1] carved to
resemble a carpet strewn with six-petalled roses, and edged

[1] **XCVI**, No. 74.

on three sides with a border of lotus blossoms alternating with buds. Two corners are hollowed to receive the door posts, and in the centre there is a square socket for the lower bolt. Another sill, made for Ashurbanipal, presents a similar design. Elsewhere, particularly between chambers with earth floors, the sills were formed of a plain brick pavement.

Many rooms had no doors, and the entrance to such was closed by a simple curtain. Where there was a door, it was normally composed of a single leaf and sometimes of two. All opened inwards ; sometimes the upright rested on a bronze ferrule, which turned in the hollow of the socket ; the latter was usually of stone as in ancient Sumerian buildings, but occasionally of brick or bronze.

The main gates of the palace were encased in precious metals. It is near the doors and passages that statues and external reliefs are generally met.

The monotony of the walls was sometimes relieved by columns and flutings—for instance, at one of the doors to the temple of Khorsabad, and on the *ziggurat* of which they form the only ornament. The walls were often surmounted by crenellated battlements, composed of two or three merlons, one above the other.

The decoration was obtained by the use of enamelled brick, stucco, or stone slabs.

Stone, employed for the plinths, protected the lower part of the walls of sun-dried bricks. The slabs, hammered on the back to facilitate adherence, were just placed side by side, sometimes connected together above by a metal fastening, and held at the corners by other stones carved as knee-pieces. In the State apartments these plinths were nearly always decorated with sculptures brightened by painting, and the palace of Khorsabad alone contained dadoes thus carved, which, if arranged in one line, would extend for over 2000 metres. At the gates the reliefs are higher, and the figures are on a larger scale. As examples, we may cite the winged bulls, of which the palace could boast at least twenty-six pairs.

The whole surface of the walls, which was not protected by such stone plinths, was covered with a chalk and plaster coating, not more than 4 millimetres thick, on which traces of fresco-paintings are often discernible.

Enamelled brick, especially at the approaches to the gates, provided ornaments of variegated colour. They were employed as plinths, as in the temple court, or as archivolts. It was from Assyria that the Neo-Babylonian kings seem to have learnt the use of this sort of decoration, which then underwent a great development in the palaces of the Achæmenids.

At Nineveh, and at Dur-Sharrukîn, the buildings were orientated by the corners as in Babylonia; at Kalah the points of the compass correspond to the centres of the walls.

Foundation rites are transmitted from one people to another. Under the palace of Esarhaddon, at Kalah, little four-winged genii were buried in the sand. At Nineveh alabaster tablets, inscribed on both faces, had been placed behind the lions, which served to adorn one of the entrances. At Dur-Sharrukîn a stone cist contained tablets [1] of different materials, and at the entrance to the city the people had thrown cylinders, cones, and various figurines into the layer of sand between the winged bulls. As in Babylonia large cylinders of clay were sometimes fitted into the interstices of the walls to ward off evil spirits and to attract the blessing of the gods.

The walls of Khorsabad, 24 metres thick, were of crude brick on a stone foundation. At some spots they still stand to a height of 23 metres above the surrounding country. They form a parallelopiped (1685 by 1760 metres square), from which 167 rectangular towers, each 13·50 metres broad in front, jut out 4 metres beyond the curtain of the walls. Judging by the bas-reliefs these towers, 31·50 metres high, ended in a corbelled vault crowned with a grating. On three sides there were two gates, one plain and the other decorated; on the fourth side, to the north-east, was a plain gate and the terrace of the palace.

The plain gates served for the entry and exit of vehicles; on the side of the plain outworks, with a low tower at each corner, projected 25 metres. A huge court extended in front of the two towers of the wall, which was here 85 metres thick. Two lateral galleries are to be met, before which, in the middle of the massive brickwork, lie the door-sockets, and,

[1] **XCVI**, p. 122.

in the wall itself, the recesses for the doors. The pavement consists of large limestone flags.

The decorative gates were reserved for pedestrians. In the out-works twenty brick steps formed a stairway. At the gate proper winged bulls seemed to support the concave and ornate vault of an archivolt. At Nineveh a gate built by Sennacherib, where traces of wheel-ruts are observable on the paving stones, was decorated with winged bulls, both on the town and on the country side.

In the city of Dur-Sharrukîn the streets, quite straight as at Babylon, were 12 metres wide and paved with irregular stones of moderate size, resting on the ground without any foundation. The town has not been excavated; some test pits brought to light plastered rooms, fragments of pottery, and household utensils.

2. SCULPTURE

The Assyrian sculpture of the first millennium springs directly out of the Babylonian art of the Kassite period and the Hittite art of the second millennium. In the representation of animals it achieved perfection; in its treatment of the human figure it did not aim, as Sumero-Akkadian art had, at indicating the forms behind clothing, but concentrated on the details of costume and ornament. In Babylonia art was above all religious; in Assyria it was primarily military, and the numerous bas-reliefs that deck the walls of the palace are devoted, for the most part, to scenes of war and the chase.

The oldest sculptures found in Assyria come from the ruins of Assur. They are stone statuettes,[1] the technique of which is that of Sumerian art in pre-Sargonic times.

In the thirteenth century an altar, whereon was carved a king between two figures of Gilgamesh, is still reminiscent of the archaic style.

Two reliefs, representing Tiglath-pileser I in different styles, show that in the twelfth century technique was still in a state of flux; that from the source of the Subnat is the more Assyrian; that on the obelisk approximates rather to the Mesopotamian style, as does the bronze statuette of Ashur-dân II (tenth century).

[1] Fig. 39, p. 240.

Beginning with the reign of Ashur-nâtsir-apla II (884–859) the monuments become more numerous, but no statue attains the artistic merit of the works of Gudea. That of Shalmaneser III, at Assur, shows sketchy workmanship; that of Ashur-nâtsir-apla, at Kalah, designed to be viewed from the front and placed near a wall, already combines the Mesopotamian with the Sumerian style. The attitude is commanding; the dress forms a rigid column. The statues of Nabu, from the reign of Adad-nirâri II (810–782), present the same defect in the lower part, but the head is better modelled.[1] Among the statuettes the demon Pazuzu of the Musée Guimet and the heads of this maleficent spirit in the round deserve notice.[2]

The bas-reliefs were multiplied in the Assyrian palaces to adorn the slabs of gypsum and alabaster, arranged as plinths along the walls, and to illustrate the records of each reign. The Babylonians had employed bas-relief almost exclusively to honour and exalt their gods; the Hittites had given the lead in the use of carved plinths; the Assyrians made out of it an art at once historical and decorative. In this new mode the smallest details of costume, gestures, and attributes have a deep significance, the landscape is faithfully treated in methods which are often very primitive, and the animals are rendered with a genuine mastery. War, the king's hunts, the great works of the reign, and sometimes even the private life of the king, were the theme of the scenes. The number of these reliefs, and the brief time allowed for their execution, did not permit of their being reserved exclusively for artists of talent: in the palace of Dur-Sharrukîn they occupy more than 6000 square metres (7175 square yards).

In the reign of Ashur-nâtsir-apla II the relief was shallow and perspective was unknown. The inscription overflowed on to the sculpture itself, and generally covered the lower part of the personages: it would remain the same under Adad-nirâri III. Sargon abandoned this practice, and had his *Annals* and *Fasti* engraved outside the pictured field. The old arrangement was, however, never completely abandoned, and reappears, for instance, on Esarhaddon's stele at Sinjerli.

[1] Fig. 46, p. 311,   [2] **XCVI**, Nos. 102 ff.

In the eighth century, under Sargon, the composition of the scenes was the same as in the time of Ashur-nâtsir-apla ; but a marked tendency to isolate the figures from the background, to enlarge their proportions, and to suppress the accessories, is becoming noticeable. In military scenes the landscape is often accurately delineated, but in themes taken from hunting not the least attempt is made to indicate the features of the background. In the next reign a reaction occurred ; a new style arose which persisted almost unchanged till the fall of Nineveh. The scenes were grouped in tiers, and this produced a more limited field on which the figures are on a smaller scale. The accessories were multiplied and the sculptor spent much pains on the accurate rendering of the landscape. The execution attained a higher degree of perfection ; the chiselling was more careful.

A certain number of conventions were adopted by the Assyrian artists. The human figure, for instance, rarely exhibits the distinctive features of race or individuality. Foemen, Hittites or Elamites, doing homage, bringing tribute, or being led off into captivity, are usually only recognizable by their costume, which differs from that of the Assyrians. The latter fall into two groups of types— the one, bearded, stood for an adult man or an official ; the other, beardless, is reserved to represent young people and servants.

The sculptor was unable to represent his characters when they were not viewed strictly in profile. When Ashur-nâtsir-apla is turning round to discharge an arrow at a lion which is trying to clamber on to the royal chariot, the general silhouette is rendered well, but respect for the sovereign's majesty or anxiety after detail has led the artist to present as full face the bust which should be seen from the back, and to make both arms visible whereas only the left one ought to be depicted. This fault was however a heritage from Sumero-Akkadian art, in which the gestures of the characters were subordinated to the geometric arrangement of the subject in symmetrical scenes. Feet are always shown in profile ; the eye appears as if viewed full face even in a profile head.

In the representations of animals, a domain in which the Assyrians had achieved perfection, conventions still recur especially in the ninth century. For instance, in that hunt-

ing scene the three horses of the royal car have only six legs
between them, just as in other sculptures the bulls have only
one horn, and the horses' manes are treated like the fringes
of the trappings.[1] The design is too geometric and the finest
products of this epoch, the lions, show a too exaggerated
musculature and rather too massive proportions.[2] Under
Ashurbanipal, the lion-hunts form the finest ensemble in
Assyrian art ; the male pierced with an arrow is a masterpiece,[3] and the wounded lioness is no less expressive.[4] A
reproduction in the round has been exhibited in the Monceau
Park.

FIG. 50.   Lion transfixed by an arrow (Palace of Ashurbanipal,
British Museum).

Assyrian art made use also of a process of sculpture
intermediate between bas-relief and modelling in the round.
It has recourse to this style in the case of plinths which had
to be unusually thick because exposed to collisions, i.e. at
the entry to halls and passages. In these the fore-part of
the genii with bodies of lions or bulls, sometimes of colossal
proportions, is detached from the base and treated like a
statue.

The man-headed bull, which in Assyria became a beneficent
genius, guardian of the gate at the entrance to the city or the
palace, seems, like Gilgamesh throttling a lion who sometimes
accompanies it, to be borrowed directly from a Sumero-
Akkadian conception ; on the other hand, the composite
beings formed of a human body joined to the limbs or head

[1] **CXXXVI**, pl. 10.   [2] *Ibid.*, pl. 31.
[3] Fig. 50.   [4] Fig. 51.

of certain animals appear rather to be copied from Egypt through the mediation of the Hittites ; for the Babylonians had remained almost entirely unacquainted with such hybrid creatures which are very rare in their monuments. Sometimes the Assyrians united a human body to an animal's head, and sometimes they appended an animal's tail and paws to a human bust as the Sumerians had pictured Enkidu. They invented also classes of genii characterized usually by one or two pairs of wings symbolizing their swiftness in executing good or evil works.

Other genii in which anthropomorphism is complete are only distinguishable from gods when they are wingless. They wear on their heads the horned tiara sometimes ovoid,

FIG. 51.   Wounded lioness (Palace of Ashurbanipal, British Museum).

and surmounted with a stylized lily, sometimes cylindrical, adorned with horns and feathered.

Like men, gods and genii are dressed in a tunic, usually short, and a long narrow shawl which does not completely cover the legs. One alone seems to be an exception ; Ashur himself is ordinarily represented by a human bust armed with a bow emerging from a winged disc. This symbolism is Hittite in origin ; sometimes even the bust disappears and the emblem is reduced to the winged disc, as in the land of the Pharaohs.

The Assyrian king is distinguished by his head-dress, a tiara in the form of a truncated cone crowned by a spike and fastened by a band or mitre, the pendants of which hang down over his shoulders and sometimes right to his girdle. Originally plain and low, this crown grew taller and taller ; by

Sargon's reign it was covered with embroideries. The royal tunic has a border and a fringe. The prince's feet are shod with sandals which only cover the heels. In the ears are massive ear-rings, on the neck often necklaces of amulets, on the wrists and above the elbows bracelets ; sometimes daggers and a sword complete the apparel.

The courtiers are dressed like the king, but with no head-dress or only a diadem. The stuffs of their garments are less rich and luxury is shown chiefly in jewellery. Some, like the soldiers, wear a short tunic which is not invariably covered by a shawl.

Foreigners are generally recognizable by details of their costume. The captive kings, through whose noses Tiglath-

Fig. 52.   King, attendants and genii (After Layard, *The Monuments of Nineveh*).

pileser I fastened rings, are characterized by their head-dresses, as are certain chiefs defeated by Ashur-nâtsir-apla.[1] Both appear to belong to the same racial type as the Assyrians ; yet they are Hittites, judging by their conical caps and high boots with turned-up toes. Similarly the tributary peoples, depicted on the black obelisk of Shalmaneser III, are chiefly distinguished by their costumes.

The bas-reliefs were enlivened with paints of dull shades used exclusively to emphasize the detail. The same colours were used in the manufacture of enamelled bricks and in fresco-painting. The palette knew little variety—black, white, red, blue, and very rarely green ; the last-named tint was only met twice in the ruins of Dur-Sharrukîn—for the ground of a fresco and for the leaves of a tree. Nor was any attention

[1] **CXXXVI**, pls. 40, 41.

shown to the real colour. On the bas-reliefs the mouths, hair, and eyebrows of men were often black; the fringes of their garments and their baldricks red or blue. On enamelled bricks the ground was usually blue, the figures yellow and white. Thus on an archivolt yellow genii are holding a situla and a cedar-cone between two bands of white rosettes. On a plinth a lion, a bull, a tree, a boat, and a bird stand out in yellow on a blue ground.

The mineral colours used for the enamelled bricks have been analysed. The blue of Kalah is an oxide of copper mixed with a little lead, that of Dur-Sharrukîn is powdered lapis lazuli, imported from Bactria. The red is the oxide of iron called oligiste. The white is tin oxide, and the yellow a mixture of antimoniate of lead and tin known to-day as Naples Yellow.

FIG. 53.   Bronze lion (Palace of Dur-Sharrukin, Louvre).

Sculpture on stone was not reserved for the decoration of palaces; tablets were covered with religious scenes, and served as amulets to drive away demons. The Louvre possesses two of these monuments designed to repulse the raids of the Labartu.[1]

3. METAL FIGURES

The Assyrians made great use of metal for the ornamentation of the palaces and the manufacture of statues and articles of furniture. A votive statuette,[2] representing a woman with clasped hands, goes back to the period of Sumerian domination. Another statuette,[3] cast in two parts, was dedicated to

---

[1] **CVIII**, Nos. 403–105–106; **I**, vol. XVIII, No. 4, 1921.
[2] **XIX**, No. 54, p. 10.   [3] **CVIII**, No. 138.

Ishtar of Arbela for the life of one of the Ashur-dâns, and is probably to be attributed to the second king of that name about the end of the tenth century. On a work of the seventh century, a god seated on a mythical animal,[1] the deity's tunic is adorned with rosettes inscribed in small squares and hollowed out. The animal's coat is likewise indicated by incised strokes, the gaping eyes must have contained pupils of another substance after the fashion traceable in Sumer and Akkad from the remotest antiquity. From the same period dates a recumbent lion (Fig. 53), embedded in the earth, and probably chained to the wall at one of the gates of Sargon's palace as guardian. Other bronze lions have been discovered at Nimrud.

The demon Pazuzu, sometimes carved in stone, was also reproduced in bronze statuettes.[2] We find him treated according to the process which in masonry combines the use of bas-relief and sculpture in the round on a bronze plaque in the de Clerq collection,[3] and on a similar plaque in the Imperial Ottoman Museum.[4]

The most important metal bas-reliefs are the bronze facings from the palace built by Shalmaneser III at Imgur-Ellil (Balawat), in the ninth century. This king had the chief events of his reign represented there in a series of friezes. Thin bronze plates of the same character had been fixed by Sargon round wooden columns in imitation of palm trunks, and overlaid with a thin gilding after a fashion illustrated by specimens dating from the ancient Sumerian period.

4. ENGRAVING ON STONE

Far fewer Assyrian cylinder-seals have come to light than Babylonian, and their classification by periods is more difficult. Those on which the legend gives the name of a historical person are rare and, as it was not the custom for the witnesses to affix their seals to documents, the number of dated impressions is likewise restricted.

The earliest dated cylinders are the seals of kings Erîba-Adad (Fig. 54) and Ashur-uballit (Fig. 55), contemporaries of the Egyptian monarchs, Amenhotep III and Amenhotep IV

---

[1] **CVIII**, No. 144.   [2] *Ibid.*, Nos. 146–147.
[3] **LXII**, vol. II, pl. 34.   [4] **II**, vol. XX, p. 69.

about 1400 B.C. The seal-impressions gathered from tablets found in the ruins of Assur only belong to this epoch when the cuneiform script had established itself as the medium for diplomatic communication throughout the Ancient East.

FIG. 54.   Cylinder of king Erîba-Adad (Assur, Berlin Museum.
After C. Weber, *Altorientalische Siegelbilder*, Fig. 316a).

Assyrian art had then abandoned the Sumerian formulæ to draw its inspiration from Hittite art, the influence of which makes itself manifest again a little later in documents from the Kerkuk region.[1]

FIG. 55.   Cylinder of king Ashur-uballit (After C. Weber,
Altorientalische Siegelbilder, Fig. 354a).

The Louvre possesses a carnelian cylinder presented by an officer of Adad-nirâri III to one of his comrades in the last years of the ninth century. In a tent, the supports of which are lances each upheld by a figure of Enkidu, an Assyrian is worshipping a warrior deity ; on the reverse another figure of Enkidu is raising its arms and seems to be supporting the symbol of the god—the upper part of a person within a circle of small spheres. This scene of adoration, omitting the tent and the secondary characters, reappears on a considerable number of cylinders, most commonly with two deities.[2] The

[1] **LXV**, pl. 119.   [2] *Ibid.*, A678.

gesture of the devotee extending one hand horizontally and raising the other with the palm outwards appears to be peculiar to Assyria (Fig. 56). A Babylonian at that period and down to the end of the empire would raise both hands and turn the palms inwards towards his face.

FIG. 56. Assyrian cylinder (Bibliothèque Nationale, No. 350).

FIG. 57. Assyrian cylinder (Louvre, A. 630).

Engraved sometimes with the graver and sometimes with the drill, real or fantastic animals form the motive of certain scenes in which a zoomorphic art, as perfect as the best works of sculpture, is sometimes revealed.[1]

FIG. 58. Assyrian cylinder (Louvre, A. 648).

Although the cylinder-engraver generally kept within the religious sphere, the themes of the bas-reliefs did not fail to influence him; at Khorsabad, some scenes from the royal hunts or wars have been found.[2] In the themes, borrowed from mythology, scenes of conflict are common. Genii, nearly always anthropomorphic and sometimes winged, are discharging arrows at a real or chimerical animal (Fig. 58), or, armed with an axe or a curved weapon with convex blade, analogous to the harpê of the Greeks, they are overcoming a quadruped or an ostrich (Fig. 59).

[1] **LXV,** K 5, 7 ; cf. **LXIII,** Nos. 115–117.
[2] **LXIV,** No. 307.

Elsewhere these genii are depicted between two animals or composite monsters standing and facing them and generally they are seizing them by a fore-limb. They appear also, as on the bas-reliefs, usually grouped in pairs, holding in one hand the situla and stretching the other out towards the cedar-cone on a sacred tree overshadowed by a winged disc.

Fig. 59.   Assyrian cylinder (Bibliothèque Nationale No. 330).

The flat seal, known by the Sumerians in the most ancient ages, but abandoned by them from the time of Lugalanda, had survived in Asia Minor where it was used on the " Cappa-docian tablets " in the twenty-fourth century and later in the Hittite Empire, and reappeared in Assyria in the first millen-nium (Fig. 60). Its use triumphed in Babylonia, and by the

Fig. 60.   Assyrian seal (Louvre A. 648).

time of the Seleucids it finally drove out the cylinder-seals throughout the Orient. It was usually shaped like a truncated cone with an elliptical base and rounded at the top. The field on such a base was more restricted than the surface of a cylinder. Though it was large enough for a battle-scene, the lapidary preferred to engrave on it a beneficent genius or divine emblems.

5. COSTUME AND FURNITURE

The bas-reliefs of the palaces are our chief source of in-formation on Assyrian dress, and we have already seen how the sculptors took great pains to distinguish between gods, genii, the king, courtiers, and foreigners by details of their clothing.

In the day of Sumerian dominion, the dress was a rectangular shawl wrapped round the loins as on the banks of the Euphrates. In the first millennium it consisted of two parts—a sleeveless tunic, sometimes short, at other times long, and a rectangular shawl draped in different fashions according to the rank of its wearer, the whole being kept in place by a belt or sometimes by cords and a baldrick. The shawl, fringed on its four edges, was often adorned with religious motives, flower-patterns, or borders.

The feet were protected by buskins in war ; in civil life by sandals with heel-pieces and fastened by leather laces encircling the big toe and passing round the instep two or three times.

The custom of shaving the head, but keeping the beard, is attested for the dawn of history by monuments found in the ruins of Assur, but it soon went out of fashion as an archaic statue from the same site shows. In the ninth century the hair was curled and fell over the shoulders, while the long beard was square cut. Only high officials and young warriors were clean-shaven.

The horned tiara was the prerogative of the gods ; the king wore a sugar-loaf cap surmounted by a spike and encircled by a diadem. Other persons generally go bareheaded in civil life ; their hair is sometimes fastened with a fillet.

Jewels of gold, silver, and gilded copper were worn by men and women alike. In the age of Sargon, olive-shaped and fluted beads were manufactured from gold-leaf with repoussé decorations for necklaces, rings, and earrings. Crystal beads were provided with a gold ferrule, precious stones used in necklaces were encircled with gold, and lapis lazuli flowers were given a centre of pure gold. Heavy unclosed bracelets, adorned at either end with animals' heads, were worn at the wrists and above the elbow. Bulky earrings and divine emblems, hung round the neck, completed the adornment. The people of humble station were content with necklaces and bracelets formed of barrel-shaped, cylindrical, olive-shaped, wheel-like or carved beads of noble stones or manufactured out of synthetic pastes imitating stone.

Like the Babylonians, the Assyrians daily used scented oils, cosmetics, and perhaps even depilatory compounds.

Furniture in the palaces was very luxurious in the first millennium, and became with every century more sumptuous and more loaded with ornaments. Sennacherib's throne rested on four feet like cedar-cones in shape, the arms on either side were supported by three rows of four figures each, one above the other, and the seat and the back were covered by a shawl of precious stuff. That of Ashur-nâtsir-apla bore bronze reliefs representing composite monsters heraldically opposed round a sacred tree. A settle of the same date was adorned with animals' heads in metal-work and covered with a fringed cushion. At Dur-Sharrukîn many seats were decorated in like fashion. Chairs, arm-chairs, beds, tables, and stools were made of precious woods richly carved, with casings or inlays of gold, silver, bronze, and precious stones.

Decorated metal vases were imported from Phœnicia and ivory objects from Egypt. Glass and stone vases were also in use, but pottery predominated. Painted vases have been found only in small numbers.

CHAPTER III

LITERATURE AND SCIENCE

1. HISTORICAL LITERATURE

THE Assyrians employed the cuneiform script, invented by the Sumerians and used by the Akkadians. Though they simplified the characters more than the Babylonians had done, they did not perfect the system. Yet in their State offices they had before them the examples of Egyptian scribes, who had already got rid of their ancient hieroglyphs, and of Aramæan clerks who were in possession of an alphabet. The art and science of the scribe remained, therefore, practically what they were in Babylonia at the same period.

Assyrian literature includes a vast number of copies or adaptation of Babylonian texts. Two classes of writings alone need detain us here—the historical and epistolatory.

The chief historical texts, drawn up to the order of Assyrian kings, are in marked contrast, from the point of view of composition, to analogous documents from Sumer and Akkad. A Babylonian king was above all the shepherd of his people ; in his inscriptions he was at pains to recall all that he had done to maintain order in his realm, to further its prosperous development, and to defend it against enemies when necessity arose. An Assyrian king, on the other hand, was a warrior ; his ideal was to enlarge the territory subject to the god Ashur and to be considered himself as a conqueror. The sculptures dispersed lavishly about the halls of his palace had no other object but to glorify him personally. The texts which accompanied the sculptures likewise extolled his glory, and the misfortunes of the reign were very seldom mentioned. If such events were recorded at all, they were treated as unimportant incidents when they were not transformed into brilliant successes.

The composition of the royal inscriptions was inspired by a canon fixed at a very remote epoch. Till the end of the eighth century scarcely any variation was introduced, and the scribes were glad to copy formulæ employed in previous reigns. Under the Sargonids the narratives assumed an increasingly personal tone which asserts itself most markedly in Ashurbanipal's texts.

Four classes of documents may be distinguished—annals in which the events are reported in chronological order, military histories allowing us to follow the progress of individual campaigns, *fasti* in which the facts are generally grouped by the regions where they happened, and finally reports in the form of letters addressed to the god Ashur on the return from each expedition, to inform him of the successes gained over the enemy.

These inscriptions, except those of the last class, were engraved on the palace walls or on foundation-cylinders. They normally consist of three main sections. The first is a panegyric on the king and gives a summary of his deeds and often his genealogy ; the next recounts the events of the reign—wars and building undertakings ; the last is made up of curses upon anyone who should destroy the inscription and, sometimes, blessings on those who should treat it with respect.

Here is the beginning of the cylinder of Tiglath-pileser I :

Beginning. Ashur, the great lord who governs the totality of the gods, who bestows the sceptre and the crown, who establishes sovereignty ; Ellil, the king of all the Anunaki, father of the gods, Lord of the lands ; Sin, the wise, Lord of the crown, exalted in splendour ; Shamash, the judge of heaven and earth who brings to nought the machinations of the foe and helps the just ; Adad the mighty who crushes the hostile regions, lands, and houses ; Inurta, the hero, who destroys the wicked and the hostile, who fulfils the heart's desire ; Ishtar the first among the gods, the lady of confusion, who unleashes terrible battles. Great gods who rule heaven and earth, whose assault signifies battle and destruction, who have magnified the kingship of Tiglath-pileser, the beloved prince, favourite of your hearts, the sublime hero whom your kindly hearts have chosen, whom you have crowned with a sublime crown, whom you have solemnly established as king of the land of Ellil, to whom you have given the dominion, the glory and the power, for whom you have decreed for ever his regal destiny for the fullness of might and his sacerdotal posterity for a place in the E-harsag-kurkura. Tiglath-pileser, the strong king, king of the whole (world) who has no peer, king of the four regions, king of all princes, lord of lords, mighty, king of kings, sublime priest, to whom by the command of Shamash a brilliant sceptre has been given, who has ruled the nations, the subjects of Ellil, in their totality, lawful shepherd whose name has been exalted above that of all princes, sublime judge whose arms Ashur has guided and whose name he has proclaimed for ever to be pastor of the four regions, conqueror of distant regions on the bounds of his realm in the upper and lower regions, brilliant day whose splendour crushes the four regions, mighty flame which falls upon the hostile lands like a bursting storm, who by the command of Ellil has no rival and has confounded the enemies of Ashur.

Ashur and the great gods who have made my reign great, have granted me strength and might, have bidden me extend the frontiers of their land, have placed in my hand their mighty arms, " the hurricane of combat."

Lands, mountains, cities, and princes, enemies of Ashur, have I conquered and their territories have I subjugated. Against sixty kings have I fought valiantly and by the conflict have I won the victory over them. Peer in combat, rival in battle, have I none. To the land of Assyria I have added other lands, to its inhabitants other inhabitants. The frontier of my land have I enlarged and the whole of their lands (i.e. of the sixty kings) have I conquered.

Ashur-nâtsir-apla II in his *Annals* relates the events of 884 B.C. thus :

In the eponymy of the year that bears my name, at the word of Ashur, my Lord, and of Inurta who loves my priesthood, while in the time of the kings, my fathers, no governor of the land of Suhi had come to Assyria, Ilu-ibni, governor of Suhi to save his life came with his brothers and his sons to bring gold and silver as tribute to Nineveh before me.

In the same eponymy while I was still at Nineveh, the news was brought to me that the Assyrians and their governor Hulaï whom Shalmaneser king of Assyria, the prince who preceded me, had established at Halzidipha (these Assyrians I say) had rebelled and had marched against Damdamusa, my royal city, to seize it.

At the word of Ashur, of Ishtar and of Adad, the great gods my helpers, I gathered together my chariots and my troops. At the source of the Subnat where the images of Tiglath-pileser and Tukulti-Inurta, kings of Assyria, my fathers, were, I formed an image of my royal person and set it up there. At that time I received tribute from the land of Itsala—flocks, herds and wine. I crossed the mountain of Kashiari and towards Kinabu, the fortress of Hulaï I advanced. With the multitude of my troops by a charge, impetuous as the tempest, I fell upon the town, I took it. I put to the sword 600 of their warriors, I delivered 3000 prisoners over to the flames and I left not a single one of them alive to serve as hostage. Hulaï, their governor, I took alive with my own hand. Their carcasses I piled up in heaps, their young men and their maidens I delivered over to the flames. Hulaï, their governor, I flayed; I stretched his skin along the wall of Damdamusa. The city I destroyed, I ravaged it, I gave it to the flames.

The city of Mariru which belongs to the same district, I captured. I put to the sword 50 of their warriors; 200 prisoners I delivered over to the flames. I slew 332 soldiers of Nirbu in a fray in open country. The people of Nirbu which lies at the foot of mount Uhira, were leagued together and shut up in their fortress, Tela. From Kinabu I set forth and I approached Tela. The city was mightily strong, girt with three ramparts. The people had confidence in their strong walls and their numerous troops; they did not come to clasp my feet. By battle and slaughter I stormed the city and took it. I put to death 3000 of their warriors; their goods and chattels, their flocks and herds, I took as booty. I gave many of them over to the flames and I took many alive. From some I cut off hands and fingers, from others noses and ears; I deprived many of sight. I made one pile of the living and another pile of the heads; I tied their heads to vine-props around the city. Their young men and maidens have I cast into the fire; I have destroyed the city, devastated it, and delivered it to the flames.

No scene of pillage is more renowned than the sack of Susa by Ashurbanipal's troops. Here is the official narrative :

I have taken Susa, the residence of their gods, the place of their oracles. At the command of Ashur and Ishtar I entered into the recesses of their palace; I have stayed there in glee. I have opened their treasuries where were accumulated the gold, the silver, the goods, and the riches which the kings of Elam from the oldest ones to my contemporaries had amassed and heaped up, whereon no enemy before me had laid hands; I have brought them forth and counted them as booty.

Silver, gold, goods and riches from Sumer and Akkad and also from Karduniash, all that the ancient kings of Elam had taken as booty in seven[1] campaigns and carried off to Elam, glittering

[1] The number " seven " is here used in the sense of " many."

tsarîru, brilliant *eshmaru,* precious stones, objects of value, royal
ornaments that the ancient kings of Akkad and Shamash-shum-
ukîn as allies had given to Elam, costly garments, royal ornaments,
ceremonial and warlike arms, ornaments for warrior's hands, all
the furniture of his palaces on which they had sat, on which they
had lain (the vessels), which they had used for eating, for drinking,
for washing and for scenting themselves ; the chariots, the cars,
the *tsumbi,*[1] adorned with *tsariru* and *zahalu,* the horses, the big
mules with golden (and) silver harness, I carried them all off as
booty to Assyria.

The ziggurat of Susa which was faced with lapis lazuli, I destroyed ; its pinnacle adorned with shining bronze I broke.
Shushinak, the god of their oracles who inhabited a secret place,
whose divine work no one had ever beheld, Shumudu, Lagamaru,
Partikira, Ammankasibar, Uduran (and) Sapak whose godhead
the kings of Elam revered, Ragibâ, Sungursarâ, Karsa, Kirsamas,
Shudânu, Aipaksina, Bilala, Panintimri, Napirtu, Kindakarpu,
Silagara, Napsâ, these gods and goddesses with their valuables,
their riches, their furniture and even the priests and the *buhlalê* I
carried off as booty to Assyria.

Thirty statues in gold, silver, bronze (and) limestone of the kings
of the cities of Susa, Madaktu, and Huradi, the statue of Ummanigash, son of Umbadara, the statue of Ishtar-nahhunte, the statue
of Hallusi, the statue of Tammaritu II who at the command of
Ashur and Ishtar had been subdued, I carried off to Assyria. I
destroyed the shedu and the lamassu[2] guardians of the temples,
as many as there were. I cast down the fierce bulls, the ornaments
of the gates. The temples of Elam I caused to disappear utterly.
God and goddess I gave to the wind. Into their sacred groves
whither no stranger had penetrated nor crossed the boundaries
thereof, my shock-troops penetrated, they beheld the mystery and
delivered them over to the flames. The coffins of their kings of
old and of recent times who did not worship Ashur and whom the
kings, my fathers, had left in peace, I broke open, I destroyed, I
brought to light. Their bones I brought to Assyria ; upon their
edimmê (manes) I imposed restlessness ; I refused them funerary
offerings and libations of water.

For a distance of one month's and twenty-five days' (march) I
devastated the districts of Elam. I spread salt and thorn-bush
there. Sons of the kings, sisters of the kings, members of Elam's
royal family, young and old, prefects, overseers of those cities as
many as I had conquered, chiefs of bowmen, governors, chariot-
eers, knights, archers, armourers, artisans as many as there were,

[1] A sort of Elamite vehicle.
[2] Protecting genii, bulls and winged lions with human heads.

inhabitants, male and female, big and little, horses, mules, asses, flocks and herds more numerous than a swarm of locusts, I carried them (all) off as booty to Assyria.

The dust of Susa, of Madaktu, of Haltemash and of their other cities I required, I carried it off to Assyria. In a month of days I subdued Elam in its whole extent. The voice of man, the steps of flocks and herds, the happy shouts of mirth I put an end to them in its fields which I left for the asses, the gazelles and all manner of wild beasts to people.

From the same cylinder of Ashurbanipal, written in 639 B.C., we shall quote the closing sentences. After recalling the restoration of the palace called Bît-riduti, the king ends his inscription with these words :

In the days to come among the kings, my descendants, may he whose name Ashur and Ishtar have appointed for the sovereignty over the land and its inhabitants, raise again from its ruins this Bît-riduti when it shall have grown old and fallen in ruins. The inscription which bears my name, that of my father, that of my father's father, the stable royal race, may he read and anoint it with oil. May he offer sacrifices and replace it beside the inscription bearing his own name. May the great gods as many as be mentioned in this inscription, grant to him, as to me, strength and might.

Whoso destroy the inscription that bears my name, that of my father, that of my father's father, and replace it not beside the inscription in his own name, may Ashur, Sin, Shamash, Adad, Bêl, Nabu, Ishtar of Nineveh, the queen of Kidmuri, Ishtar of Arbela, Inurta, Nergal (and) Nusku take vengeance upon him in respect of the mention of my name.

2. EPISTOLATORY LITERATURE

In Assyria as in Babylonia the epistolatory literature includes official documents and private correspondence. The majority of the documents come from Ashurbanipal's library and consequently refer to public business. Some are written in Assyrian, others in Babylonian. They allow of a reconstruction of certain chapters in history for which royal inscriptions are wanting and reveal how the central Government kept itself abreast of events on the frontiers and in neighbour states.

In a certain year, 713 B.C. or later, Sargon was at Babylon.

His son, Sennacherib forwards to him reports sent in by various officials on affairs in Urartu. His letters begin with phrases of greeting : " To the king, my master, Sennacherib, thy servant. Peace to the king, my master ! There is peace in Assyria, peace in the temples, peace in all the fortresses of the king. Let the heart of the king, my master, rejoice completely."[1] Then follow the reports copied without even a change in the phraseology used by the correspondents. From the land of the Ukkæans it is reported that the king of Urartu had been utterly routed when he went to the Cimmerians' land. For his part Ashur-ritsua reports a great slaughter among the troops of this prince. The nobles are dead, the commander-in-chief is a prisoner, the king himself is in the land of Uazaun (Bitlis ?). The prefect of Haltsu has sent to make investigations on the frontier. The victory of the Cimmerians has been reported to him ; three Urartian nobles with their troops have been cut to pieces ; the king has been able to make good his escape and return to his territory ; up to the moment of writing his camp has not been attacked. The garrisons of the frontier forts send similar news. The king of Mutsatsir, his brother, and his son have gone to greet the king of Urartu. The king of Hupushkia has sent a messenger to him. The letter ends with a note of the despatch directly to the king of a tablet from Nabu-li', chief-steward of the lady Ahat-abisha. This lady seems to be a daughter of Sargon, married to the king of Tabal, Ambaridi, who was led away captive in 713 B.C. with his whole family.

Another group of reports is presented in the same manner.[2] They deal first with an attempt by the king of Urartu to capture the Assyrian prefects assembled at Kumai. The correspondent mentions a letter received from Ashur-ritsua, according to which the king of Armenia has come with a small contingent of troops and entered the city of Uasi. Ashur-ritsua, for his part, writes directly that he has sent his body-guard to the land of the Ukkæans who have revolted against Arzabia.

Nine reports relating to affairs in Urartu from the same Ashur-ritsua have been discovered. In one he announces a movement of troops :[3] " At the beginning of Nisan, the king

[1] CXVI, No. 197. Cf. XXV, vol. III, p. xv.
[2] CXVI, No. 198.   [3] Ibid., No. 492.

of Urartu has set out from Thurushpîa and gone to Elitsada;
Kakkadânu, his commander-in-chief, has made his way to
the city of Uasi and the armies of Urartu are concentrated at
Elitsada." In another[1] he confirms the king's presence at
Uasi and reports " 3000 Urartian infantry on the march for
Mutsatsir under the command of Sêtini who has camels with
him; they have crossed the river by night." A body of
troops, under the leadership of Shunâ, was likewise marching
towards Mutsatsir across the Ukkæans' territory. These
two messages are certainly later than the second statement
from Sennacherib, dealing with the entry of the king of Urartu
into Uasi, and than the first, which is almost entirely devoted
to his defeat by the Cimmerians; the latter is consequently
of later date.

These movements of troops described by the royal officials
were not to the taste of the king of Assyria, and gave him
umbrage. He ordered the Mayor of the Palace to request
the king of Mutsatsir not to allow the princes, who visited his
town for purposes of worship, to bring their soldiers with
them. An impertinent reply came to prove the existence of a
belief in their capacity to resist their mighty rival. " Tablet
of Urzana to the Mayor of the Palace.[2] Greetings to thee.
Referring to what thou has written me, to wit : ' The king
of Urartu with his troops, is it thee he visits ? Where is he ? '
(here is my reply). ' The prefect of Uasi and the prefect of
the territory of the Ukkæans have come, they have paid
their devotions to the temple. They say : " The king will
come; he is at Uasi. The (other) prefects are late ; they
will come." At Mutsatsir they have made their devotions.
Concerning what thou hast written me, to wit : " Without
acknowledgment as vassals by the king, no one may bring
his troops with him to his devotions." When the king of
Assyria has come, have I hindered him ? What he has done,
that other has done. How then should I hinder that other ? ' "

Another period for which epistolary literature supplies
interesting information is the close of the reign of Shamash-
shum-ukîn, king of Babylon, the period of the attempted
revolt against the Assyrian power and the conflict with
Elam.

---

[1] **CXVI**, No. 380.
[2] *Ibid.*, No. 409. Cf. **XXV**, vol. III, pp. xii-xiii (translation).

Nabu-bêl-shumâte, perhaps the king of the Land of the Sea, writes :[1] " From what I have learnt, the king of Elam has been deposed and several cities have rebelled against him, saying : ' We do not wish to throw ourselves into thy hands.' As I have heard, I report it to the king, my master. I have dwelt in the Land of the Sea since the days of Na'id-Marduk. The brigands and the fugitives who had come to the Gurun-amæans, 500 of them, Sin-balâtsu-iqbi when he had captured them put in irons (and) surrendered to their master, Natânu, king of the Uttæans to whom the king (of Assyria) had given them."

Nabu-bêl-shumâte, grandson of Merodach-baladan, had become king of the Land of the Sea on the death of his uncle, Na'id-Marduk. When Shamash-shum-ukîn had revolted, the king of Assyria sent him troops to attack the rebel on the south, but Nabu-bêl-shumâte, also desiring to regain his independence, tried to win over to his side the Assyrian soldiers and succeeded in securing the allegiance of a certain number. When he became convinced that disaster was in-evitable, he fled with them to Elam. In 650 B.C. Ashur-banipal replaced him by a certain Bêl-ibni, and addressed the following proclamation to the population : " The king's command to the people of the Land of the Sea, young and old, my servants :[2] My peace be with you ! May your hearts be satisfied. Behold, now, how my consideration extends over you. Before the sin of Nabu-bêl-shumâte, I had set over you the hierodulos (temple prostitute) of Menanu ; now I have sent you Bêl-ibni, my *dubashu*, to march before you." The end of the text is fragmentary ; the king demands obedience, otherwise he threatens to send troops. However, in Elam, Indabigash had received Nabu-bêl-shumâte and his partisans. Ashurbanipal sent an ambassador to demand their surrender. " If thou dost not surrender these men," he wrote, " I will come and destroy thy towns, I will carry off the people of Susa, Madaktu, and Haïdalu ; I will cast thee down from thy throne and enthrone another in thy stead. As once I crushed Teumman, I will annihilate thee." During the negotiations a Susian general, Ummanaldash, assassinated Indabigash and seized the throne. In 645 B.C. he wrote to the king of Assyria about Nabu-bêl-shumâte : " Tablet

---

[1] **CXVI**, No. 839.   [2] *Ibid.*, No. 289.

of Ummanaldash, king of Elam, to Ashurbanipal, king of Assyria.[1] Peace to my brother ! From the beginning the people of the Land of the Sea have sinned against thee. Nabu-bêl-shumâte has come thence. . . . Thou hast sent to me to command : ' Send Nabu-bêl-shumâte.' I am going to arrest Nabu-bêl-shumâte and shall send him to thee. The people of the Land of the Sea whom from the beginning Nabu-bêl-shumâte has brought with him to us, . . . these are people come by water of . . . ; they have entered by force into Lahiru and are there. I am going to send against them into their borders my servants, and by their hand I shall send thee those who have sinned against us. If they be on my territory, I will send them by their hands, but if they have crossed the river, take them thyself." Nabu-bêl-shumâte, seeing himself lost, would not be surrendered alive and made his squire slay him. His body was handed over to the king of Assyria who had it decapitated and forbade its burial.

Bêl-ibni, installed as king of the Land of the Sea after the flight of Nabu-bêl-shumâte, drew up a lengthy report on affairs in Elam.[2] He had sent 500 soldiers to Tsabdânu with orders to fortify themselves in that town, to make raids into Elam, to massacre the people and to bring back captives. These troops had advanced as far as Irzidu, a short distance from Susa, and had slain the governor, Amma-ladin, his two brothers, three of his uncles, two of his nephews, and two hundred notables. A hundred and fifty prisoners had been taken. The inhabitants of Lahiru and Nugu had immediately made overtures to Mushêzib-Marduk, Bêl-ibni's nephew and commandant at Tsabdênu. They had sworn allegiance to the king of Assyria, had mobilized their bowmen and had put them at the disposal of the governor. Bêl-ibni announced he would send all the spoils to the king and terminated his letter with news from the court of Elam : it was reported that Ummanigash had revolted against Ummanaldash ; both armies were encamped facing one another on the banks of the Hudhud. Iqîsha-aplu, whom he had sent to the palace, was conversant with their plans ; he should be interrogated.

[1] CXXXII, p. 350.   [2] CXVI, No. 280.

Mushêzib-Marduk, Bêl-ibni's nephew, enjoyed the royal favour. He had been summoned two or three times to an audience with the sovereign, and one day Ashurbanipal wrote to his uncle thus :[1] "Message from the king to Bêl-ibni. I am well. May thy heart be satisfied. Mushêzib-Marduk, about whom I have given thee directions, shall in the fulness of time be admitted into my presence. I shall determine the path for his feet."

Kudur, governor of Uruk, to whom the king had sent a doctor to tend him in a serious illness, had started on his journey to thank the king. Recalled to his post where a letter from the king had reached him, he would not postpone any longer the expression of his gratitude and wrote what follows :[2] "To the king of the lands, my master, thy servant, Kudur. May Uruk and the Eana be propitious to the king of the lands, my master. Iqîsha-aplu, the doctor whom the king, my master, has sent to cure me, has restored me to life. May the great gods of heaven and earth be propitious to the king, my master, and may they establish the throne of the king, my master, in the midst of the heavens for all eternity. I was as one dead and the king, my master, has restored me to life. The benefits of the king, my master, towards me are numerous ; I wish to go and see the king, my master. I have said to myself : ' I shall go and behold the face of the king, my master, then I shall return and live.' The key-bearer has made me return to Uruk sending me word to say : ' A special messenger has brought a sealed letter coming from the Palace for thee ; thou must come with me to Uruk.' He has sent this order and made me return to Uruk. The king, my master, should be made aware of this."

Another letter illustrates the care with which certain kings of Assyria had search made for ancient texts, especially those relating to magic, to enrich their libraries.[3]

Magic was, in fact, highly esteemed at court as among the people. The king would not embark upon any important enterprise without consulting the gods and obtaining favourable omens. The least event gave rise to interpretations which were based on data collected from the earliest days of the Sumero-Akkadian civilization. Here is probably an example. It is a letter from a certain Nabua, a resident of Assur, from

[1] **CXVI**, No. 398.   [2] *Ibid.*, No. 274.   [3] Above p. 223.

whom we possess a certain number of astrological reports.[1] " To the king, my master, thy servant Nabua. May Nabu and Marduk be propitious to the king, my master. On the 7th of Kislimu a fox entered the city and fell into a pit in the sacred grove of Ashur. It was caught and killed."

When Ashur-mukîn-palêa, one of Ashurbanipal's younger brothers, a man of feeble health, wanted to go on a journey, the king asked advice and received this reply : " To the king, our master, thy servants, Balasi and Nabu-ahê-êriba. Peace to the king, our master ! May Nabu and Marduk be propitious to the king, our master. Concerning Ashur-mukîn-palêa about whom the king, our master, has written to us, may Ashur, Bêl, Sin, Shamash and Adad be propitious to him. May the king, our master, see him in good health. The omens are favourable for a journey. The second is propitious, the fourth very propitious."

Balasi and Nabu-ahê-êriba are among the king's most frequent correspondents about astrological observations. Adad-shum-utsur was likewise an astrologer. He gave consultations in respect of illnesses, favourable days, an eclipse and so forth, but he did not neglect the interests of his family, and liked to end a long letter of adulation by a recommendation for one of his sons : [2] " To the king, my master, thy servant Adad-shum-utsur. Peace to the king, my master. May Nabu and Marduk be extremely propitious to the king, my master. The king of the gods has decreed the name of the king, my master, for the kingdom of Assyria. Shamash and Adad in their immovable regard for the king, my master, have confirmed him for the empire over all lands. A favourable reign, stable days, years of justice, abundant rains, plenteous floods, high prices. The gods are honoured, the fear of the divinity increases, the temples are prosperous, the great gods of heaven and earth are exalted under the rule of the king, my master. The old men dance, the young people sing, women and maidens are given in marriage, the widows remarry, marriages are consummated, boys and girls are begotten and children are born. To those who have sinned and await death, the king, my master, has given a new life. Those who have been in prison for many years, hast thou set at liberty. Those who have been sick for long days, have recovered their health.

[1] **CXVI**, No. 142.   [2] *Ibid.*, No. 2.

Hunger is appeased, the lean grow fat. The orchards are full of fruit. Only Arad-Gula and I are languishing in spirit and anxious at heart. Recently the king has manifested his love for Nineveh, her people and her chiefs, saying : ' Bring hither your sons, let them stand before me.' May Arad-Gula, my son, stand with them before the king, my lord. In truth we shall rejoice with all the people and dance with joy. My eyes are fixed on the king, my master. Those who stand in the palace are all, none excepted, without affection for me. I have no friend among them to whom I can offer a present who would accept it and take my cause in hand. May the king, my master, take pity on his servant. Among all these people I pray that none of my slanderers may see the accomplishment of their plans against me."

Some letters refer to medical treatment. The majority are hard to interpret because, despite the large number of medical tablets preserved in the British Museum, we are too often ignorant of the exact meaning of the terms used to designate the diseases and their remedies. Shamash-mîtu-uballit, Ashurbanipal's youngest brother, asks the king to send a doctor to treat a woman of the Palace.[1] " To the king, my master, thy servant, Shamash-mîtu-uballit : Peace to the king, my master ! May Nabu and Marduk be extremely favourable to the king, my master. Bau-gâmelat, the king's maid-servant, is very sick ; she cannot eat. Let the king, my master, order a doctor to be sent to see her." The medical treatises prescribe remedies for the various diseases which might attack all parts of the body. They are roots, oils, and powders ; very often they include, in addition, incantations to dispel the influence of the evil spirits to whom the maladies and indispositions are due. Arad-Nanaï has treated a man in whom king Esarhaddon was personally interested. He gives him an account of the state of the sick man who suffered from some affection of the eyes, perhaps erysipelis. " It is well with the poor man who has eye trouble. I have applied a dressing to his whole face. Last night I undid the bandage which fastened the dressing and took it off. There was pus on the dressing, a spot as big as the tip of my little finger. If one of thy gods has taken the matter in hand, he has put everything right. All is going quite well. Let the heart of

[1] **CXVI**, No. 341.

the king, my master, rejoice. In seven or eight days he will be cured." The same Arad-Nanaï tended the young prince Ashur-mukîn-palêa who, as we have seen, was very delicate.

One day he wrote to the king, his father, that there was no occasion to worry about this ;[1] another time he gave advice to the sovereign himself[2] and, when the latter complained that the nature of the malady had not been diagnosed, the doctor replied :[3] " I have already said to the king, my master : ' The ulcer is incurable (?) ; I can prescribe nothing for this case.' Now, however, I have sealed a letter and send it. In the presence of the king, my master, let it be read. I am going to make a prescription for the king, my master. If it be agreeable to the king, my master, let a magician perform his operations over him ; let the king apply a lotion and the pain shall soon disappear. This lotion of oil (?) let the king apply two or three times."

The beginning of the month was dependent upon the appearance of the crescent moon in the heavens. From the 29th day the astronomers of Assur watched the heavens, and immediately reported whether or no it was time to pass on to the next month. Here is a typical specimen of their reports :[4] " On the 29th we have taken observations ; we have not seen the moon. May Nabu and Marduk be propitious to the king, my master. From Nabuâ of Assur."

The epistolary collections confirm and emphasize the great influence in Assyrian society enjoyed by certain women. Zakutu, Sennacherib's wife, played an important rôle at court and in the State. On the death of her son, Esarhaddon, she sided with Ashurbanipal, and Na'id-Marduk, king of the Land of the Sea and a vassal of Assyria, regarded her as regent while her son was waging war in the west, and addressed reports to her : " To the mother of the king, my master, thy servant, Na'id-Marduk. Peace to the mother of the king, my master. May Ashur, Shamash, and Marduk grant health to the king, my master ; may they decree joy of heart for the mother of the king, my master. From Elam a messenger is come to announce : ' The bridge has been taken away.' As soon as he came, I sent to the mother of the king, my master. Let now the bridge be restored and the bolts strengthened."

---

[1] **XCVI**, No. 109.   [2] *Ibid.*, No. 110.
[3] *Ibid.*, No. 391.   [4] *Ibid.*, No. 825.

Another letter from a certain Aplîa brings her news of her son :[1] " To the mother of the king, my lady, thy servant Aplîa. May Bêl and Nabu be propitious to the mother of the king, my lady. Every day I pray to Nabu and Nanaï for the life, health, and longevity of the king of the lands, my master, and of the mother of the king, my lady. Let the mother of the king, my lady, be glad. A message of good tidings from Bêl and Nabu is come from the king of the lands, my master." The king himself wrote to his mother using the usual introduction employed in all his letters :[2] " Message from the king to the mother of the king. I am well. Peace to the mother of the king. Concerning the serving-woman of Amushe whom you have sent me, in accordance with what the mother of the king has told me, I am immediately going to give orders. What thou has said is perfectly good. Why will Hamunai depart ? "

3. SCIENCES

The Assyrian system of weights and measures was borrowed from the Babylonians, but it underwent some modifications. The unit of volume was still the *qa* or *sila*. Its multiple was no longer the *gur* of 300 or 180 *qa*, but the *imêru* or ass-load of 100 *qa* (84·2 litres or 19 gallons). This measure, like the *gur* at Babylon from the Kassite domination, served likewise as a land-measure, the block of land being valued according to the quantity of seed required for a unit of area.

The ancient Sumerians had used copper as money before employing silver. The Assyrians used it too, even in the period of the Sargonids, but they had adopted lead very early ; in the penal clauses of the Assyrian laws, from the second millennium, it was the metal in current use. Silver likewise functioned in transactions ; it appears in the form of ingots, rings, and plaques, the weight and quality of which are indicated by stamp marks. Gold also occurs in the period of the Sargonids, albeit more rarely.

The Assyrian year consisted of twelve or thirteen lunar months as in Babylonia. No scientific rules seem to have existed to determine the order in which ordinary years and leap-years should occur.

[1] **XCVI**, No. 303.   [2] *Ibid.*, No. 324.

From the earliest times and down to the end of the empire, every year bore the name of an important personage who was called *limmu*. This practice, attested already on the Cappadocian documents of the twenty-fourth century, reappears in tablets dating from the second millennium discovered at Assur. In the time of the Sargonids, the king was *limmu* in the first complete year of his reign, and his turn to enjoy the privilege came again thirty years later; after him the title was assigned in turn to the grand vizir, the turtan, and the other leading officials.

Assyrian medicine had the same foundation and methods as the Babylonian. Astronomical science does not appear to have made any progress; even more than at Babylon the stars were only studied with a view to omens about the events of public life or private affairs. In geography the only standpoint taken up by the Assyrians was apparently to note down the names of localities, the distances between two given points, and the lands crossed in travelling from one place to another for the use of military expeditions, caravans of merchants, or the scribes charged with drawing up the royal annals. Very often the geographical documents are just copies of Babylonian tablets.

The Assyrians do not seem to have sought or achieved any progress worth mentioning in any science whatsoever. But we are indebted to them for having preserved in their archives and libraries a great number of texts derived from Babylonia. Some of these are unknown from other sources; others present variants, glosses or additions which render them invaluable for us.

CONCLUSION

WE do not know whence came the Semites who colonized the plain of the Lower Euphrates. Still, it would be of prime importance if we could determine whether their former habitat was Arabia, as has long been maintained, or rather the Amorite region of Syria and Palestine according to a more modern thesis.[1] This question is of capital importance especially for estimating to what extent Babylonian civilization has exerted its own peculiar influence upon the various people who have occupied Asia Minor and the Syrian coast of Mesopotamia. If the theory that the first Semites to settle among the Sumerians were a branch sprung from the group of the Western Semites be confirmed, if the Amorite origin of the earliest kings of Kish and Uruk be definitely established, if the foundation for the legends about these kings turn out to be events which happened in Syria at an epoch anterior to the oldest facts attested by contemporary documents still extant, then the Pan-Babylonist thesis falls to the ground completely. The civilization of Israel would then no longer be wholly a reflection of that of Babylon ; the traditions preserved in the Book of Genesis would not then be importations from Chaldæa ; on the contrary, it would be the Semites who introduced them in the last stage of their eastward wandering to the Sumerians and the latter who adopted them. The Sumero-Akkadians did, in any case, develop their culture more rapidly than the Semites left behind in Amurru, and consequently exercised a profound influence in that region because they were obliged to go thither to seek stone and timber, and they engaged on a large scale in all sorts of commerce. This influence is still patent in the fifteenth century in the Amarna Age. The Assyrians developed it by their system of conquest, and the foundation of colonies in the regions annexed to their empire. The

[1] **XXXVII**, vol. VI, vol. V, 3.

Neo-Babylonians put the finishing touches to the work, notably in the case of the Jews, upon whom they stamped their imprint deeply during the years of the Exile.

Reciprocal influences between the Babylonian and Egyptian civilizations at very ancient times are admitted by many Orientalists. Still, serious divergences appear in the views on particular cases. They would be better explained if the Amorite origin of Akkadians be admitted. The points of contact between the two ethnic groups are the cities on the Syrian coast ; there, by the beginning of the historical period, Egypt had established rich trading settlements which served as bases for the exploitation of the forest of Lebanon in the time of the Third Dynasty apparently contemporary with Lugalzaggisi of Uruk.

In the Cappadocian region it was first a colony of traders, given to the worship of Ashur, in the third millennium, then later the Hittites who diffused Babylonian culture. Both employed the cuneiform script and were inspired by Sumero-Akkadian art, but they created different forms of expression which reappear on the banks of the Tigris and prelude the growth of classical Assyrian art.

Assyrian civilization reacted chiefly upon the mountaineers of the upper valleys of the Tigris and Euphrates—on Mutsatsir and Urartu, for instance, in the days of Sargon.

Elsewhere the labours of the Délégation en Perse have emphasized the stimuli exerted by Sumer and Akkad upon Elam. The kings of Agade and the kings of Ur imposed their language as well as their script upon the Elamites without, however, causing the disappearance of the Anzanite speech or preventing the survival of the local script. The art of Elam, too, resisted to some extent the foreign models ; the large collection of cylinders and impressions found at Susa shows in glyptic a series of motives which do not recur in the Euphrates valley. Babylonian inspiration is traceable again in the reliefs of Malamir about 1000 B.C., and still later in writing, art, and architecture at the period of the Achæmenid Persians.

The Greek world came under the spell of Babylon chiefly after that city had vanished as a political power. Through the Syrian coast and Asia Minor she may have exercised more or less effective influence. It had reached Cyprus before the age of Hammurabi, and perhaps Crete as well, but the Greeks proper knew the great city only in her decline under the dominion of the Persians and even more under the Seleucids. Then the Chaldæan priests, heirs of the antique traditions of Sumer and Akkad, indefatigable copyists of liturgical tablets, spread their science throughout the whole Mediterranean world. The best known of them was named Berosus.

From such influences, radiated over so many different peoples, something survives even to-day. Here are two obvious examples : the present Israelite calendar is derived directly from the Babylonian ; the division of the circle into 360 degrees and of the day into twenty-four hours, both incompatible with the principles of the metric system, go back to the Sumerians.

In less than a century regular or clandestine excavations have brought to light thousands of documents. Unexplored *tells* in hundreds still cumber the soil of Mesopotamia and contain the answer to numerous unsolved questions. The Service of the Antiquities of Egypt and similar organizations in Syria and Palestine have obtained very satisfactory results in their respective territories, and discourage clandestine diggers who destroy much of the evidential value of the documents they unearth. It is essential that the exploration of the ruins of Mesopotamia should be pursued on a like plan modified to meet local conditions.

The excavations of Khorsabad were limited almost entirely to the ruins of Sargon's palace and of the city gates. In the town itself only trial excavations were conducted, but this city only dates from the seventh century and would not be likely to furnish documents of archæological value comparable to what might be expected from other sites. At Nineveh the palaces are known ; the town has not been dug down to virgin soil. Assur has yielded up the secret of its remote origins, of the Sumerian influence upon its inhabitants in the first half of the third millennium. In other localities in Assyria a little surface scratching has been done, but neither in the Kerkuk region, where Hittite art is manifest from about the fifteenth century, nor at Arbela, where rose one of the most famous temples, nor yet at several other promising sites has any scientifically conducted exploration been carried out.

In Babylonia the German mission was unable to explore the deeper strata on the site of Babylon; its researches were hindered by the water which, at present in normal seasons, reaches a level above that of the city towards the end of the second millennium. At Niffer the University of Pennyslvania is continuing its important and fruitful operations which will last several years still before the disinterment of this ancient religious capital of Sumer will be complete. The British and American excavations at Ur and Kish already give promise of brilliant results. At Tello the work of Ernest de Sarzee and Col. Cros, so precious for the history and archæology of the third millennium, remains unfinished. The first excavator has died at his task, the second has fallen gloriously on the field of honour; it remains for a Frenchman to take up their tools and pursue the exploration of Gudea's town. How many other cities the importance of which is known are awaiting an explorer! Warka, for instance, is the site of the ancient Uruk, a centre of scientific culture in the Seleucid period, where clandestine diggings have brought to light a number of tablets. This was the city of Gilgamesh, that ancient king, earlier than the period as yet historical; the lower strata of the town ought to cover the ruins of the original fortification-wall which tradition attributed to him. Perhaps we might find there materials for a new page of history—not of local history only, though that by itself would be fascinating, but also of the relations between the Sumerians and the people of Northern Syria whose memory the *Epic* of this hero has sanctified.

And how many ruins in appearance less imposing might yield fruitful results to study! The example of Tepe Mussian in Susiana, where M. J.-E. Gautier has personally borne all the costs of his own researches, is an admirable proof thereof. The pursuit of the works on the ruins of Susa is not irrelevant to our subject; for there are found points of comparison for the reconstruction of Babylonian history and sometimes even direct documents. Long ago J. de Morgan discovered there the Code of Hammurabi, the Stele of Narâm-Sin, and other spoils from a vanquished Babylonia, side by side with documen's demonstrating the effective domination of the kings of Ur over the land of Elam. He brought to light there that archaic necropolis so important for its double series of painted vases. To-day M. de Mecquenem is exploring another necropolis, the earliest monuments of which go back to the epoch of the kings of Ur, while the latest are hardly older than the Achæmenid domination.

Other regions might add their testimony to the growth and expansion of Babylonian or Assyrian civilization. For instance, we know the site of Mari, that town on the Middle Euphrates which imposed its domination upon Sumer and Akkad about the time of the early king of Lagash, Ur-Ninâ, and whence came some centuries later Ishbi-Ira, the founder of the Dynasty of Isin. We know the site of Tirqa, the capital of the realm of Hana, which flourished about 2000 B.C. The methodical exploration of the ruins of these two towns would certainly yield very striking results.

In the circumstances of the day, governments are less than ever able to grant the substantial subventions now indispensable for the pursuit of archæological excavation, that veritable laboratory of the history of the Orient. If this be true, it is left to individuals to take charge of them and to join those powerful societies in every country which esteem it a point of honour to provide excavators with the material means for exhuming the documents of these ancient civilizations, the common heritage of mankind.

BIBLIOGRAPHY

I. PERIODICALS

II. COLLECTIVE WORKS

The Babylonian Expedition of the University of Pennsylvania :—
     Series A : *Cuneiform Texts*   **XXXII**
     Series D : *Researches and treatises*   **XXXIII**
University of Chicago. Oriental Institute   **XXXIV**
University of Pennsylvania. The Museum, Publications of the
     Babylonian Section   **XXXV**
Yale Oriental Series : Babylonian Texts, 1915 ff.   **XXXVI**
                 Researches   **XXXVII**
Oxford Edition of Cuneiform Texts. The Weld-Blundell Collection **XXXVIII**
Assyriologische Bibliothek   **XXXIX**
Keilinschriftliche Bibliothek, 1880 ff.   **XL**
Boghaz-Koi Studien   **XLI**
Königliche Museen zu Berlin. Mitteilungen aus den orientalischen
     Sammlungen, 1889 ff.   **XLII**
Vorderasiatische Bibliothek   **XLIII**
Vorderasiatische Schriftdenkmäler der königlichen Museen zu Berlin,
     1902 ff.   **XLIV**
Wissenschaftliche Veröffentlichungen der deutschen Orient-Gesell-
     schaft   **XLV**
Der alte Orient   **XLVI**

III. INDIVIDUAL WORKS

Allotte de la Fuye, *Documents présargoniques*, 1908 ff.   **XLVII**
Alfred Boissier, *Documents assyriens relatifs aux présages*, 1894   **XLVIII**
P. E. Botta and E. Flandin, *Monuments de Ninive*, 1849   **XLIX**
Etienne Combe, *Histoire du culte de Sin*, 1908   **L**
Georges Contenau, *Contribution à l'histoire économique d'Umma*   **LI**
Georges Contenau, *La déesse nue babylonienne*, 1904   **LII**
Georges Contenau, *La civilisation assyro-babylonienne*, 1922   **LIII**
Gaston Cros, Léon Heuzey and Fr. Thureau-Dangin, *Nouvelles*
     fouilles de Tello, 1910   **LIV**
Edouard Cuq, *Le mariage à Babylone d'après les lois de Hammurabi*   **LV**
Edouard Cuq, *Notes d'épigraphie et de la papyrologie juridiques*,
     1908–9   **LVI**
Edouard Cuq, *La propriété foncière en Chaldée*, 1906   **LVII**
Edouard Cuq, *Études sur les contrats de l'époque de la 1re dynastie*
     babylonienne, 1910   **LVIII**
Edouard Cuq, *Les nouveaux fragments du Code de Hammurabi sur*
     la prêt à interêt et les sociétés, 1918   **LIX**
Edouard Cuq, *Le cautionnement en Chaldée*, 1918   **LX**
Edouard Cuq, *Les pierres de bornage babyloniennes du British*
     Museum, 1920   **LXI**
De Clerq and Joachim Menant, *Collection de Clercq. Catalogue*
     méthodique et raisonné, 1888   **LXII**
Louis Delaporte, *Catalogue des cylindres orientaux du Musée Guimet*,
     1906   **LXIII**
Louis Delaporte, *Catalogue des cylindres orientaux de la Bibliothèque*
     nationale, 1910   **LXIV**

Louis Delaporte and Fr. Thureau-Dangin, *Catalogue des cylindres orientaux du Musée du Louvre*, 1920–1922 — LXV

Paul Dhorme, *Choix de textes religieux assyro-babyloniens*, 1907 — LXVI

Paul Dhorme, *La religion assyro-babylonienne*, 1910 — LXVII

Marcel Dieulafoy, *L'acropole de Suse*, 1893 — LXVIII

J. E. Gautier, *Archives d'une famille de Dilbat* — LXIX

Leon Heuzey, *Les origines orientales de l'art* — LXX

Leon Heuzey, *Musée du Louvre. Catalogue des antiquités chaldéenes*, 1902 — LXXI

Charles Fossey, *Manuel d'assyriologie*, 1904 — LXXII

Charles Fossey, *La Magie assyrienne*, 1902 — LXXIII

Charles Fossey, *Texts assyriens et babyloniens relatifs à la divination*, 1905 — LXXIV

Charles F. Jean, *Le milieu biblique avant Jésus-Christ*, 1923 — LXXV

Charles F. Jean, *Sumer et Akkad*, 1923 — LXXVI

Charles F. Jean, *La littérature des Babyloniens et des Assyriens*, 1924 — LXXVII

Henri de Genouillac, *Tablettes sumériennes archaiques*, 1909 — LXXVIII

Henri de Genouillac, *La trouvaille de Dréhem*, 1911 — LXXIX

Henri de Genouillac, *Fouilles françaises d'El-Akhynte. Premières recherches archéologiques à Kich*, 1924 — LXXX

M. J. Lagrande, *Études sur les religions sémitiques*, 2nd edit., 1905 — LXXXI

Stephen Langdon, *Le poème sumérien de Paradis, du Déluge, et de la chute de l'homme* — LXXXII

Léon Légrain, *Le temps des rois d'Ur*, 1912 — LXXXIII

Léon Légrain, *Catalogue des cylindres orientaux de la collection Louis Cugnin*, 1911 — LXXXIV

François Martin, *Lettres néo-babyloniennes* — LXXXV

François Martin, *Textes religieux assyriens et babyloniens*, 1910 — LXXXVI

Gaston Maspero, *Histoire ancienne des peuples de l'Orient classique*, 1895 — LXXXVII

Gaston Maspero, *Histoire ancienne des peuples de l'Orient*, 8th edit., 1909 — LXXXVIII

Joachim Menant, *Les écritures cuneiformes*, 1864 — LXXXIX

Joachim Menant, *Catalogues des cylindres orientaux du cabinet royal de Médailles de La Haye*, 1878 — XC

Jules Oppert, *Expédition scientifique en Mésopotamie*, 1869 — XCI

Victor Place, *Ninive et l'Assyrie*, 1867 — XCII

G. Perrot and Ch. Chipiez, *Histoire de l'art dans l'antiquité* (Vol. II), 1884 — XCIII

L. Pillet, *Le Palais de Darius I à Suse*, 1914 — XCIV

J. Plessis, *Études sur les texts concernant Ishtar-Astarté*, 1921 — XCV

Edmond Pottier, *Musée de Louvre, les antiquités assyriennes*, 1917 — XCVI

Max Ringelmann, *Essai sur l'histoire du génie rural* (Vol. II), 1907 — XCVII

Ernest de Sarzec and Léon Heuzey, *Découvertes en Chaldée*, 1884 — XCVIII

Vincent Scheil, *Une saison de fouilles à Sippar* — XCIX

Vincent Scheil, *La loi de Hammurabi*, 1904 (cf. XXIII, Vol IV) — C

Vincent Scheil, *Recueil des lois assyriennes*, 1921 — CI

Vincent Scheil and M. Dieulafoy, *Esagil ou le temple de Bél-Marduk à Babylone*, 1913 — CII

Louis Speelers, *Catalogue des intailles et empreintes orientales des Musées royaux du Cinquantonaire*, 1917 — CIII

François Thureau-Dangin, *Recueil des tablettes chaldéennes* — CIV

François Thureau-Dangin, *Les inscriptions de Sumer et d'Akkad*, 1905 — CV

François Thureau-Dangin, *Chronologie des dynasties de Sumer et d'Akkad*, 1918 — CVI

François Thureau-Dangin, *Rituels accadiens*, 1921 — CVII

Charles Virolleaud, *L'astrologie chaldéenne*, 1908, etc. — CVIII

Edgar James Banks, *Bismya, or the lost city of Adab*, 1912 — CIX

G. A. Barton, *Haverford Library Collection of Cuneiform Tablets*, 1910 — CX

J. H. Breasted, *Ancient Times, a History of the Early World*, 1916 — CXI

E. A. Wallis-Budge, *Assyrian Sculptures in the British Museum, Reign of Ashur-nasir-pal*, 1914 — CXII

E. A. Wallis-Budge and L. W. King, *Annals of the Kings of Assyria*, 1902 — CXIII

J. Gadd, *The Fall of Nineveh*, 1924 — CXIV

H. R. Hall, *The Ancient History of the Near East* (5th edit.), 1922 — CXV

Harper, *Assyrian and Babylonian Letters* — CXVI

H. V. Hillprecht, *Exploration in Bible Lands during the 19th Century*, 1907 — CXVII

Mary Inda Hussey, *Sumerian Tablets in the Harvard Semitic Museum*, 1912 — CXVIII

Morris Jastrow, *Aspects of Religious Belief and Practice in Babylonia and Assyria*, 1911 — CXIX

Morris Jastrow, *The Civilization of Babylonia and Assyria*, 1919 — CXX

Morris Jastrow, *The Medicine of the Babylonians and Assyrians*, 1914 — CXXI

Morris Jastrow, *The Religion of Babylonia and Assyria* — CXXII

Leonard W. King, *A History of Sumer and Akkad*, 1910 — CXXIII

Leonard W. King, *A History of Babylon*, 1915 — CXXIV

Leonard W. King, *Studies in Eastern History*, 1904 — CXXV

Leonard W. King, *The Letters and Inscriptions of Hammurabi*, 1898 — CXXVI

Leonard W. King, *Babylonian Boundary Stones and Memorial Tablets in the British Museum*, 1912 — CXXVII

Leonard W. King, *Bronze Reliefs from the Gates of Shalmaneser, King of Assyria* — CXXVIII

Leonard W. King, *The Seven Tablets of Creation*, 1902 — CXXIX

Leonard W. King, *Babylonian Magic and Sorcery*, 1896 — CXXX

C. H. W. Johns, *Assyrian Deeds and Documents*, 1898 — CXXXI

C. H. W. Johns, *Babylonian and Assyrian Laws, Contracts and Tablets*, 1904 — CXXXII

Stephen Langdon, *Tablets from the Archives of Drehem*, 1911 — CXXXIII

Stephen Langdon, *Sumerian and Babylonian Psalms*, 1909 — CXXXIV

Stephen Langdon, *Babylonian Liturgies*, 1913 — CXXXV

Layard, *The Monuments of Nineveh* — CXXXVI

D. A. Mackenzie, *Myths of Babylonia and Assyria*, 1919 — CXXXVII

Samuel Mercer, *Religious and Moral Ideas in Babylonia and Assyria*, 1919   **CXXXVIII**

A. T. Olmstead, *History of Assyria*, 1923   **CXXXIX**

Archibald Paterson, *Assyrian Sculptures*   **CXL**

Archibald Paterson, *Assyrian Sculptures, Palace of Sinacherib*   **CXLI**

Theophilies G. Pinches, *The Amherst Tablets*, 1908   **CXLII**

R. W. Rogers, *A History of Babylonia and Assyria*, 6th edit., 1919   **CXLIII**

L. Spence, *Myths and Legends of Babylonia and Assyria*, 1916   **CXLIV**

R. Campbell Thompson, *The Devils and Evil Spirits of Babylonia*   **CXLV**

William Hayes Ward, *Cylinders and other Oriental Seals in the Library of J. Pierpont Morgan*, 1909   **CXLVI**

William Hayes Ward, *The Seal Cylinders of Western Asia*, 1910   **CXLVII**

The Cambridge Ancient History, Vol. I, 1923 ; II, 1924   **CXLVIII**

E. K. Klauber, *Politisch-religiöse Texte aus der Sargonidenzeit*, 1913   **CXLIX**

J. Kohler and F. E. Peiser, *Aus dem babylonischen Rechtsleben*, 1890   **CL**

J. Kohler and F. E. Peiser, *Hammurabi's Gesetz*, 1904   **CLI**

J. Kohler and F. E. Peiser, *Urkunden aus der Zeit der dritten babylonischen Dynastie*, 1905   **CLII**

J. Kohler and F. E. Peiser, *Babylonische Verträge des Berliner Museums*, 1920   **CLIII**

J. Kohler and A. Ungnad, *Assyrische Rechtsurkunden*   **CLIV**

J. Kohler and A. Ungnad, *Hundert ausgewählte Rechtsurkunden aus der Spätzeit des babylonischen Schrifttums von Xerxes bis Mithridates II* (485–93 *v Chr*)   **CLV**

Koldeway, *Das neuerscheinende Babylon*, 1913   **CLVI**

F. X. Kugler, *Die babylonische Mondrechnung*, 1900   **CLVII**

F. X. Kugler, *Sternkunde und Sterndienst in Babel*, 1907 ff.   **CLVIII**

Bruno Meissner, *Babylonien und Assyrien*, 1920   **CLIX**

Edouard Meyer, *Geschichte des Altertums*   **CLX**

J. N. Strassmaier, *Babylonische Texte*   **CLXI**

K. L. Tallquist, *Die assyrische Beschwörungsserie Maqlû*, 1894   **CLXII**

M. V. Nikolski, *Economic Documents from the Early Period of Chaldœa* (in Russian)   **CLXIII**

INDEX